# Love Hin

LOVE HINA
7
Sarah
7
Love Hina


by Ken Akamatsu

Vol.7

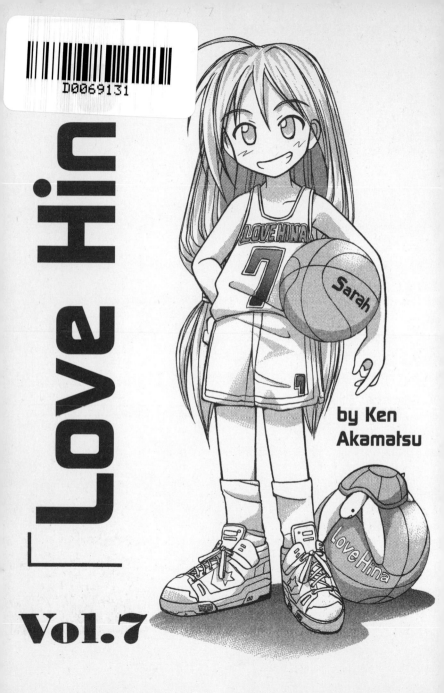

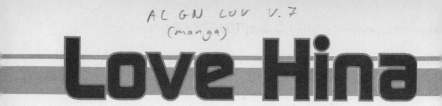

# Love Hina

By

## Ken Akamatsu

## Volume 7

Los Angeles • Tokyo

Translator - Nan Rymer
English Adaption - Adam Arnold
Associate Editor - Julie Taylor
Retouch - Tim Law
Lettering - Monalisa J. deAsis
Cover Layout - Anna Kernbaum

Senior Editor - Luis Reyes
Production Manager - Jennifer Miller
Art Director - Matthew Alford
VP of Production & Manufacturing - Ron Klamert
President & C.O.O. - John Parker
Publisher - Stuart Levy

Email: editor@TOKYOPOP.com
Come visit us online at www.TOKYOPOP.com

A **TOKYOPOP**® Manga
TOKYOPOP® is an imprint of Mixx Entertainment Inc.
5900 Wilshire Blvd. Suite 2000, Los Angeles, CA 90036

ISBN: 1-59182-018-9

First TOKYOPOP® printing: November 2002

10  9  8  7  6  5  4  3  2
Printed in Canada

# Love Hina

## The Story Thus Far ...

Fifteen years ago, Keitaro Urashima made a promise to a girl that they would go to Tokyo University together. The promise is nothing more than a hazy memory now, but to Keitaro, it's the only thing that brings meaning to his life. Having failed the entrance exam several times, he's found it more and more difficult to keep that promise, much less being able to find the girl he made it to... until now.

But before we get into that, let's set the scene. He's inherited from his globetrotting grandmother the Hinata House, a quiet residential dorm where he could work as the landlord and prepare for his upcoming exams in peace... if it wasn't for the fact that Hinata House is actually a girls' dormitory with a clientele none too pleased that their new, live-in landlord is a man – or as close to a man as poor Keitaro can be. The lanky loser incessantly (and accidentally) crashes their sessions in the hot springs, walks in on them changing... and pokes his nose pretty much everywhere it can get broken, if not by the hot-headed Naru, then by one of the other Hinata inmates – Kitsune, a late-teen alcoholic with a diesel libido; Motoko, a swordswoman who struggles with a feminine identity; Shinobu, a pre-teen princess with a colossal crush on Keitaro; and Su, a foreign girl with a big appetite.

So, about that "... until now." Naru has just discovered a photograph that strongly suggests that her and Keitaro's mutual friend Mutsumi might very well be the girl from Ketiaro's memory... which strongly suggests that Keitaro and Mutsumi belong together... which strongly suggests that Naru has been chopped to second fiddle in the hierarchy of Keitaro's affections. Bad timing, considering that the stern, studious Naru has just developed an unyielding crush on her klutzy study partner.

# CONTENTS

LOVE♡HINA

LOVE♡HINA

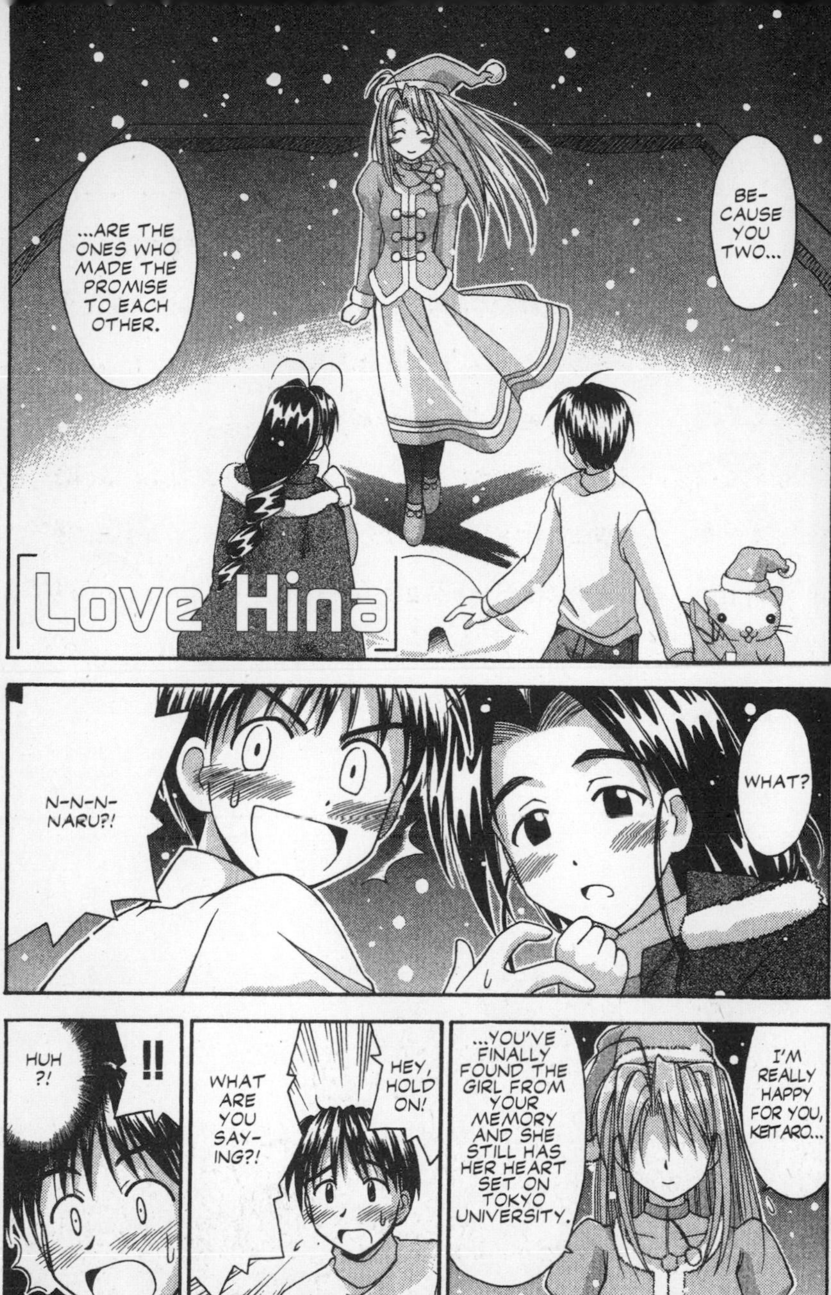
BE-CAUSE YOU TWO...
...ARE THE ONES WHO MADE THE PROMISE TO EACH OTHER.
Love Hina
WHAT?
N-N-N-NARU?!
I'M REALLY HAPPY FOR YOU, KEITARO...
...YOU'VE FINALLY FOUND THE GIRL FROM YOUR MEMORY AND SHE STILL HAS HER HEART SET ON TOKYO UNIVERSITY.
HEY, HOLD ON!
WHAT ARE YOU SAY-ING?!
!!
HUH?!

## HINATA.52 A Little Lost Sheep on a Holy Night?!

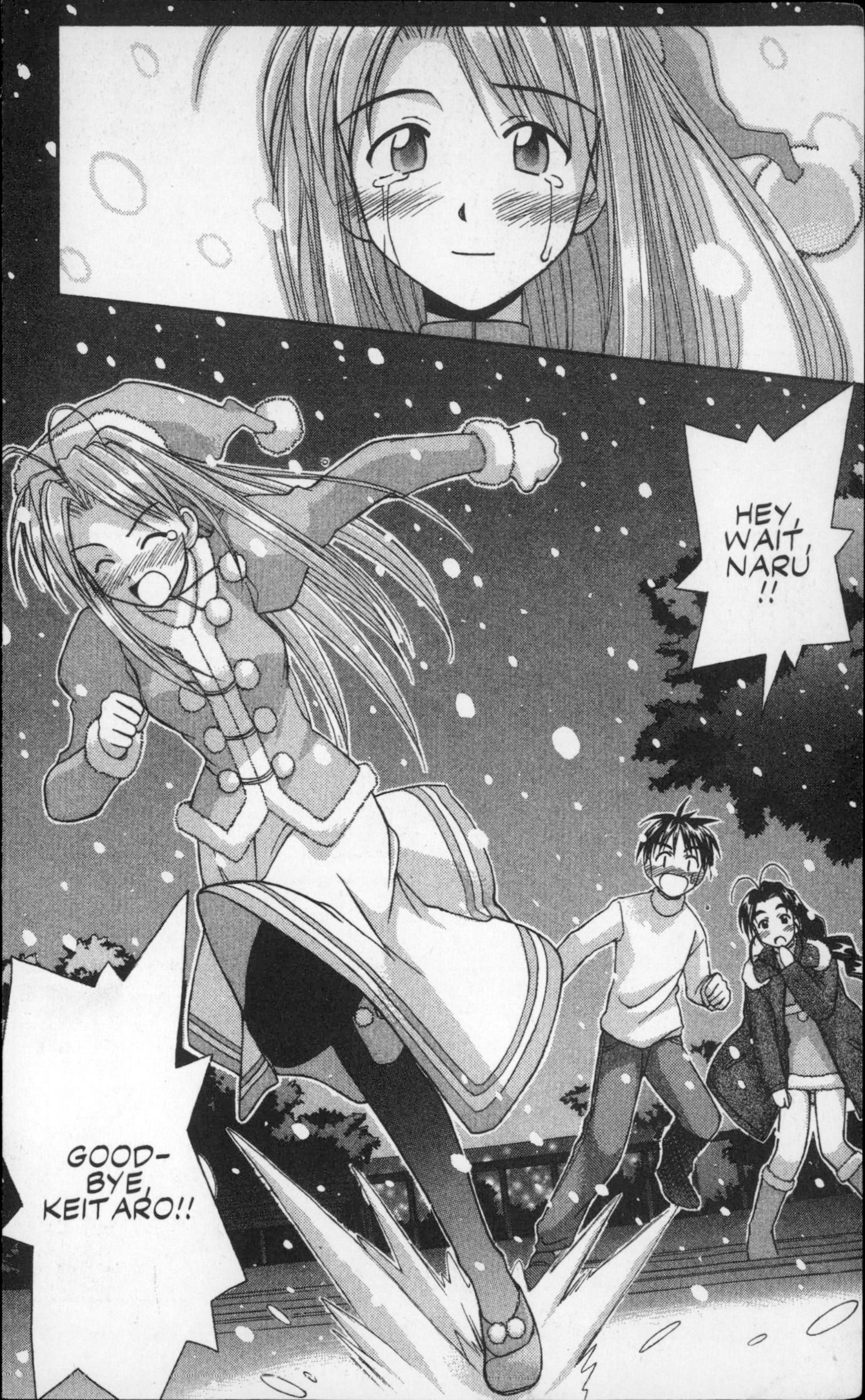
HEY, WAIT, NARU!!
GOOD-BYE, KEITARO!!

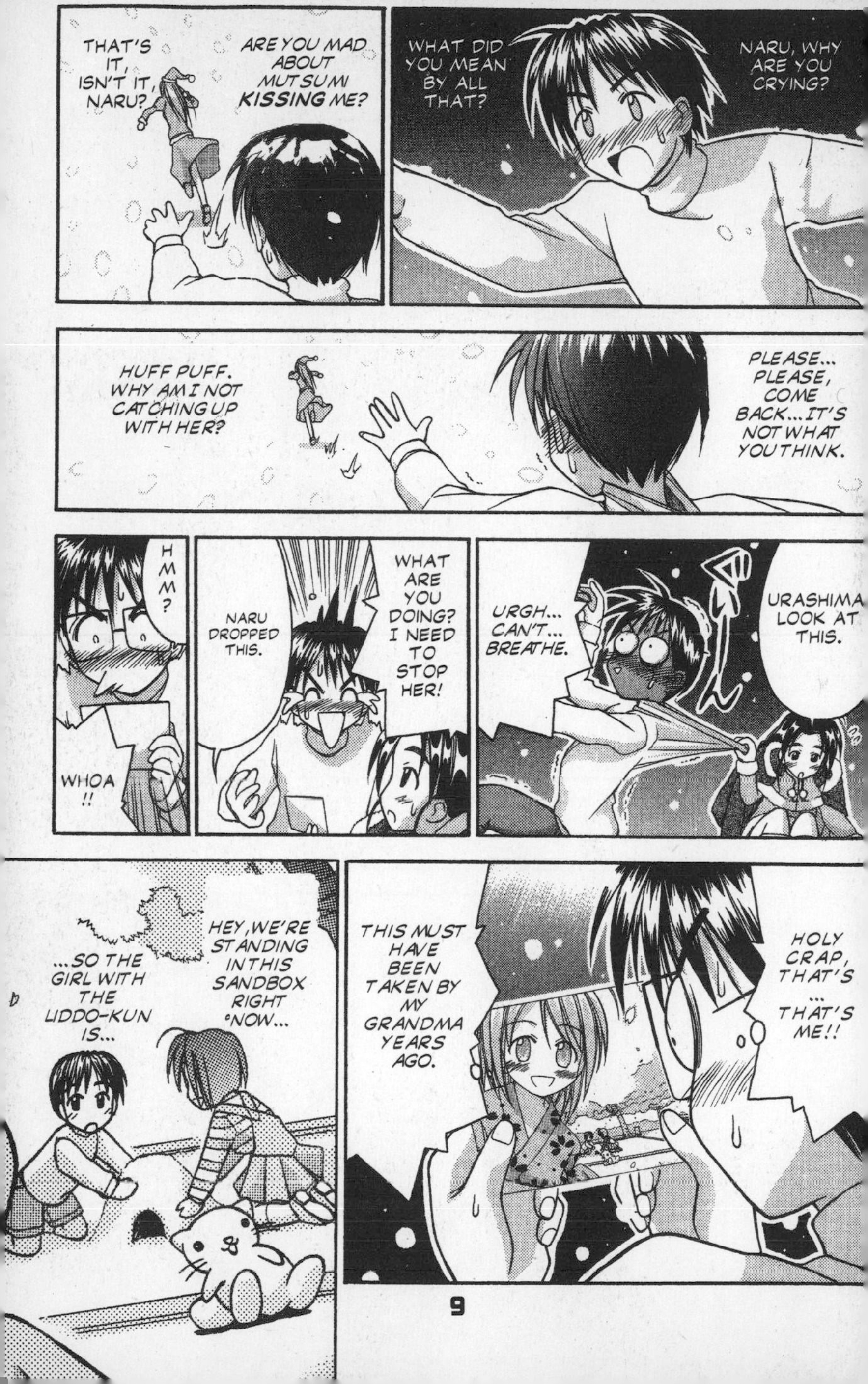
NARU, WHY ARE YOU CRYING?
WHAT DID YOU MEAN BY ALL THAT?
ARE YOU MAD ABOUT MUTSUMI KISSING ME?
THAT'S IT, ISN'T IT, NARU?
PLEASE... PLEASE, COME BACK... IT'S NOT WHAT YOU THINK.
HUFF PUFF. WHY AM I NOT CATCHING UP WITH HER?
URASHIMA LOOK AT THIS.
URGH... CAN'T... BREATHE.
WHAT ARE YOU DOING? I NEED TO STOP HER!
NARU DROPPED THIS.
HMM?
WHOA!!
HOLY CRAP, THAT'S ... THAT'S ME!!
THIS MUST HAVE BEEN TAKEN BY MY GRANDMA YEARS AGO.
HEY, WE'RE STANDING IN THIS SANDBOX RIGHT NOW...
...SO THE GIRL WITH THE LIDDO-KUN IS...

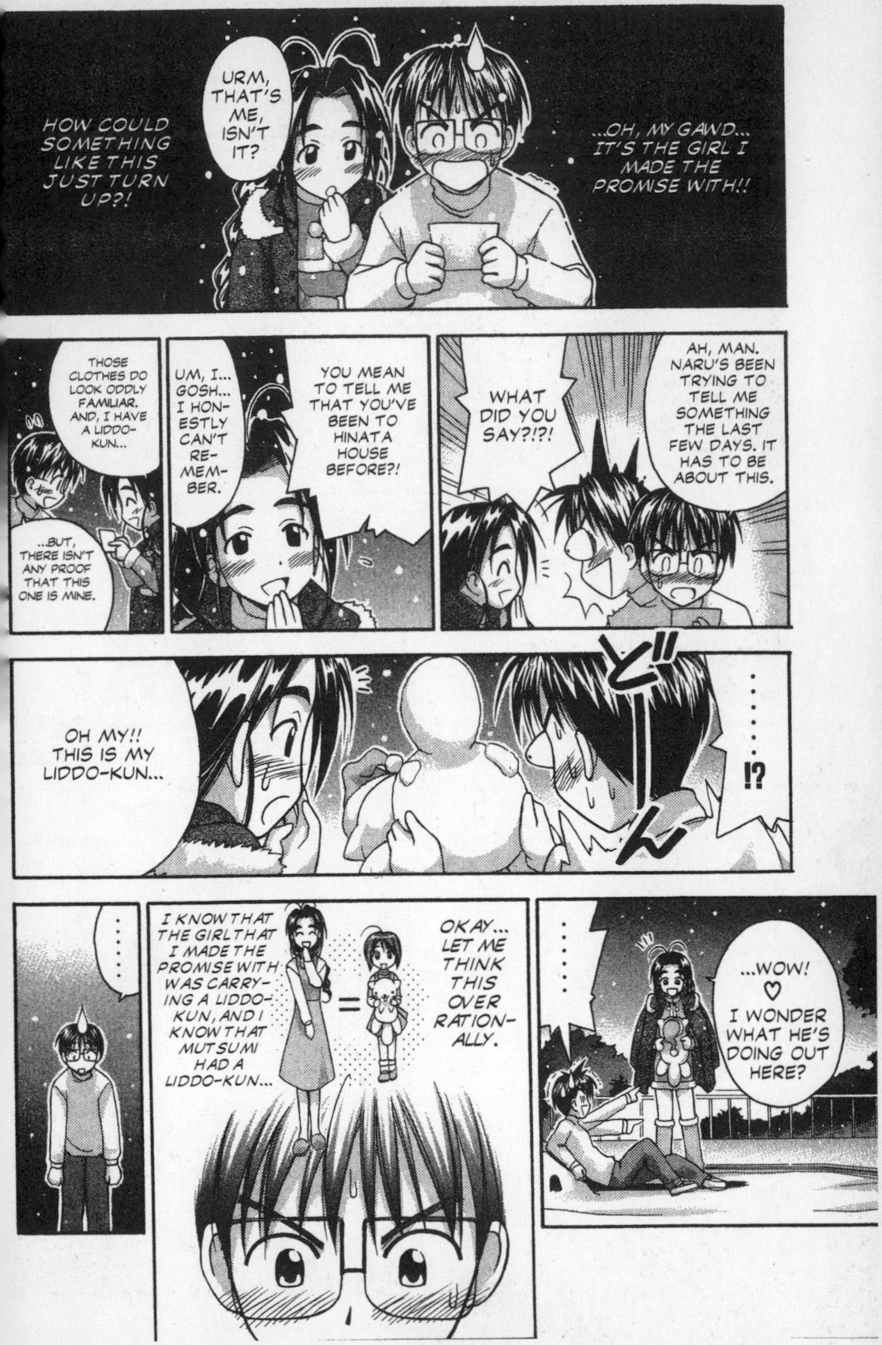

...OH, MY GAWD... IT'S THE GIRL I MADE THE PROMISE WITH!!
URM, THAT'S ME, ISN'T IT?
HOW COULD SOMETHING LIKE THIS JUST TURN UP?!
AH, MAN. NARU'S BEEN TRYING TO TELL ME SOMETHING THE LAST FEW DAYS. IT HAS TO BE ABOUT THIS.
WHAT DID YOU SAY?!?!
YOU MEAN TO TELL ME THAT YOU'VE BEEN TO HINATA HOUSE BEFORE?!
UM, I... GOSH... I HON-ESTLY CAN'T RE-MEM-BER.
THOSE CLOTHES DO LOOK ODDLY FAMILIAR. AND, I HAVE A LIDDO-KUN...
...BUT, THERE ISN'T ANY PROOF THAT THIS ONE IS MINE.
......
!?
どん
OH MY!! THIS IS MY LIDDO-KUN...
...WOW! ♡ I WONDER WHAT HE'S DOING OUT HERE?
......
OKAY... LET ME THINK THIS OVER RATION-ALLY.
I KNOW THAT THE GIRL THAT I MADE THE PROMISE WITH WAS CARRY-ING A LIDDO-KUN, AND I KNOW THAT MUTSUMI HAD A LIDDO-KUN...
=
......

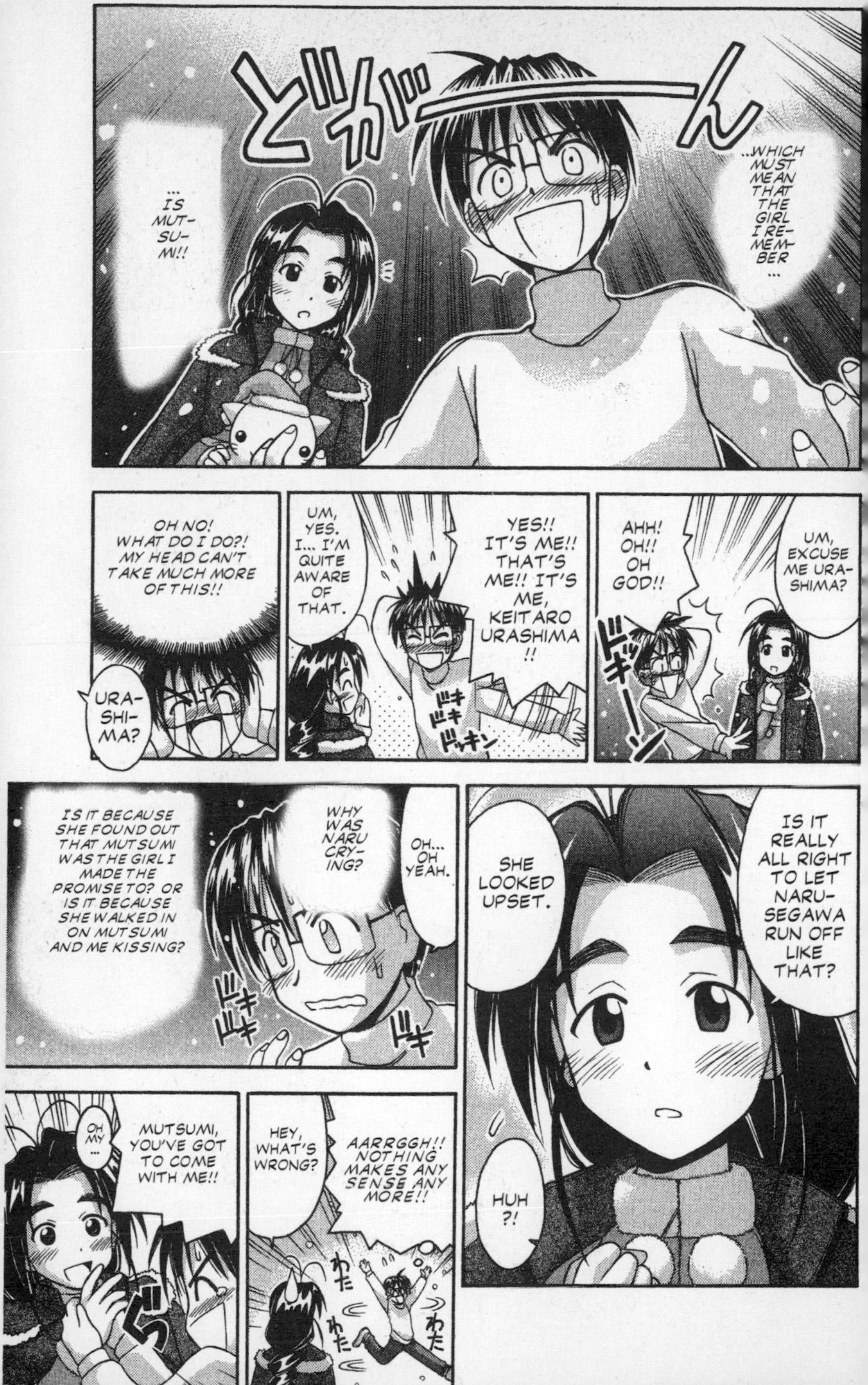

どがーん
...WHICH MUST MEAN THAT THE GIRL I REMEMBER...
...IS MUTSUMI!!
UM, EXCUSE ME URASHIMA?
AHH! OH!! OH GOD!!
ドッキーン
YES!! IT'S ME!! THAT'S ME!! IT'S ME, KEITARO URASHIMA!!
UM, YES. I... I'M QUITE AWARE OF THAT.
ドキドキドッキン
OH NO! WHAT DO I DO?! MY HEAD CAN'T TAKE MUCH MORE OF THIS!!
URASHIMA?
IS IT REALLY ALL RIGHT TO LET NARUSEGAWA RUN OFF LIKE THAT?
SHE LOOKED UPSET.
HUH?!
OH... OH YEAH.
WHY WAS NARU CRYING?
IS IT BECAUSE SHE FOUND OUT THAT MUTSUMI WAS THE GIRL I MADE THE PROMISE TO? OR IS IT BECAUSE SHE WALKED IN ON MUTSUMI AND ME KISSING?
ドキドキ
ドキ
AARRGGH!! NOTHING MAKES ANY SENSE ANY MORE!!
HEY, WHAT'S WRONG?
わたわた
わた
MUTSUMI, YOU'VE GOT TO COME WITH ME!!
OH MY...
ぐっ

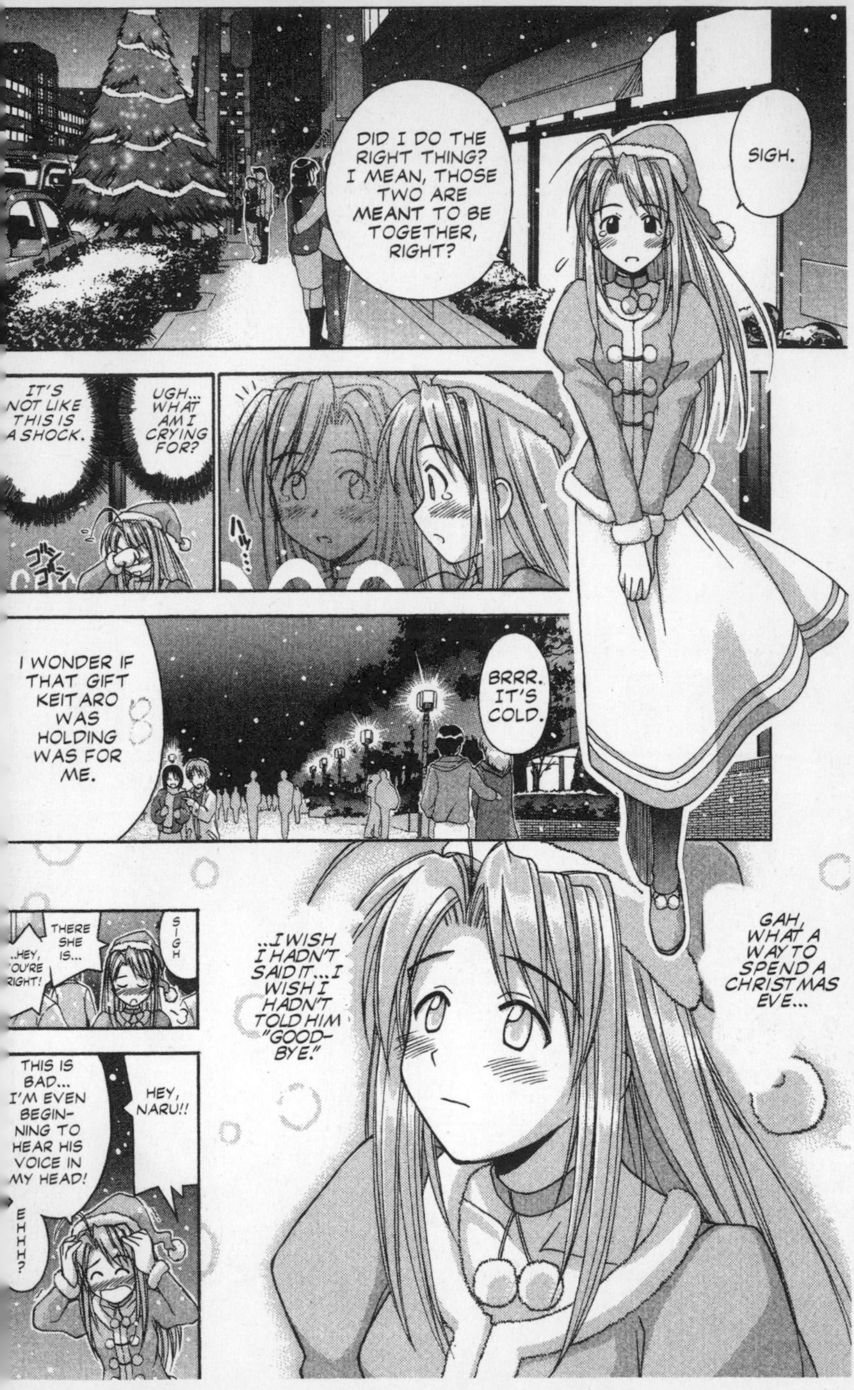
SIGH.
DID I DO THE RIGHT THING? I MEAN, THOSE TWO ARE MEANT TO BE TOGETHER, RIGHT?
UGH... WHAT AM I CRYING FOR?
IT'S NOT LIKE THIS IS A SHOCK.
BRRR. IT'S COLD.
I WONDER IF THAT GIFT KEITARO WAS HOLDING WAS FOR ME.
GAH, WHAT A WAY TO SPEND A CHRISTMAS EVE...
...I WISH I HADN'T SAID IT... I WISH I HADN'T TOLD HIM "GOOD-BYE."
SIGH
THERE SHE IS...
..HEY, YOU'RE RIGHT!
HEY, NARU!!
THIS IS BAD... I'M EVEN BEGIN-NING TO HEAR HIS VOICE IN MY HEAD!
EHHH?

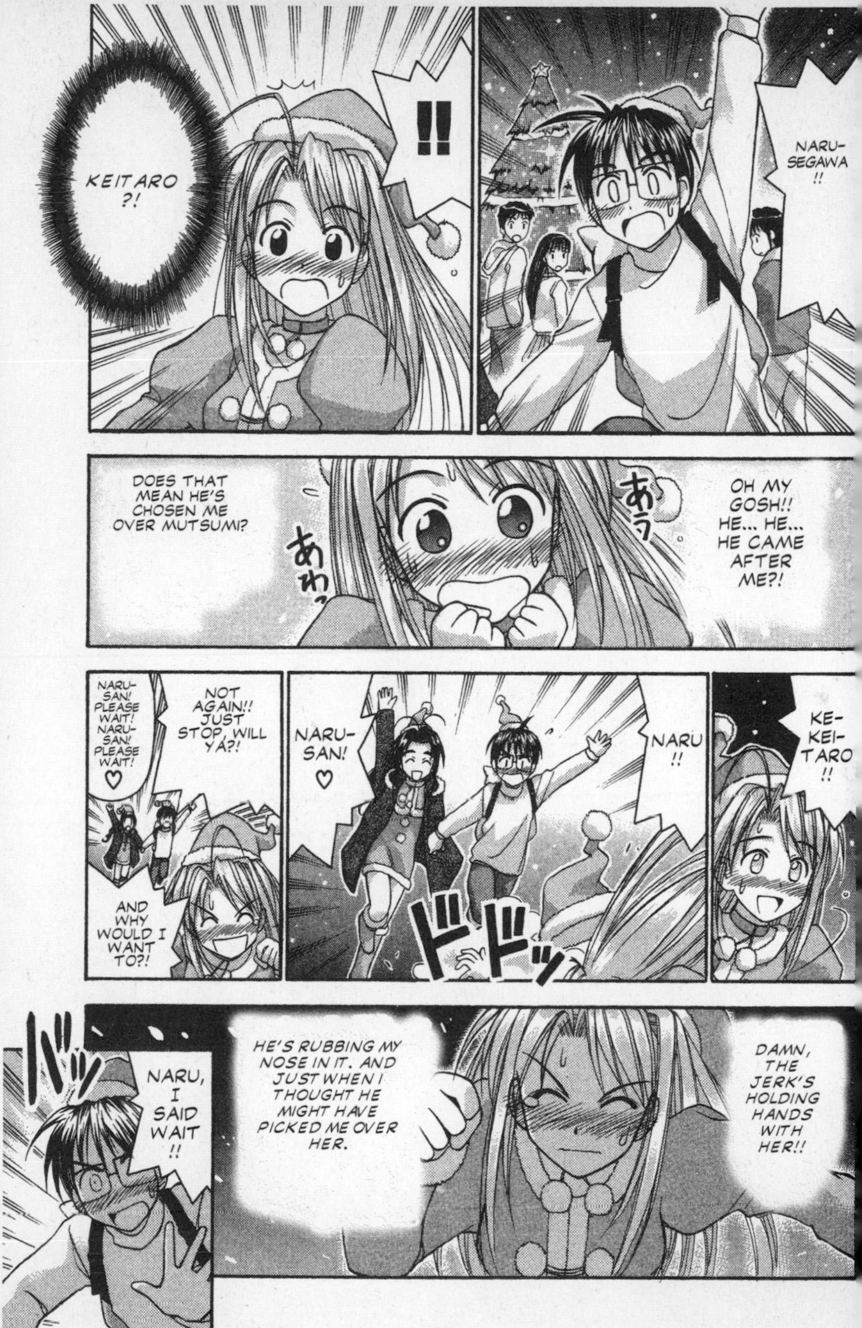
NARU-SEGAWA !!
!!
KEITARO ?!
OH MY GOSH!! HE... HE... HE CAME AFTER ME?!
あぅ
あわっ
DOES THAT MEAN HE'S CHOSEN ME OVER MUTSUMI?
KE-KEI-TARO !!
NARU !!
NARU-SAN! ♡
ドドッ
NOT AGAIN!! JUST STOP, WILL YA?!
NARU-SAN! PLEASE WAIT! NARU-SAN! PLEASE WAIT! ♡
AND WHY WOULD I WANT TO?!
DAMN, THE JERK'S HOLDING HANDS WITH HER!!
HE'S RUBBING MY NOSE IN IT. AND JUST WHEN I THOUGHT HE MIGHT HAVE PICKED ME OVER HER.
NARU, I SAID WAIT !!
バッ

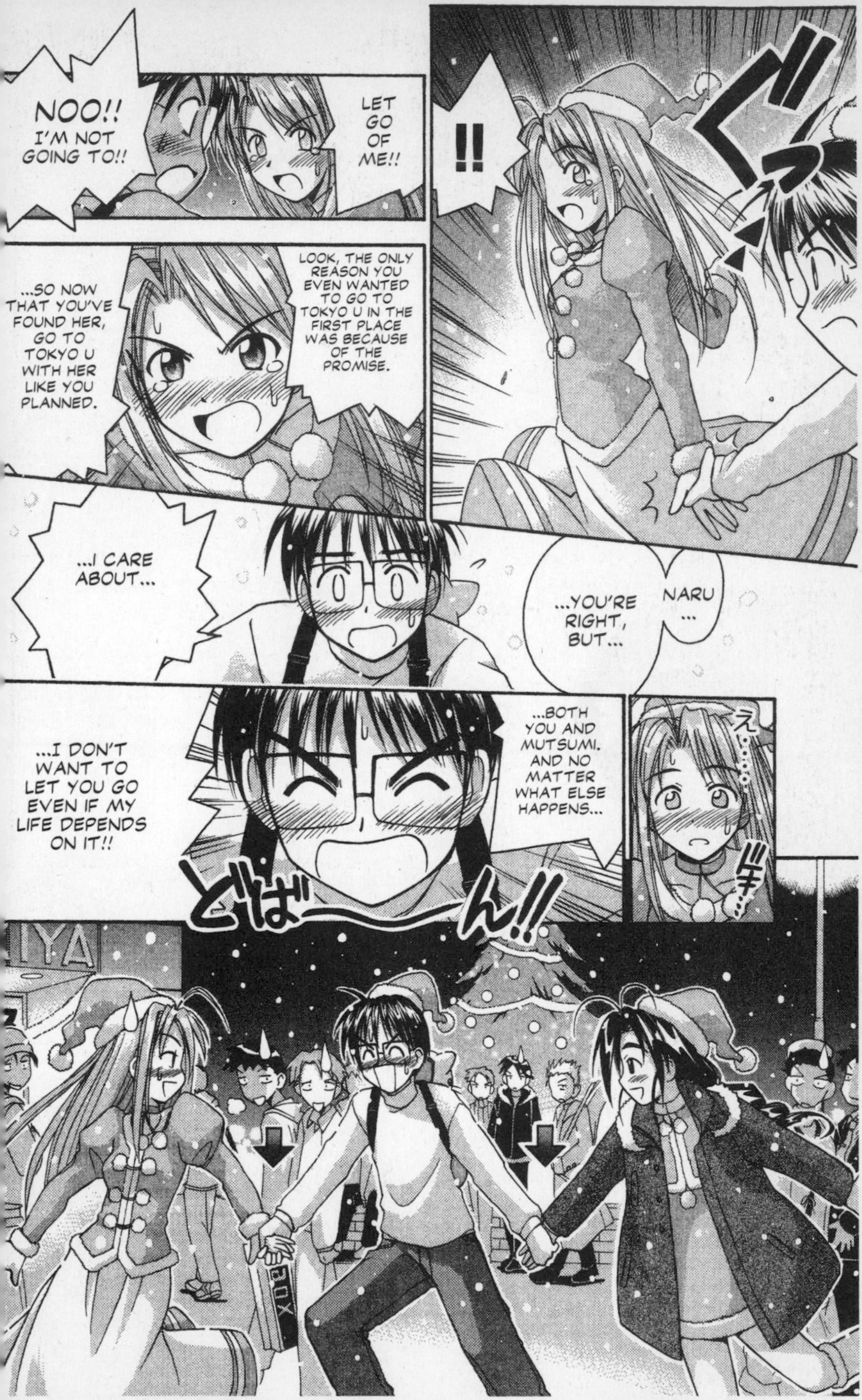
!!
ぐっ
LET GO OF ME!!
NOO!! I'M NOT GOING TO!!
LOOK, THE ONLY REASON YOU EVEN WANTED TO GO TO TOKYO U IN THE FIRST PLACE WAS BECAUSE OF THE PROMISE.
...SO NOW THAT YOU'VE FOUND HER, GO TO TOKYO U WITH HER LIKE YOU PLANNED.
NARU ...
...YOU'RE RIGHT, BUT...
...I CARE ABOUT...
え……
ドキ…
...BOTH YOU AND MUTSUMI. AND NO MATTER WHAT ELSE HAPPENS...
...I DON'T WANT TO LET YOU GO EVEN IF MY LIFE DEPENDS ON IT!!
どば——ん!!
IYA

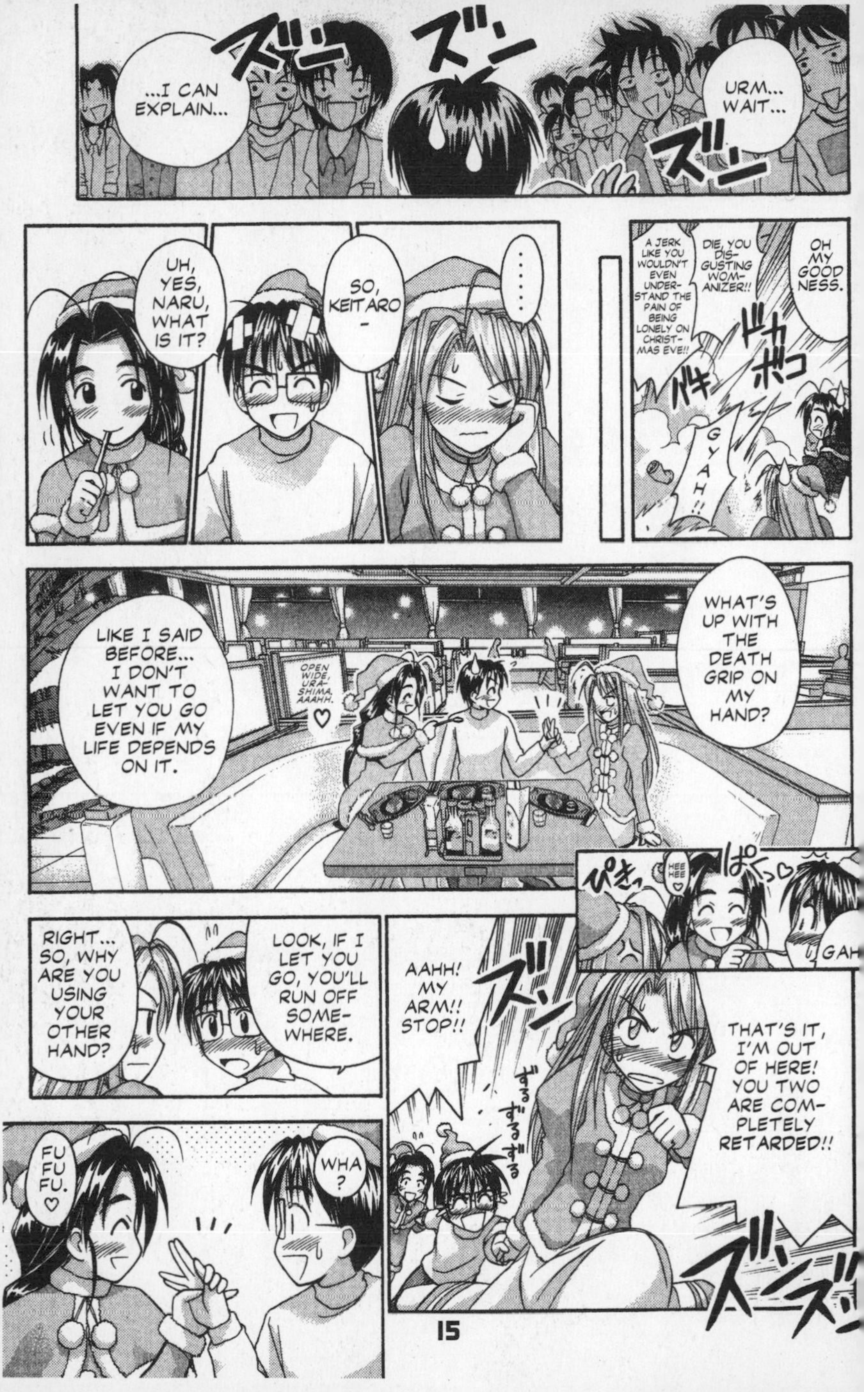
URM... WAIT...
ズン
ズン
ズーン
...I CAN EXPLAIN...
OH MY GOODNESS.
DIE, YOU DISGUSTING WOMANIZER!!
A JERK LIKE YOU WOULDN'T EVEN UNDERSTAND THE PAIN OF BEING LONELY ON CHRISTMAS EVE!!
ドカボコ
バキ
GYAH!!
......
SO, KEITARO -
UH, YES, NARU, WHAT IS IT?
WHAT'S UP WITH THE DEATH GRIP ON MY HAND?
OPEN WIDE, URASHIMA. AAAHH. ♥
LIKE I SAID BEFORE... I DON'T WANT TO LET YOU GO EVEN IF MY LIFE DEPENDS ON IT.
ぱくっ♥
HEE HEE ♥
ぴきっ
GAH
THAT'S IT, I'M OUT OF HERE! YOU TWO ARE COMPLETELY RETARDED!!
ズン
AAHH! MY ARM!! STOP!!
ずるずるずる
ズン、ズン
LOOK, IF I LET YOU GO, YOU'LL RUN OFF SOMEWHERE.
RIGHT... SO, WHY ARE YOU USING YOUR OTHER HAND?
WHA?
FUFUFU. ♥

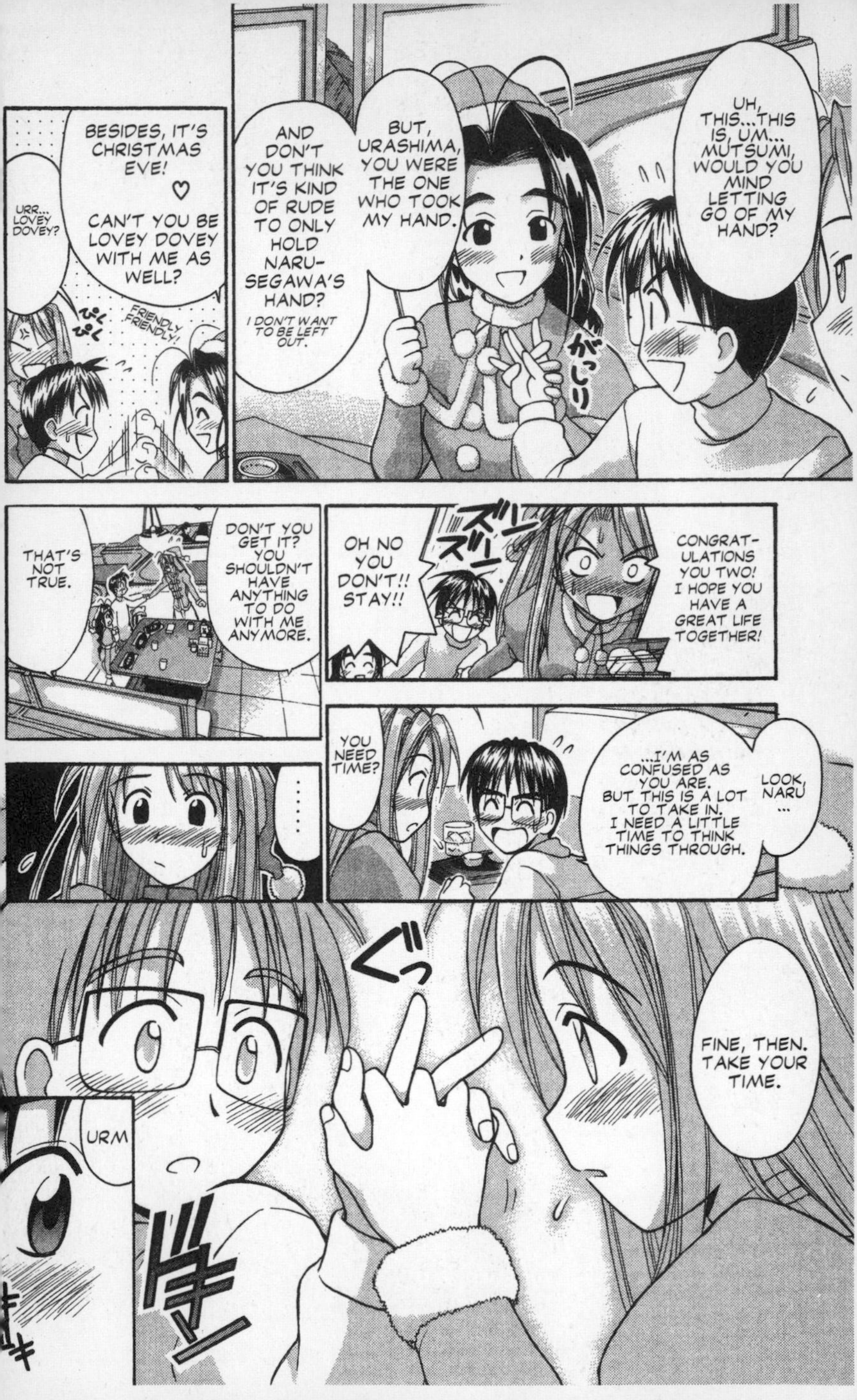
UH, THIS...THIS IS, UM... MUTSUMI, WOULD YOU MIND LETTING GO OF MY HAND?
BUT, URASHIMA, YOU WERE THE ONE WHO TOOK MY HAND.
AND DON'T YOU THINK IT'S KIND OF RUDE TO ONLY HOLD NARU-SEGAWA'S HAND?
I DON'T WANT TO BE LEFT OUT.
がっしり
BESIDES, IT'S CHRISTMAS EVE! ♡ CAN'T YOU BE LOVEY DOVEY WITH ME AS WELL?
URR... LOVEY DOVEY?
FRIENDLY FRIENDLY!
ぷくぷく
CONGRAT-ULATIONS YOU TWO! I HOPE YOU HAVE A GREAT LIFE TOGETHER!
ズリ ズリ
OH NO YOU DON'T!! STAY!!
DON'T YOU GET IT? YOU SHOULDN'T HAVE ANYTHING TO DO WITH ME ANYMORE.
THAT'S NOT TRUE.
LOOK, NARU...
...I'M AS CONFUSED AS YOU ARE. BUT THIS IS A LOT TO TAKE IN. I NEED A LITTLE TIME TO THINK THINGS THROUGH.
YOU NEED TIME?
......
ぐっ
FINE, THEN. TAKE YOUR TIME.
URM

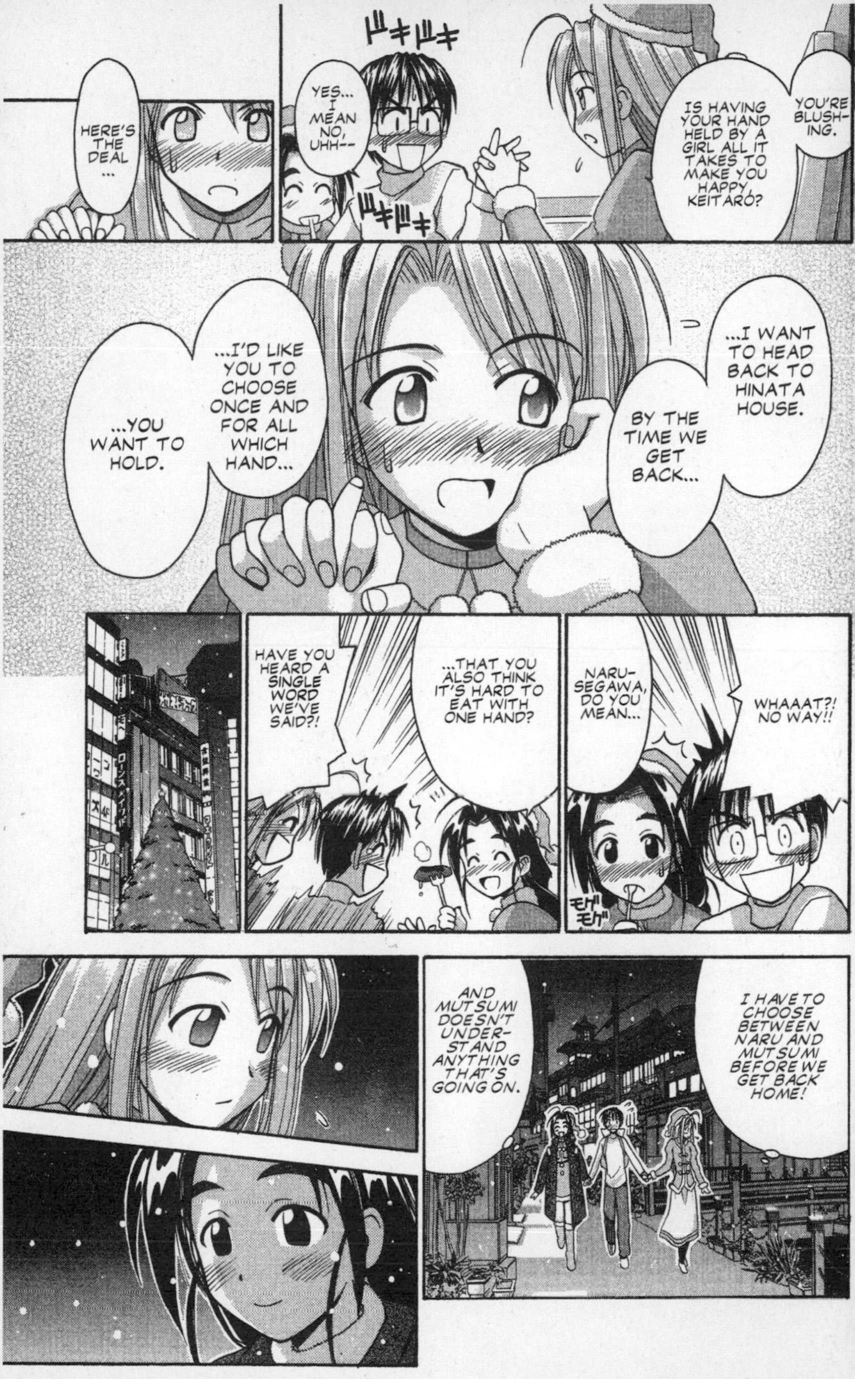
YOU'RE BLUSHING.
IS HAVING YOUR HAND HELD BY A GIRL ALL IT TAKES TO MAKE YOU HAPPY, KEITARÓ?
ドキドキ
YES... I MEAN NO, UHH--
ドキドキ
HERE'S THE DEAL ...
...I WANT TO HEAD BACK TO HINATA HOUSE.
BY THE TIME WE GET BACK...
...I'D LIKE YOU TO CHOOSE ONCE AND FOR ALL WHICH HAND...
...YOU WANT TO HOLD.
WHAAAT?! NO WAY!!
NARU-SEGAWA, DO YOU MEAN...
モグモグ
...THAT YOU ALSO THINK IT'S HARD TO EAT WITH ONE HAND?
HAVE YOU HEARD A SINGLE WORD WE'VE SAID?!
I HAVE TO CHOOSE BETWEEN NARU AND MUTSUMI BEFORE WE GET BACK HOME!
AND MUTSUMI DOESN'T UNDERSTAND ANYTHING THAT'S GOING ON.

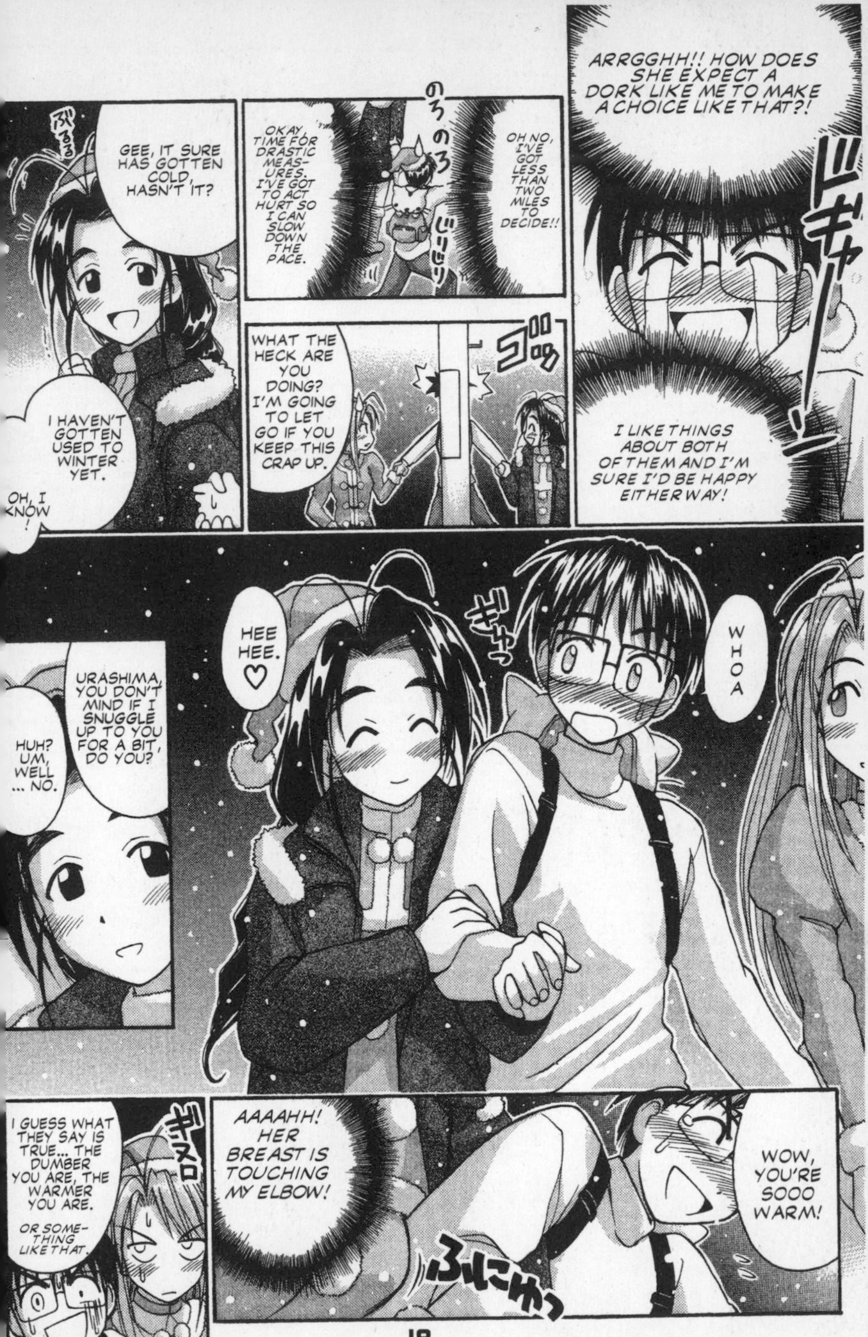
ARRGGHH!! HOW DOES SHE EXPECT A DORK LIKE ME TO MAKE A CHOICE LIKE THAT?!
ドギャー
I LIKE THINGS ABOUT BOTH OF THEM AND I'M SURE I'D BE HAPPY EITHER WAY!
OH NO, I'VE GOT LESS THAN TWO MILES TO DECIDE!!
のろのろ
OKAY, TIME FOR DRASTIC MEASURES. I'VE GOT TO ACT HURT SO I CAN SLOW DOWN THE PACE.
じりじり
ゴッ
WHAT THE HECK ARE YOU DOING? I'M GOING TO LET GO IF YOU KEEP THIS CRAP UP.
ぶるる
GEE, IT SURE HAS GOTTEN COLD, HASN'T IT?
I HAVEN'T GOTTEN USED TO WINTER YET.
OH, I KNOW!
WHOA
ぎゅっ
HEE HEE. ♡
URASHIMA, YOU DON'T MIND IF I SNUGGLE UP TO YOU FOR A BIT, DO YOU?
HUH? UM, WELL ... NO.
WOW, YOU'RE SOOO WARM!
AAAAHH! HER BREAST IS TOUCHING MY ELBOW!
ふにゅっ
ギヌロ
I GUESS WHAT THEY SAY IS TRUE... THE DUMBER YOU ARE, THE WARMER YOU ARE.
OR SOMETHING LIKE THAT.

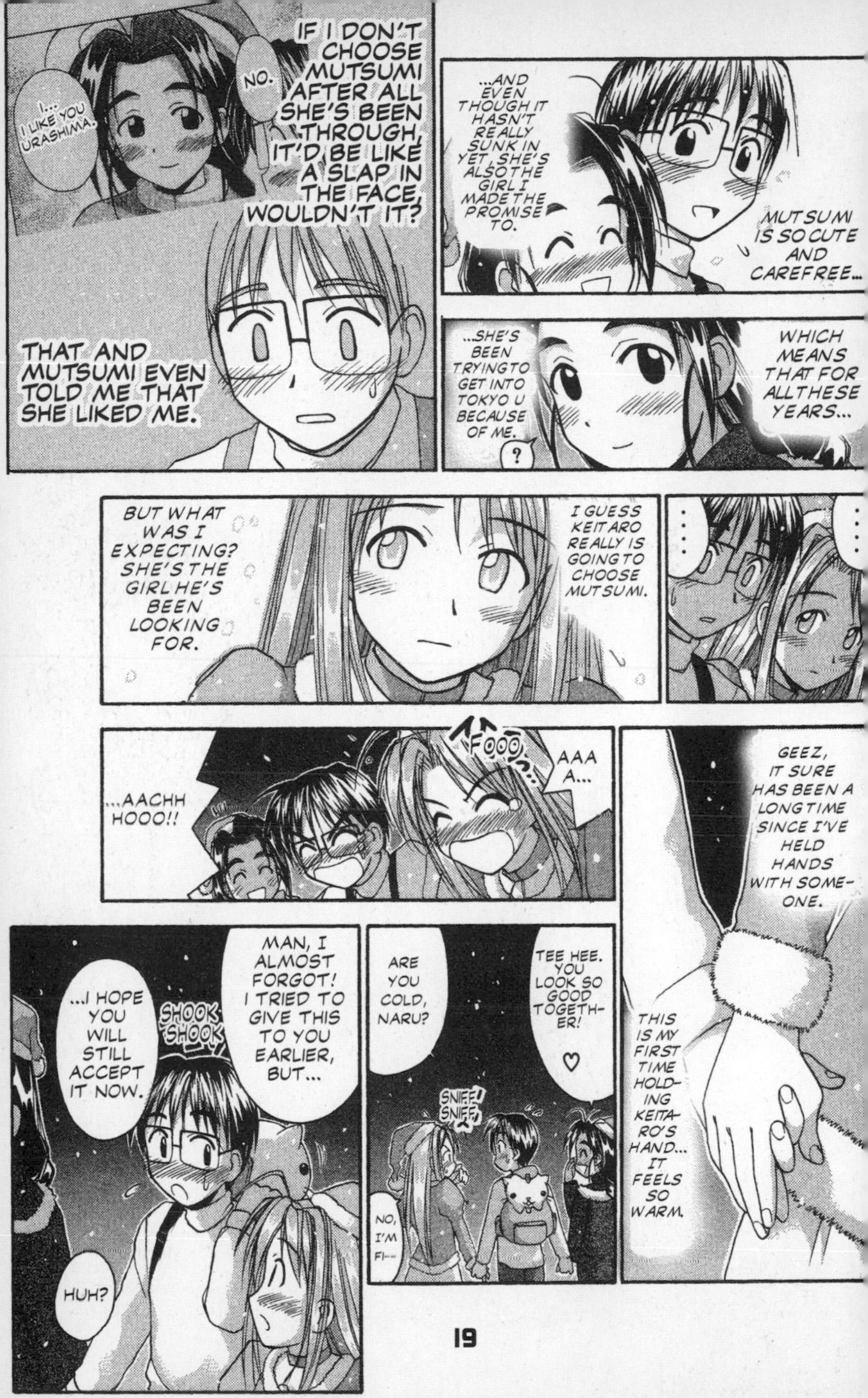
MUTSUMI IS SO CUTE AND CAREFREE...
...AND EVEN THOUGH IT HASN'T REALLY SUNK IN YET, SHE'S ALSO THE GIRL I MADE THE PROMISE TO.
WHICH MEANS THAT FOR ALL THESE YEARS...
...SHE'S BEEN TRYING TO GET INTO TOKYO U BECAUSE OF ME.
?
IF I DON'T CHOOSE MUTSUMI AFTER ALL SHE'S BEEN THROUGH, IT'D BE LIKE A SLAP IN THE FACE, WOULDN'T IT?
NO.
I... I LIKE YOU URASHIMA.
THAT AND MUTSUMI EVEN TOLD ME THAT SHE LIKED ME.
.....
.....
I GUESS KEITARO REALLY IS GOING TO CHOOSE MUTSUMI.
BUT WHAT WAS I EXPECTING? SHE'S THE GIRL HE'S BEEN LOOKING FOR.
GEEZ, IT SURE HAS BEEN A LONG TIME SINCE I'VE HELD HANDS WITH SOME-ONE.
THIS IS MY FIRST TIME HOLD-ING KEITA-RO'S HAND... IT FEELS SO WARM.
AAA A...
FOOO
...AACHH HOOO!!
TEE HEE. YOU LOOK SO GOOD TOGETH-ER! ♡
ARE YOU COLD, NARU?
SNIFF! SNIFF!
NO, I'M FI--
MAN, I ALMOST FORGOT! I TRIED TO GIVE THIS TO YOU EARLIER, BUT...
SHOOK SHOOK
...I HOPE YOU WILL STILL ACCEPT IT NOW.
HUH?

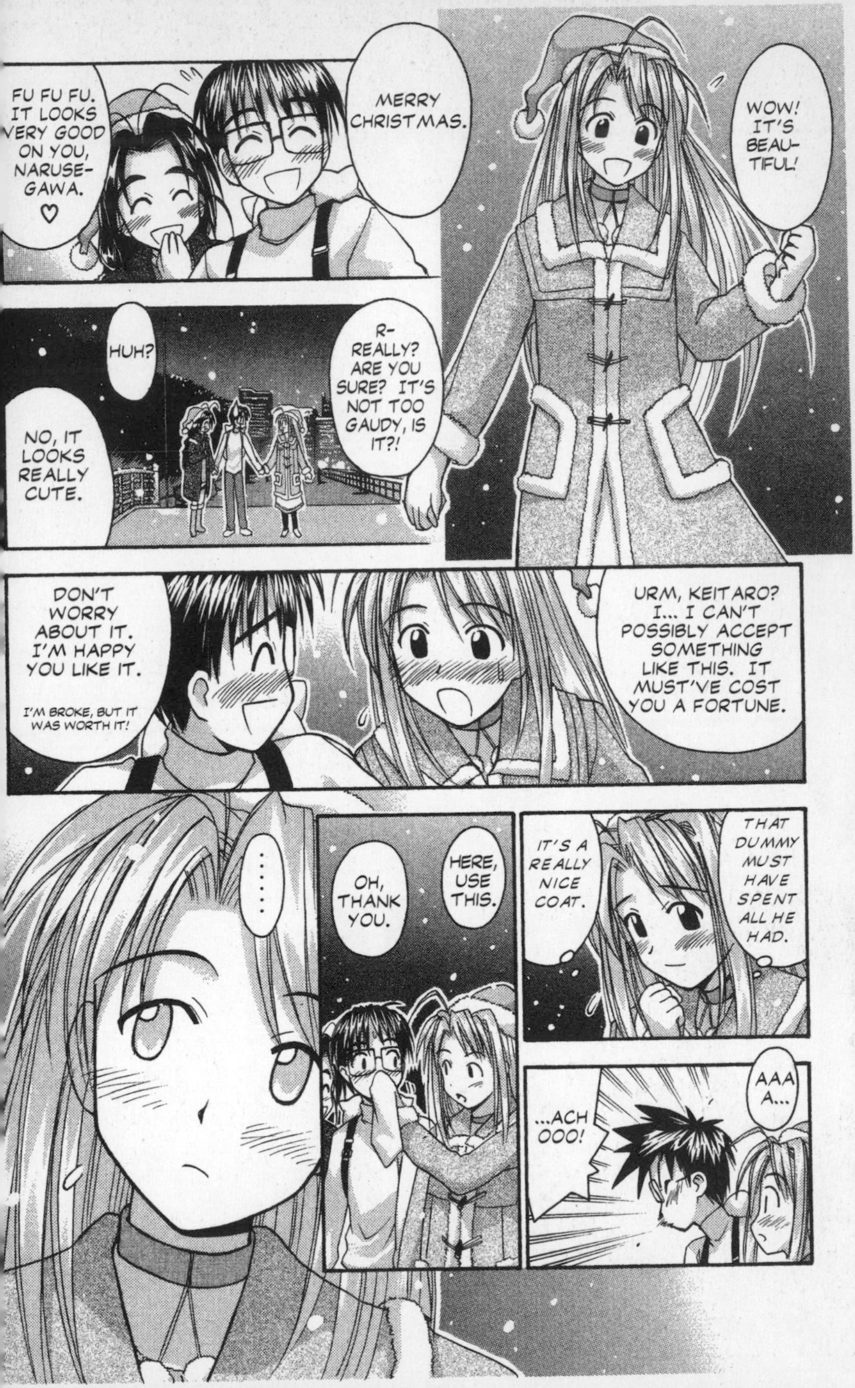
WOW! IT'S BEAU-TIFUL!
MERRY CHRISTMAS.
FU FU FU. IT LOOKS VERY GOOD ON YOU, NARUSE-GAWA. ♡
R-REALLY? ARE YOU SURE? IT'S NOT TOO GAUDY, IS IT?!
HUH?
NO, IT LOOKS REALLY CUTE.
URM, KEITARO? I... I CAN'T POSSIBLY ACCEPT SOMETHING LIKE THIS. IT MUST'VE COST YOU A FORTUNE.
DON'T WORRY ABOUT IT. I'M HAPPY YOU LIKE IT.
I'M BROKE, BUT IT WAS WORTH IT!
THAT DUMMY MUST HAVE SPENT ALL HE HAD.
IT'S A REALLY NICE COAT.
AAAA...
...ACHOOO!
HERE, USE THIS.
OH, THANK YOU.
......

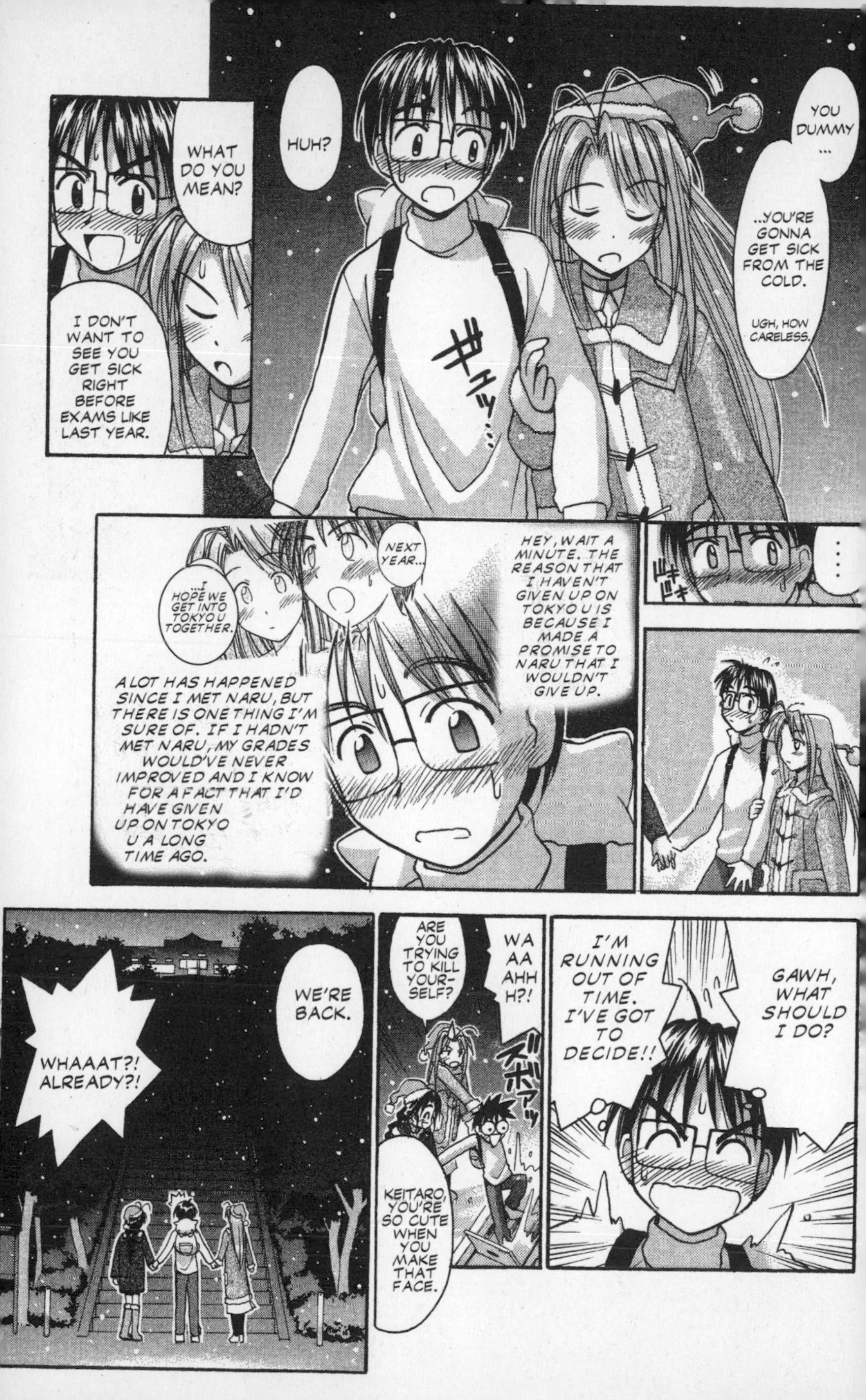
YOU DUMMY...
...YOU'RE GONNA GET SICK FROM THE COLD.
UGH, HOW CARELESS.
HUH?
ギュッ…
WHAT DO YOU MEAN?
I DON'T WANT TO SEE YOU GET SICK RIGHT BEFORE EXAMS LIKE LAST YEAR.
....
HEY, WAIT A MINUTE. THE REASON THAT I HAVEN'T GIVEN UP ON TOKYO U IS BECAUSE I MADE A PROMISE TO NARU THAT I WOULDN'T GIVE UP.
NEXT YEAR...
...I HOPE WE GET INTO TOKYO U TOGETHER.
A LOT HAS HAPPENED SINCE I MET NARU, BUT THERE IS ONE THING I'M SURE OF. IF I HADN'T MET NARU, MY GRADES WOULD'VE NEVER IMPROVED AND I KNOW FOR A FACT THAT I'D HAVE GIVEN UP ON TOKYO U A LONG TIME AGO.
GAWH, WHAT SHOULD I DO?
I'M RUNNING OUT OF TIME. I'VE GOT TO DECIDE!!
WA AA AHH H?!
ARE YOU TRYING TO KILL YOUR-SELF?
KEITARO, YOU'RE SO CUTE WHEN YOU MAKE THAT FACE.
WE'RE BACK.
WHAAAT?! ALREADY?!

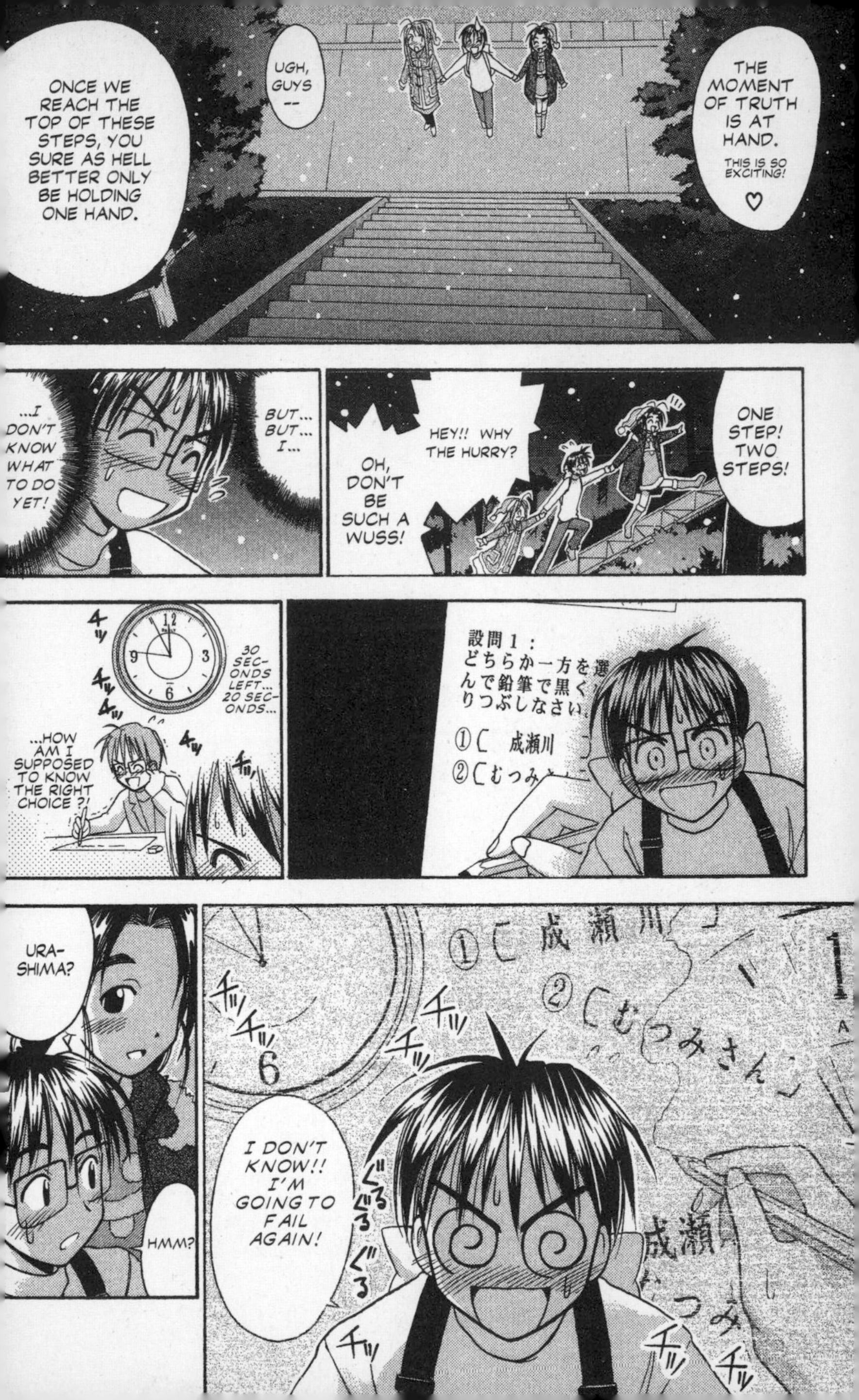

THE MOMENT OF TRUTH IS AT HAND.
THIS IS SO EXCITING! ♡
UGH, GUYS --
ONCE WE REACH THE TOP OF THESE STEPS, YOU SURE AS HELL BETTER ONLY BE HOLDING ONE HAND.
ONE STEP! TWO STEPS!
HEY!! WHY THE HURRY?
OH, DON'T BE SUCH A WUSS!
BUT... BUT... I...
...I DON'T KNOW WHAT TO DO YET!
設問１：
どちらか一方を選
んで鉛筆で黒く
りつぶしなさい。
①〔　成瀬川
②〔むつみ
チッ
30 SECONDS LEFT... 20 SECONDS...
...HOW AM I SUPPOSED TO KNOW THE RIGHT CHOICE?!
①〔成瀬川
②〔むつみさん〕
チッ
I DON'T KNOW!! I'M GOING TO FAIL AGAIN!
ぐるぐるぐる
成瀬
つみ
URA-SHIMA?
HMM?

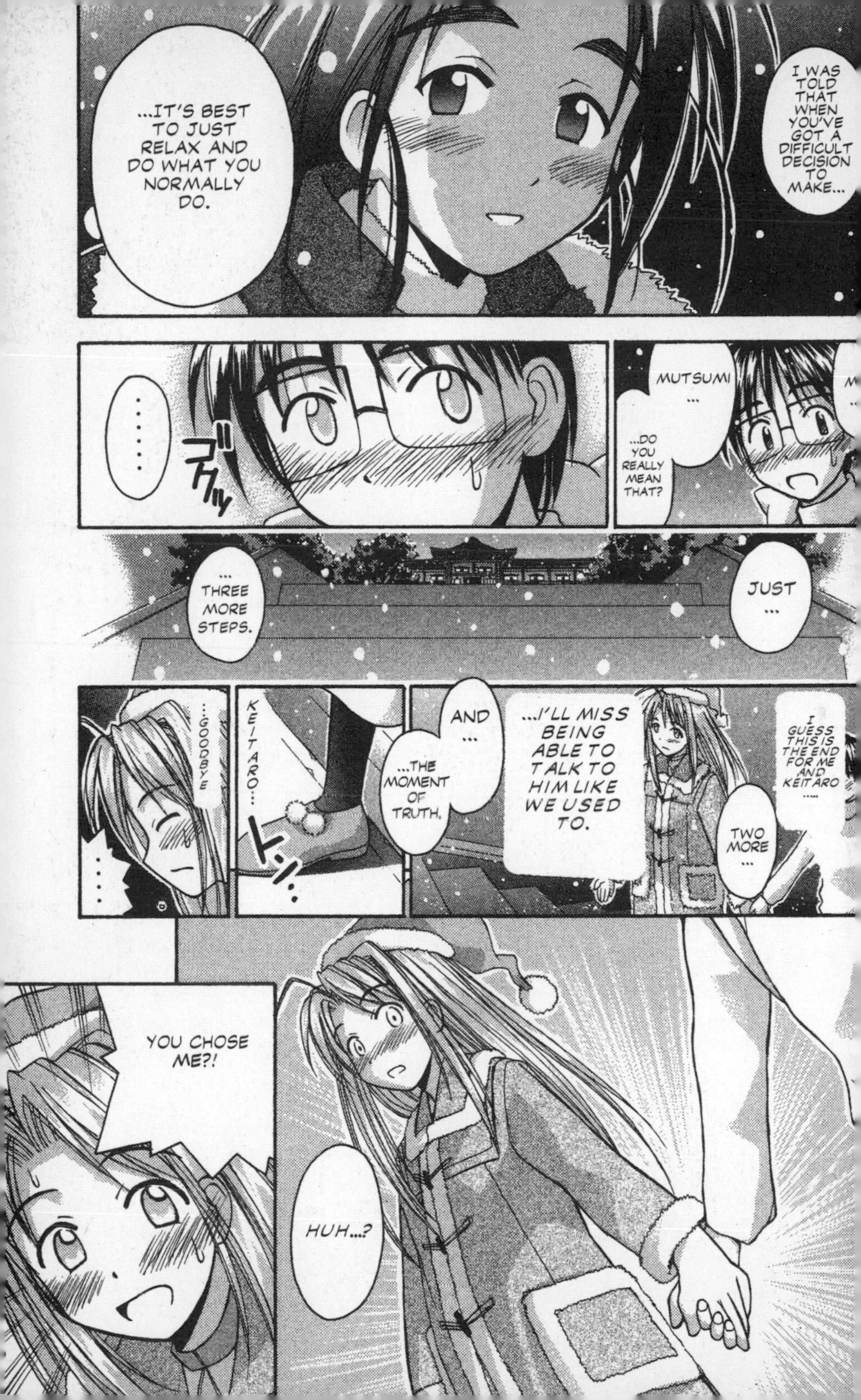
I WAS TOLD THAT WHEN YOU'VE GOT A DIFFICULT DECISION TO MAKE...
...IT'S BEST TO JUST RELAX AND DO WHAT YOU NORMALLY DO.
MUTSUMI ...
...DO YOU REALLY MEAN THAT?
......
JUST ...
... THREE MORE STEPS.
I GUESS THIS IS THE END FOR ME AND KEITARO .....
TWO MORE ...
...I'LL MISS BEING ABLE TO TALK TO HIM LIKE WE USED TO.
AND ...
...THE MOMENT OF TRUTH.
KEITARO...
...GOODBYE
.....
HUH...?
YOU CHOSE ME?!

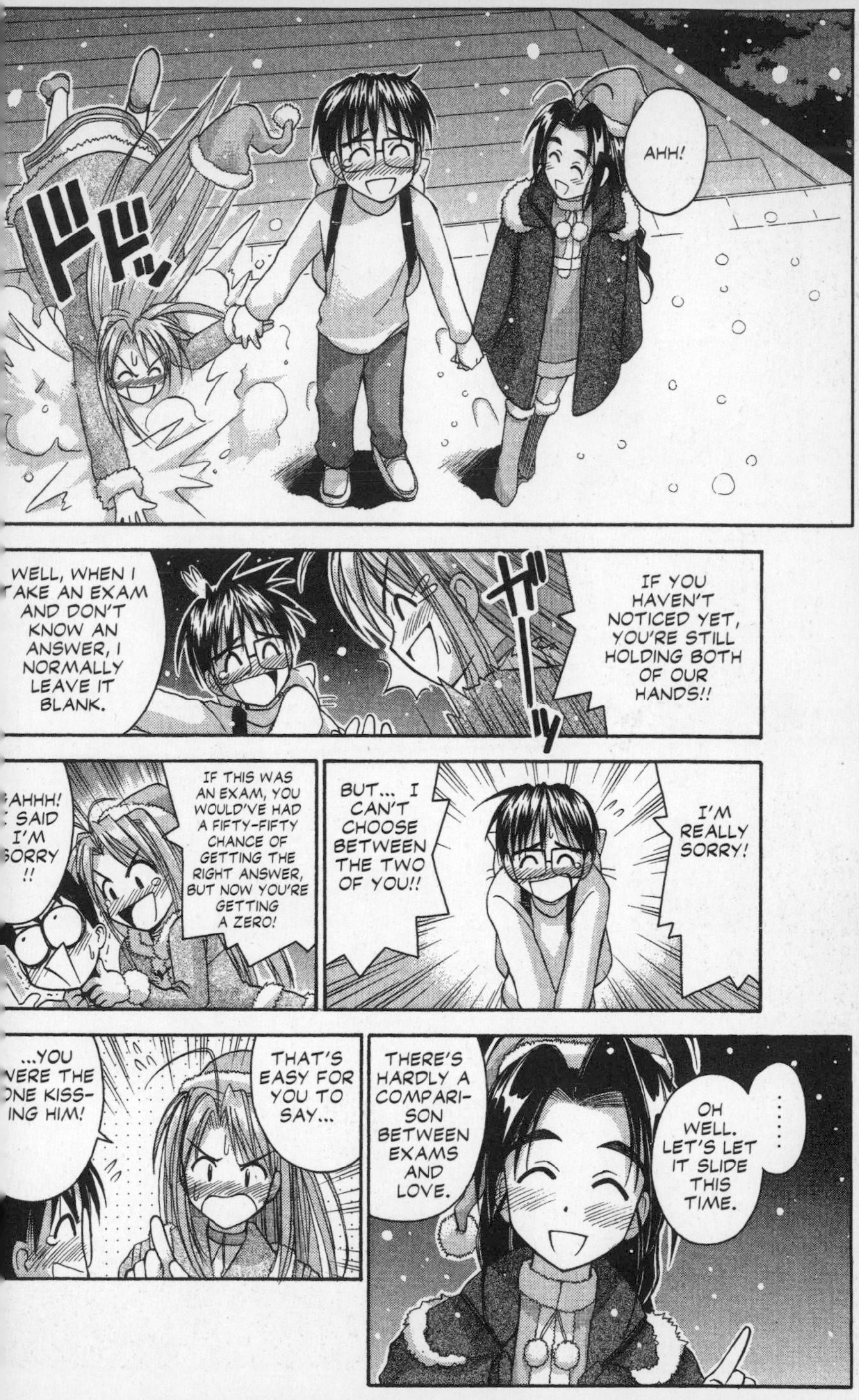
AHH!
ドドッ
IF YOU HAVEN'T NOTICED YET, YOU'RE STILL HOLDING BOTH OF OUR HANDS!!
WELL, WHEN I TAKE AN EXAM AND DON'T KNOW AN ANSWER, I NORMALLY LEAVE IT BLANK.
I'M REALLY SORRY!
BUT... I CAN'T CHOOSE BETWEEN THE TWO OF YOU!!
IF THIS WAS AN EXAM, YOU WOULD'VE HAD A FIFTY-FIFTY CHANCE OF GETTING THE RIGHT ANSWER, BUT NOW YOU'RE GETTING A ZERO!
AHHH! SAID I'M SORRY !!
......
OH WELL. LET'S LET IT SLIDE THIS TIME.
THERE'S HARDLY A COMPARI- SON BETWEEN EXAMS AND LOVE.
THAT'S EASY FOR YOU TO SAY...
...YOU WERE THE ONE KISS- ING HIM!

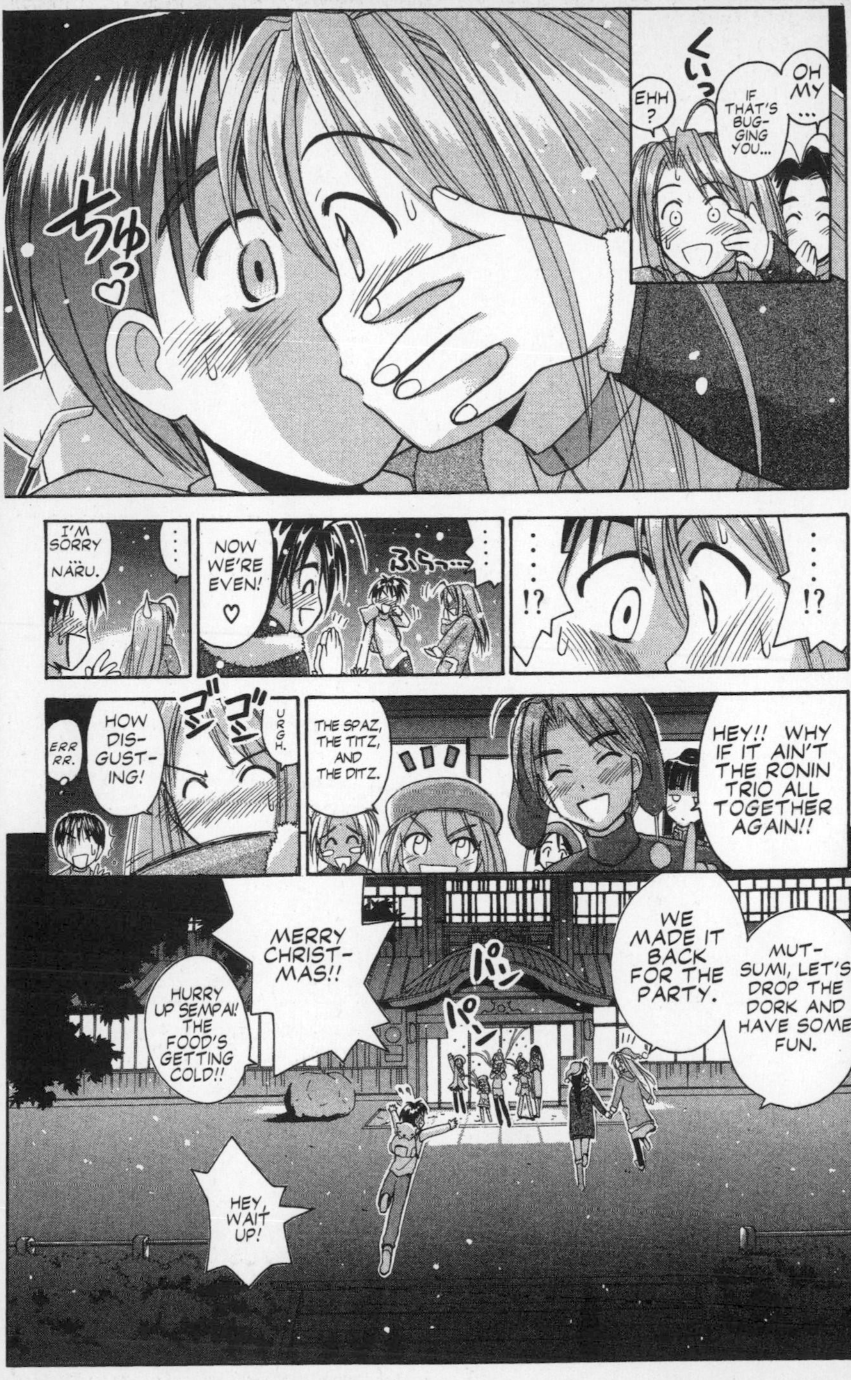

OH MY...
IF THAT'S BUGGING YOU...
くいっ
EHH?
ちゅっ♡
...!?
...!?
...
ふら…
NOW WE'RE EVEN! ♡
...
I'M SORRY ... NÄRU.
HEY!! WHY IF IT AIN'T THE RONIN TRIO ALL TOGETHER AGAIN!!
THE SPAZ, THE TITZ, AND THE DITZ.
URGH.
ゴゴ
HOW DISGUSTING!
ERR RR.
MUTSUMI, LET'S DROP THE DORK AND HAVE SOME FUN.
WE MADE IT BACK FOR THE PARTY.
パン
パン
MERRY CHRISTMAS!!
HURRY UP SEMPAI! THE FOOD'S GETTING COLD!!
HEY, WAIT UP!

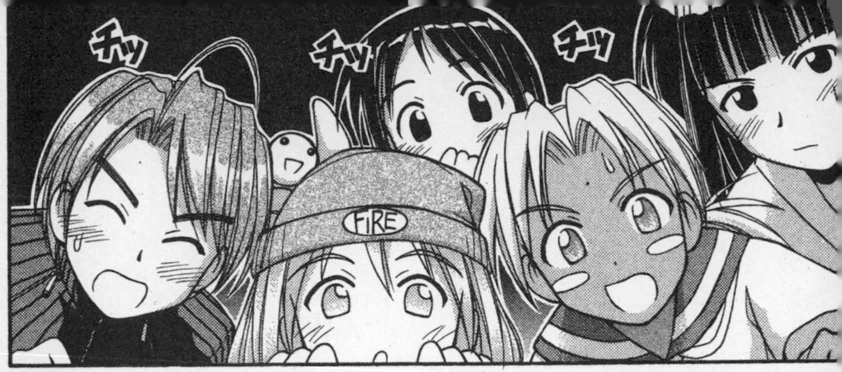
チッ
チッ
チッ
FIRE

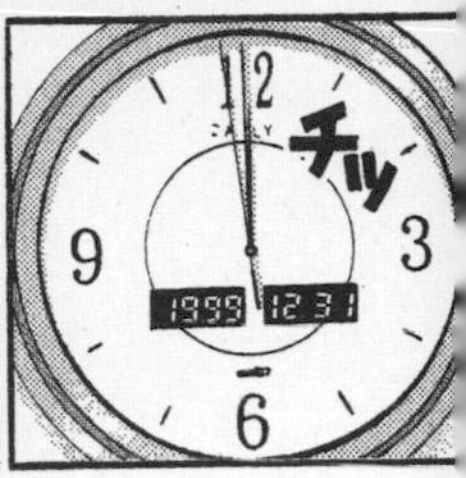
チッ
1999 12 31

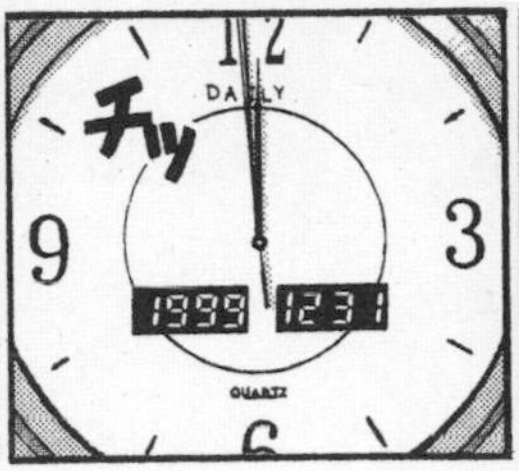
チッ
1999 12 31

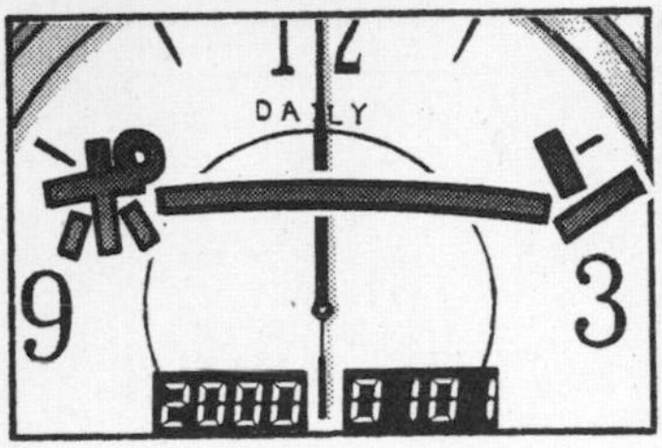
ポーーーン
2000 01 01

Love Hina

## HINATA.53
## The Heart-Pounding ♡ Bad Luck Cleansing Scheme?!

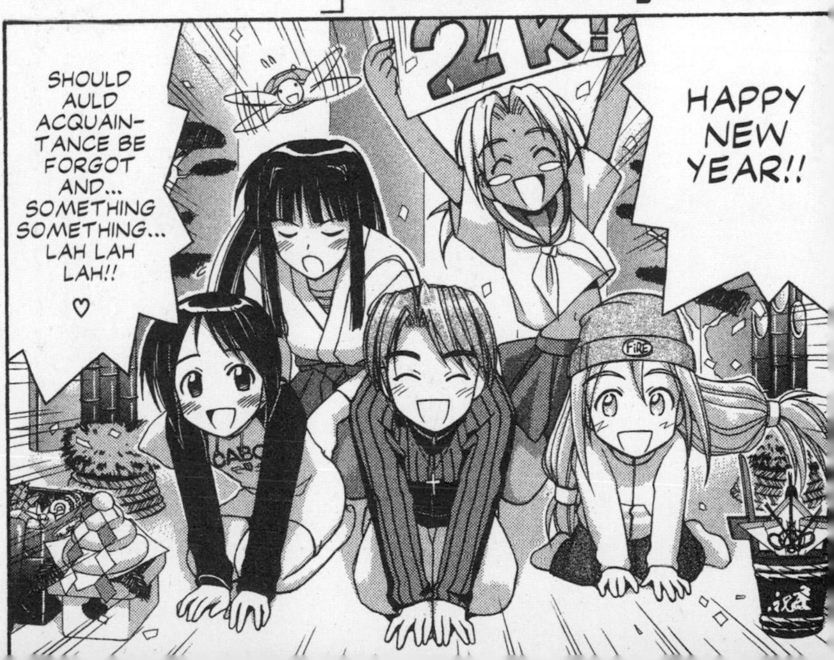
2K!
HAPPY NEW YEAR!!
SHOULD AULD ACQUAIN-TANCE BE FORGOT AND... SOMETHING SOMETHING... LAH LAH LAH!! ♡

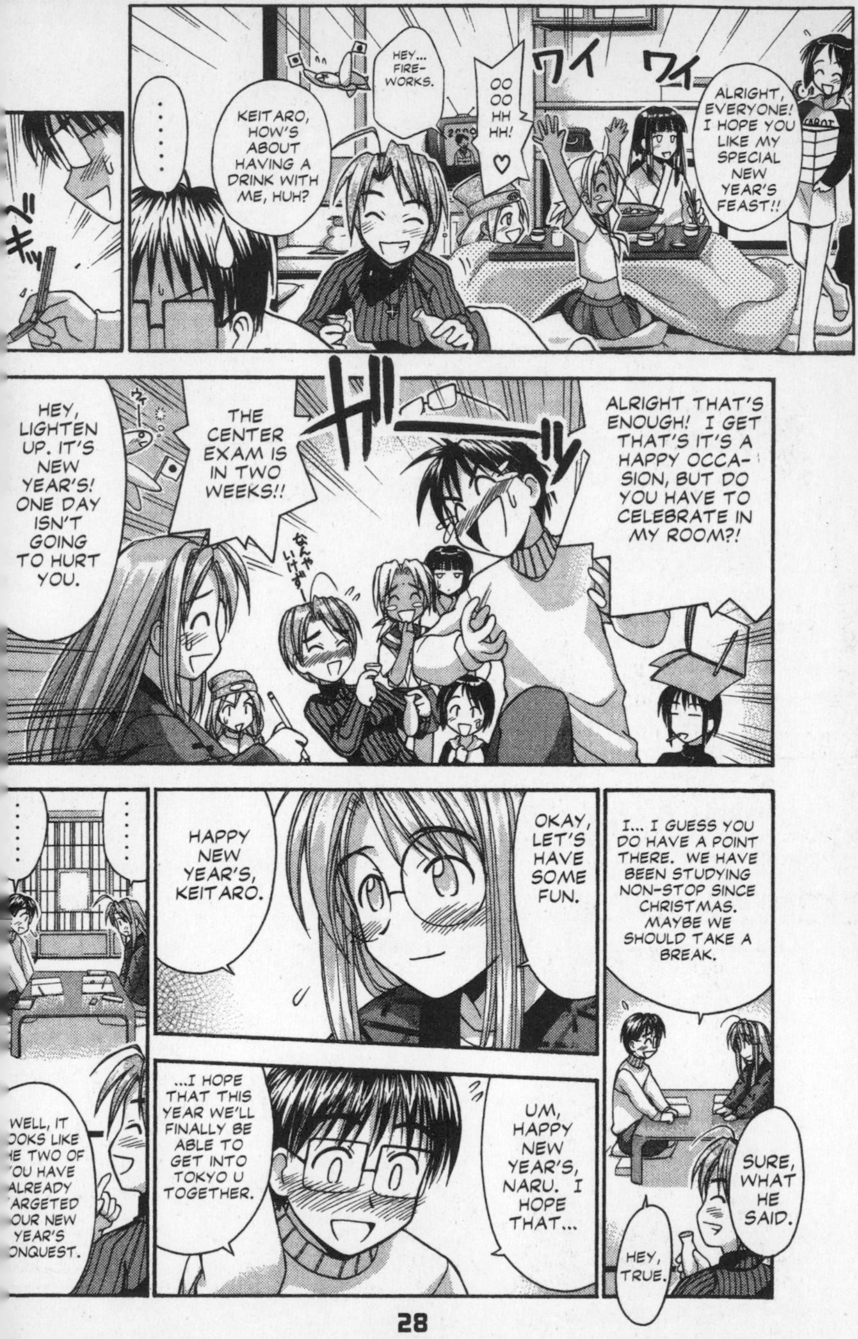
ALRIGHT, EVERYONE! I HOPE YOU LIKE MY SPECIAL NEW YEAR'S FEAST!!
ワイ ワイ
OOOOHHHH! ♥
HEY... FIRE-WORKS.
KEITARO, HOW'S ABOUT HAVING A DRINK WITH ME, HUH?
......
ベキッ
ALRIGHT THAT'S ENOUGH! I GET THAT'S IT'S A HAPPY OCCA-SION, BUT DO YOU HAVE TO CELEBRATE IN MY ROOM?!
ガーッ
THE CENTER EXAM IS IN TWO WEEKS!!
なんやいけずー
HEY, LIGHTEN UP. IT'S NEW YEAR'S! ONE DAY ISN'T GOING TO HURT YOU.
I... I GUESS YOU DO HAVE A POINT THERE. WE HAVE BEEN STUDYING NON-STOP SINCE CHRISTMAS. MAYBE WE SHOULD TAKE A BREAK.
SURE, WHAT HE SAID.
HEY, TRUE.
OKAY, LET'S HAVE SOME FUN.
HAPPY NEW YEAR'S, KEITARO.
UM, HAPPY NEW YEAR'S, NARU. I HOPE THAT...
...I HOPE THAT THIS YEAR WE'LL FINALLY BE ABLE TO GET INTO TOKYO U TOGETHER.
......
......
WELL, IT OOKS LIKE HE TWO OF OU HAVE LREADY ARGETED OUR NEW YEAR'S ONQUEST.

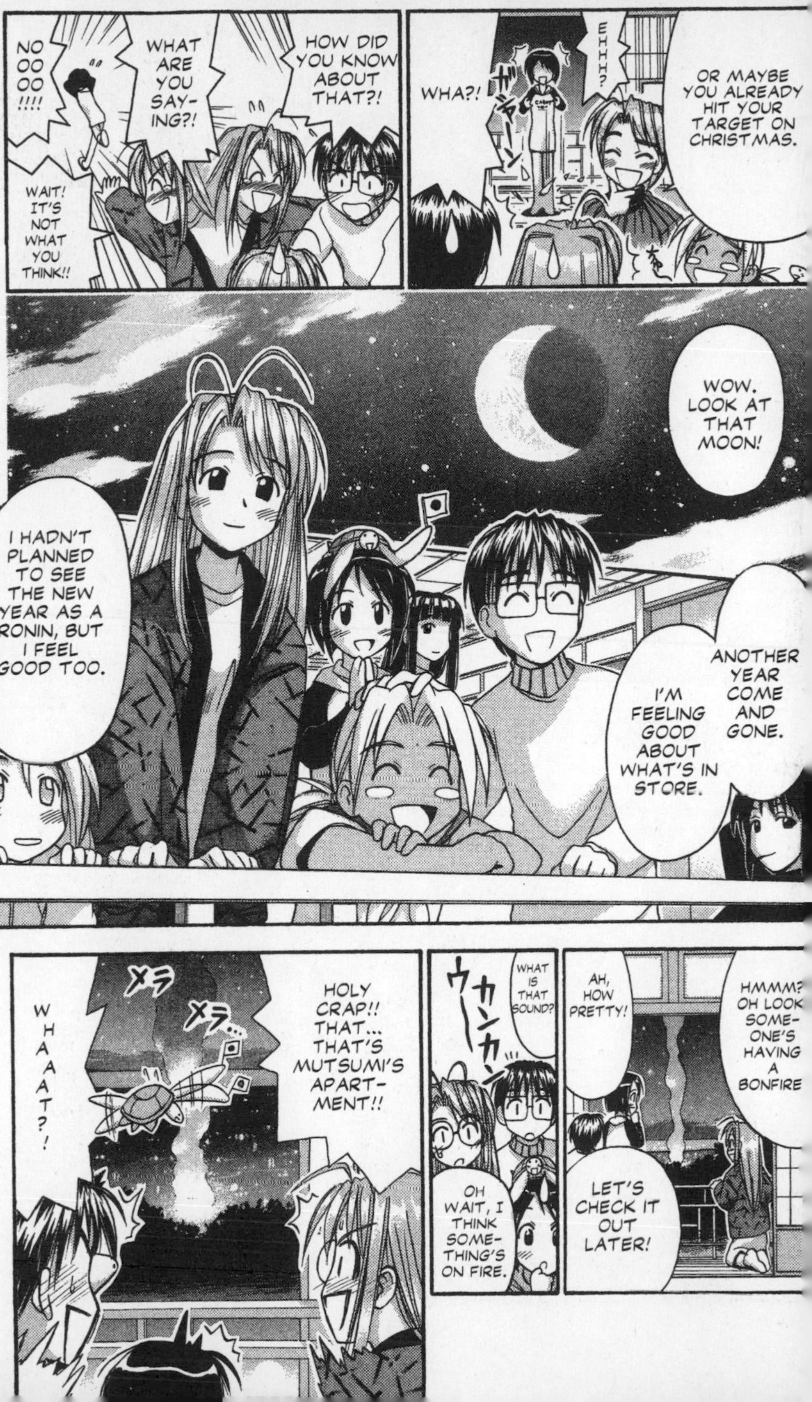
OR MAYBE YOU ALREADY HIT YOUR TARGET ON CHRISTMAS.
EHHH?
WHA?!
HOW DID YOU KNOW ABOUT THAT?!
WHAT ARE YOU SAY-ING?!
NOOOOOO!!!!
WAIT! IT'S NOT WHAT YOU THINK!!
WOW. LOOK AT THAT MOON!
ANOTHER YEAR COME AND GONE.
I'M FEELING GOOD ABOUT WHAT'S IN STORE.
I HADN'T PLANNED TO SEE THE NEW YEAR AS A RONIN, BUT I FEEL GOOD TOO.
HMMM? OH LOOK SOME-ONE'S HAVING A BONFIRE
AH, HOW PRETTY!
LET'S CHECK IT OUT LATER!
WHAT IS THAT SOUND?
OH WAIT, I THINK SOME-THING'S ON FIRE.
HOLY CRAP!! THAT... THAT'S MUTSUMI'S APART-MENT!!
WHAAAT?!

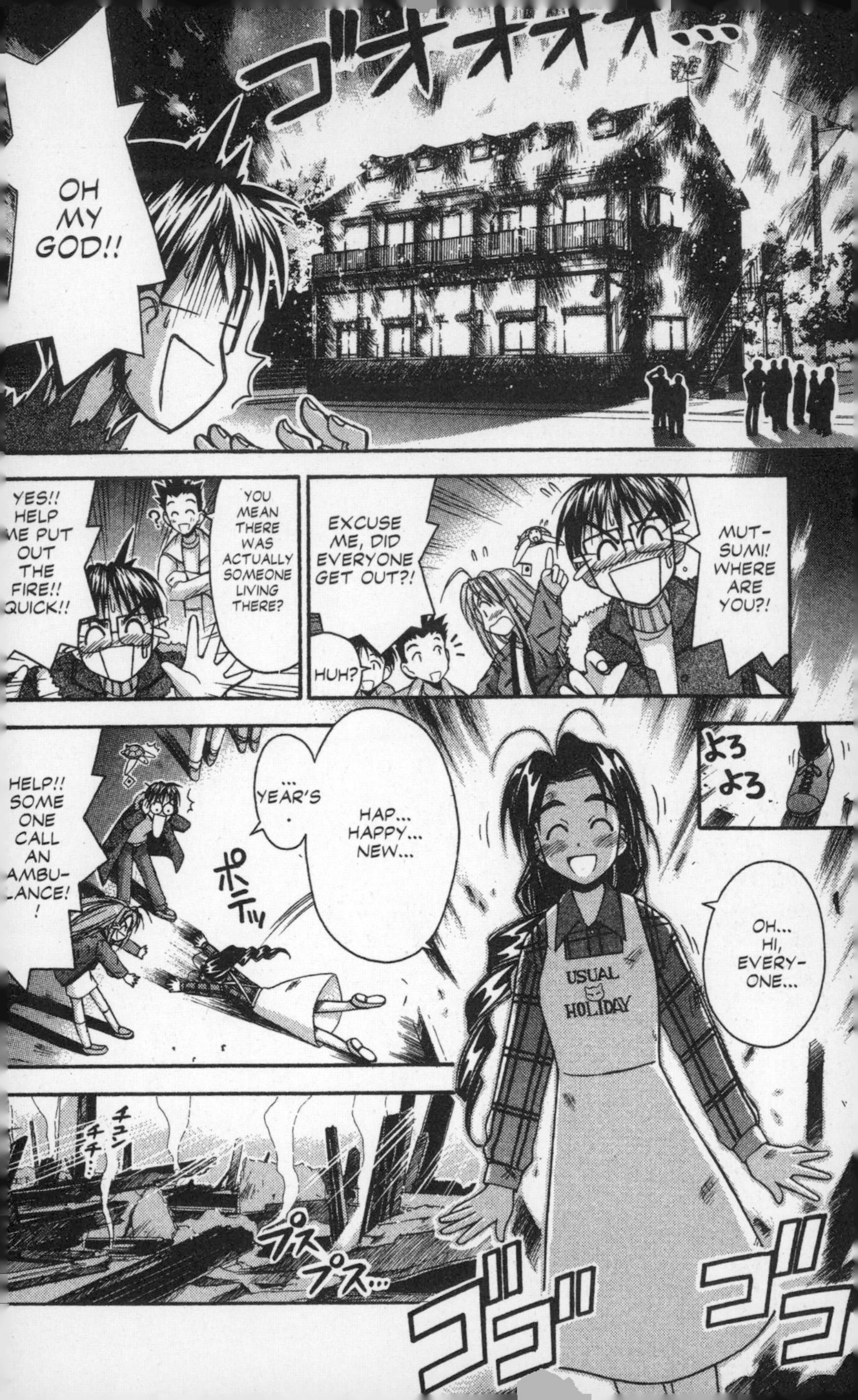
ゴオオオオ…
OH MY GOD!!
MUT-SUMI! WHERE ARE YOU?!
EXCUSE ME, DID EVERYONE GET OUT?!
HUH?
YOU MEAN THERE WAS ACTUALLY SOMEONE LIVING THERE?
YES!! HELP ME PUT OUT THE FIRE!! QUICK!!
よろよろ
OH... HI, EVERY-ONE...
USUAL HOLIDAY
HAP... HAPPY... NEW...
...YEAR'S.
ポテッ
HELP!! SOME ONE CALL AN AMBU-LANCE!!
ゴゴ
ゴゴ
プスプス…
チュン チチ…

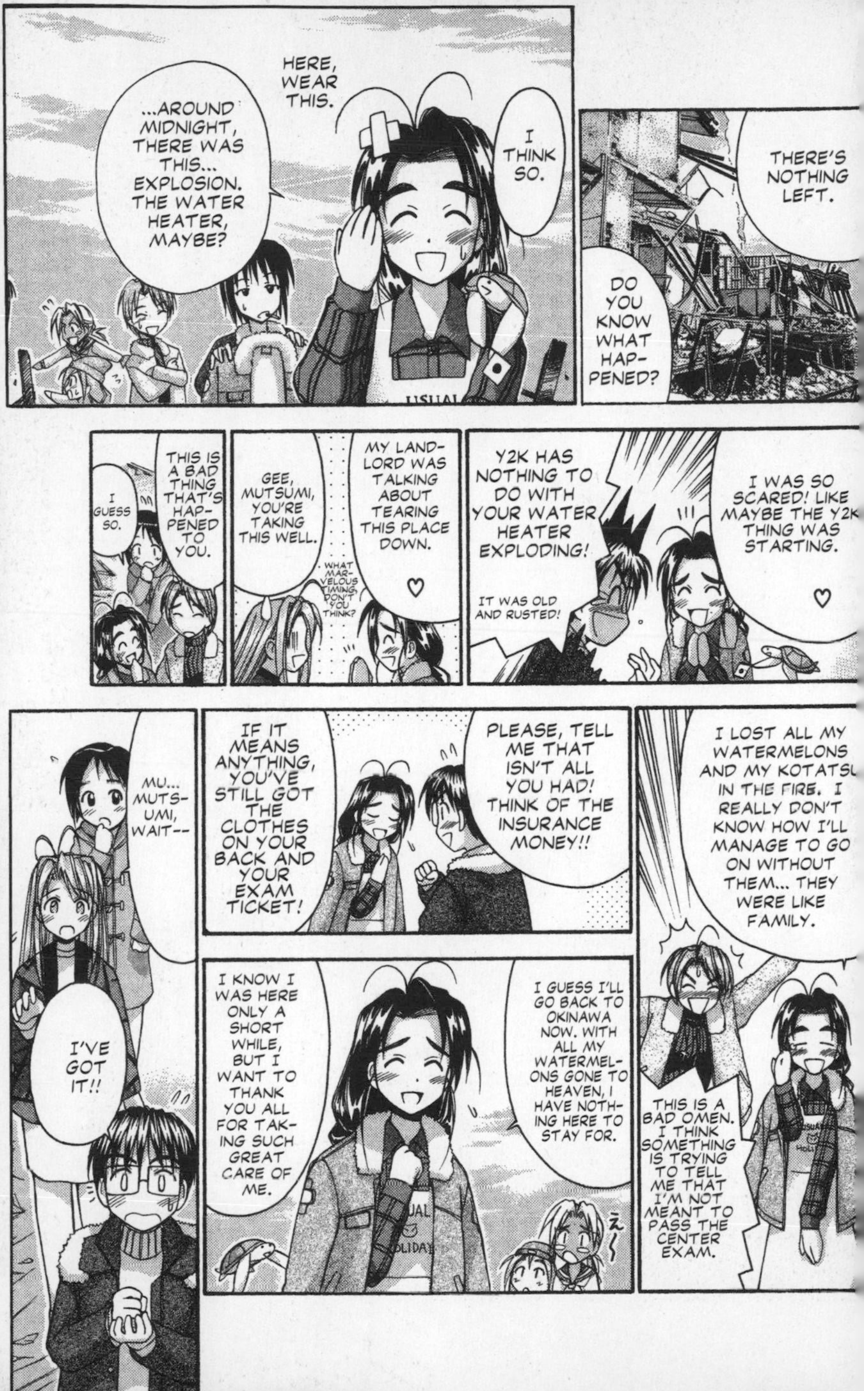
THERE'S NOTHING LEFT.
DO YOU KNOW WHAT HAPPENED?
I THINK SO.
...AROUND MIDNIGHT, THERE WAS THIS... EXPLOSION. THE WATER HEATER, MAYBE?
HERE, WEAR THIS.
I WAS SO SCARED! LIKE MAYBE THE Y2K THING WAS STARTING. ♡
Y2K HAS NOTHING TO DO WITH YOUR WATER HEATER EXPLODING!
IT WAS OLD AND RUSTED!
MY LANDLORD WAS TALKING ABOUT TEARING THIS PLACE DOWN. ♡
WHAT MARVELOUS TIMING, DON'T YOU THINK?
GEE, MUTSUMI, YOU'RE TAKING THIS WELL.
THIS IS A BAD THING THAT'S HAPPENED TO YOU.
I GUESS SO.
I LOST ALL MY WATERMELONS AND MY KOTATSU IN THE FIRE. I REALLY DON'T KNOW HOW I'LL MANAGE TO GO ON WITHOUT THEM... THEY WERE LIKE FAMILY.
THIS IS A BAD OMEN. I THINK SOMETHING IS TRYING TO TELL ME THAT I'M NOT MEANT TO PASS THE CENTER EXAM.
PLEASE, TELL ME THAT ISN'T ALL YOU HAD! THINK OF THE INSURANCE MONEY!!
IF IT MEANS ANYTHING, YOU'VE STILL GOT THE CLOTHES ON YOUR BACK AND YOUR EXAM TICKET!
I GUESS I'LL GO BACK TO OKINAWA NOW. WITH ALL MY WATERMELONS GONE TO HEAVEN, I HAVE NOTHING HERE TO STAY FOR.
I KNOW I WAS HERE ONLY A SHORT WHILE, BUT I WANT TO THANK YOU ALL FOR TAKING SUCH GREAT CARE OF ME.
えー
MU... MUTSUMI, WAIT--
I'VE GOT IT!!

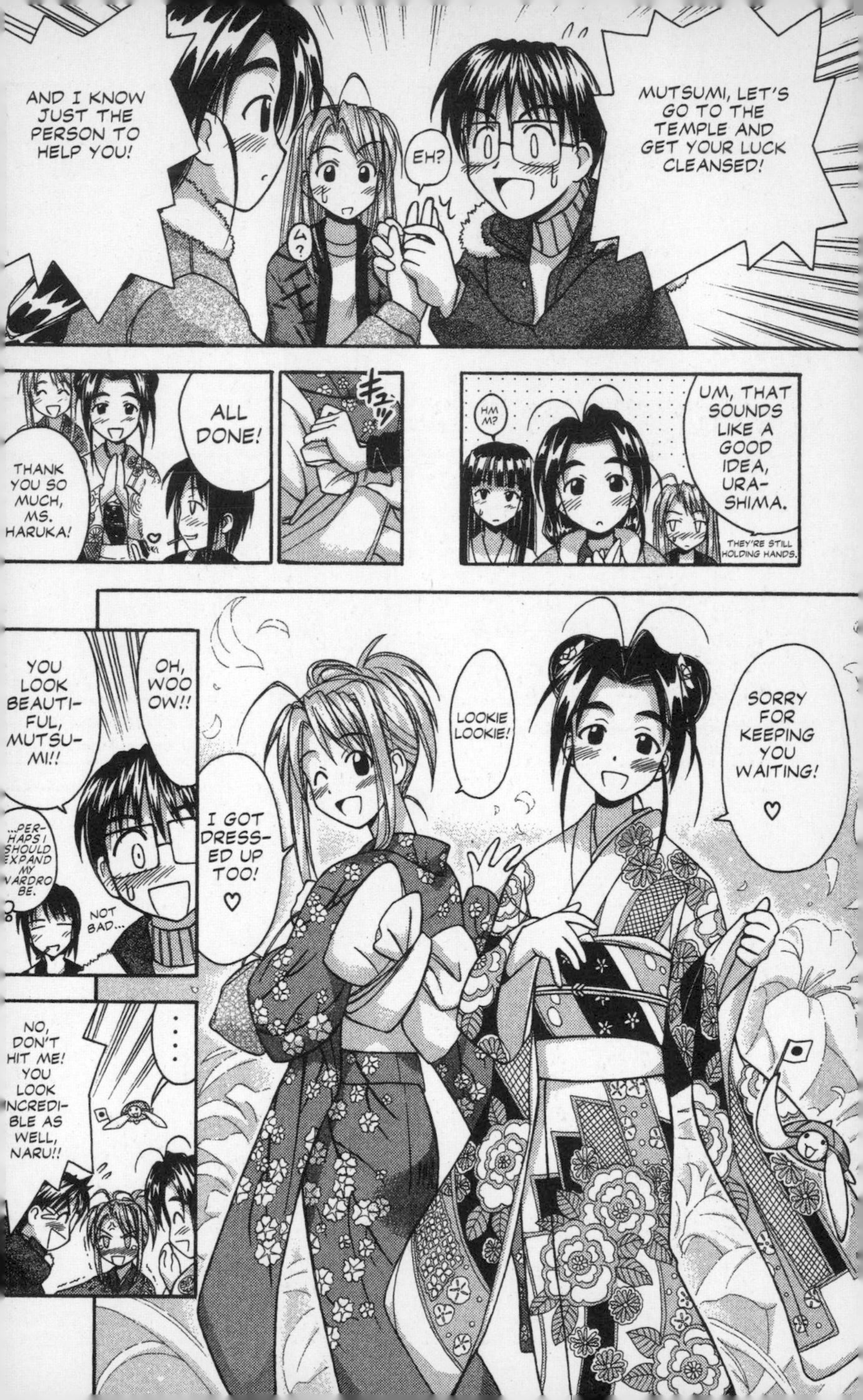
MUTSUMI, LET'S GO TO THE TEMPLE AND GET YOUR LUCK CLEANSED!
EH?
ム?
AND I KNOW JUST THE PERSON TO HELP YOU!
UM, THAT SOUNDS LIKE A GOOD IDEA, URASHIMA.
HM M?
THEY'RE STILL HOLDING HANDS.
キュッ
ALL DONE!
THANK YOU SO MUCH, MS. HARUKA!
SORRY FOR KEEPING YOU WAITING! ♡
LOOKIE LOOKIE!
I GOT DRESSED UP TOO! ♡
OH, WOOOW!!
YOU LOOK BEAUTIFUL, MUTSUMI!!
...PERHAPS I SHOULD EXPAND MY WARDROBE.
NOT BAD...
....
NO, DON'T HIT ME! YOU LOOK INCREDIBLE AS WELL, NARU!!

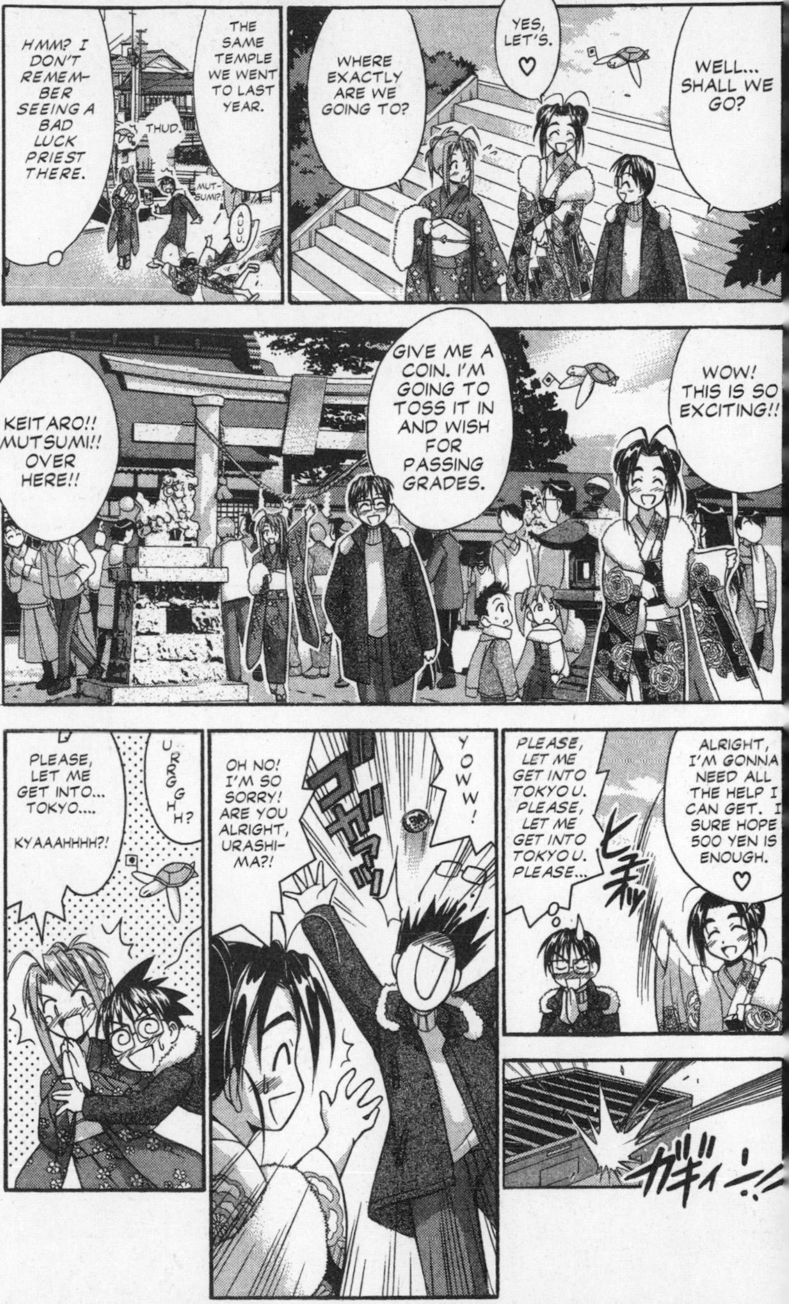
WELL... SHALL WE GO?
YES, LET'S. ♡
WHERE EXACTLY ARE WE GOING TO?
THE SAME TEMPLE WE WENT TO LAST YEAR.
HMM? I DON'T REMEMBER SEEING A BAD LUCK PRIEST THERE.
THUD.
MUT-SUMI?!
AUUU.
WOW! THIS IS SO EXCITING!!
GIVE ME A COIN. I'M GOING TO TOSS IT IN AND WISH FOR PASSING GRADES.
KEITARO!! MUTSUMI!! OVER HERE!!
ALRIGHT, I'M GONNA NEED ALL THE HELP I CAN GET. I SURE HOPE 500 YEN IS ENOUGH. ♡
PLEASE, LET ME GET INTO TOKYO U. PLEASE, LET ME GET INTO TOKYO U. PLEASE...
YOWW!
OH NO! I'M SO SORRY! ARE YOU ALRIGHT, URASHIMA?!
URRGGH?
PLEASE, LET ME GET INTO... TOKYO....
KYAAAHHHH?!

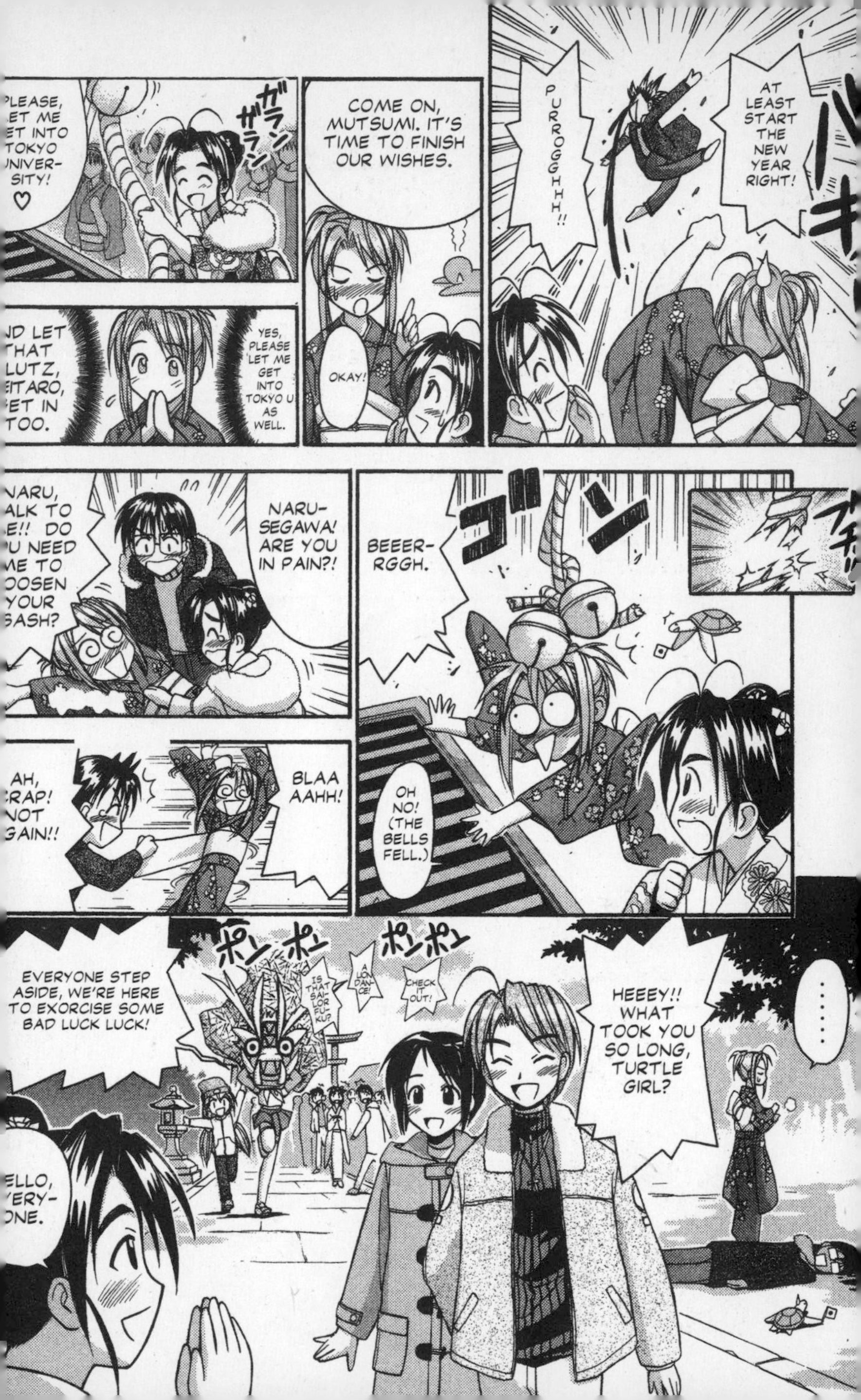

バキ
AT LEAST START THE NEW YEAR RIGHT!
PURROGGHHH!!
COME ON, MUTSUMI. IT'S TIME TO FINISH OUR WISHES.
OKAY!
ガラン ガラン
PLEASE, ET ME ET INTO TOKYO NIVER-SITY! ♡
YES, PLEASE LET ME GET INTO TOKYO U AS WELL.
ND LET THAT LUTZ, EITARO, ET IN TOO.
ブチ
ゴン
BEEER-RGGH.
OH NO! (THE BELLS FELL.)
NARU-SEGAWA! ARE YOU IN PAIN?!
NARU, ALK TO E!! DO U NEED ME TO OOSEN YOUR SASH?
BLAA AAHH!
AH, RAP! NOT GAIN!!
......
HEEEY!! WHAT TOOK YOU SO LONG, TURTLE GIRL?
ポンポン
CHECK IT OUT!
A LION DANCE!
IS THAT SAILOR FUKU?
ポンポン
EVERYONE STEP ASIDE, WE'RE HERE TO EXORCISE SOME BAD LUCK LUCK!
ELLO, ERY-ONE.

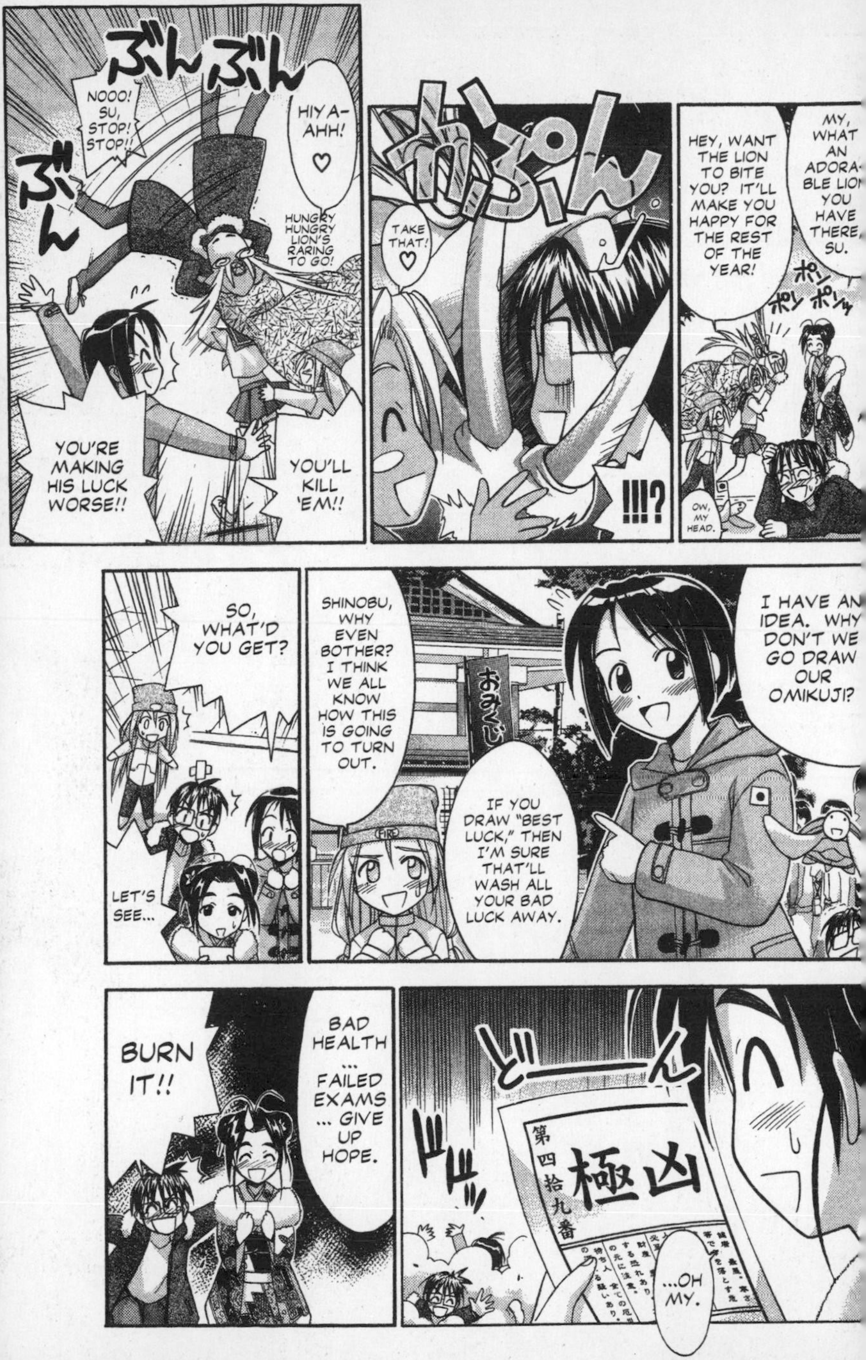
MY, WHAT AN ADORABLE LION YOU HAVE THERE, SU.
HEY, WANT THE LION TO BITE YOU? IT'LL MAKE YOU HAPPY FOR THE REST OF THE YEAR!
ポン ポン ポンッ
OW, MY HEAD.
かぷん
TAKE THAT! ♡
!!!?
ぶんぶん
HIYA-AHH! ♡
NOOO! SU, STOP! STOP!!
ぶん
HUNGRY HUNGRY LION'S RARING TO GO!
YOU'LL KILL 'EM!!
YOU'RE MAKING HIS LUCK WORSE!!
I HAVE AN IDEA. WHY DON'T WE GO DRAW OUR OMIKUJI!?
IF YOU DRAW "BEST LUCK," THEN I'M SURE THAT'LL WASH ALL YOUR BAD LUCK AWAY.
SHINOBU, WHY EVEN BOTHER? I THINK WE ALL KNOW HOW THIS IS GOING TO TURN OUT.
おみくじ
SO, WHAT'D YOU GET?
LET'S SEE...
どーーん
第四拾九番
極凶
...OH MY.
BAD HEALTH ... FAILED EXAMS ... GIVE UP HOPE.
BURN IT!!

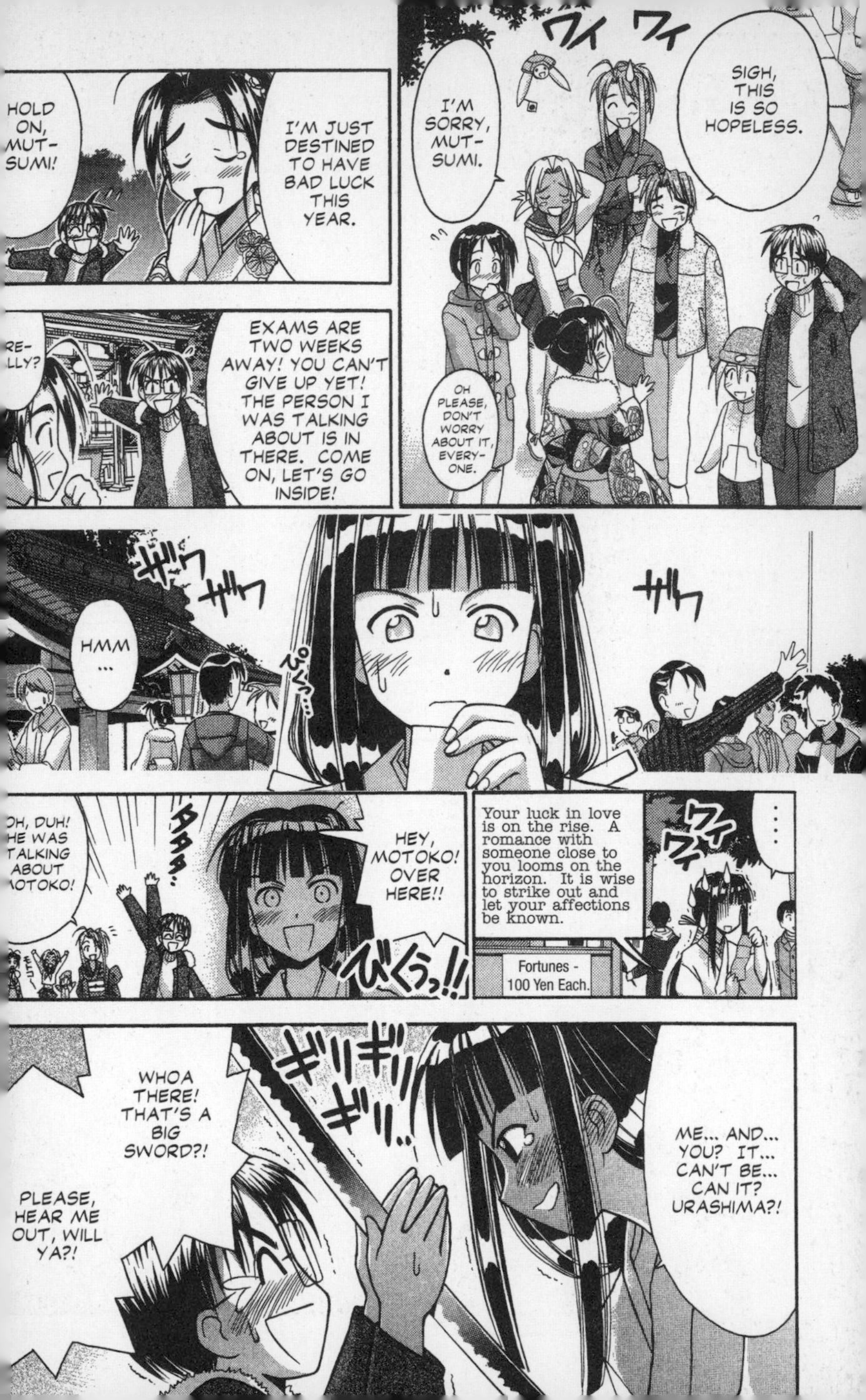
ワイワイ
SIGH, THIS IS SO HOPELESS.
I'M SORRY, MUT-SUMI.
OH PLEASE, DON'T WORRY ABOUT IT, EVERY-ONE.
I'M JUST DESTINED TO HAVE BAD LUCK THIS YEAR.
HOLD ON, MUT-SUMI!
EXAMS ARE TWO WEEKS AWAY! YOU CAN'T GIVE UP YET! THE PERSON I WAS TALKING ABOUT IS IN THERE. COME ON, LET'S GO INSIDE!
RE-LLY?
ザワ
ぴくっ…
HMM...
ザワザワ
....
ワイワイ
Your luck in love is on the rise. A romance with someone close to you looms on the horizon. It is wise to strike out and let your affections be known.
Fortunes - 100 Yen Each.
HEY, MOTOKO! OVER HERE!!
タタタ
びくっ!!
OH, DUH! HE WAS TALKING ABOUT MOTOKO!
ME... AND... YOU? IT... CAN'T BE... CAN IT? URASHIMA?!
ギリギリギリ...
WHOA THERE! THAT'S A BIG SWORD?!
PLEASE, HEAR ME OUT, WILL YA?!

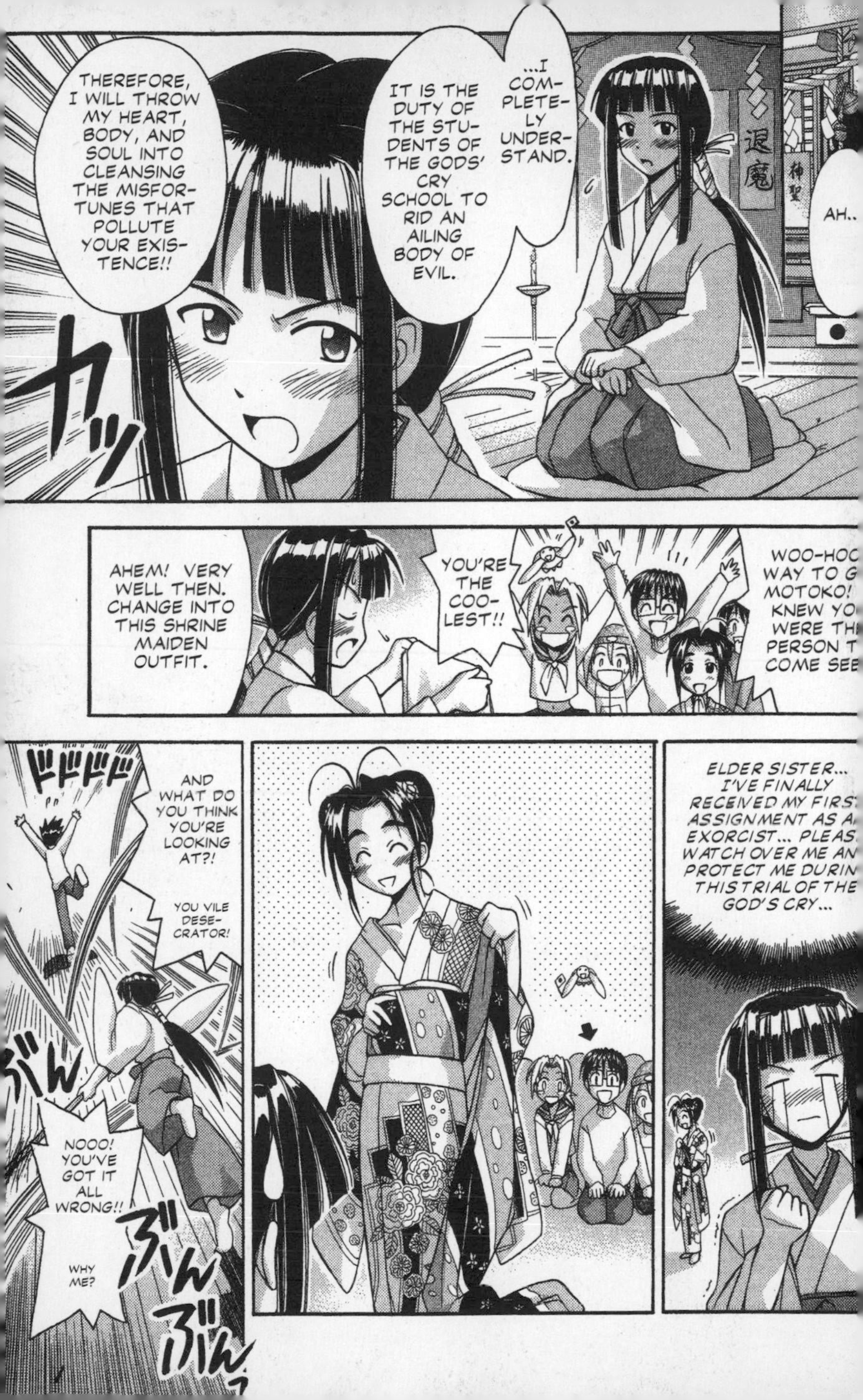
AH..
...I COMPLETELY UNDERSTAND.
IT IS THE DUTY OF THE STUDENTS OF THE GODS' CRY SCHOOL TO RID AN AILING BODY OF EVIL.
THEREFORE, I WILL THROW MY HEART, BODY, AND SOUL INTO CLEANSING THE MISFORTUNES THAT POLLUTE YOUR EXISTENCE!!
退魔
カッ
WOO-HOC WAY TO G MOTOKO! KNEW YO WERE TH PERSON T COME SEE
YOU'RE THE COOLEST!!
AHEM! VERY WELL THEN. CHANGE INTO THIS SHRINE MAIDEN OUTFIT.
ELDER SISTER... I'VE FINALLY RECEIVED MY FIRS ASSIGNMENT AS A EXORCIST... PLEAS WATCH OVER ME AN PROTECT ME DURIN THIS TRIAL OF THE GOD'S CRY...
ドドドド
AND WHAT DO YOU THINK YOU'RE LOOKING AT?!
YOU VILE DESECRATOR!
ぶん
NOOO! YOU'VE GOT IT ALL WRONG!!
WHY ME?
ぶんぶん

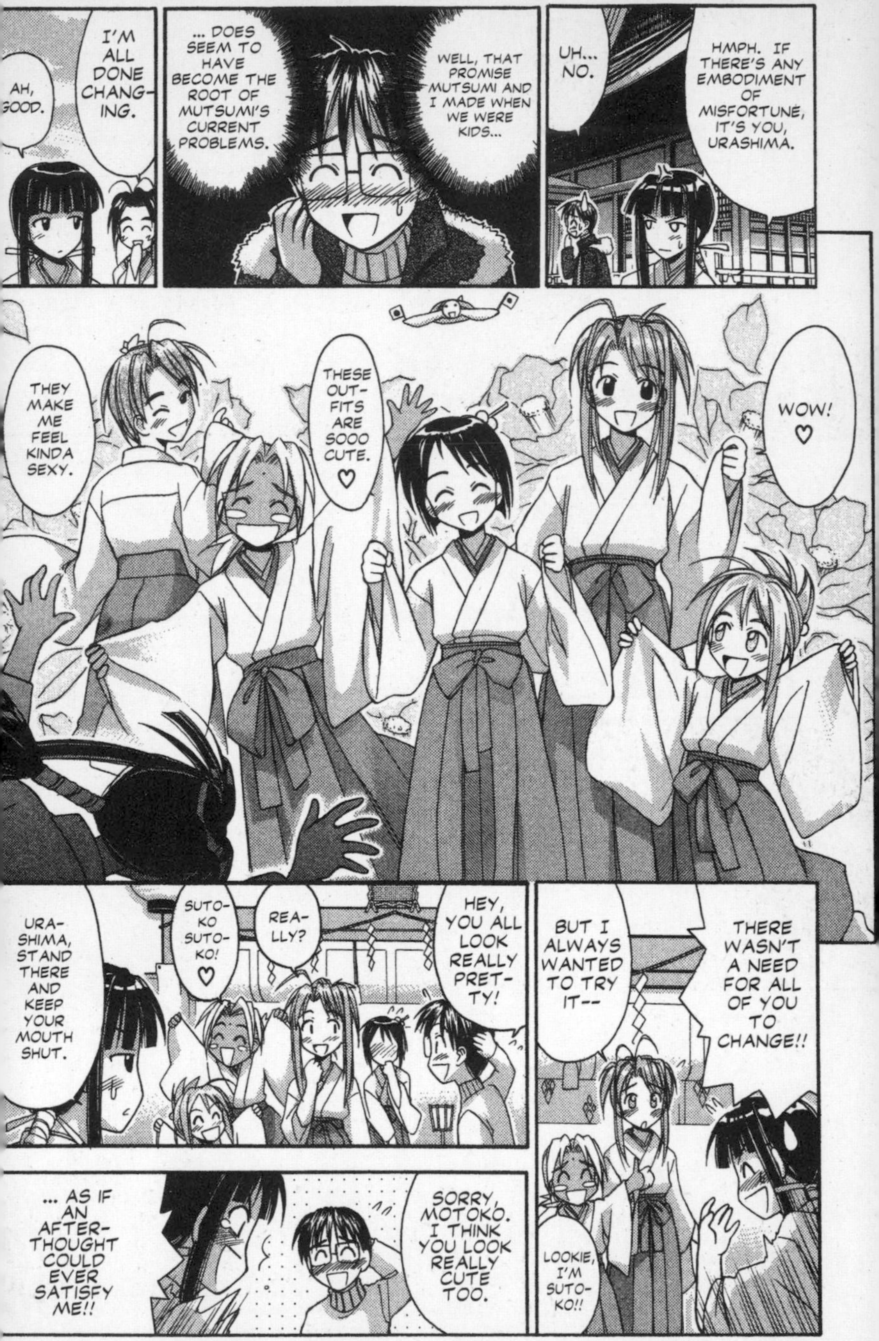
HMPH. IF THERE'S ANY EMBODIMENT OF MISFORTUNE, IT'S YOU, URASHIMA.
UH... NO.
WELL, THAT PROMISE MUTSUMI AND I MADE WHEN WE WERE KIDS...
... DOES SEEM TO HAVE BECOME THE ROOT OF MUTSUMI'S CURRENT PROBLEMS.
I'M ALL DONE CHANGING.
AH, GOOD.
WOW! ♡
THESE OUTFITS ARE SOOO CUTE. ♡
THEY MAKE ME FEEL KINDA SEXY.
THERE WASN'T A NEED FOR ALL OF YOU TO CHANGE!!
BUT I ALWAYS WANTED TO TRY IT--
LOOKIE, I'M SUTOKO!!
HEY, YOU ALL LOOK REALLY PRETTY!
REALLY?
SUTOKO SUTOKO! ♡
URASHIMA, STAND THERE AND KEEP YOUR MOUTH SHUT.
SORRY, MOTOKO. I THINK YOU LOOK REALLY CUTE TOO.
... AS IF AN AFTERTHOUGHT COULD EVER SATISFY ME!!

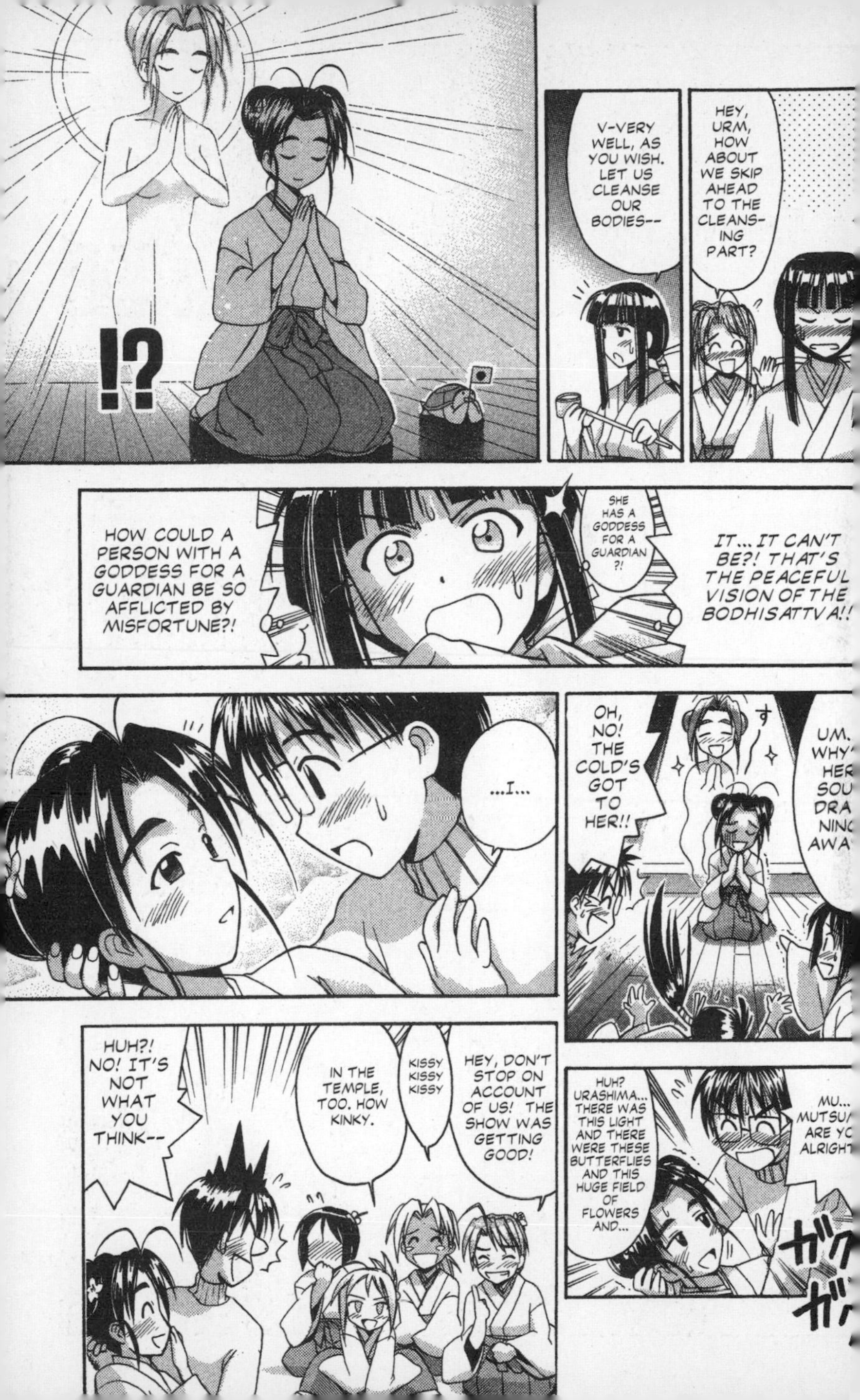

HEY, URM, HOW ABOUT WE SKIP AHEAD TO THE CLEANSING PART?
V-VERY WELL, AS YOU WISH. LET US CLEANSE OUR BODIES--
!?
IT... IT CAN'T BE?! THAT'S THE PEACEFUL VISION OF THE BODHISATTVA!!
SHE HAS A GODDESS FOR A GUARDIAN ?!
HOW COULD A PERSON WITH A GODDESS FOR A GUARDIAN BE SO AFFLICTED BY MISFORTUNE?!
OH, NO! THE COLD'S GOT TO HER!!
す
HUH? URASHIMA... THERE WAS THIS LIGHT AND THERE WERE THESE BUTTERFLIES AND THIS HUGE FIELD OF FLOWERS AND...
...I...
HEY, DON'T STOP ON ACCOUNT OF US! THE SHOW WAS GETTING GOOD!
KISSY KISSY KISSY
IN THE TEMPLE, TOO. HOW KINKY.
HUH?! NO! IT'S NOT WHAT YOU THINK--

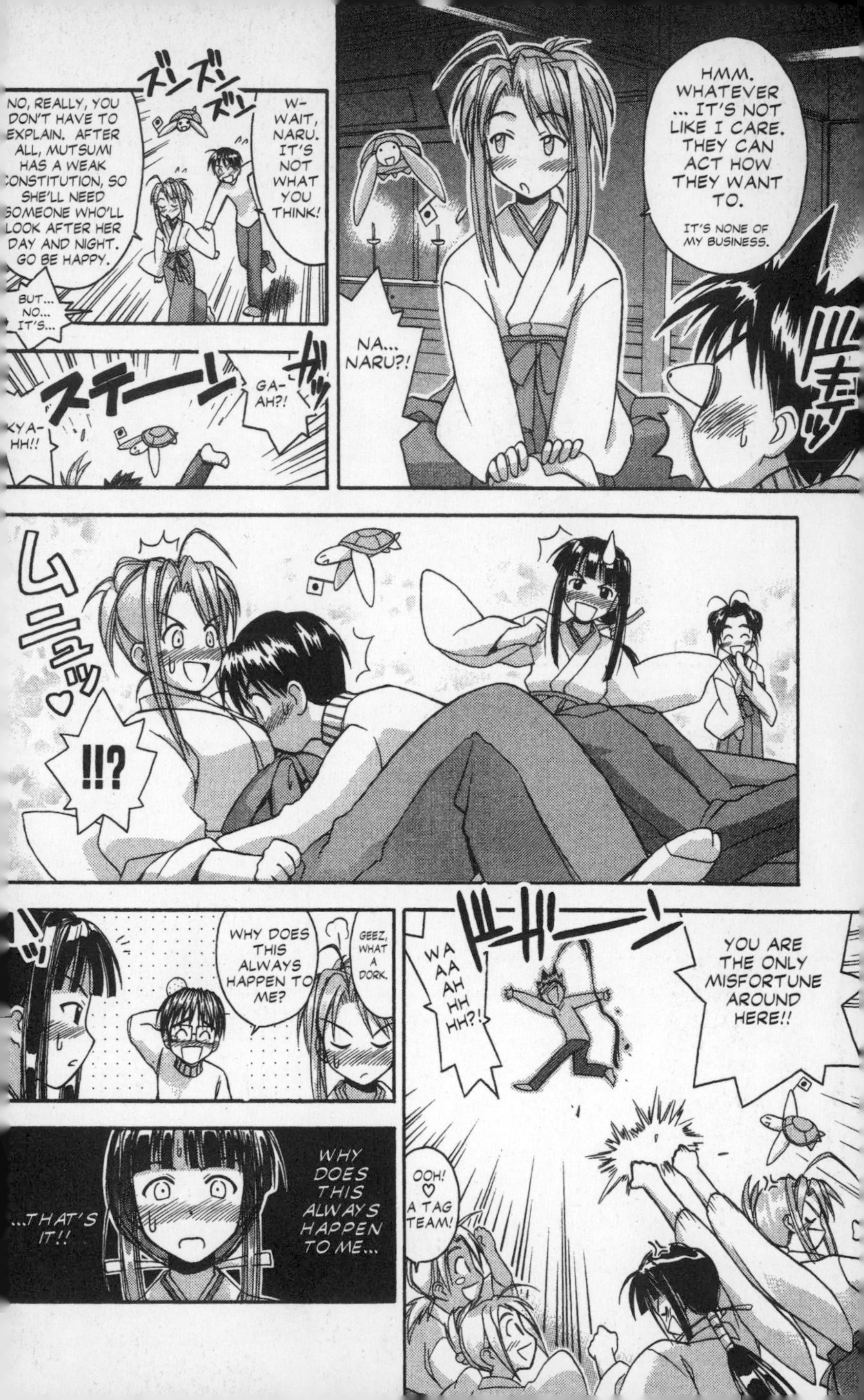
HMM. WHATEVER ... IT'S NOT LIKE I CARE. THEY CAN ACT HOW THEY WANT TO.
IT'S NONE OF MY BUSINESS.
NA... NARU?!
ズンズンズン
W-WAIT, NARU. IT'S NOT WHAT YOU THINK!
NO, REALLY, YOU DON'T HAVE TO EXPLAIN. AFTER ALL, MUTSUMI HAS A WEAK CONSTITUTION, SO SHE'LL NEED SOMEONE WHO'LL LOOK AFTER HER DAY AND NIGHT. GO BE HAPPY.
BUT... NO... IT'S...
GA-AH?!
ステーン
KYA-HH!!
ムニュッ
!!?
YOU ARE THE ONLY MISFORTUNE AROUND HERE!!
WA AA AH HH HH?!
OOH! ♡ A TAG TEAM!
GEEZ, WHAT A DORK.
WHY DOES THIS ALWAYS HAPPEN TO ME?
WHY DOES THIS ALWAYS HAPPEN TO ME...
...THAT'S IT!!

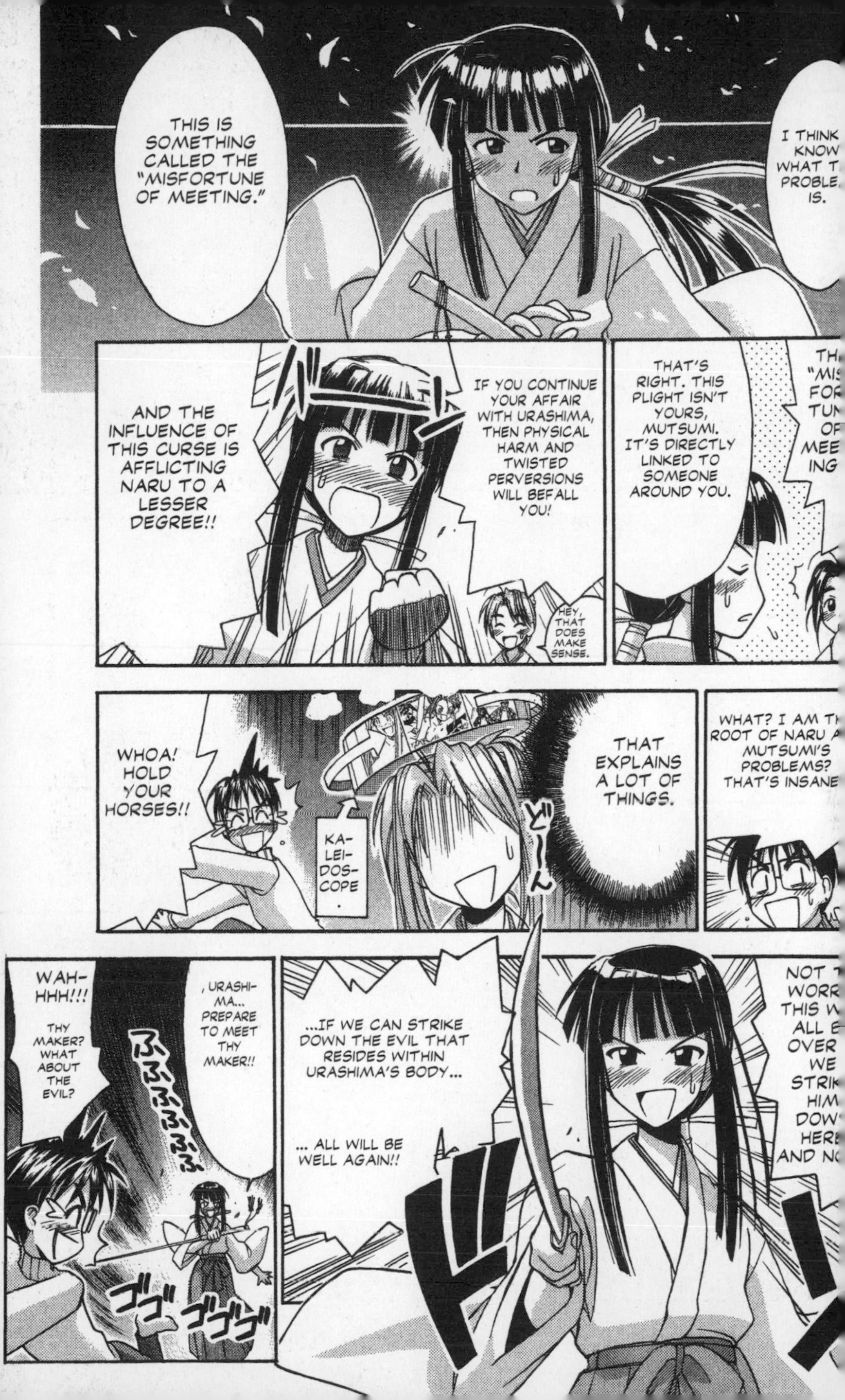
I THINK
KNOW
WHAT T
PROBLE
IS.
THIS IS SOMETHING CALLED THE "MISFORTUNE OF MEETING."
TH "MIS FOR TUN OF MEE ING
THAT'S RIGHT. THIS PLIGHT ISN'T YOURS, MUTSUMI. IT'S DIRECTLY LINKED TO SOMEONE AROUND YOU.
IF YOU CONTINUE YOUR AFFAIR WITH URASHIMA, THEN PHYSICAL HARM AND TWISTED PERVERSIONS WILL BEFALL YOU!
AND THE INFLUENCE OF THIS CURSE IS AFFLICTING NARU TO A LESSER DEGREE!!
HEY, THAT DOES MAKE SENSE.
WHAT? I AM T
ROOT OF NARU A
MUTSUMI'S PROBLEMS?
THAT'S INSANE
THAT EXPLAINS A LOT OF THINGS.
どーん
KA-LEI-DOS-COPE.
WHOA! HOLD YOUR HORSES!!
NOT T
WORR
THIS W
ALL E
OVER
WE
STRIK
HIM
DOW
HERE
AND N
...IF WE CAN STRIKE DOWN THE EVIL THAT RESIDES WITHIN URASHIMA'S BODY...
... ALL WILL BE WELL AGAIN!!
, URASHIMA... PREPARE TO MEET THY MAKER!!
ふふふふふ
WAH-HHH!!!
THY MAKER? WHAT ABOUT THE EVIL?
ゴゴ
ゴゴゴ

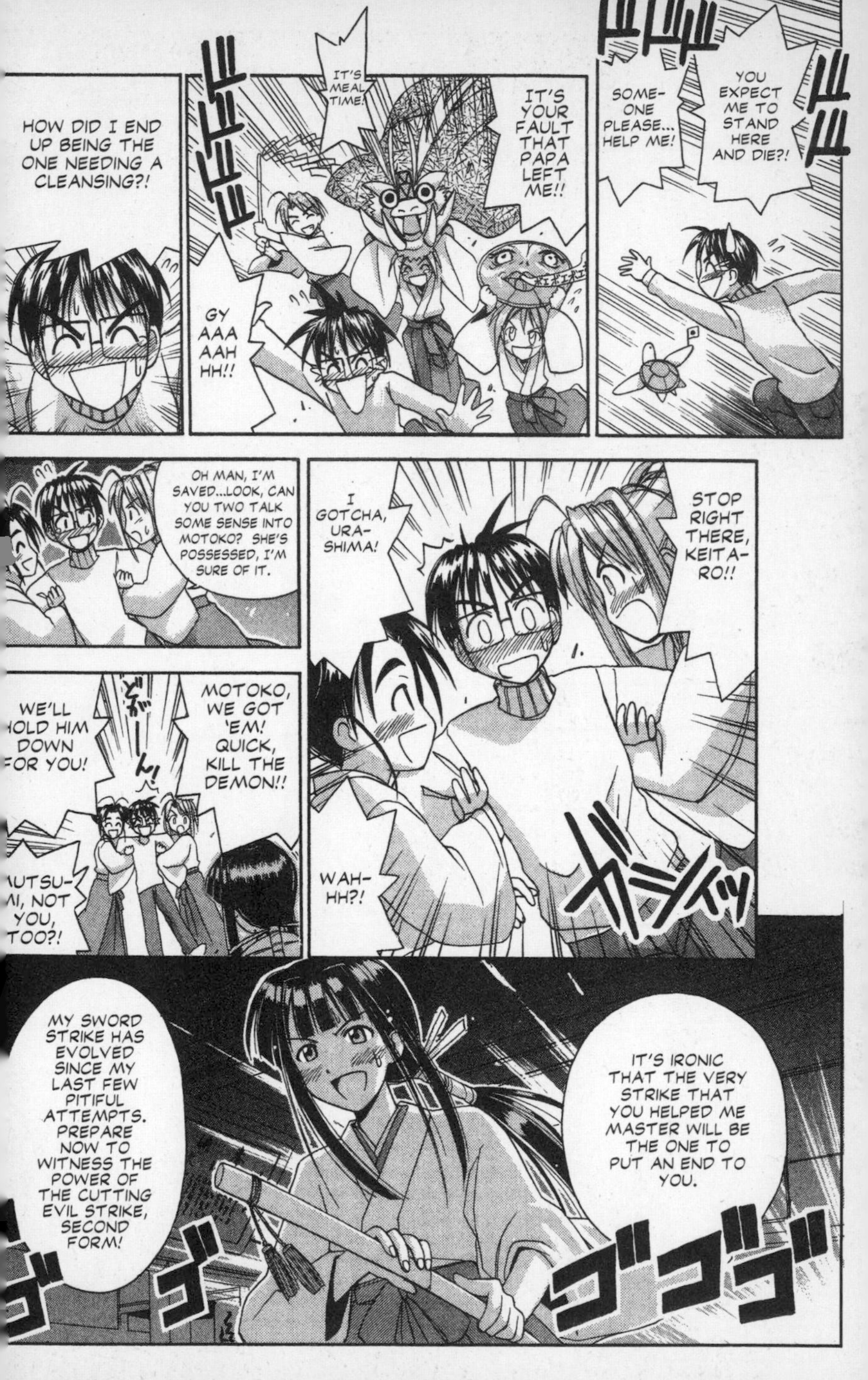
YOU EXPECT ME TO STAND HERE AND DIE?!
SOME-ONE PLEASE... HELP ME!
IT'S MEAL TIME!
IT'S YOUR FAULT THAT PAPA LEFT ME!!
GY AAA AAH HH!!
HOW DID I END UP BEING THE ONE NEEDING A CLEANSING?!
STOP RIGHT THERE, KEITA-RO!!
I GOTCHA, URA-SHIMA!
WAH-HH?!
OH MAN, I'M SAVED...LOOK, CAN YOU TWO TALK SOME SENSE INTO MOTOKO? SHE'S POSSESSED, I'M SURE OF IT.
MOTOKO, WE GOT 'EM! QUICK, KILL THE DEMON!!
WE'LL HOLD HIM DOWN FOR YOU!
MUTSU-MI, NOT YOU, TOO?!
IT'S IRONIC THAT THE VERY STRIKE THAT YOU HELPED ME MASTER WILL BE THE ONE TO PUT AN END TO YOU.
MY SWORD STRIKE HAS EVOLVED SINCE MY LAST FEW PITIFUL ATTEMPTS. PREPARE NOW TO WITNESS THE POWER OF THE CUTTING EVIL STRIKE, SECOND FORM!

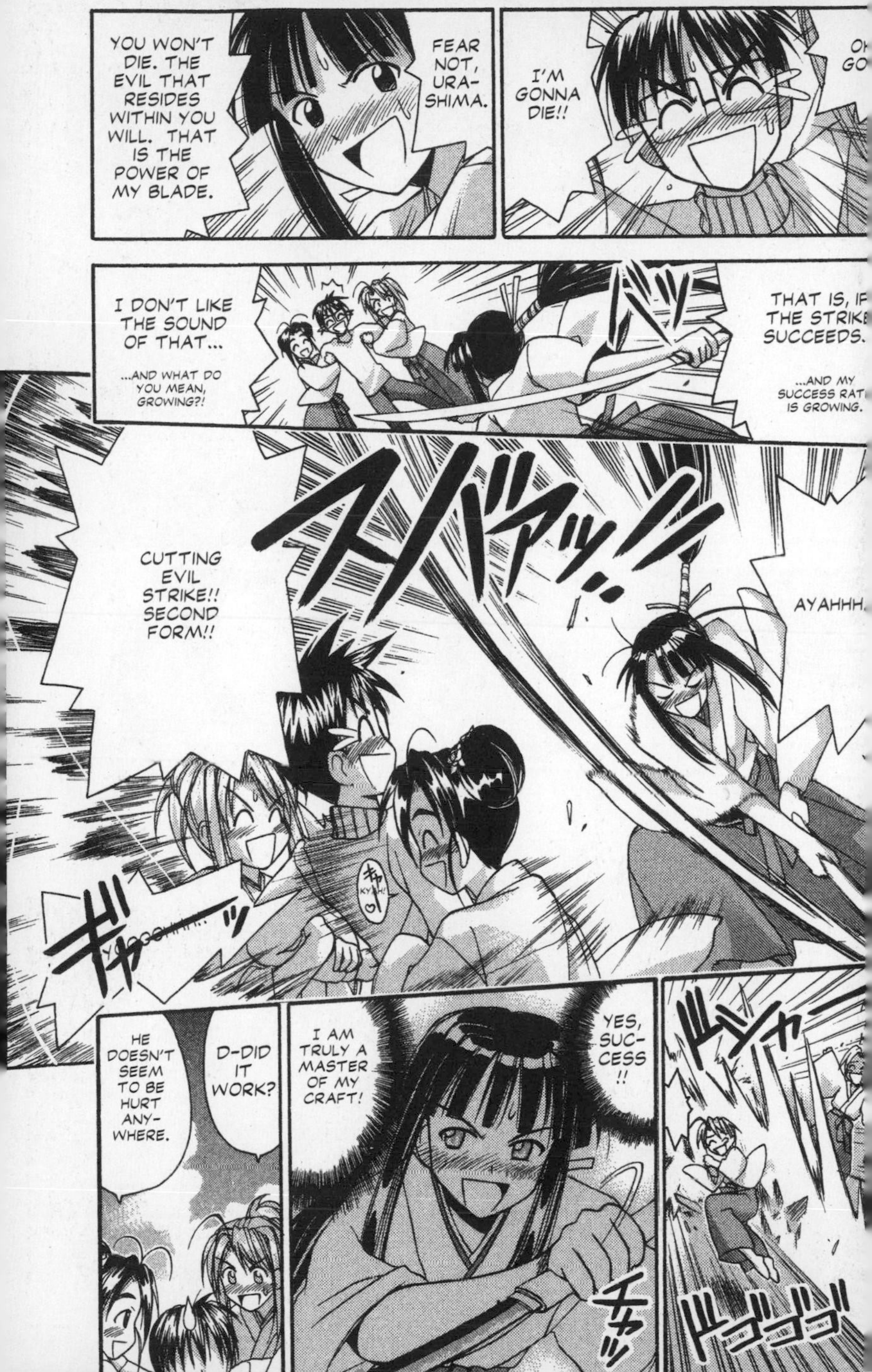
I'M GONNA DIE!!
FEAR NOT, URA-SHIMA.
YOU WON'T DIE. THE EVIL THAT RESIDES WITHIN YOU WILL. THAT IS THE POWER OF MY BLADE.
THAT IS, IF THE STRIKE SUCCEEDS.
...AND MY SUCCESS RAT IS GROWING.
I DON'T LIKE THE SOUND OF THAT...
...AND WHAT DO YOU MEAN, GROWING?!
AYAHHH.
CUTTING EVIL STRIKE!! SECOND FORM!!
KYAH! ♡
YES, SUC-CESS!!
I AM TRULY A MASTER OF MY CRAFT!
D-DID IT WORK?
HE DOESN'T SEEM TO BE HURT ANY-WHERE.

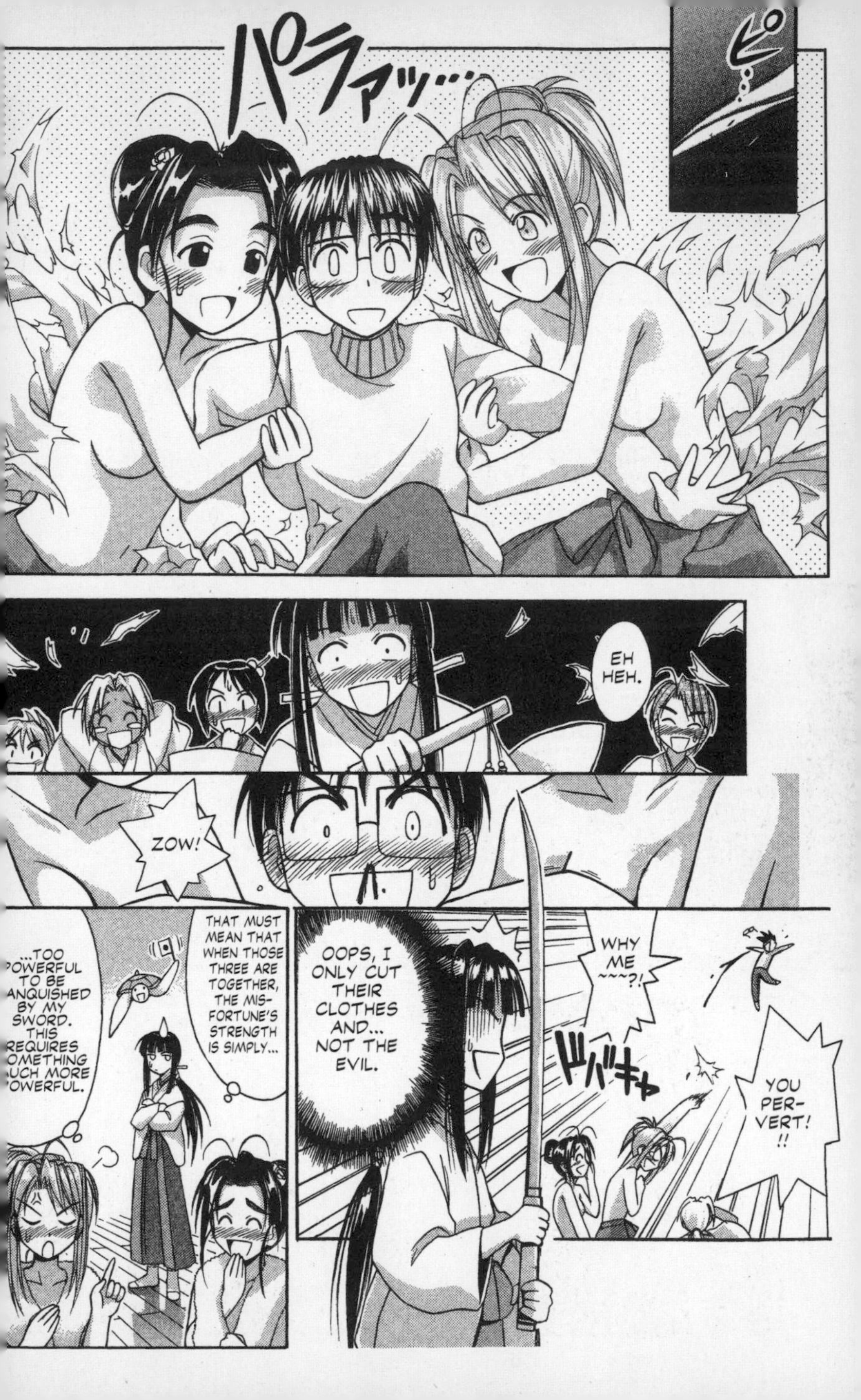
ピ
パラァッ…
EH HEH.
ZOW!
YOU PER-VERT! !!
ドバキャ
WHY ME ~~~?!
OOPS, I ONLY CUT THEIR CLOTHES AND... NOT THE EVIL.
THAT MUST MEAN THAT WHEN THOSE THREE ARE TOGETHER, THE MIS-FORTUNE'S STRENGTH IS SIMPLY...
...TOO POWERFUL TO BE ANQUISHED BY MY SWORD. THIS REQUIRES OMETHING UCH MORE OWERFUL.

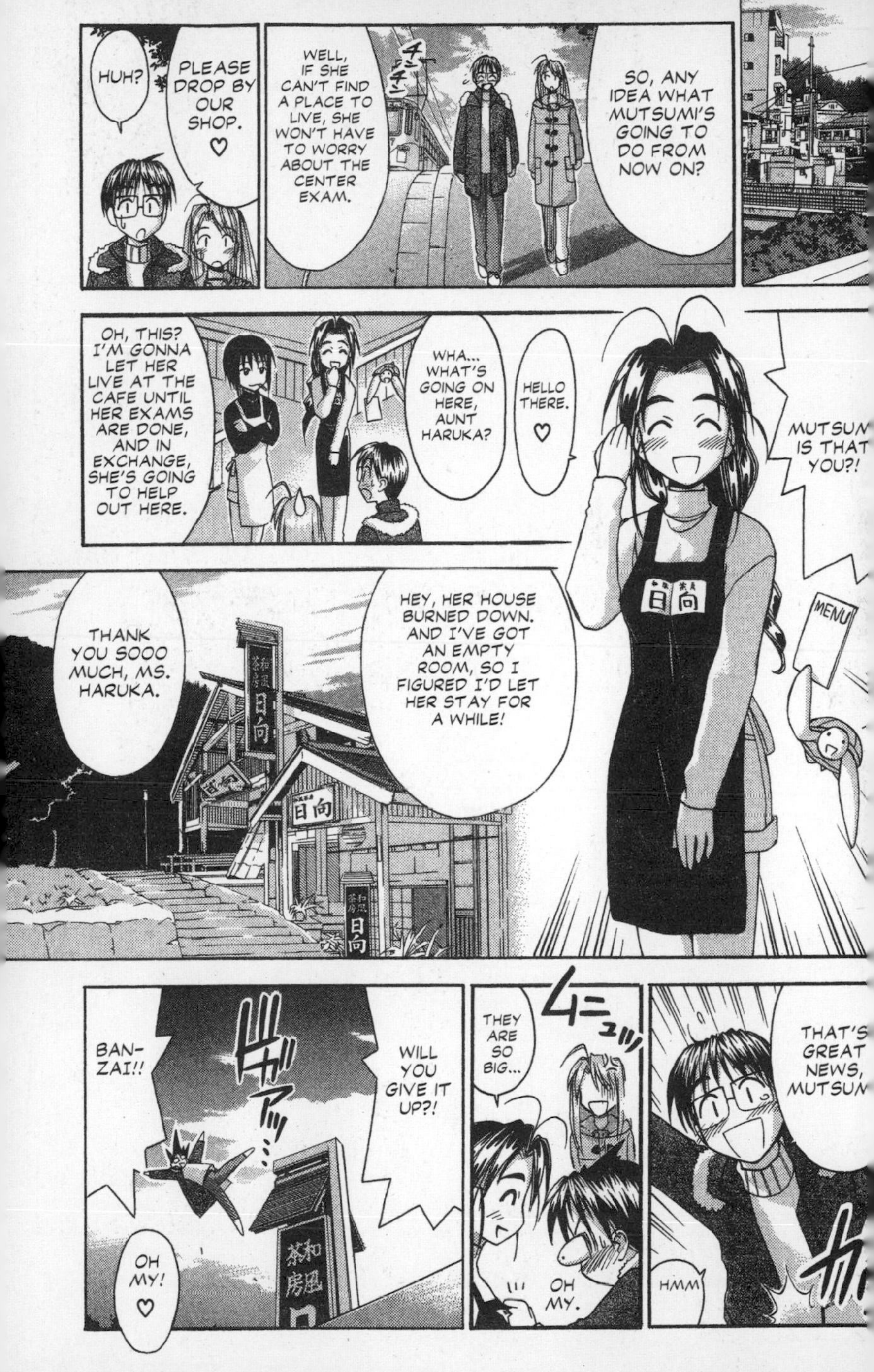
SO, ANY IDEA WHAT MUTSUMI'S GOING TO DO FROM NOW ON?
WELL, IF SHE CAN'T FIND A PLACE TO LIVE, SHE WON'T HAVE TO WORRY ABOUT THE CENTER EXAM.
PLEASE DROP BY OUR SHOP. ♡
HUH?
MUTSUM IS THAT YOU?!
MENU
日向
HELLO THERE. ♡
WHA... WHAT'S GOING ON HERE, AUNT HARUKA?
OH, THIS? I'M GONNA LET HER LIVE AT THE CAFE UNTIL HER EXAMS ARE DONE, AND IN EXCHANGE, SHE'S GOING TO HELP OUT HERE.
HEY, HER HOUSE BURNED DOWN. AND I'VE GOT AN EMPTY ROOM, SO I FIGURED I'D LET HER STAY FOR A WHILE!
THANK YOU SOOO MUCH, MS. HARUKA.
THAT'S GREAT NEWS, MUTSUM
HMM
ムニュッ
THEY ARE SO BIG...
OH MY.
WILL YOU GIVE IT UP?!
BAN-ZAI!!
OH MY! ♡

「Love Hina」

# HINATA.54

## Love Confession on Ice?!

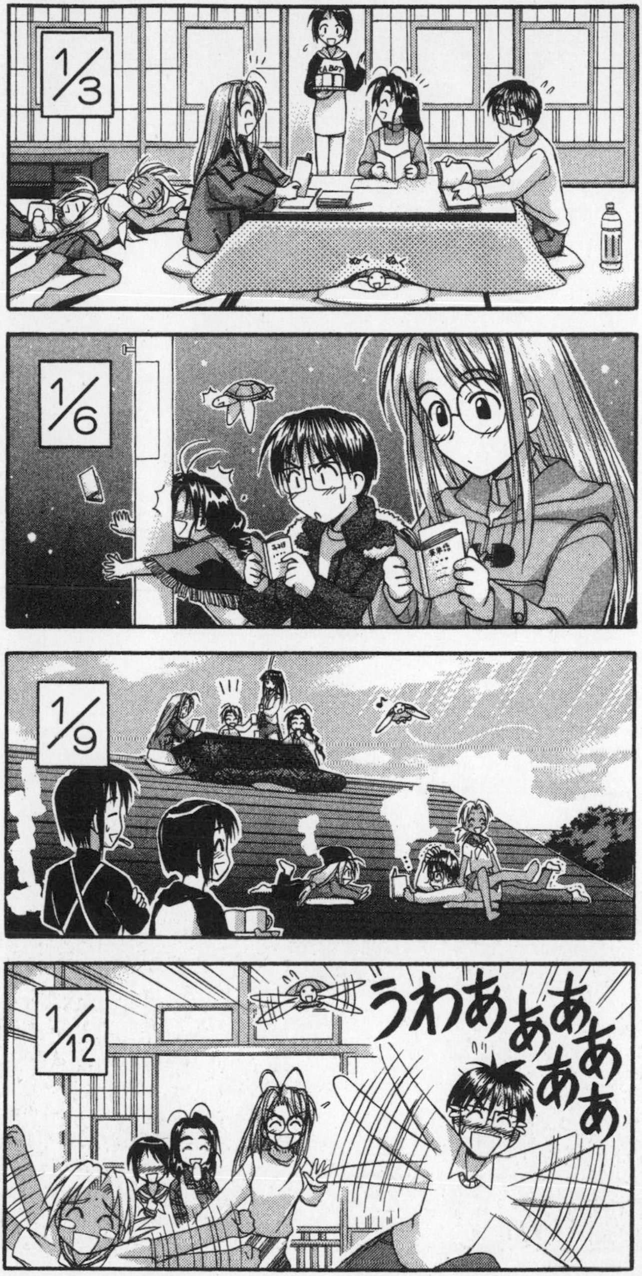
1/3
ぬく ぬく
1/6
1/9
1/12
うわああああああ

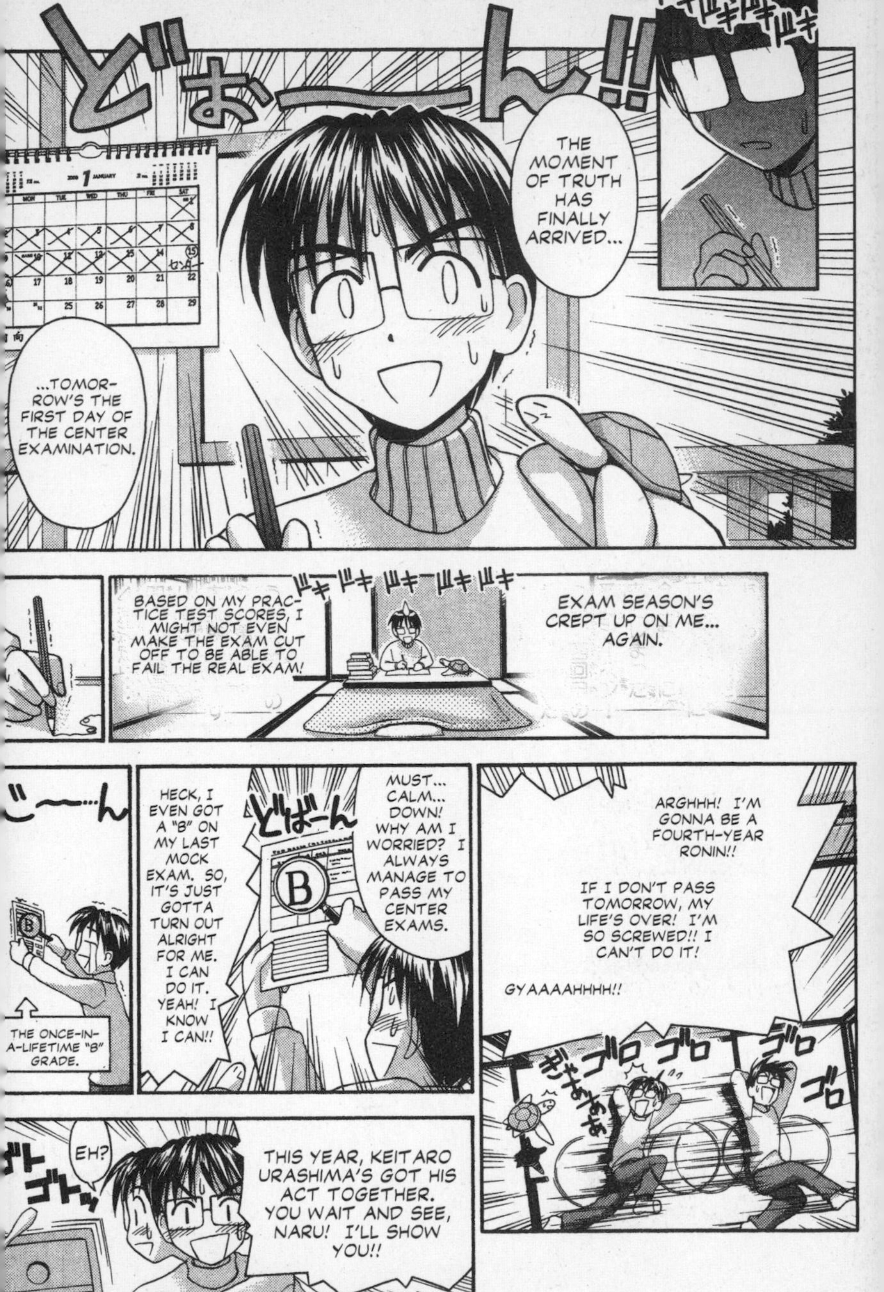
ドキドキドキドキ
どぉーーん!!
THE MOMENT OF TRUTH HAS FINALLY ARRIVED...
...TOMORROW'S THE FIRST DAY OF THE CENTER EXAMINATION.
EXAM SEASON'S CREPT UP ON ME... AGAIN.
ドキドキドキドキドキ
BASED ON MY PRACTICE TEST SCORES, I MIGHT NOT EVEN MAKE THE EXAM CUT OFF TO BE ABLE TO FAIL THE REAL EXAM!
ARGHHH! I'M GONNA BE A FOURTH-YEAR RONIN!!
IF I DON'T PASS TOMORROW, MY LIFE'S OVER! I'M SO SCREWED!! I CAN'T DO IT!
GYAAAAHHHH!!
ぎゃあああ
ゴロゴロゴロゴロ
MUST... CALM... DOWN! WHY AM I WORRIED? I ALWAYS MANAGE TO PASS MY CENTER EXAMS.
どばーん
HECK, I EVEN GOT A "B" ON MY LAST MOCK EXAM. SO, IT'S JUST GOTTA TURN OUT ALRIGHT FOR ME. I CAN DO IT. YEAH! I KNOW I CAN!!
ごーーん
THE ONCE-IN-A-LIFETIME "B" GRADE.
THIS YEAR, KEITARO URASHIMA'S GOT HIS ACT TOGETHER. YOU WAIT AND SEE, NARU! I'LL SHOW YOU!!
EH?
ゴトッ

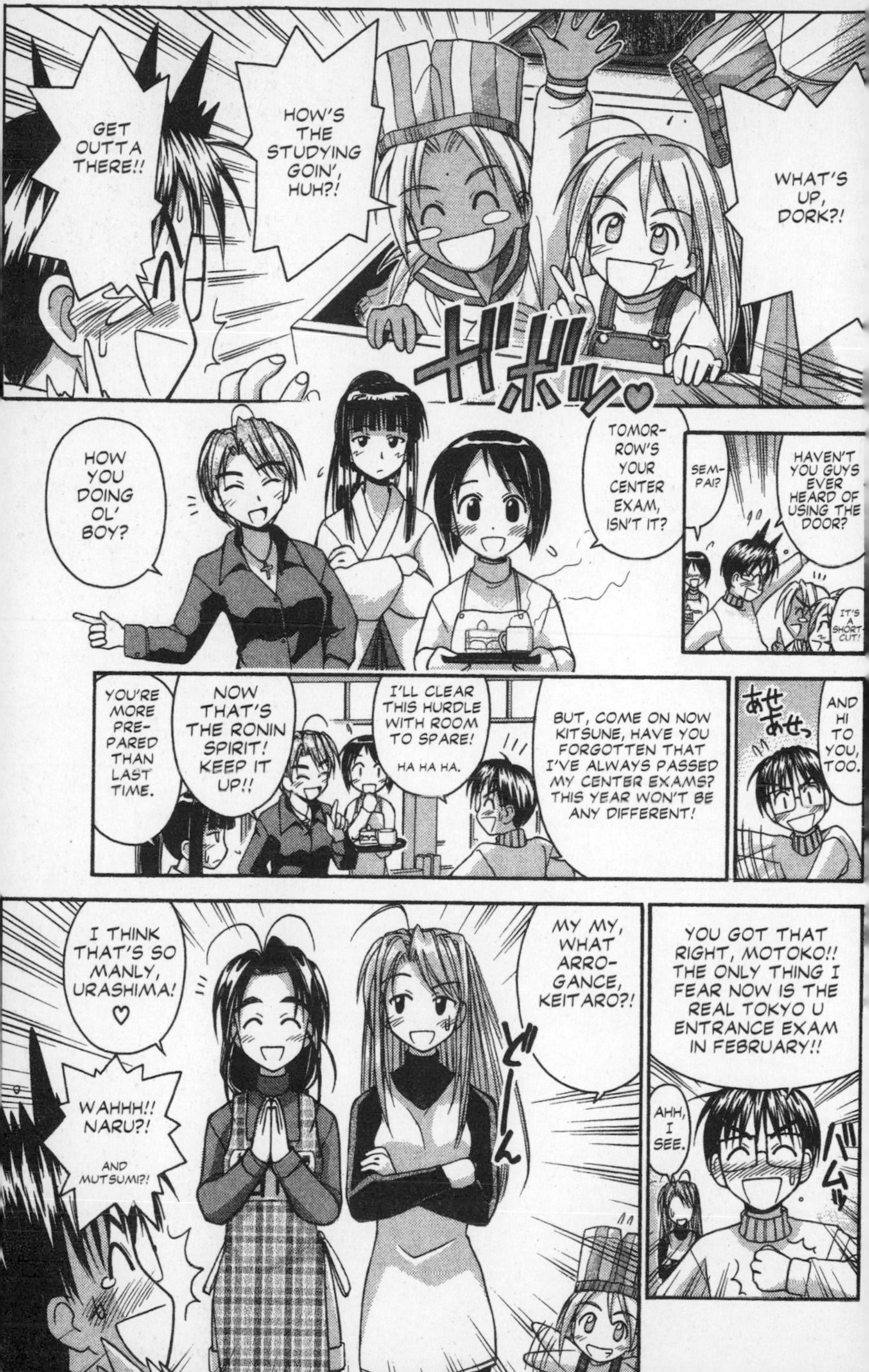
WHAT'S UP, DORK?!
HOW'S THE STUDYING GOIN', HUH?!
GET OUTTA THERE!!
HAVEN'T YOU GUYS EVER HEARD OF USING THE DOOR?
SEM-PAI?
IT'S A SHORT-CUT!
TOMOR-ROW'S YOUR CENTER EXAM, ISN'T IT?
HOW YOU DOING OL' BOY?
あせあせっ
AND HI TO YOU, TOO.
BUT, COME ON NOW KITSUNE, HAVE YOU FORGOTTEN THAT I'VE ALWAYS PASSED MY CENTER EXAMS? THIS YEAR WON'T BE ANY DIFFERENT!
I'LL CLEAR THIS HURDLE WITH ROOM TO SPARE!
HA HA HA.
NOW THAT'S THE RONIN SPIRIT! KEEP IT UP!!
YOU'RE MORE PRE-PARED THAN LAST TIME.
YOU GOT THAT RIGHT, MOTOKO!! THE ONLY THING I FEAR NOW IS THE REAL TOKYO U ENTRANCE EXAM IN FEBRUARY!!
AHH, I SEE.
バムッ
MY MY, WHAT ARRO-GANCE, KEITARO?!
どーん
I THINK THAT'S SO MANLY, URASHIMA! ♡
WAHHH!! NARU?!
AND MUTSUMI?!

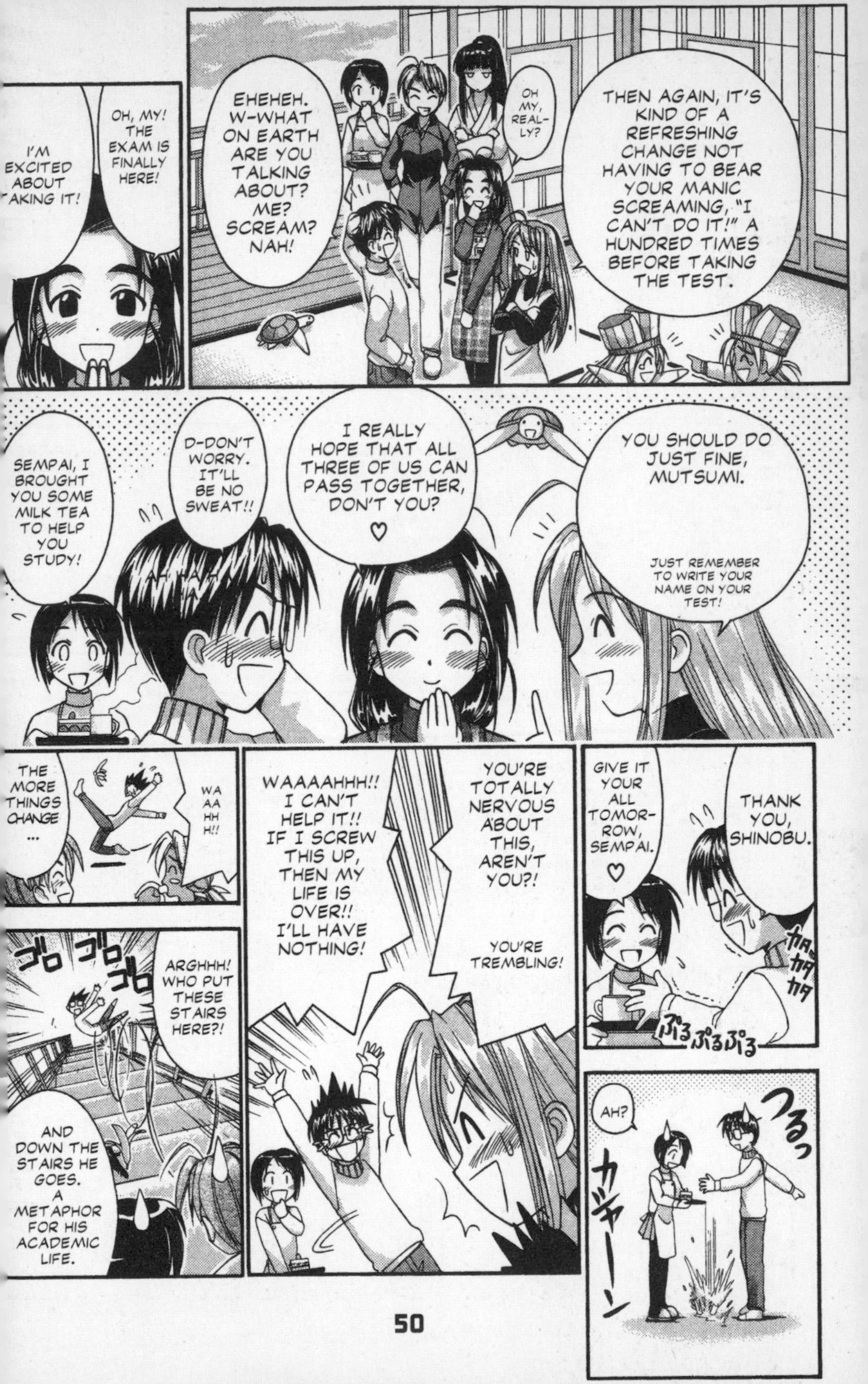
THEN AGAIN, IT'S KIND OF A REFRESHING CHANGE NOT HAVING TO BEAR YOUR MANIC SCREAMING, "I CAN'T DO IT!" A HUNDRED TIMES BEFORE TAKING THE TEST.
OH MY, REALLY?
EHEHEH. W-WHAT ON EARTH ARE YOU TALKING ABOUT? ME? SCREAM? NAH!
OH, MY! THE EXAM IS FINALLY HERE!
I'M EXCITED ABOUT TAKING IT!
YOU SHOULD DO JUST FINE, MUTSUMI.
JUST REMEMBER TO WRITE YOUR NAME ON YOUR TEST!
I REALLY HOPE THAT ALL THREE OF US CAN PASS TOGETHER, DON'T YOU? ♡
D-DON'T WORRY. IT'LL BE NO SWEAT!!
SEMPAI, I BROUGHT YOU SOME MILK TEA TO HELP YOU STUDY!
THANK YOU, SHINOBU.
GIVE IT YOUR ALL TOMORROW, SEMPAI. ♡
カタカタカタ
ぷるぷるぷる
AH?
つるっ
カシャーン
YOU'RE TOTALLY NERVOUS ABOUT THIS, AREN'T YOU?!
YOU'RE TREMBLING!
WAAAAHHH!! I CAN'T HELP IT!! IF I SCREW THIS UP, THEN MY LIFE IS OVER!! I'LL HAVE NOTHING!
WA AA HH H!!
THE MORE THINGS CHANGE ...
ARGHHH! WHO PUT THESE STAIRS HERE?!
ゴロゴロゴロ
AND DOWN THE STAIRS HE GOES. A METAPHOR FOR HIS ACADEMIC LIFE.

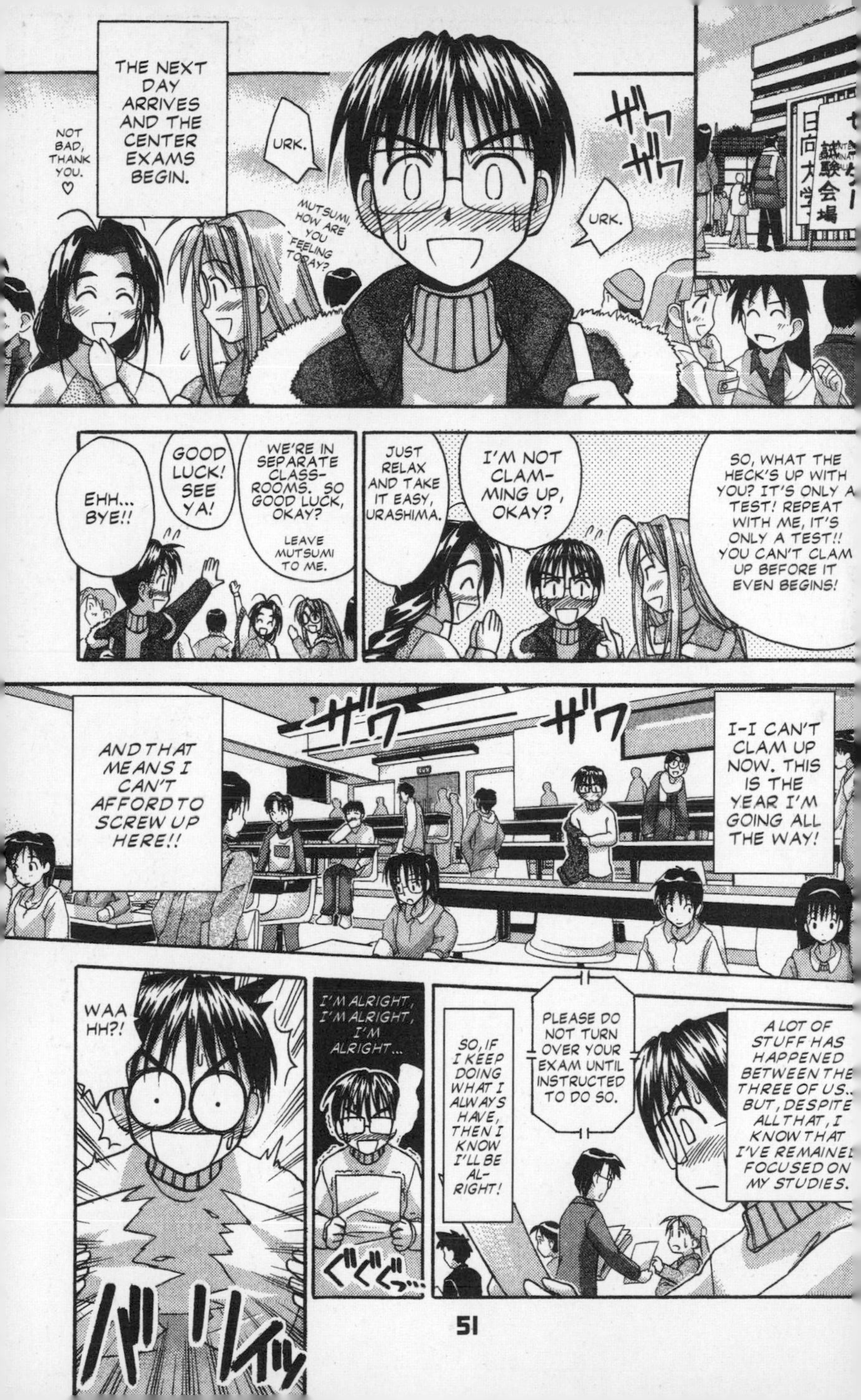
試験会場
ザワザワ
URK.
URK.
MUTSUMI, HOW ARE YOU FEELING TODAY?
THE NEXT DAY ARRIVES AND THE CENTER EXAMS BEGIN.
NOT BAD, THANK YOU. ♡
SO, WHAT THE HECK'S UP WITH YOU? IT'S ONLY A TEST! REPEAT WITH ME, IT'S ONLY A TEST!! YOU CAN'T CLAM UP BEFORE IT EVEN BEGINS!
I'M NOT CLAMMING UP, OKAY?
JUST RELAX AND TAKE IT EASY, URASHIMA.
WE'RE IN SEPARATE CLASSROOMS. SO GOOD LUCK, OKAY?
LEAVE MUTSUMI TO ME.
GOOD LUCK! SEE YA!
EHH... BYE!!
I-I CAN'T CLAM UP NOW. THIS IS THE YEAR I'M GOING ALL THE WAY!
ザワ ザワ
AND THAT MEANS I CAN'T AFFORD TO SCREW UP HERE!!
A LOT OF STUFF HAS HAPPENED BETWEEN THE THREE OF US... BUT, DESPITE ALL THAT, I KNOW THAT I'VE REMAINED FOCUSED ON MY STUDIES.
PLEASE DO NOT TURN OVER YOUR EXAM UNTIL INSTRUCTED TO DO SO.
SO, IF I KEEP DOING WHAT I ALWAYS HAVE, THEN I KNOW I'LL BE ALRIGHT!
I'M ALRIGHT, I'M ALRIGHT, I'M ALRIGHT...
ぐぐぐっ...
WAAHH?!
バリィッ

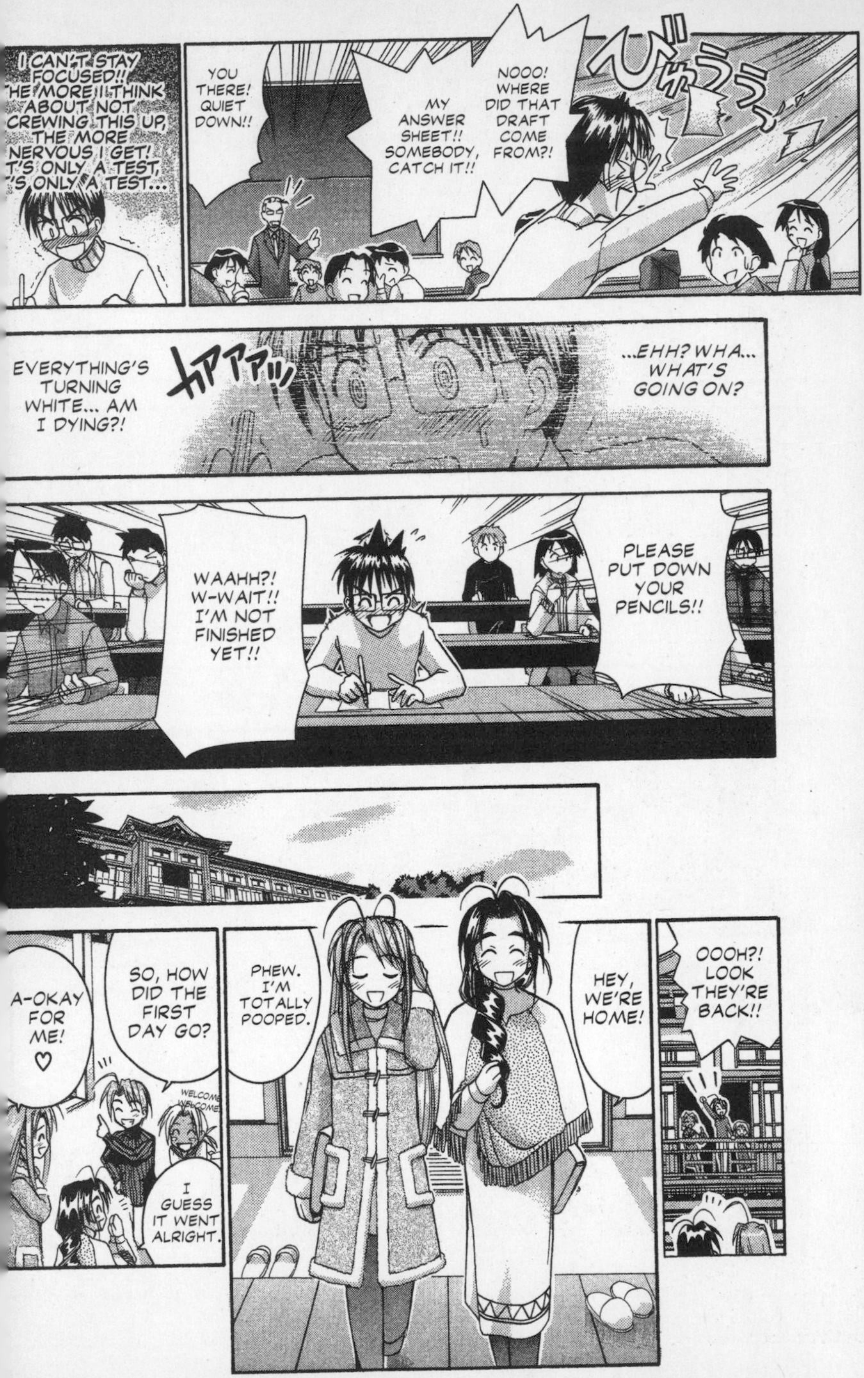
びゅううっ
NOOO! WHERE DID THAT DRAFT COME FROM?!
MY ANSWER SHEET!! SOMEBODY, CATCH IT!!
YOU THERE! QUIET DOWN!!
I CAN'T STAY FOCUSED!! THE MORE I THINK ABOUT NOT CREWING THIS UP, THE MORE NERVOUS I GET! T'S ONLY A TEST, 'S ONLY A TEST...
...EHH? WHA... WHAT'S GOING ON?
カァアァッ
EVERYTHING'S TURNING WHITE... AM I DYING?!
PLEASE PUT DOWN YOUR PENCILS!!
WAAHH?! W-WAIT!! I'M NOT FINISHED YET!!
OOOH?! LOOK THEY'RE BACK!!
HEY, WE'RE HOME!
PHEW. I'M TOTALLY POOPED.
SO, HOW DID THE FIRST DAY GO?
A-OKAY FOR ME! ♡
WELCOME WELCOME
I GUESS IT WENT ALRIGHT.

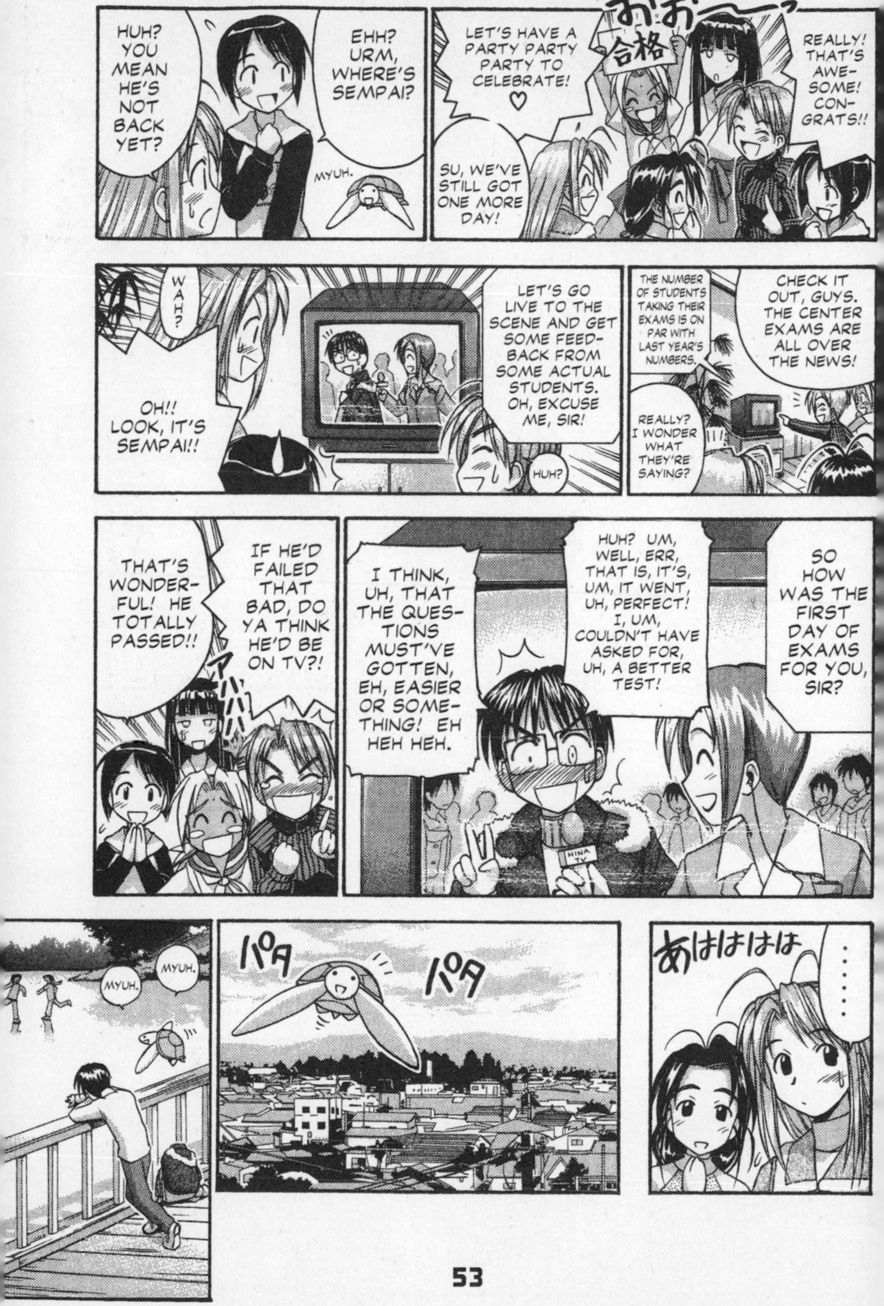

おお——っ
合格
REALLY! THAT'S AWE-SOME! CON-GRATS!!
LET'S HAVE A PARTY PARTY PARTY TO CELEBRATE! ♡
SU, WE'VE STILL GOT ONE MORE DAY!
EHH? URM, WHERE'S SEMPAI?
HUH? YOU MEAN HE'S NOT BACK YET?
MYUH.
CHECK IT OUT, GUYS. THE CENTER EXAMS ARE ALL OVER THE NEWS!
THE NUMBER OF STUDENTS TAKING THEIR EXAMS IS ON PAR WITH LAST YEAR'S NUMBERS.
REALLY? I WONDER WHAT THEY'RE SAYING?
LET'S GO LIVE TO THE SCENE AND GET SOME FEED-BACK FROM SOME ACTUAL STUDENTS. OH, EXCUSE ME, SIR!
HUH?
WAH?
OH!! LOOK, IT'S SEMPAI!!
SO HOW WAS THE FIRST DAY OF EXAMS FOR YOU, SIR?
HUH? UM, WELL, ERR, THAT IS, IT'S, UM, IT WENT, UH, PERFECT! I, UM, COULDN'T HAVE ASKED FOR, UH, A BETTER TEST!
HINA TV
I THINK, UH, THAT THE QUES-TIONS MUST'VE GOTTEN, EH, EASIER OR SOME-THING! EH HEH HEH.
IF HE'D FAILED THAT BAD, DO YA THINK HE'D BE ON TV?!
THAT'S WONDER-FUL! HE TOTALLY PASSED!!
アハハハ
あはははは
......
パタ
パタ
MYUH.
MYUH.

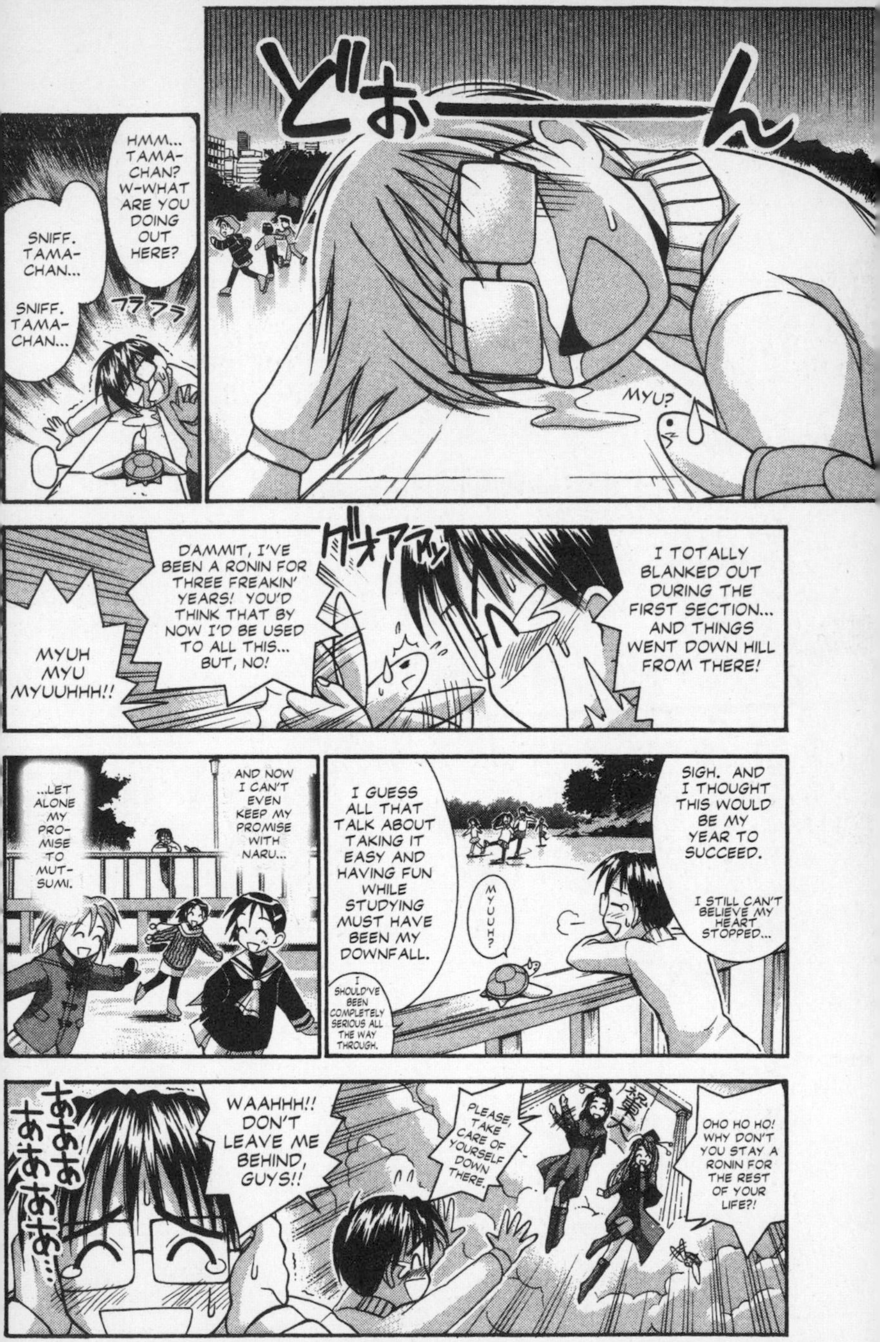
どぉーーん
MYU?
HMM... TAMA-CHAN? W-WHAT ARE YOU DOING OUT HERE?
SNIFF. TAMA-CHAN...
フラフラ
SNIFF. TAMA-CHAN...
I TOTALLY BLANKED OUT DURING THE FIRST SECTION... AND THINGS WENT DOWN HILL FROM THERE!
グオアアッ
DAMMIT, I'VE BEEN A RONIN FOR THREE FREAKIN' YEARS! YOU'D THINK THAT BY NOW I'D BE USED TO ALL THIS... BUT, NO!
MYUH MYU MYUUHHH!!
SIGH. AND I THOUGHT THIS WOULD BE MY YEAR TO SUCCEED.
I STILL CAN'T BELIEVE MY HEART STOPPED...
MYUUH?
I GUESS ALL THAT TALK ABOUT TAKING IT EASY AND HAVING FUN WHILE STUDYING MUST HAVE BEEN MY DOWNFALL.
I SHOULD'VE BEEN COMPLETELY SERIOUS ALL THE WAY THROUGH.
AND NOW I CAN'T EVEN KEEP MY PROMISE WITH NARU...
...LET ALONE MY PROMISE TO MUTSUMI.
OHO HO HO! WHY DON'T YOU STAY A RONIN FOR THE REST OF YOUR LIFE?!
PLEASE, TAKE CARE OF YOURSELF DOWN THERE.
WAAHHH!! DON'T LEAVE ME BEHIND, GUYS!!
あああ あああああ...

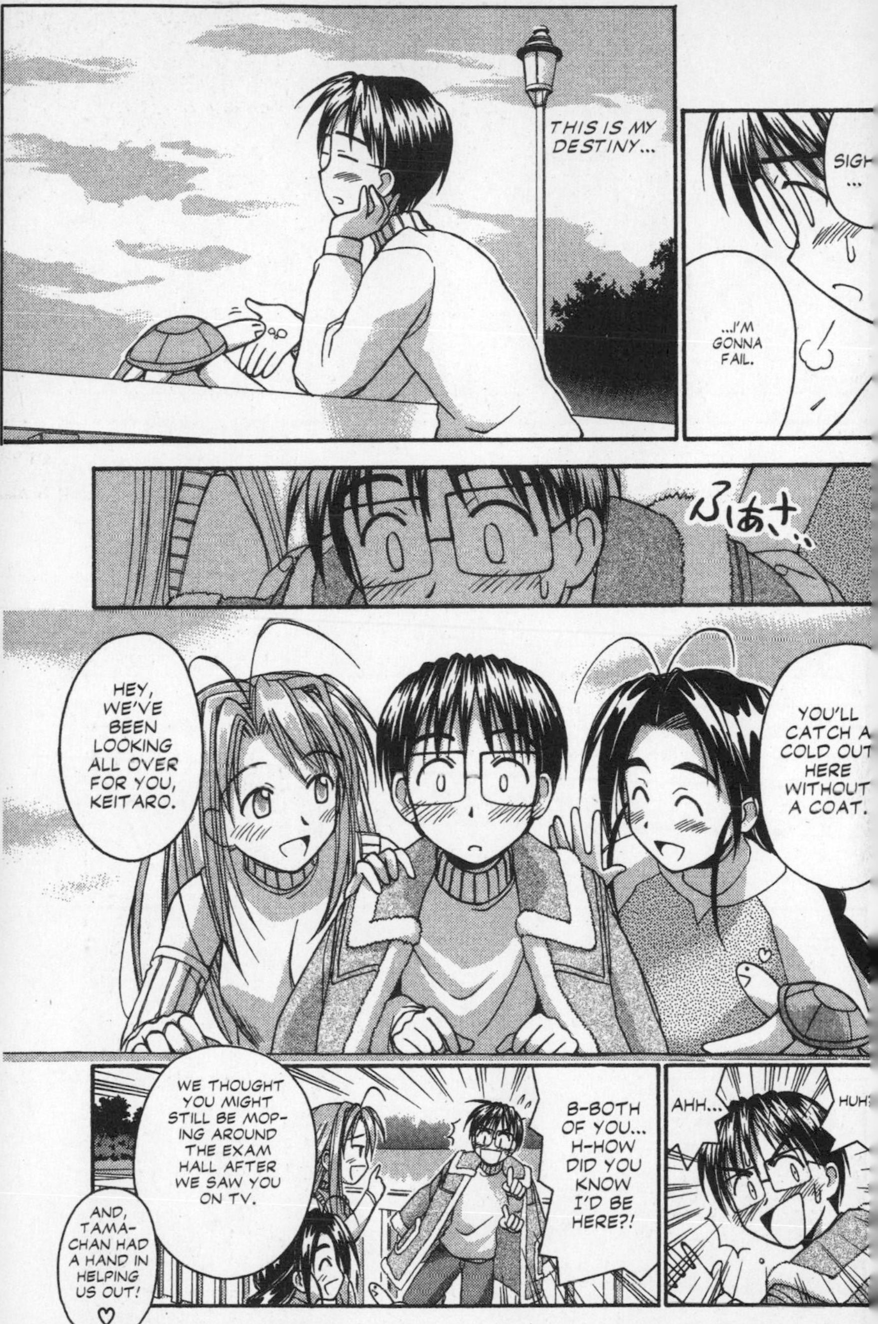
SIGH...
...I'M GONNA FAIL.
THIS IS MY DESTINY...
ふぁさ..
YOU'LL CATCH A COLD OUT HERE WITHOUT A COAT.
HEY, WE'VE BEEN LOOKING ALL OVER FOR YOU, KEITARO.
HUH
AHH...
B-BOTH OF YOU... H-HOW DID YOU KNOW I'D BE HERE?!
WE THOUGHT YOU MIGHT STILL BE MOPING AROUND THE EXAM HALL AFTER WE SAW YOU ON TV.
AND, TAMA-CHAN HAD A HAND IN HELPING US OUT! ♡

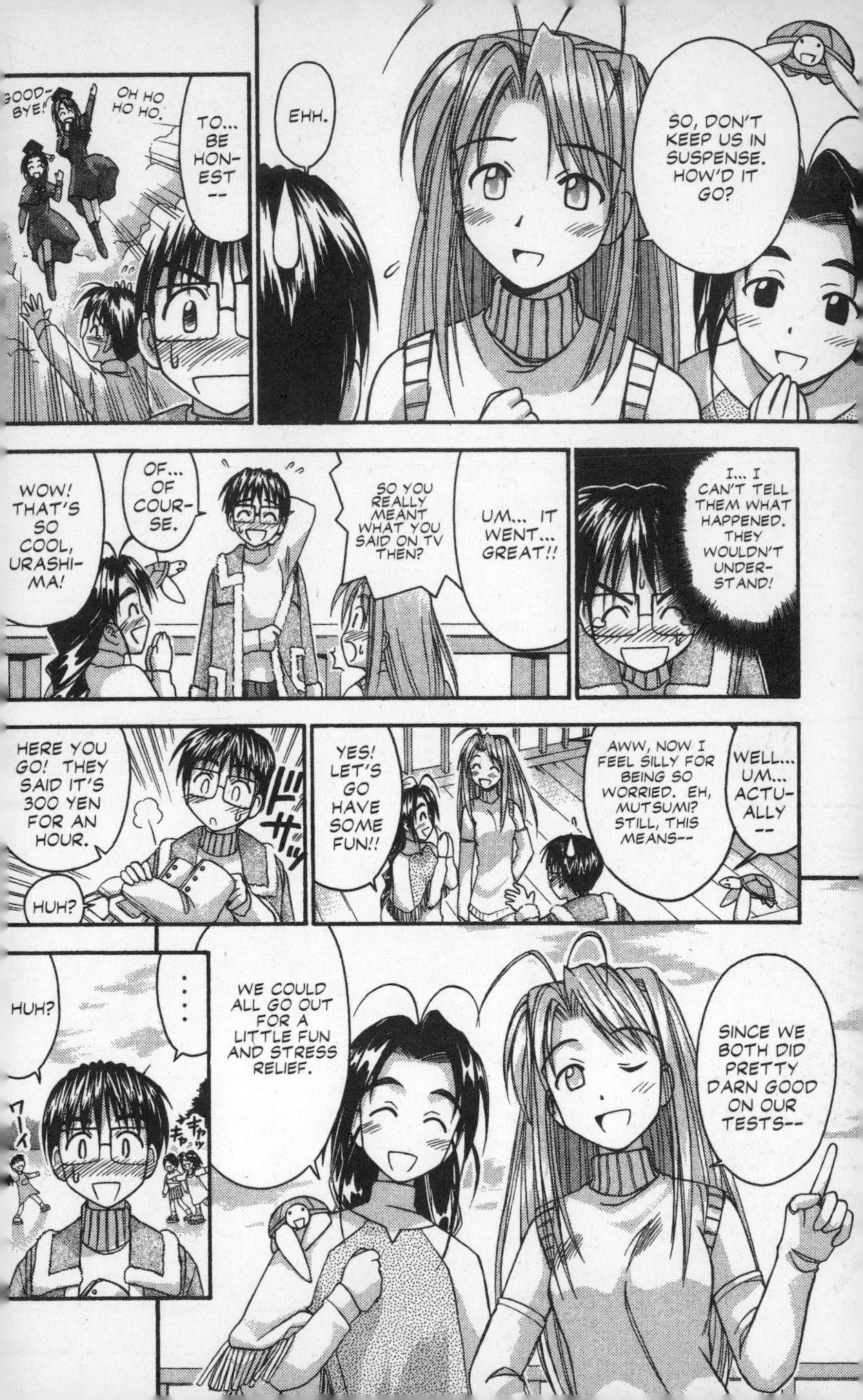
SO, DON'T KEEP US IN SUSPENSE. HOW'D IT GO?
EHH.
TO... BE HON-EST --
OH HO HO HO.
GOOD-BYE!
I... I CAN'T TELL THEM WHAT HAPPENED. THEY WOULDN'T UNDER-STAND!
UM... IT WENT... GREAT!!
SO YOU REALLY MEANT WHAT YOU SAID ON TV THEN?
OF... OF COURSE.
WOW! THAT'S SO COOL, URASHIMA!
WELL... UM... ACTU-ALLY --
AWW, NOW I FEEL SILLY FOR BEING SO WORRIED. EH, MUTSUMI? STILL, THIS MEANS--
YES! LET'S GO HAVE SOME FUN!!
HERE YOU GO! THEY SAID IT'S 300 YEN FOR AN HOUR.
HUH?
SINCE WE BOTH DID PRETTY DARN GOOD ON OUR TESTS--
WE COULD ALL GO OUT FOR A LITTLE FUN AND STRESS RELIEF.
....
HUH?

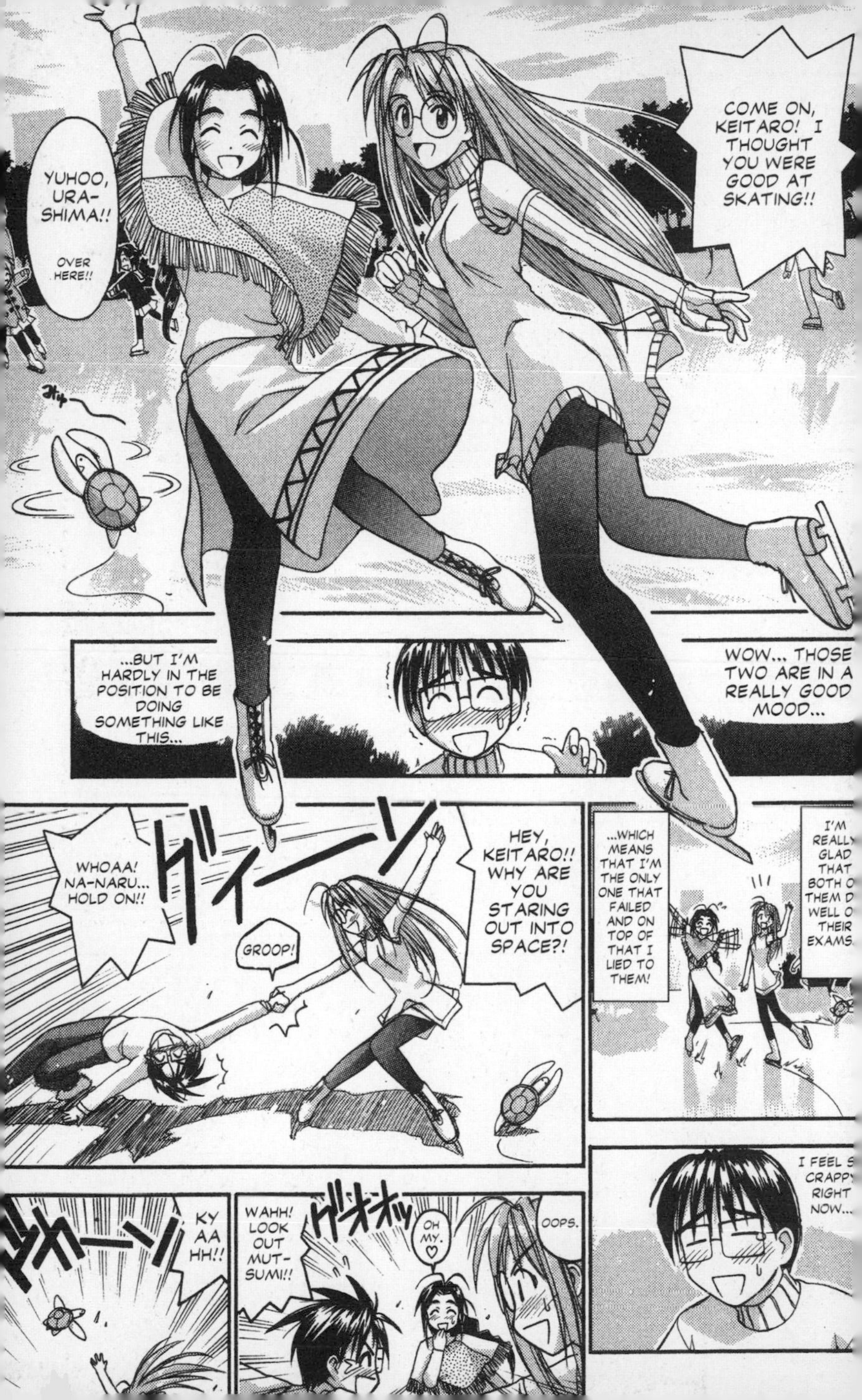
COME ON, KEITARO! I THOUGHT YOU WERE GOOD AT SKATING!!
YUHOO, URA-SHIMA!!
OVER HERE!!
WOW... THOSE TWO ARE IN A REALLY GOOD MOOD...
...BUT I'M HARDLY IN THE POSITION TO BE DOING SOMETHING LIKE THIS...
I'M REALLY GLAD THAT BOTH O THEM D WELL O THEIR EXAMS.
...WHICH MEANS THAT I'M THE ONLY ONE THAT FAILED AND ON TOP OF THAT I LIED TO THEM!
HEY, KEITARO!! WHY ARE YOU STARING OUT INTO SPACE?!
GROOP!
WHOAA! NA-NARU... HOLD ON!!
I FEEL S CRAPPY RIGHT NOW...
OOPS.
OH MY. ♡
WAHH! LOOK OUT MUT-SUMI!!
KY AA HH!!

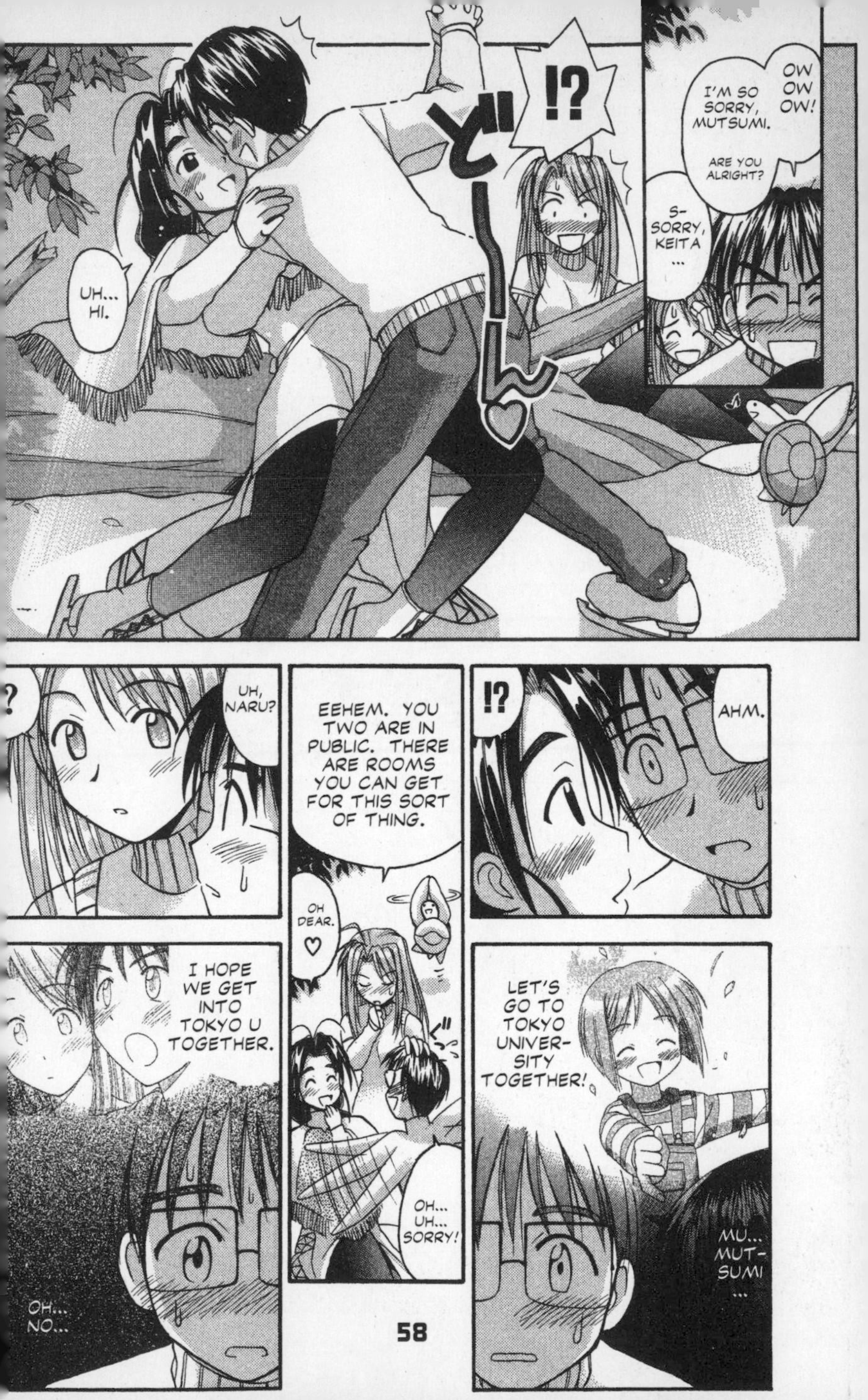
OW OW OW!
I'M SO SORRY, MUTSUMI.
ARE YOU ALRIGHT?
S-SORRY, KEITA ...
!?
どしん
UH... HI.
!?
AHM.
LET'S GO TO TOKYO UNIVER-SITY TOGETHER!
MU... MUT-SUMI ...
EEHEM. YOU TWO ARE IN PUBLIC. THERE ARE ROOMS YOU CAN GET FOR THIS SORT OF THING.
OH DEAR. ♡
OH... UH... SORRY!
?
UH, NARU?
I HOPE WE GET INTO TOKYO U TOGETHER.
OH... NO...

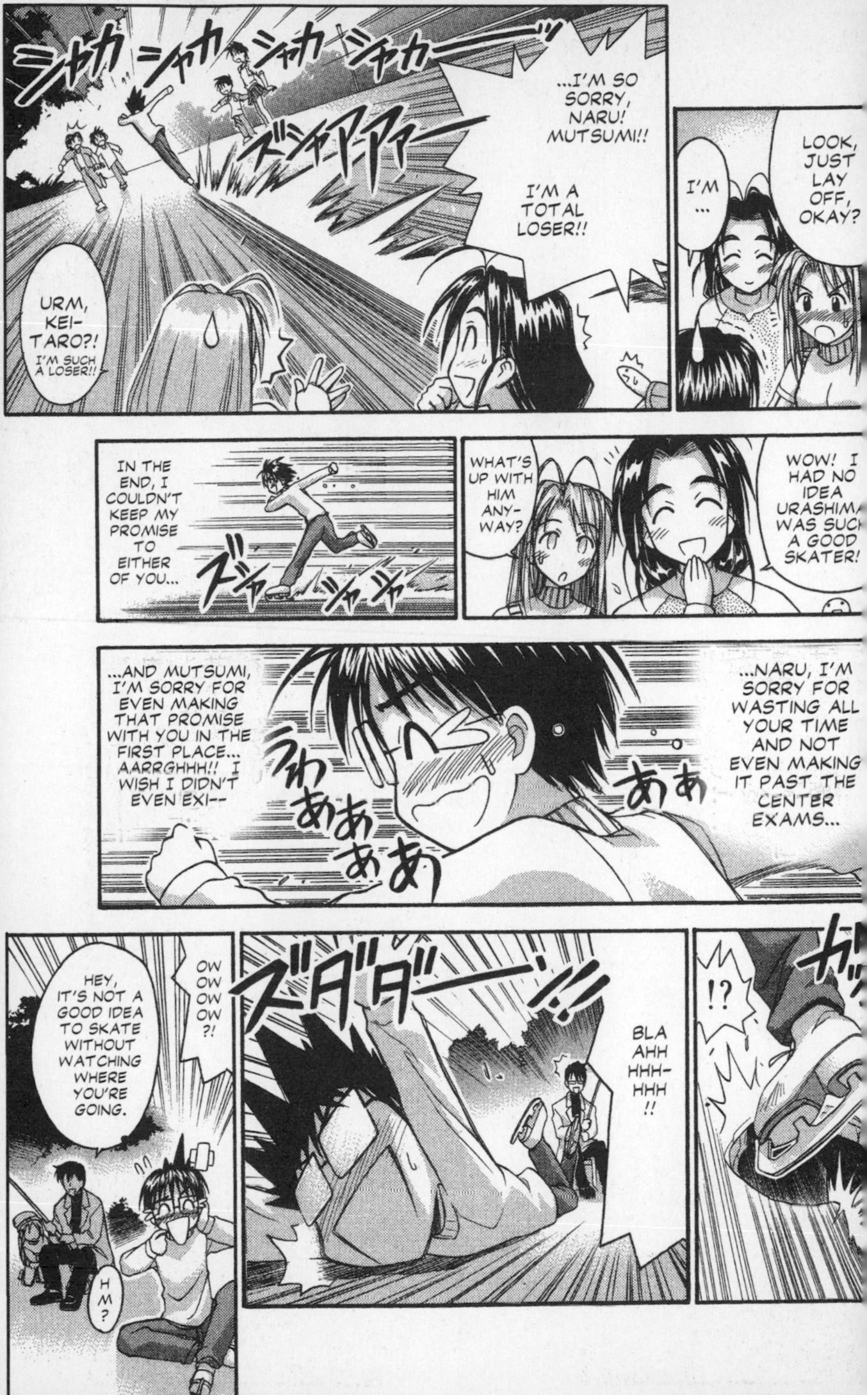
I'M ...
LOOK, JUST LAY OFF, OKAY?
シャカ シャカ シャカ シャカーッ
ズシャアァー
...I'M SO SORRY, NARU! MUTSUMI!!
I'M A TOTAL LOSER!!
URM, KEI-TARO?!
I'M SUCH A LOSER!!
WOW! I HAD NO IDEA URASHIMA WAS SUCH A GOOD SKATER!
WHAT'S UP WITH HIM ANY-WAY?
IN THE END, I COULDN'T KEEP MY PROMISE TO EITHER OF YOU...
ズシャ シャ シャ
...NARU, I'M SORRY FOR WASTING ALL YOUR TIME AND NOT EVEN MAKING IT PAST THE CENTER EXAMS...
...AND MUTSUMI, I'M SORRY FOR EVEN MAKING THAT PROMISE WITH YOU IN THE FIRST PLACE... AARRGHHH!! I WISH I DIDN'T EVEN EXI--
うわあああ ああ
!?
ズダダーッ!!
BLA AHH HHH- HHH !!
OW OW OW OW ?!
HEY, IT'S NOT A GOOD IDEA TO SKATE WITHOUT WATCHING WHERE YOU'RE GOING.
HM?

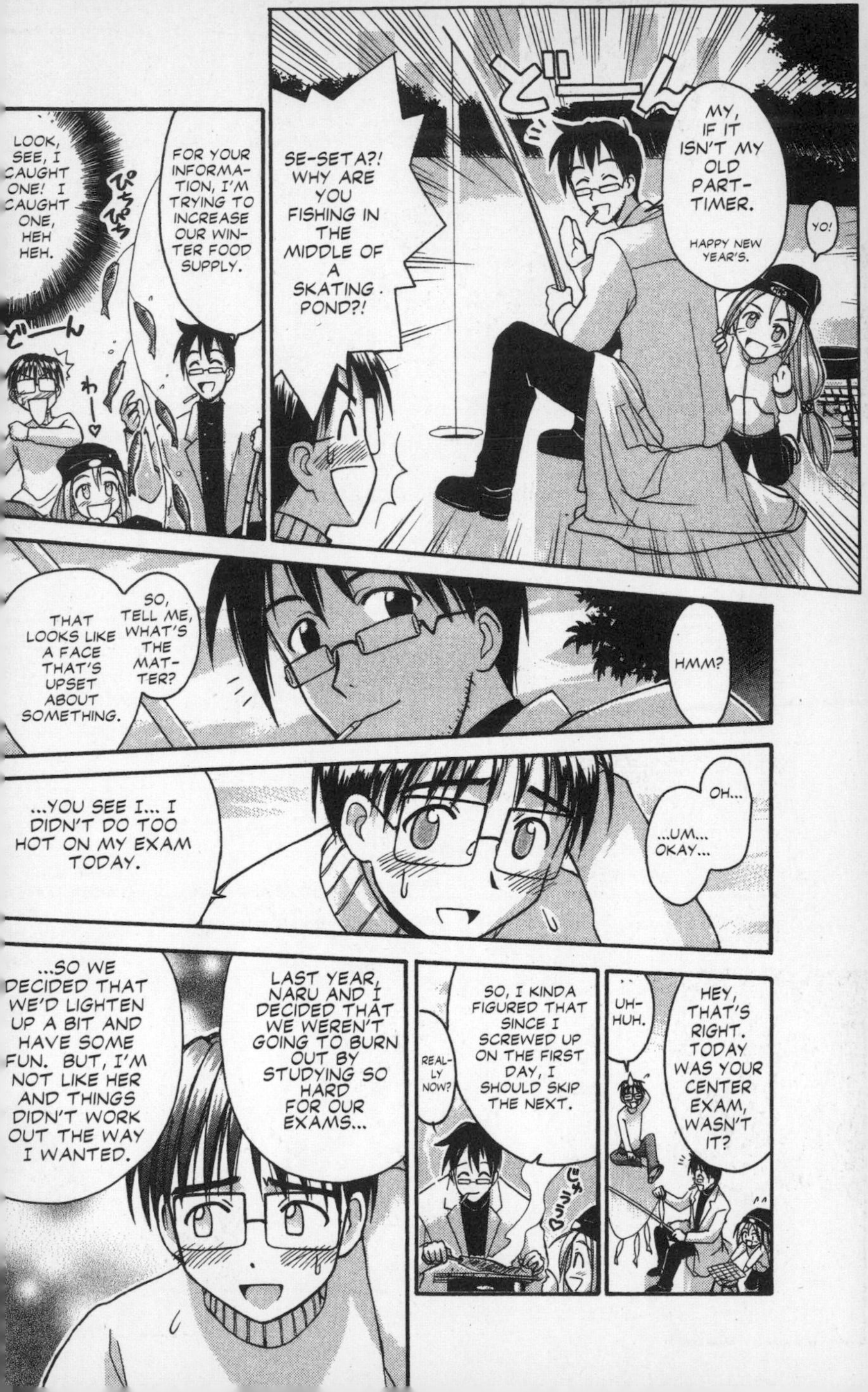
どーん
MY, IF IT ISN'T MY OLD PART-TIMER.
HAPPY NEW YEAR'S.
YO!
SE-SETA?! WHY ARE YOU FISHING IN THE MIDDLE OF A SKATING POND?!
FOR YOUR INFORMATION, I'M TRYING TO INCREASE OUR WINTER FOOD SUPPLY.
LOOK, SEE, I CAUGHT ONE! I CAUGHT ONE, HEH HEH.
ぴちぴち
どーん
わー♡
HMM?
SO, TELL ME, WHAT'S THE MATTER?
THAT LOOKS LIKE A FACE THAT'S UPSET ABOUT SOMETHING.
OH...
...UM... OKAY...
...YOU SEE I... I DIDN'T DO TOO HOT ON MY EXAM TODAY.
HEY, THAT'S RIGHT. TODAY WAS YOUR CENTER EXAM, WASN'T IT?
UH-HUH.
SO, I KINDA FIGURED THAT SINCE I SCREWED UP ON THE FIRST DAY, I SHOULD SKIP THE NEXT.
REALLY NOW?
LAST YEAR, NARU AND I DECIDED THAT WE WEREN'T GOING TO BURN OUT BY STUDYING SO HARD FOR OUR EXAMS...
...SO WE DECIDED THAT WE'D LIGHTEN UP A BIT AND HAVE SOME FUN. BUT, I'M NOT LIKE HER AND THINGS DIDN'T WORK OUT THE WAY I WANTED.

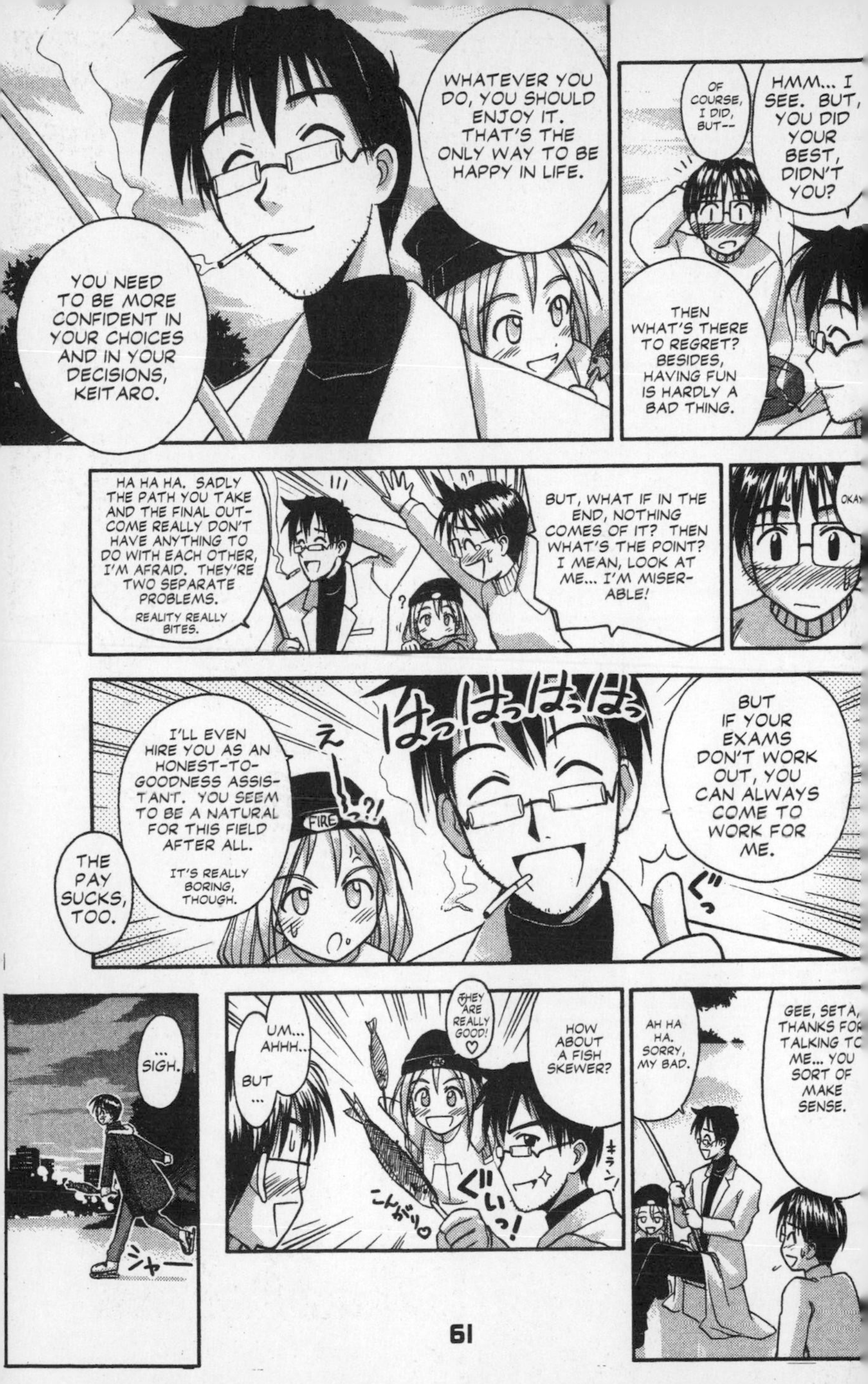

HMM... I SEE. BUT, YOU DID YOUR BEST, DIDN'T YOU?
OF COURSE, I DID, BUT--
THEN WHAT'S THERE TO REGRET? BESIDES, HAVING FUN IS HARDLY A BAD THING.
WHATEVER YOU DO, YOU SHOULD ENJOY IT. THAT'S THE ONLY WAY TO BE HAPPY IN LIFE.
YOU NEED TO BE MORE CONFIDENT IN YOUR CHOICES AND IN YOUR DECISIONS, KEITARO.
OKAY
BUT, WHAT IF IN THE END, NOTHING COMES OF IT? THEN WHAT'S THE POINT? I MEAN, LOOK AT ME... I'M MISERABLE!
HA HA HA. SADLY THE PATH YOU TAKE AND THE FINAL OUTCOME REALLY DON'T HAVE ANYTHING TO DO WITH EACH OTHER, I'M AFRAID. THEY'RE TWO SEPARATE PROBLEMS.
REALITY REALLY BITES.
BUT IF YOUR EXAMS DON'T WORK OUT, YOU CAN ALWAYS COME TO WORK FOR ME.
ぐっ
はっはっはっはっ
え
っ?!
FIRE
I'LL EVEN HIRE YOU AS AN HONEST-TO-GOODNESS ASSISTANT. YOU SEEM TO BE A NATURAL FOR THIS FIELD AFTER ALL.
IT'S REALLY BORING, THOUGH.
THE PAY SUCKS, TOO.
GEE, SETA, THANKS FOR TALKING TO ME... YOU SORT OF MAKE SENSE.
AH HA HA. SORRY, MY BAD.
HOW ABOUT A FISH SKEWER?
キラン!
THEY ARE REALLY GOOD! ♡
ぐいっ!
こんがり♡
UM... AHHH...
BUT ...
... SIGH.
シャー

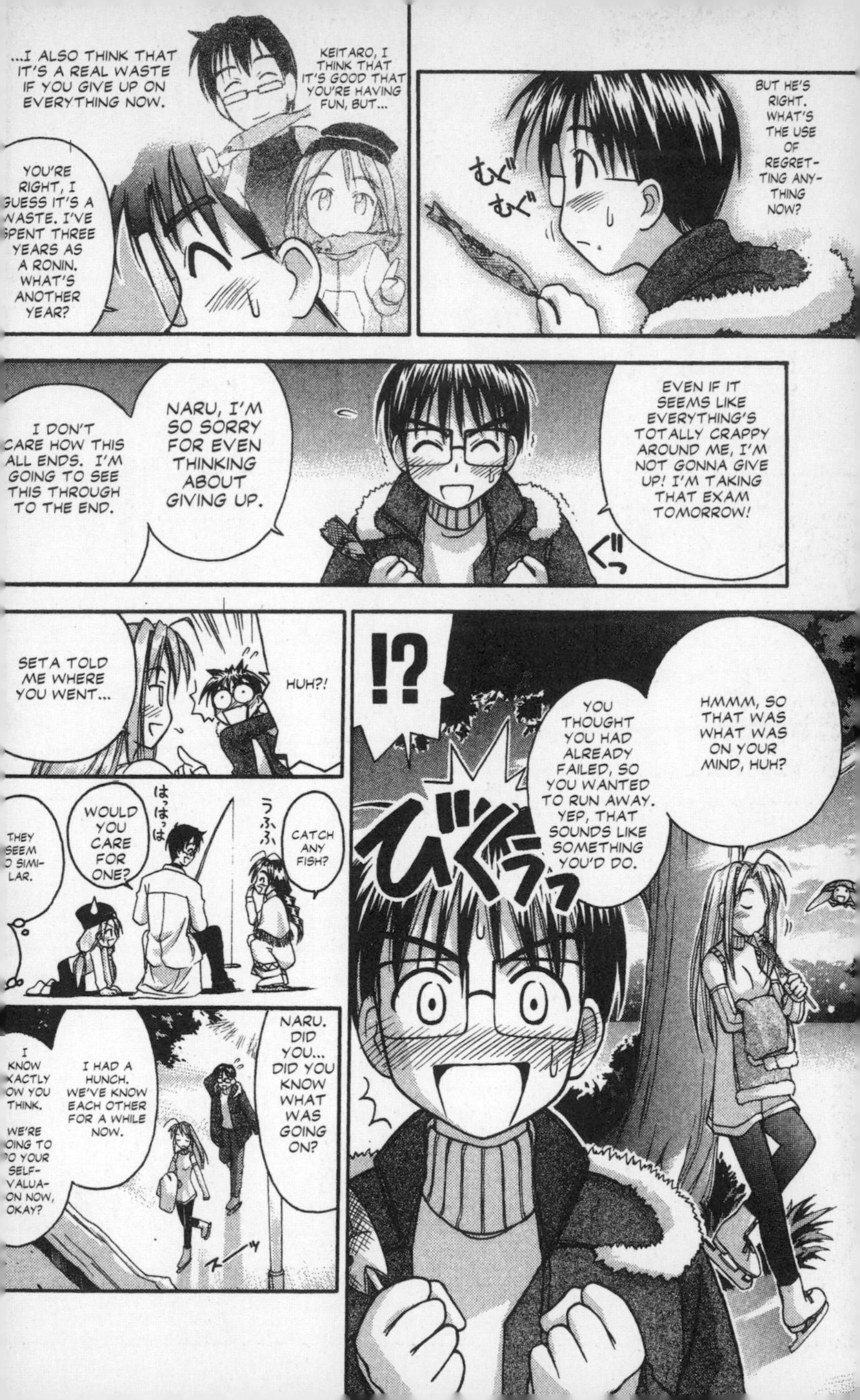
むぐ むぐ
BUT HE'S RIGHT. WHAT'S THE USE OF REGRETTING ANYTHING NOW?
KEITARO, I THINK THAT IT'S GOOD THAT YOU'RE HAVING FUN, BUT...
...I ALSO THINK THAT IT'S A REAL WASTE IF YOU GIVE UP ON EVERYTHING NOW.
YOU'RE RIGHT, I GUESS IT'S A ASTE. I'VE PENT THREE YEARS AS A RONIN. WHAT'S ANOTHER YEAR?
EVEN IF IT SEEMS LIKE EVERYTHING'S TOTALLY CRAPPY AROUND ME, I'M NOT GONNA GIVE UP! I'M TAKING THAT EXAM TOMORROW!
ぐっ
NARU, I'M SO SORRY FOR EVEN THINKING ABOUT GIVING UP.
I DON'T CARE HOW THIS ALL ENDS. I'M GOING TO SEE THIS THROUGH TO THE END.
HMMM, SO THAT WAS WHAT WAS ON YOUR MIND, HUH?
YOU THOUGHT YOU HAD ALREADY FAILED, SO YOU WANTED TO RUN AWAY. YEP, THAT SOUNDS LIKE SOMETHING YOU'D DO.
!?
びくぅっ
HUH?!
SETA TOLD ME WHERE YOU WENT...
うふふ
CATCH ANY FISH?
はっはっは
WOULD YOU CARE FOR ONE?
THEY SEEM O SIMILAR.
NARU. DID YOU... DID YOU KNOW WHAT WAS GOING ON?
I HAD A HUNCH. WE'VE KNOW EACH OTHER FOR A WHILE NOW.
I KNOW XACTLY OW YOU THINK. WE'RE OING TO O YOUR SELF-VALUA-ON NOW, OKAY?
スーッ

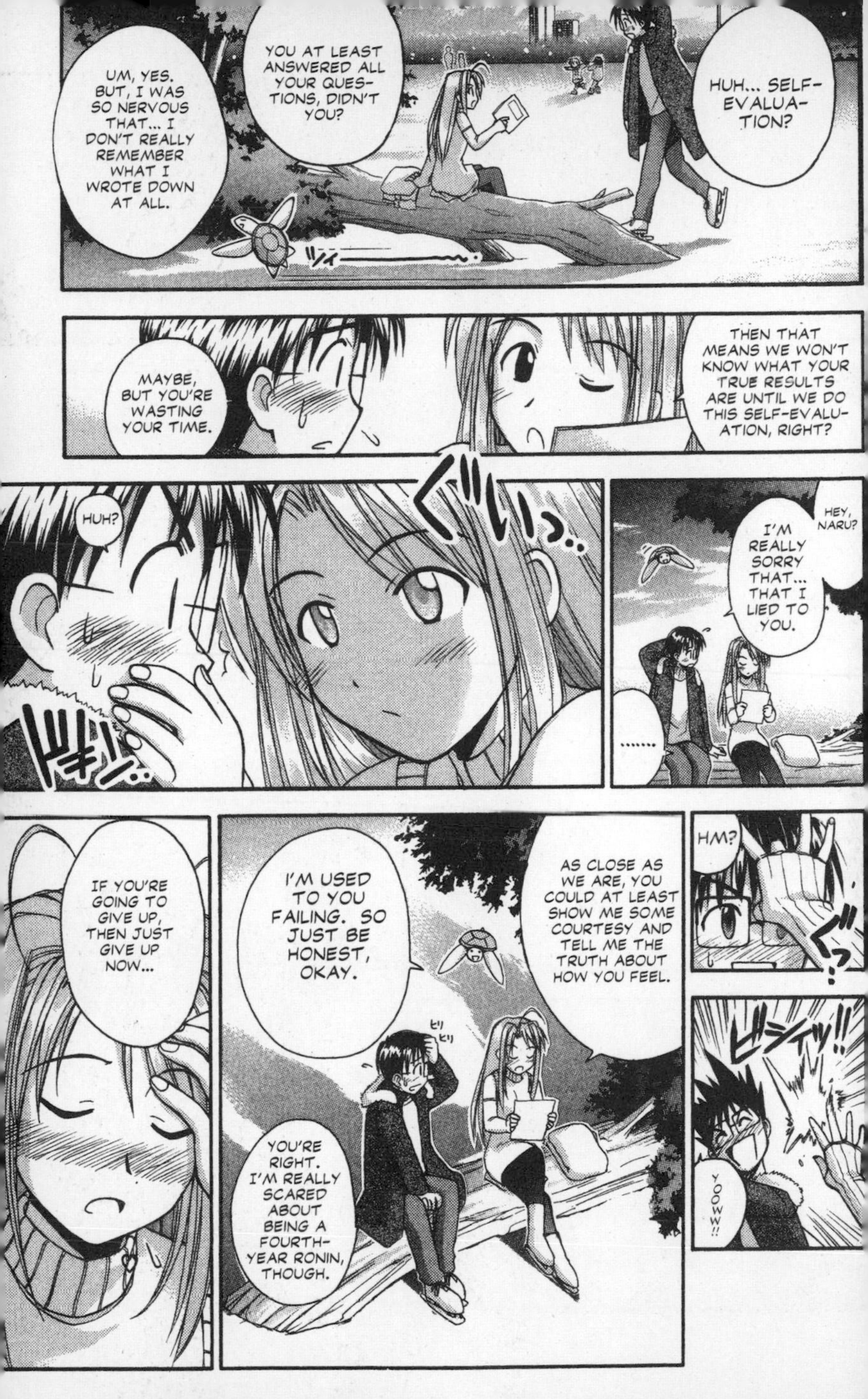
HUH... SELF-EVALUATION?
YOU AT LEAST ANSWERED ALL YOUR QUESTIONS, DIDN'T YOU?
UM, YES. BUT, I WAS SO NERVOUS THAT... I DON'T REALLY REMEMBER WHAT I WROTE DOWN AT ALL.
THEN THAT MEANS WE WON'T KNOW WHAT YOUR TRUE RESULTS ARE UNTIL WE DO THIS SELF-EVALUATION, RIGHT?
MAYBE, BUT YOU'RE WASTING YOUR TIME.
HEY, NARU?
I'M REALLY SORRY THAT... THAT I LIED TO YOU.
......
HUH?
HM?
YOOWW!!
AS CLOSE AS WE ARE, YOU COULD AT LEAST SHOW ME SOME COURTESY AND TELL ME THE TRUTH ABOUT HOW YOU FEEL.
I'M USED TO YOU FAILING. SO JUST BE HONEST, OKAY.
YOU'RE RIGHT. I'M REALLY SCARED ABOUT BEING A FOURTH-YEAR RONIN, THOUGH.
IF YOU'RE GOING TO GIVE UP, THEN JUST GIVE UP NOW...

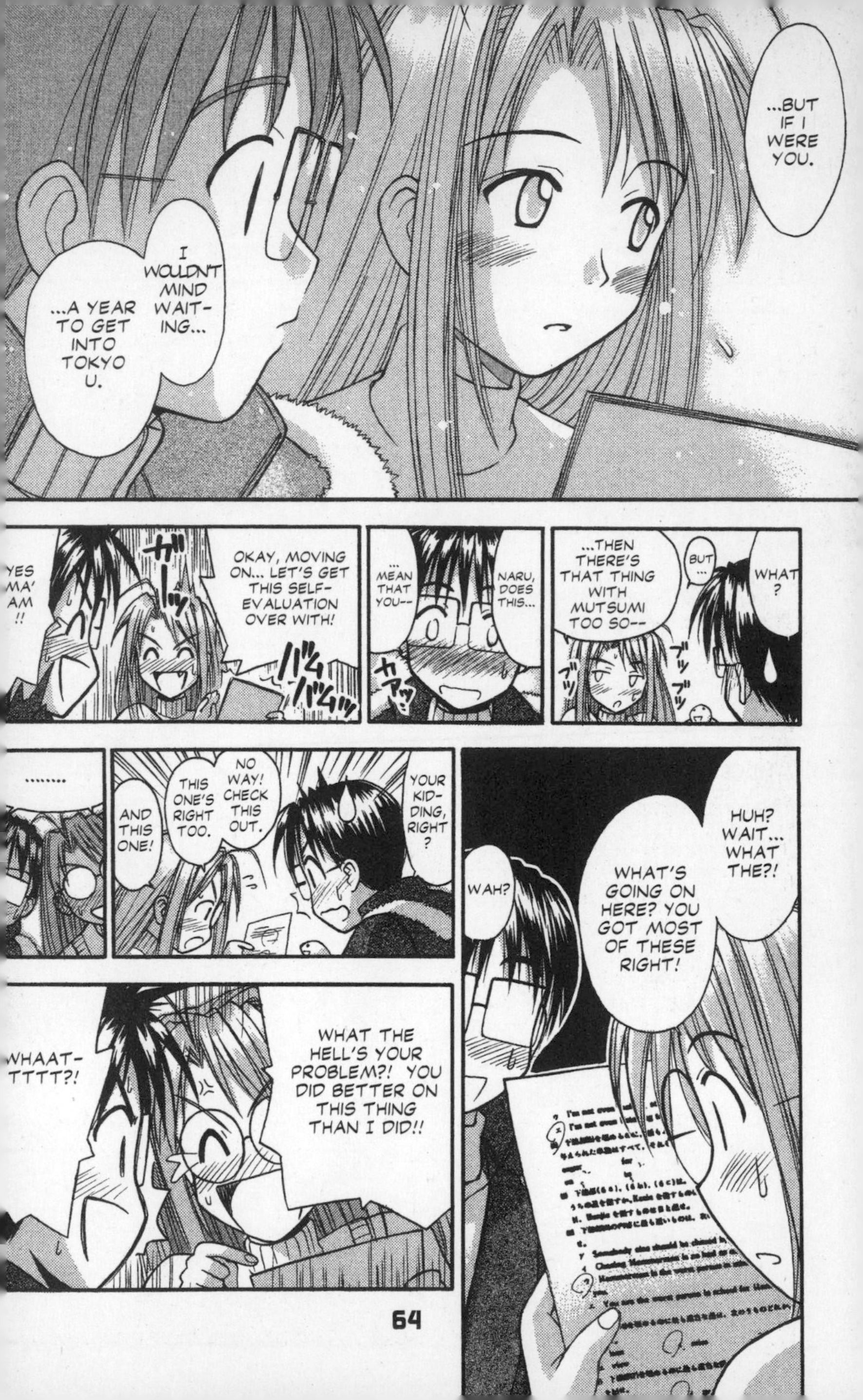
...BUT IF I WERE YOU.
I WOULDN'T MIND WAIT-ING...
...A YEAR TO GET INTO TOKYO U.
WHAT?
BUT...
...THEN THERE'S THAT THING WITH MUTSUMI TOO SO--
NARU, DOES THIS...
...MEAN THAT YOU--
OKAY, MOVING ON... LET'S GET THIS SELF-EVALUATION OVER WITH!
YES MA'AM!!
HUH? WAIT... WHAT THE?!
WHAT'S GOING ON HERE? YOU GOT MOST OF THESE RIGHT!
WAH?
YOUR KID-DING, RIGHT?
NO WAY! CHECK THIS OUT.
THIS ONE'S RIGHT TOO.
AND THIS ONE!
........
WHAT THE HELL'S YOUR PROBLEM?! YOU DID BETTER ON THIS THING THAN I DID!!
WHAAT-TTTT?!

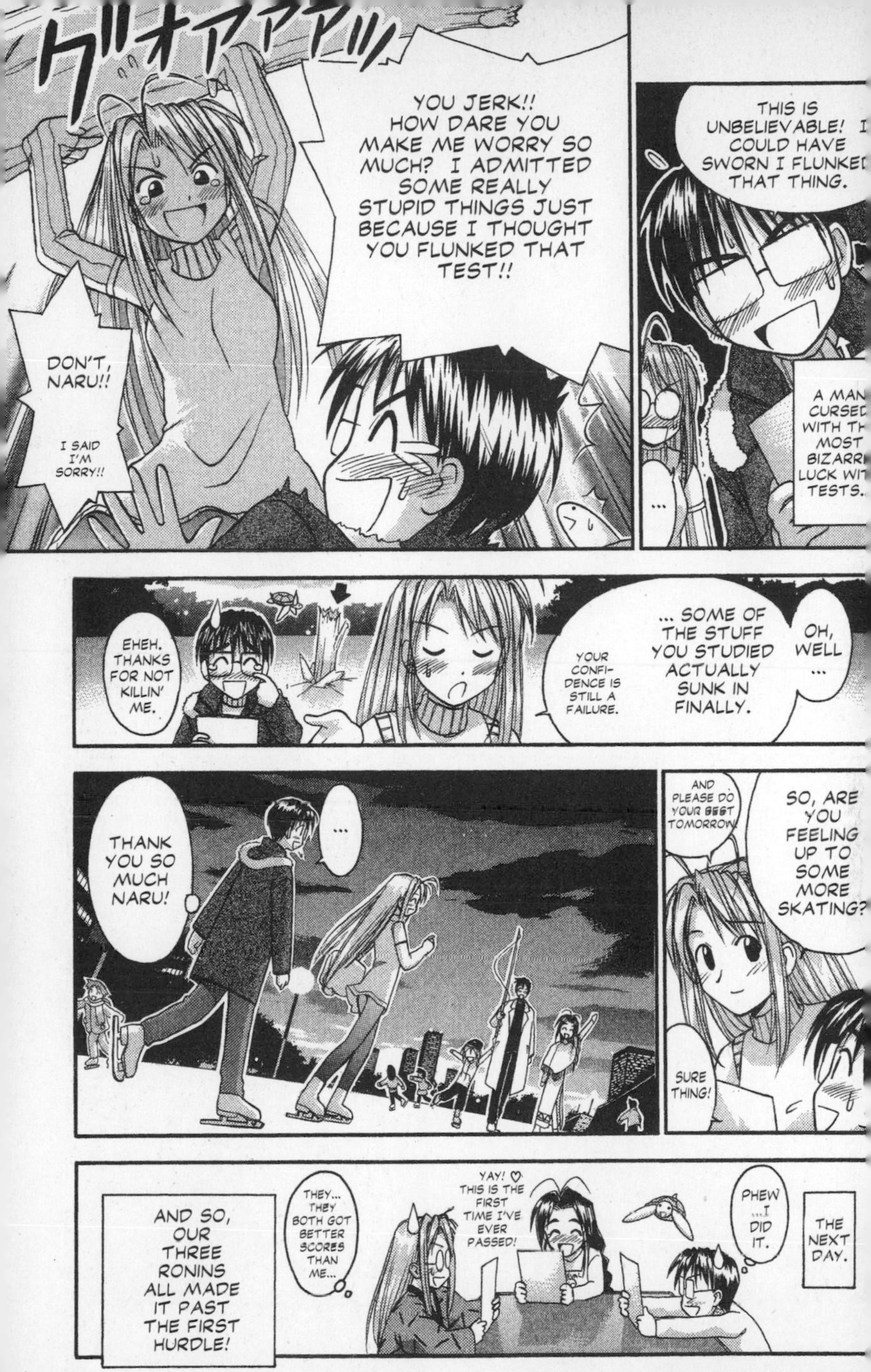
THIS IS UNBELIEVABLE! I COULD HAVE SWORN I FLUNKE THAT THING.
...
A MAN CURSE WITH TH MOST BIZARR LUCK WIT TESTS...
グオアアアッ
YOU JERK!! HOW DARE YOU MAKE ME WORRY SO MUCH? I ADMITTED SOME REALLY STUPID THINGS JUST BECAUSE I THOUGHT YOU FLUNKED THAT TEST!!
DON'T, NARU!!
I SAID I'M SORRY!!
OH, WELL ...
... SOME OF THE STUFF YOU STUDIED ACTUALLY SUNK IN FINALLY.
YOUR CONFI-DENCE IS STILL A FAILURE.
EHEH. THANKS FOR NOT KILLIN' ME.
SO, ARE YOU FEELING UP TO SOME MORE SKATING?
AND PLEASE DO YOUR BEST TOMORROW.
SURE THING!
...
THANK YOU SO MUCH NARU!
THE NEXT DAY.
PHEW ...I DID IT.
YAY! ♡ THIS IS THE FIRST TIME I'VE EVER PASSED!
THEY... THEY BOTH GOT BETTER SCORES THAN ME...
AND SO, OUR THREE RONINS ALL MADE IT PAST THE FIRST HURDLE!

# Love Hina

## HINATA.55
## That Serious Guy is a Criminal?!

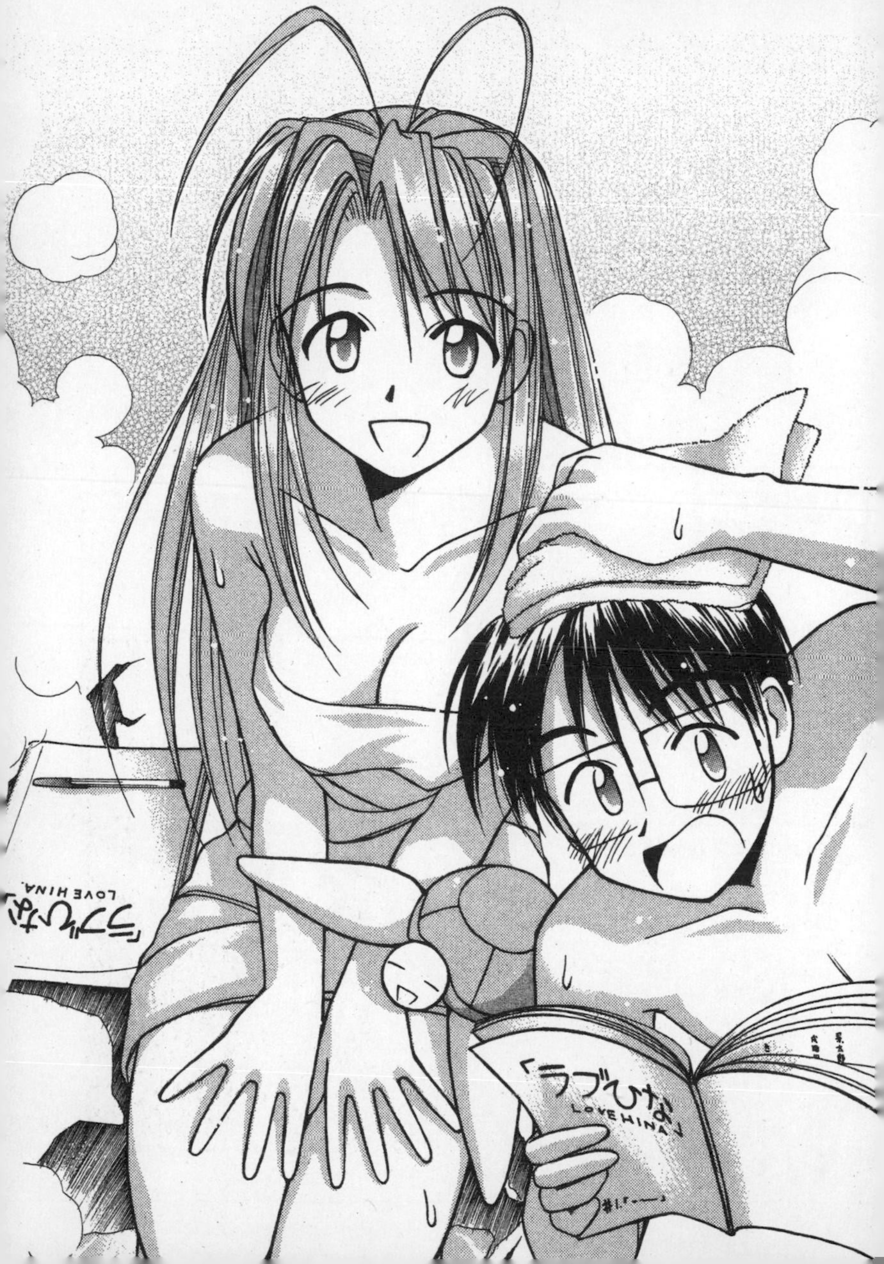
「ラブひな」
LOVE HINA
「ラブひな
LOVE HINA」

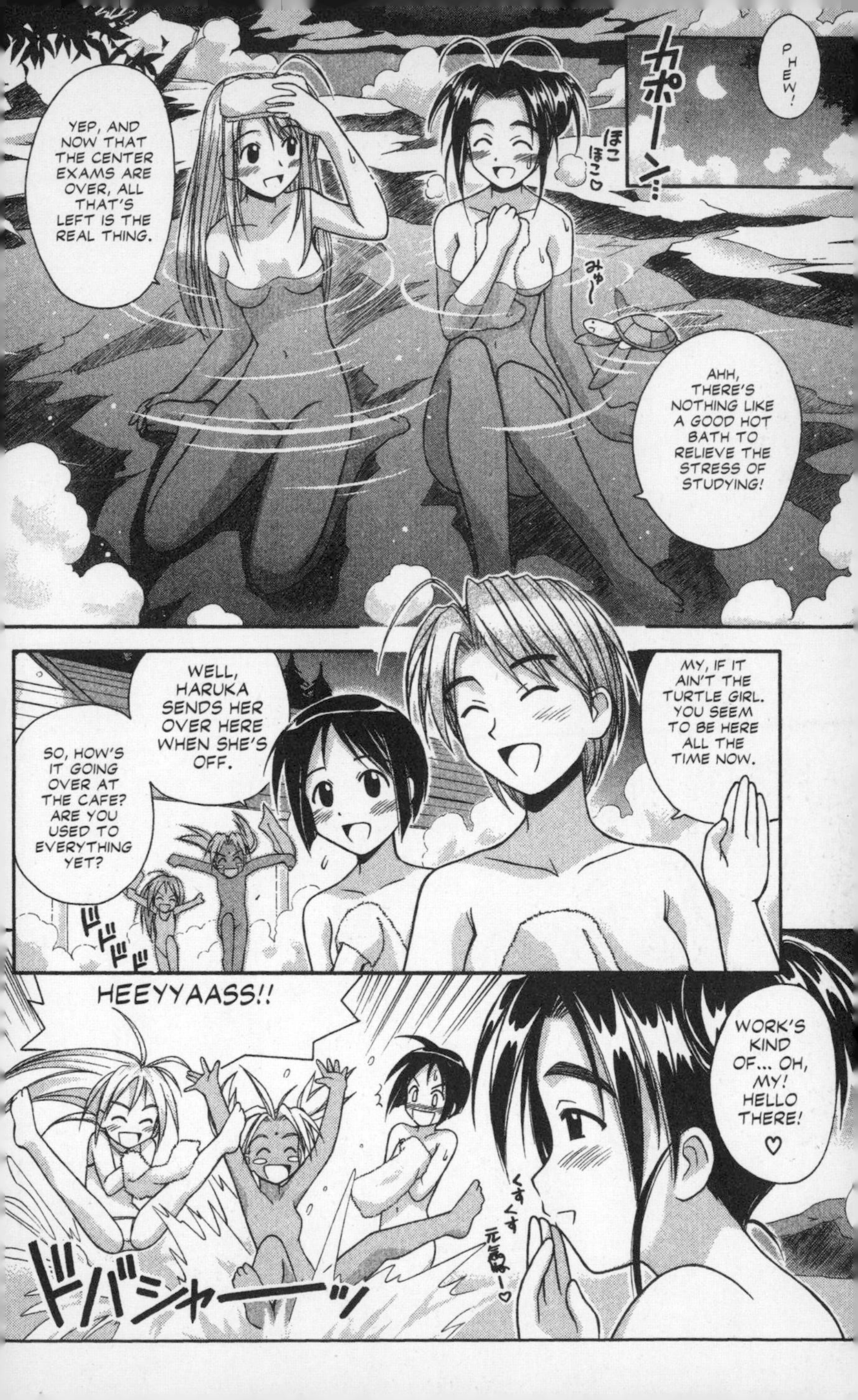
PHEW!
カポーン…
ほこほこ♡
みゅ～
AHH, THERE'S NOTHING LIKE A GOOD HOT BATH TO RELIEVE THE STRESS OF STUDYING!
YEP, AND NOW THAT THE CENTER EXAMS ARE OVER, ALL THAT'S LEFT IS THE REAL THING.
MY, IF IT AIN'T THE TURTLE GIRL. YOU SEEM TO BE HERE ALL THE TIME NOW.
WELL, HARUKA SENDS HER OVER HERE WHEN SHE'S OFF.
SO, HOW'S IT GOING OVER AT THE CAFE? ARE YOU USED TO EVERYTHING YET?
ドドドド
WORK'S KIND OF... OH, MY! HELLO THERE! ♡
くすくす
元気ねー♡
HEEYYAASS!!
ドバシャーーッ

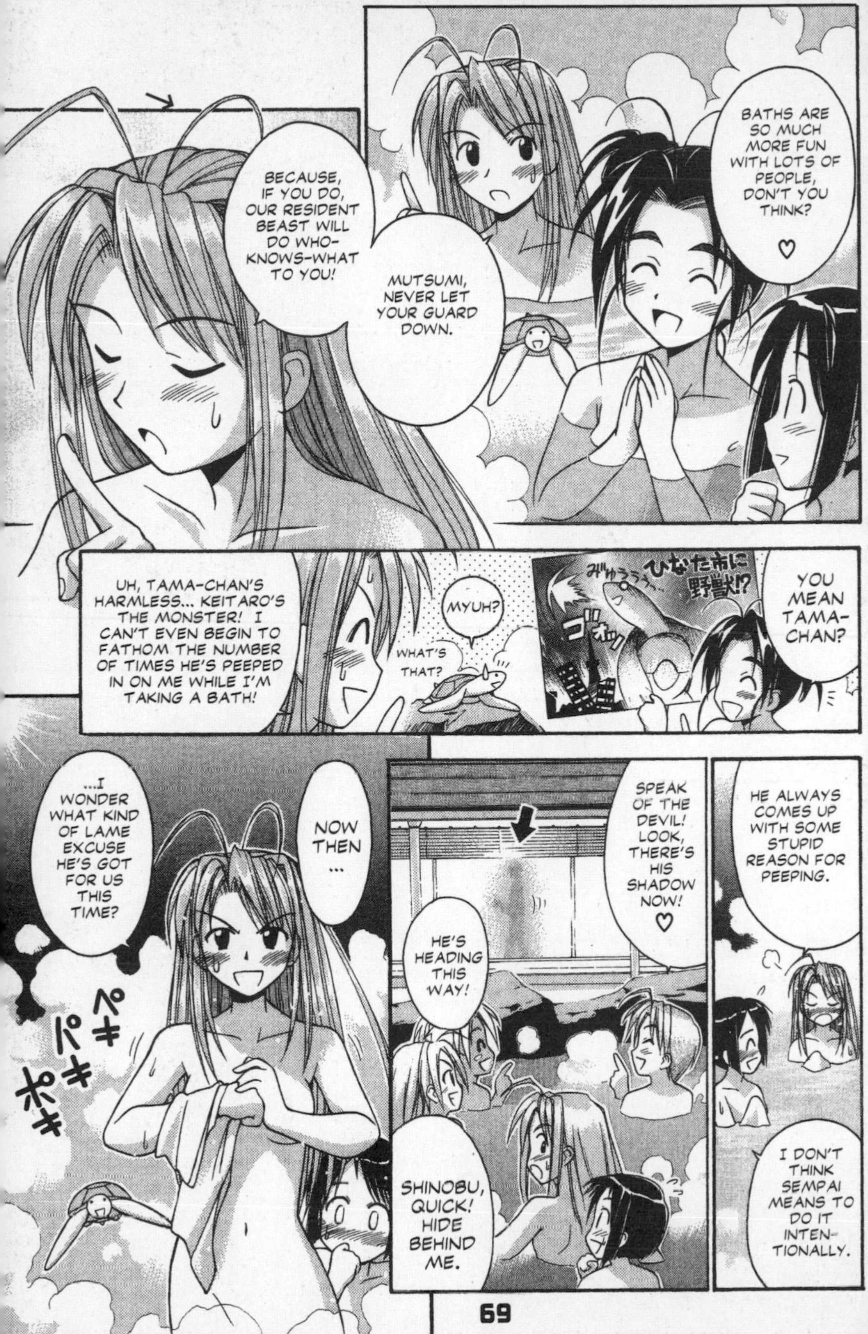

BATHS ARE SO MUCH MORE FUN WITH LOTS OF PEOPLE, DON'T YOU THINK? ♡
MUTSUMI, NEVER LET YOUR GUARD DOWN.
BECAUSE, IF YOU DO, OUR RESIDENT BEAST WILL DO WHO-KNOWS-WHAT TO YOU!
YOU MEAN TAMA-CHAN?
ひなた市に野獣!?
ゴォッ
MYUH?
WHAT'S THAT?
UH, TAMA-CHAN'S HARMLESS... KEITARO'S THE MONSTER! I CAN'T EVEN BEGIN TO FATHOM THE NUMBER OF TIMES HE'S PEEPED IN ON ME WHILE I'M TAKING A BATH!
HE ALWAYS COMES UP WITH SOME STUPID REASON FOR PEEPING.
I DON'T THINK SEMPAI MEANS TO DO IT INTEN-TIONALLY.
SPEAK OF THE DEVIL! LOOK, THERE'S HIS SHADOW NOW! ♡
HE'S HEADING THIS WAY!
SHINOBU, QUICK! HIDE BEHIND ME.
NOW THEN ...
...I WONDER WHAT KIND OF LAME EXCUSE HE'S GOT FOR US THIS TIME?
ペキ
パキ
ポキ

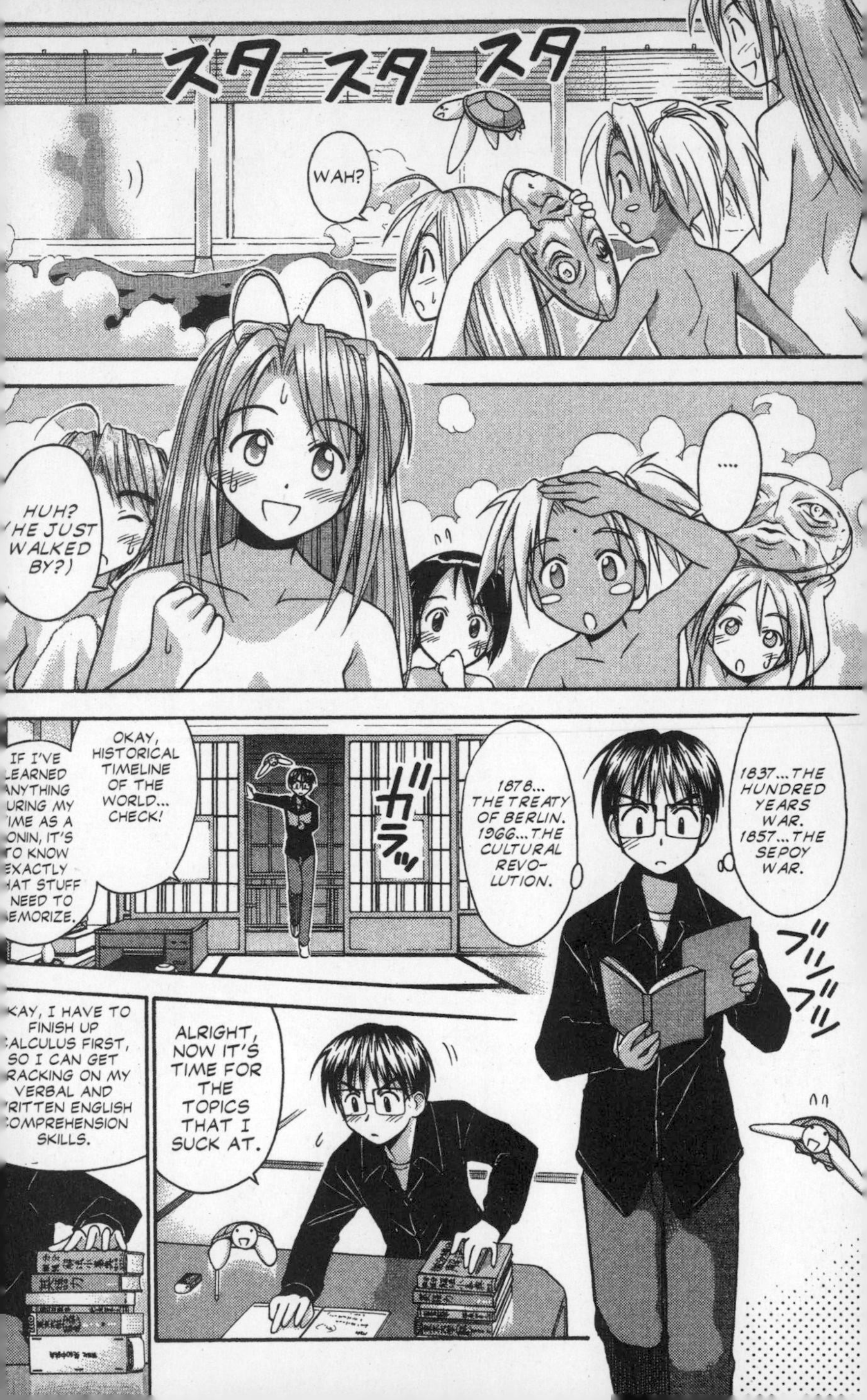

スタ スタ スタ
WAH?
....
HUH? (HE JUST WALKED BY?)
1837...THE HUNDRED YEARS WAR. 1857...THE SEPOY WAR.
1878... THE TREATY OF BERLIN. 1966...THE CULTURAL REVOLUTION.
ブツブツ
ガラッ
OKAY, HISTORICAL TIMELINE OF THE WORLD... CHECK!
IF I'VE LEARNED ANYTHING URING MY IME AS A ONIN, IT'S O KNOW EXACTLY HAT STUFF NEED TO EMORIZE.
ALRIGHT, NOW IT'S TIME FOR THE TOPICS THAT I SUCK AT.
KAY, I HAVE TO FINISH UP CALCULUS FIRST, SO I CAN GET RACKING ON MY VERBAL AND RITTEN ENGLISH COMPREHENSION SKILLS.

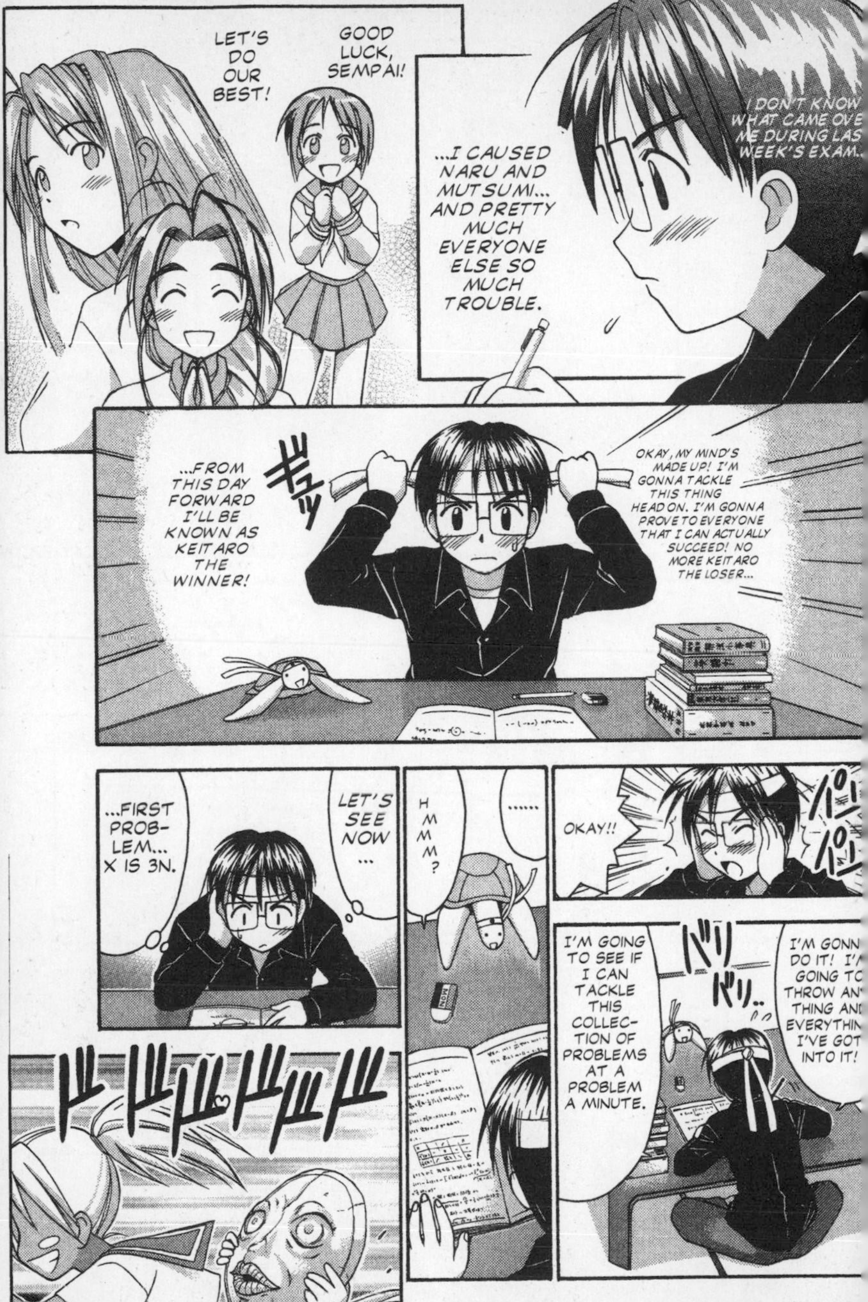
I DON'T KNOW WHAT CAME OVE ME DURING LAS WEEK'S EXAM...
...I CAUSED NARU AND MUTSUMI... AND PRETTY MUCH EVERYONE ELSE SO MUCH TROUBLE.
GOOD LUCK, SEMPAI!
LET'S DO OUR BEST!
OKAY, MY MIND'S MADE UP! I'M GONNA TACKLE THIS THING HEAD ON. I'M GONNA PROVE TO EVERYONE THAT I CAN ACTUALLY SUCCEED! NO MORE KEITARO THE LOSER...
ギュッ
...FROM THIS DAY FORWARD I'LL BE KNOWN AS KEITARO THE WINNER!
パン
パン
OKAY!!
I'M GONN DO IT! I'/ GOING TO THROW AN' THING AND EVERYTHIN I'VE GOT INTO IT!
バリ
バリ..
I'M GOING TO SEE IF I CAN TACKLE THIS COLLECTION OF PROBLEMS AT A PROBLEM A MINUTE.
......
HMMM?
LET'S SEE NOW...
...FIRST PROBLEM... X IS 3N.
ドドドドドド

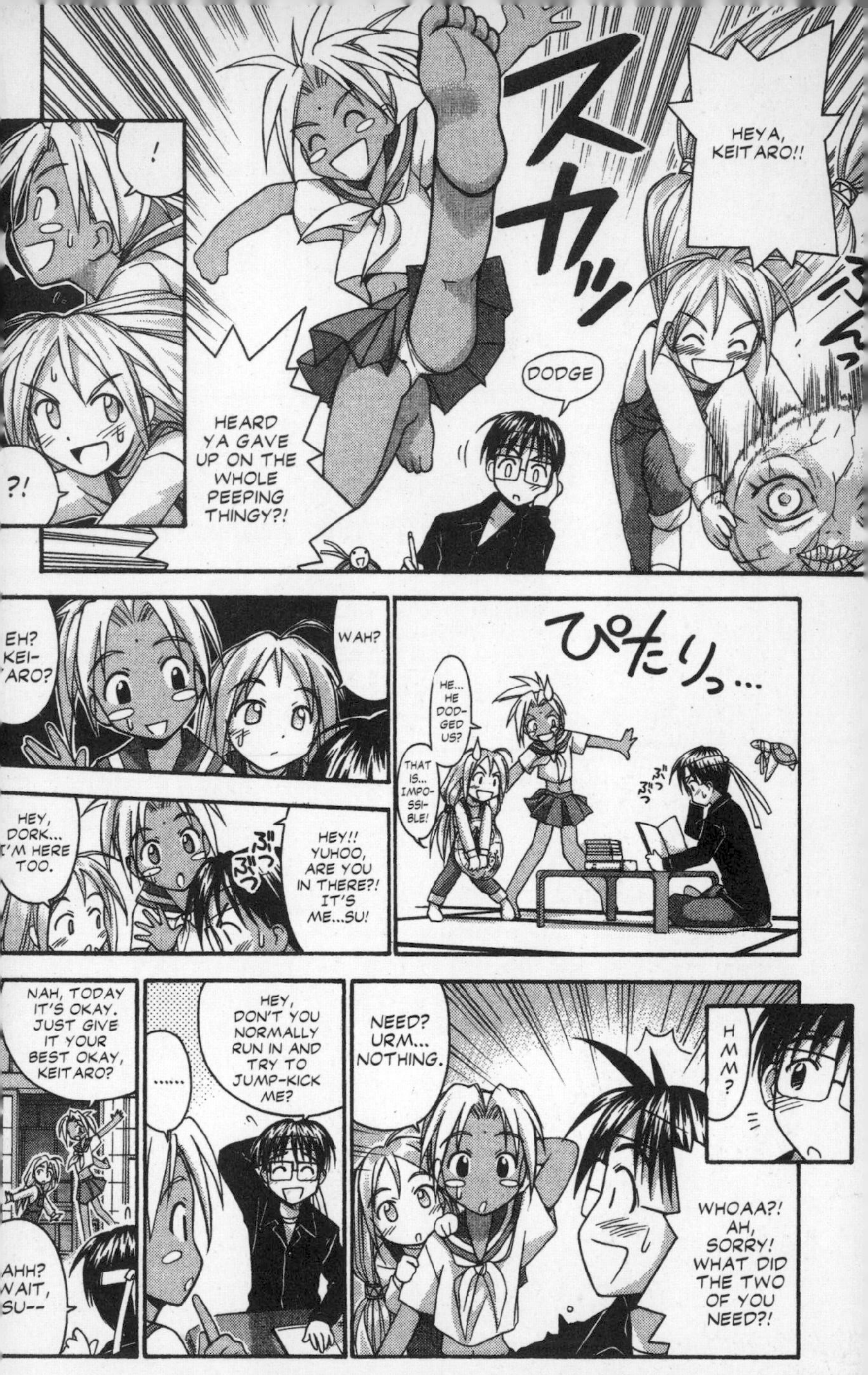
HEYA, KEITARO!!
スカッ
HEARD YA GAVE UP ON THE WHOLE PEEPING THINGY?!
DODGE
!
?!
ぴたりっ...
HE... HE DODGED US?
THAT IS... IMPOSSIBLE!
ぶつぶつ
WAH?
EH? KEITARO?
HEY!! YUHOO, ARE YOU IN THERE?! IT'S ME...SU!
ぶつぶつ
HEY, DORK... I'M HERE TOO.
HMM?
WHOAA?! AH, SORRY! WHAT DID THE TWO OF YOU NEED?!
NEED? URM... NOTHING.
HEY, DON'T YOU NORMALLY RUN IN AND TRY TO JUMP-KICK ME?
......
NAH, TODAY IT'S OKAY. JUST GIVE IT YOUR BEST OKAY, KEITARO?
AHH? WAIT, SU--

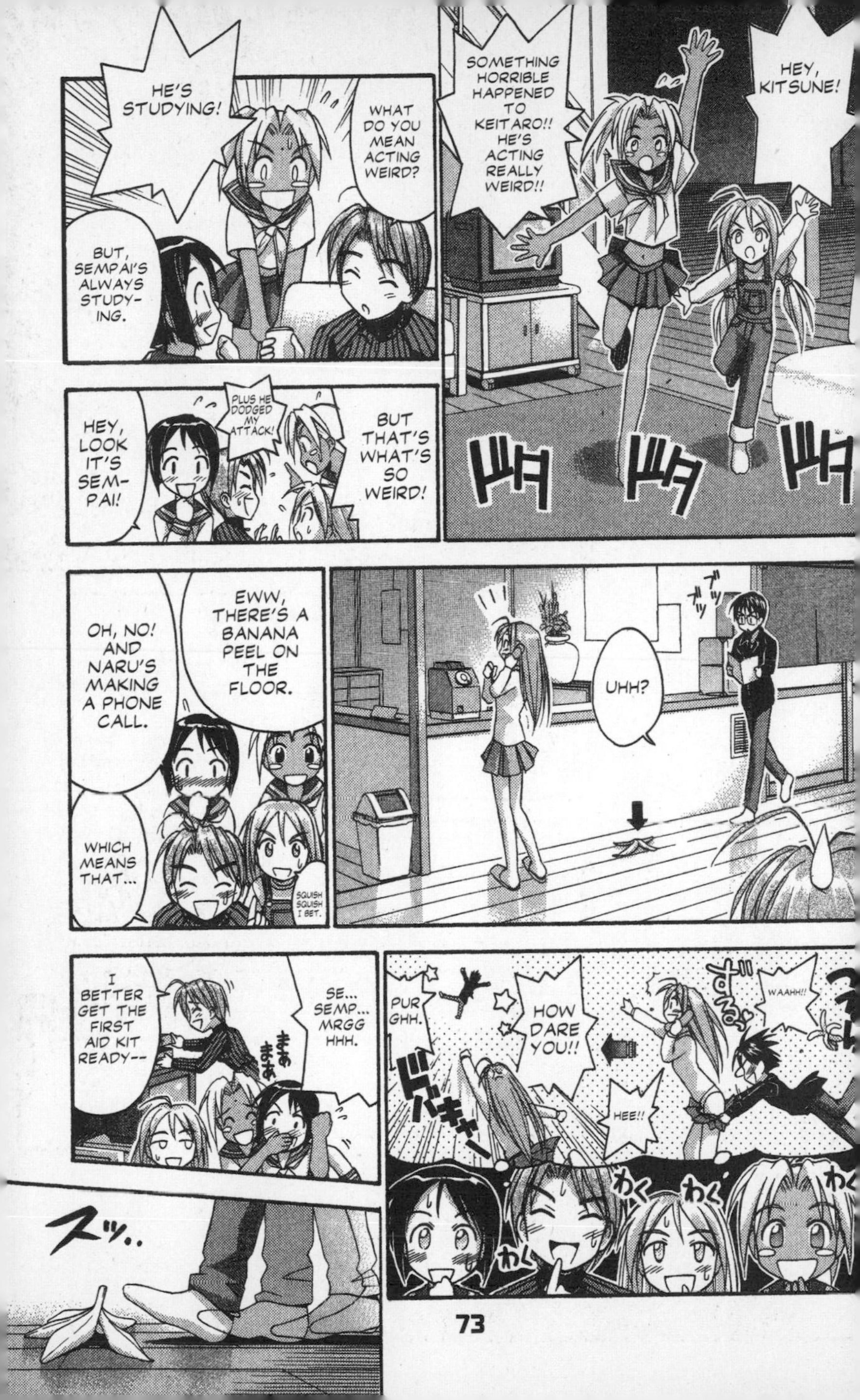
HEY, KITSUNE!
SOMETHING HORRIBLE HAPPENED TO KEITARO!! HE'S ACTING REALLY WEIRD!!
WHAT DO YOU MEAN ACTING WEIRD?
HE'S STUDYING!
BUT, SEMPAI'S ALWAYS STUDY-ING.
BUT THAT'S WHAT'S SO WEIRD!
PLUS HE DODGED MY ATTACK!
HEY, LOOK IT'S SEM-PAI!
UHH?
EWW, THERE'S A BANANA PEEL ON THE FLOOR.
OH, NO! AND NARU'S MAKING A PHONE CALL.
WHICH MEANS THAT...
SQUISH SQUISH I BET.
WAAHH!!
HOW DARE YOU!!
PURGHH.
HEE!!
わく わく わく わく
SE... SEMP... MRGG HHH.
I BETTER GET THE FIRST AID KIT READY--

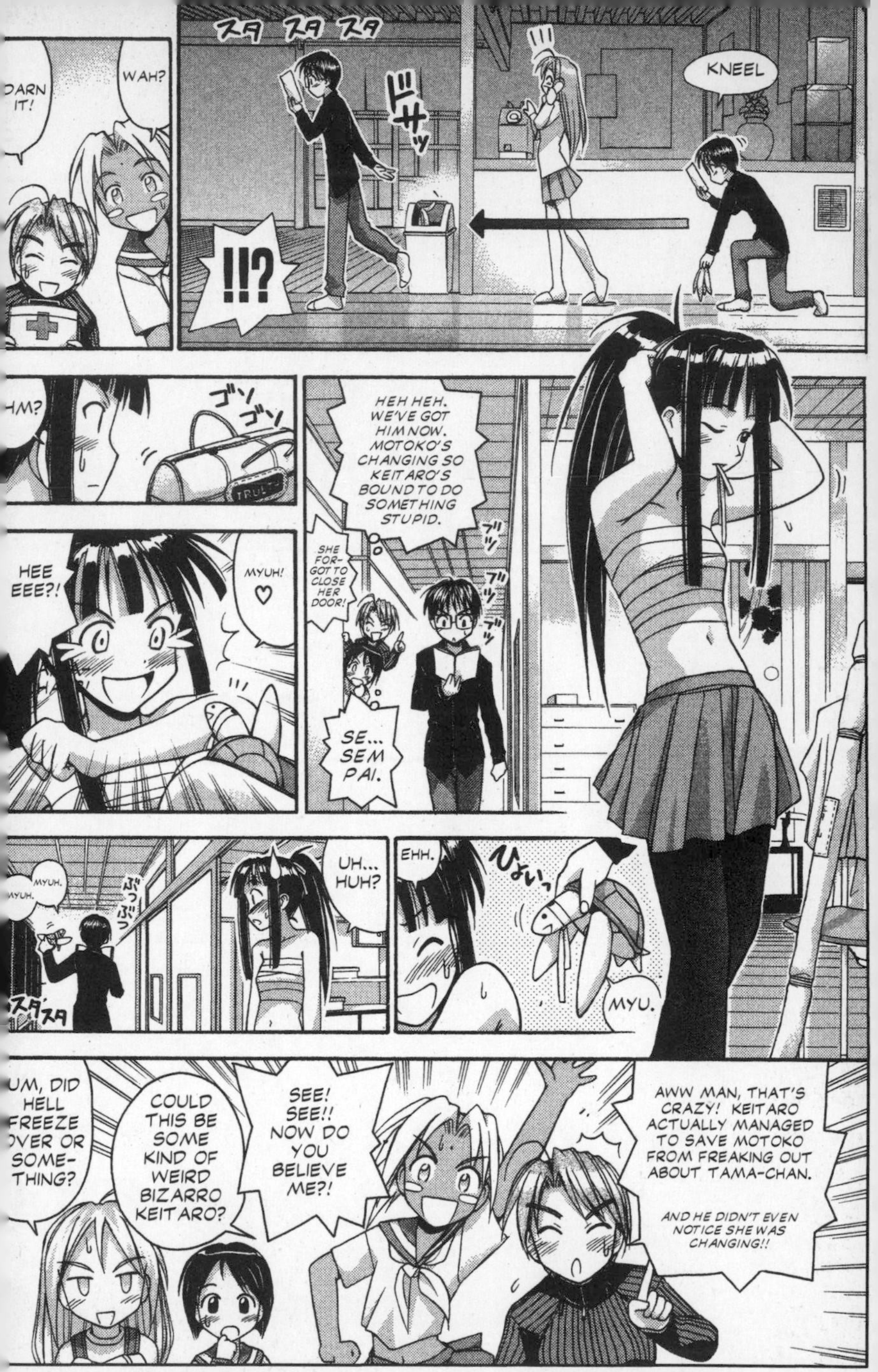
KNEEL
スタ スタ スタ
ドサッ
!!?
WAH?
DARN IT!
HEH HEH. WE'VE GOT HIM NOW. MOTOKO'S CHANGING SO KEITARO'S BOUND TO DO SOMETHING STUPID.
ブツ ブツ ブツ
SHE FORGOT TO CLOSE HER DOOR!
SE... SEMPAI.
HM?
ゴソ ゴソ
HEE EEE?!
MYUH! ♡
EHH.
ひょいっ
MYU.
UH... HUH?
ぶつぶつ
MYUH. MYUH.
スタ スタ
AWW MAN, THAT'S CRAZY! KEITARO ACTUALLY MANAGED TO SAVE MOTOKO FROM FREAKING OUT ABOUT TAMA-CHAN.
AND HE DIDN'T EVEN NOTICE SHE WAS CHANGING!!
SEE! SEE!! NOW DO YOU BELIEVE ME?!
COULD THIS BE SOME KIND OF WEIRD BIZARRO KEITARO?
UM, DID HELL FREEZE OVER OR SOME-THING?

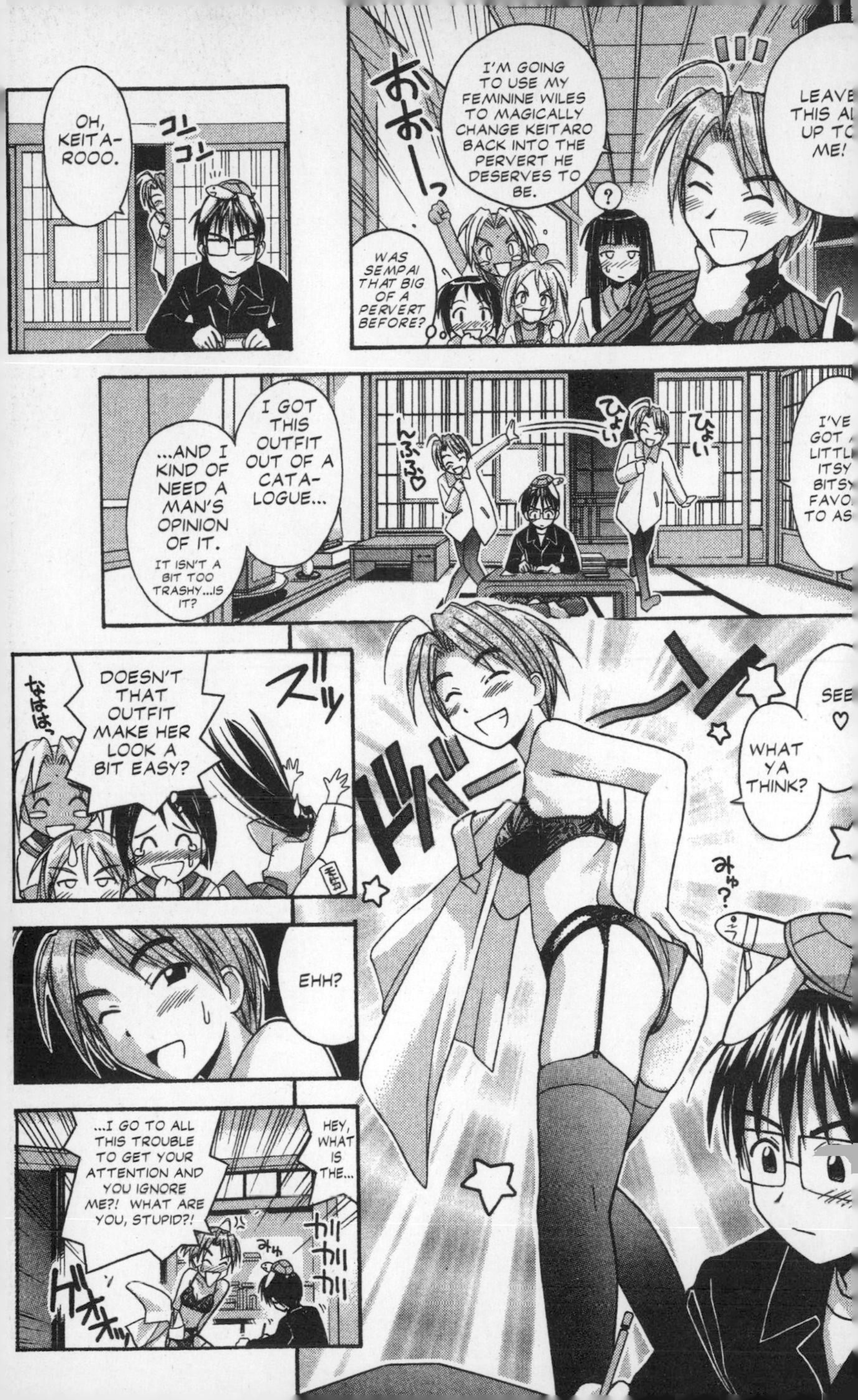
LEAVE THIS AL UP TO ME!
I'M GOING TO USE MY FEMININE WILES TO MAGICALLY CHANGE KEITARO BACK INTO THE PERVERT HE DESERVES TO BE.
おおーっ
?
WAS SEMPAI THAT BIG OF A PERVERT BEFORE?
コンコン
OH, KEITA-ROOO.
I'VE GOT A LITTL ITSY BITSY FAVO TO AS
ひょい
ひょい
んふふ♡
I GOT THIS OUTFIT OUT OF A CATA-LOGUE...
...AND I KIND OF NEED A MAN'S OPINION OF IT.
IT ISN'T A BIT TOO TRASHY...IS IT?
SEE ♡
WHAT YA THINK?
ドバーン
みゅ?
ズッ
DOESN'T THAT OUTFIT MAKE HER LOOK A BIT EASY?
なははっ
EHH?
HEY, WHAT IS THE...
...I GO TO ALL THIS TROUBLE TO GET YOUR ATTENTION AND YOU IGNORE ME?! WHAT ARE YOU, STUPID?!
カリカリカリ
みゅ
ドオオッ

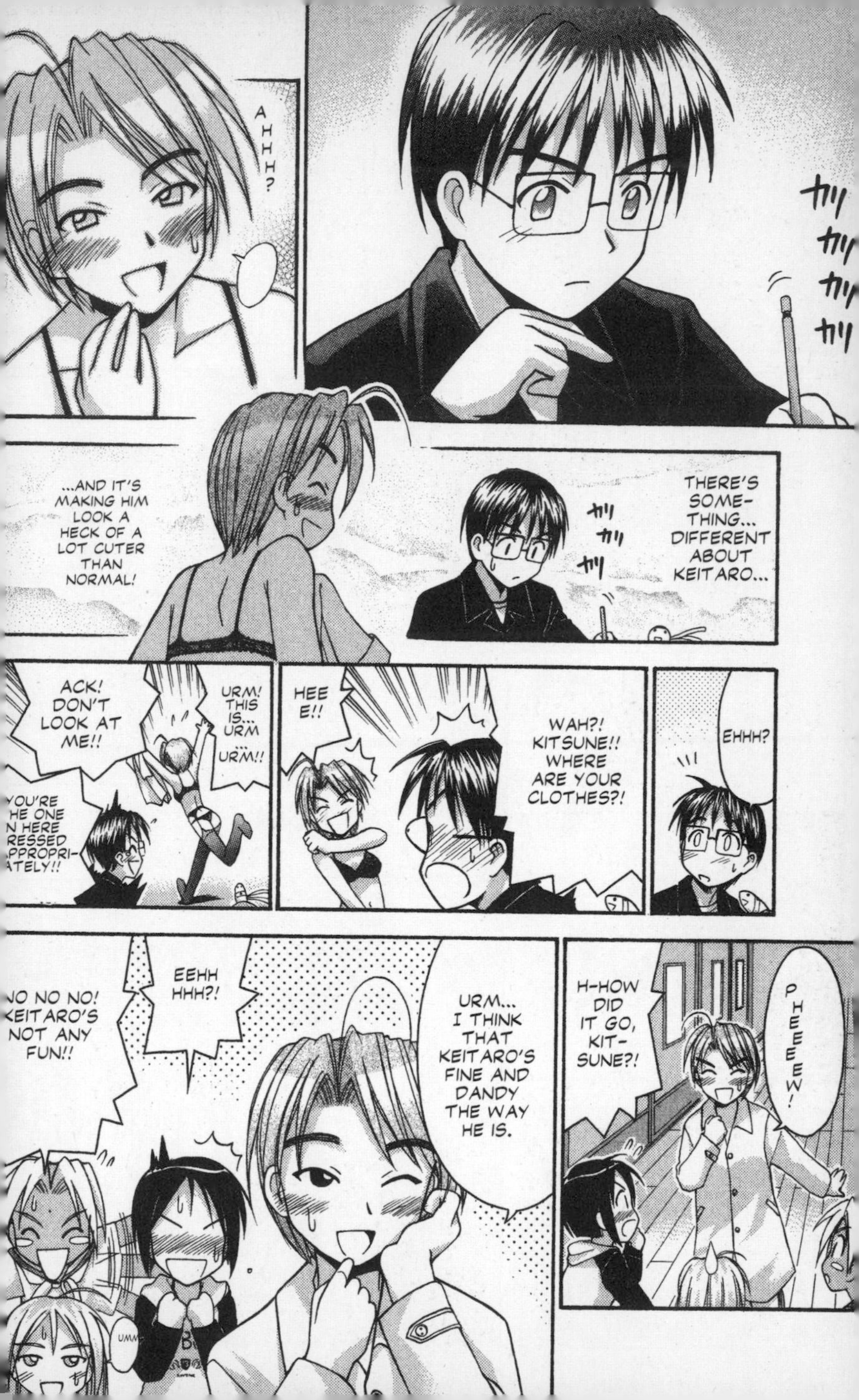
カリ カリ カリ カリ
AHHH?
THERE'S SOME-THING... DIFFERENT ABOUT KEITARO...
カリ カリ カリ
...AND IT'S MAKING HIM LOOK A HECK OF A LOT CUTER THAN NORMAL!
EHHH?
WAH?! KITSUNE!! WHERE ARE YOUR CLOTHES?!
HEE E!!
URM! THIS IS... URM ... URM!!
ACK! DON'T LOOK AT ME!!
OU'RE HE ONE N HERE RESSED APPROPRI-ATELY!!
PHEEEEW!
H-HOW DID IT GO, KIT-SUNE?!
URM... I THINK THAT KEITARO'S FINE AND DANDY THE WAY HE IS.
EEHH HHH?!
O NO NO! EITARO'S NOT ANY FUN!!
UMM

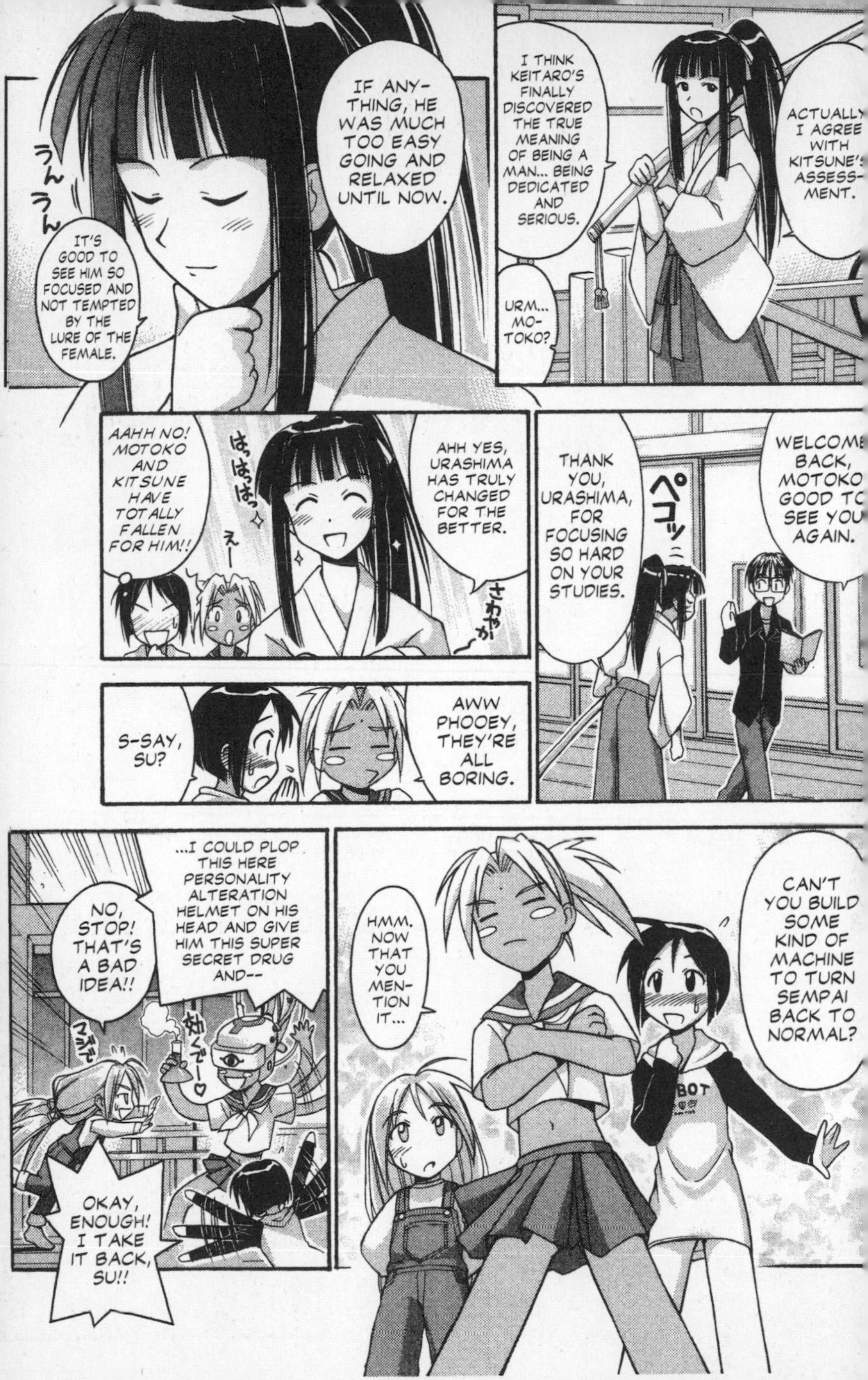

ACTUALLY I AGREE WITH KITSUNE'S ASSESSMENT.
I THINK KEITARO'S FINALLY DISCOVERED THE TRUE MEANING OF BEING A MAN... BEING DEDICATED AND SERIOUS.
URM... MO-TOKO?
IF ANY-THING, HE WAS MUCH TOO EASY GOING AND RELAXED UNTIL NOW.
うんうん
IT'S GOOD TO SEE HIM SO FOCUSED AND NOT TEMPTED BY THE LURE OF THE FEMALE.
WELCOME BACK, MOTOKO. GOOD TO SEE YOU AGAIN.
ペコッ
THANK YOU, URASHIMA, FOR FOCUSING SO HARD ON YOUR STUDIES.
AHH YES, URASHIMA HAS TRULY CHANGED FOR THE BETTER.
さわやか~
はっはっはっ
え~
AAHH NO! MOTOKO AND KITSUNE HAVE TOTALLY FALLEN FOR HIM!!
AWW PHOOEY, THEY'RE ALL BORING.
S-SAY, SU?
CAN'T YOU BUILD SOME KIND OF MACHINE TO TURN SEMPAI BACK TO NORMAL?
HMM. NOW THAT YOU MEN-TION IT...
...I COULD PLOP THIS HERE PERSONALITY ALTERATION HELMET ON HIS HEAD AND GIVE HIM THIS SUPER SECRET DRUG AND--
NO, STOP! THAT'S A BAD IDEA!!
効くでー♡
マジで
OKAY, ENOUGH! I TAKE IT BACK, SU!!

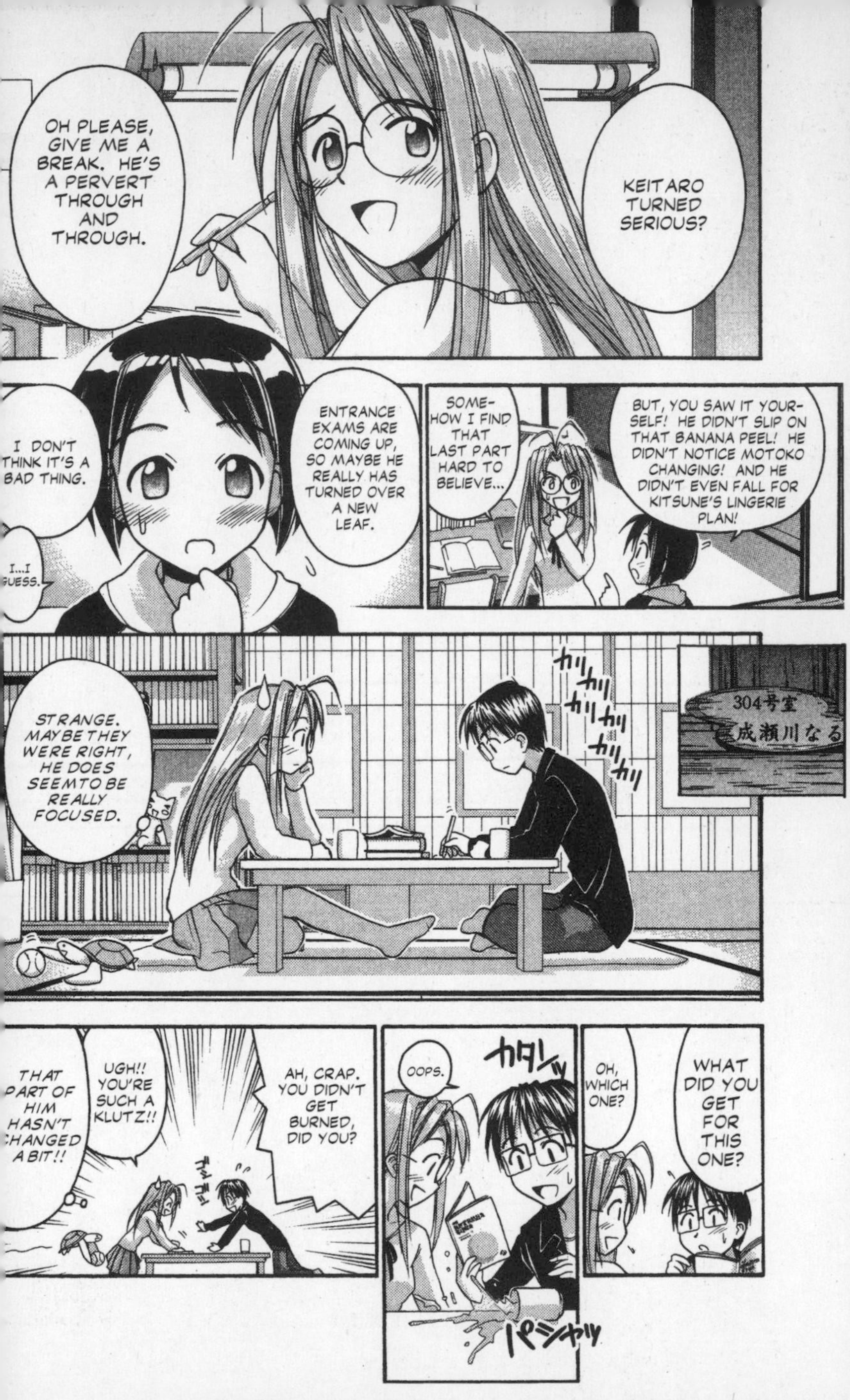
KEITARO TURNED SERIOUS?
OH PLEASE, GIVE ME A BREAK. HE'S A PERVERT THROUGH AND THROUGH.
BUT, YOU SAW IT YOURSELF! HE DIDN'T SLIP ON THAT BANANA PEEL! HE DIDN'T NOTICE MOTOKO CHANGING! AND HE DIDN'T EVEN FALL FOR KITSUNE'S LINGERIE PLAN!
SOMEHOW I FIND THAT LAST PART HARD TO BELIEVE...
ENTRANCE EXAMS ARE COMING UP, SO MAYBE HE REALLY HAS TURNED OVER A NEW LEAF.
I DON'T THINK IT'S A BAD THING.
I...I GUESS.
304号室
成瀬川なる
カリカリカリカリカリカリ
STRANGE. MAYBE THEY WERE RIGHT, HE DOES SEEM TO BE REALLY FOCUSED.
WHAT DID YOU GET FOR THIS ONE?
OH, WHICH ONE?
カタンッ
OOPS.
パシャッ
AH, CRAP. YOU DIDN'T GET BURNED, DID YOU?
UGH!! YOU'RE SUCH A KLUTZ!!
THAT PART OF HIM HASN'T CHANGED A BIT!!

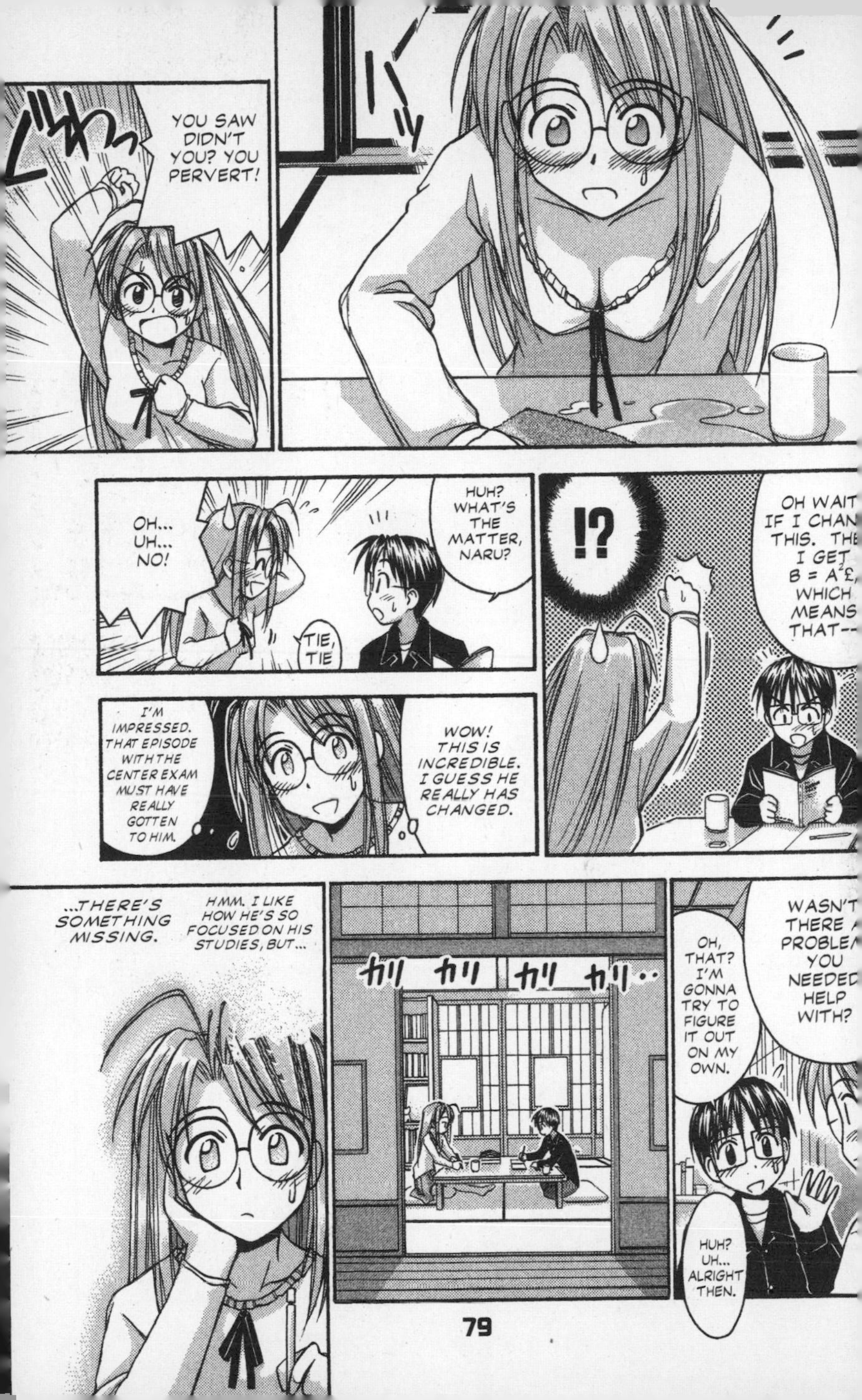

ぐわっ
YOU SAW DIDN'T YOU? YOU PERVERT!
!?
OH WAIT IF I CHAN THIS. THE I GET B = $A^2$£, WHICH MEANS THAT--
HUH? WHAT'S THE MATTER, NARU?
OH... UH... NO!
TIE, TIE
WOW! THIS IS INCREDIBLE. I GUESS HE REALLY HAS CHANGED.
I'M IMPRESSED. THAT EPISODE WITH THE CENTER EXAM MUST HAVE REALLY GOTTEN TO HIM.
WASN'T THERE A PROBLEM YOU NEEDED HELP WITH?
OH, THAT? I'M GONNA TRY TO FIGURE IT OUT ON MY OWN.
HUH? UH... ALRIGHT THEN.
カリ カリ カリ カリ..
HMM. I LIKE HOW HE'S SO FOCUSED ON HIS STUDIES, BUT...
...THERE'S SOMETHING MISSING.

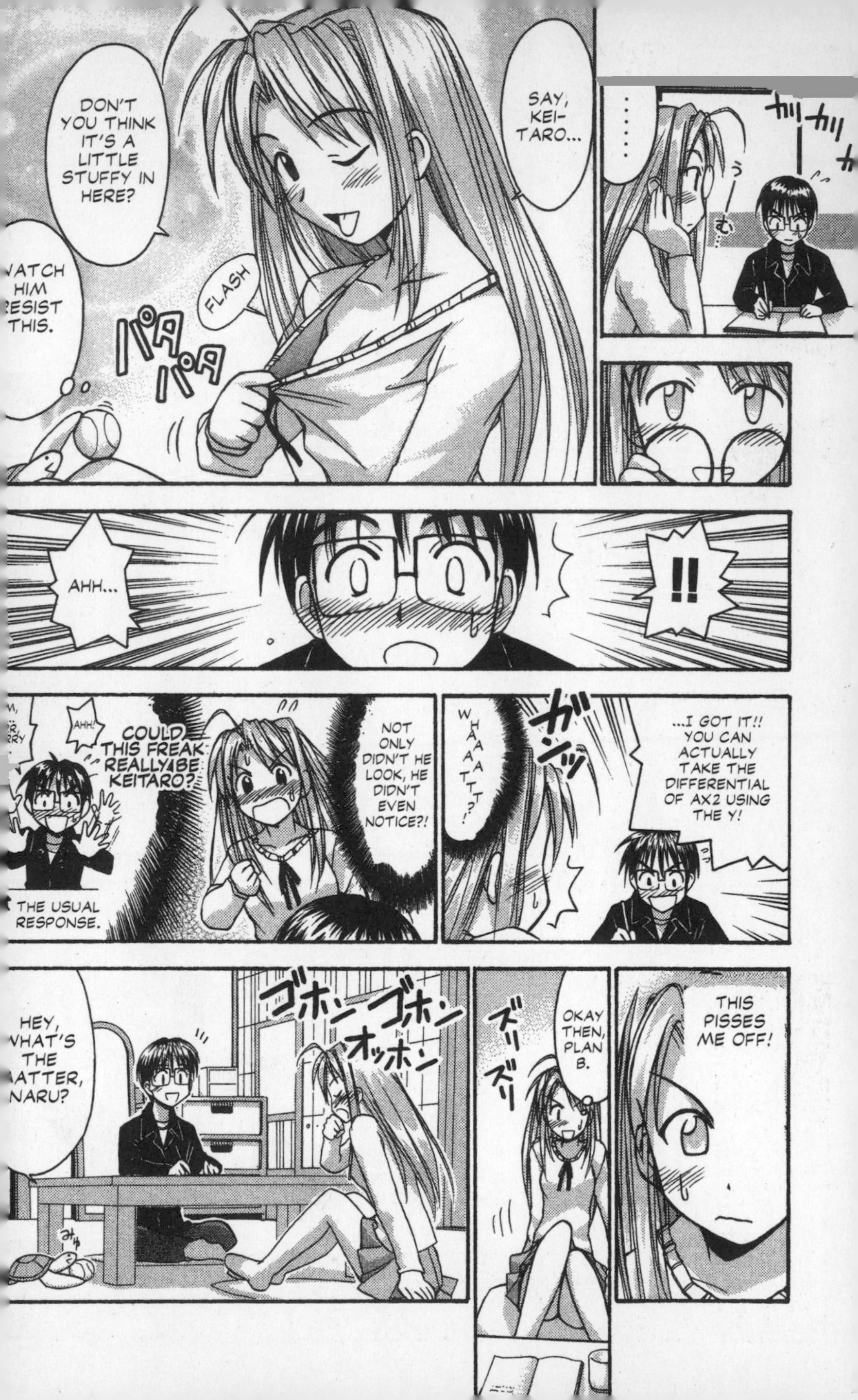

......
カリカリカリ
うーむ
SAY, KEI-TARO...
DON'T YOU THINK IT'S A LITTLE STUFFY IN HERE?
FLASH
パタパタ
WATCH HIM RESIST THIS.
!!
AHH...
...I GOT IT!! YOU CAN ACTUALLY TAKE THE DIFFERENTIAL OF AX2 USING THE Y!
ガンッ
WHAAATT?!
NOT ONLY DIDN'T HE LOOK, HE DIDN'T EVEN NOTICE?!
COULD THIS FREAK REALLY BE KEITARO?
AHH!
THE USUAL RESPONSE.
THIS PISSES ME OFF!
OKAY THEN, PLAN B.
ズリズリ
ゴホン ゴホン オッホン
HEY, WHAT'S THE MATTER, NARU?

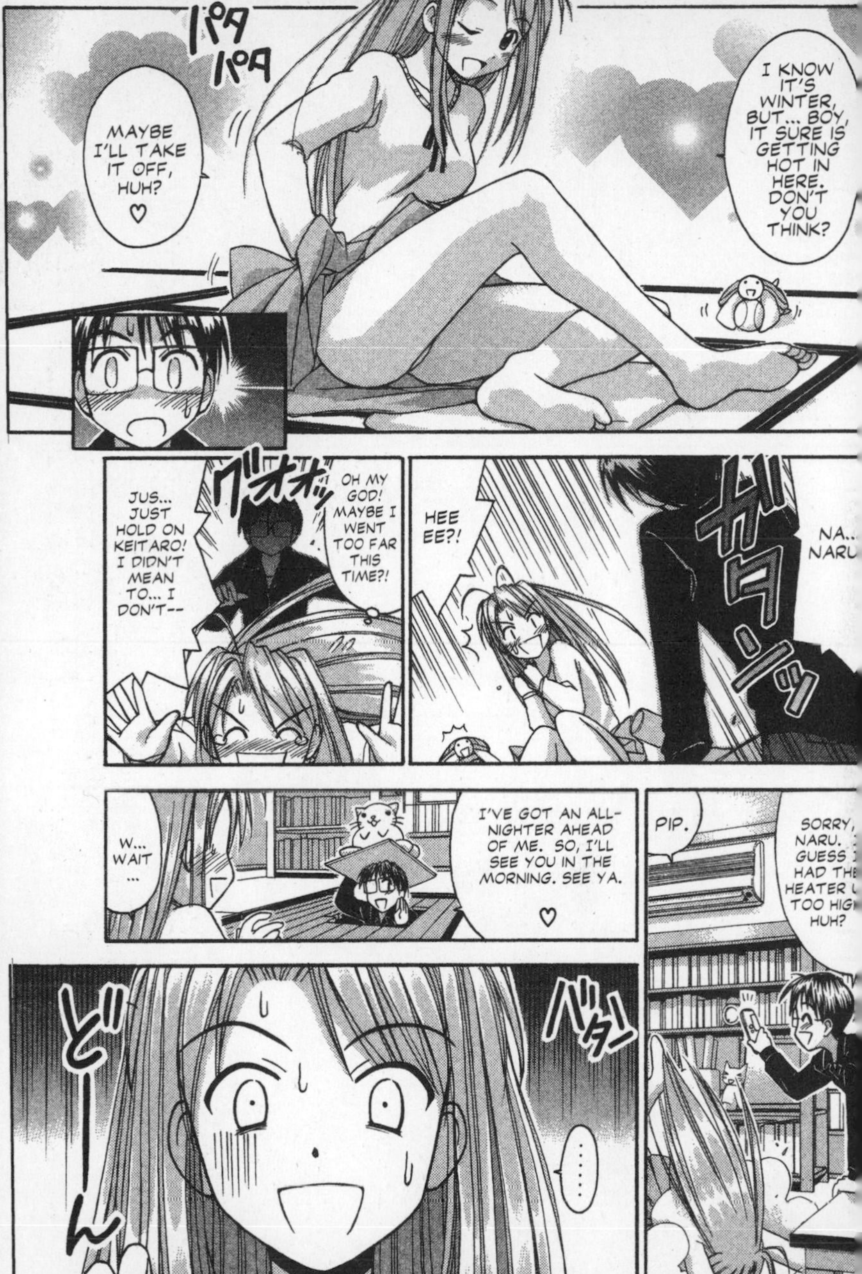
I KNOW IT'S WINTER, BUT... BOY, IT SURE IS GETTING HOT IN HERE. DON'T YOU THINK?
パタパタ
MAYBE I'LL TAKE IT OFF, HUH? ♡
NA... NARU
ガタンッ
HEE EE?!
OH MY GOD! MAYBE I WENT TOO FAR THIS TIME?!
グオオッ
JUS... JUST HOLD ON KEITARO! I DIDN'T MEAN TO... I DON'T--
SORRY, NARU. GUESS HAD THE HEATER TOO HIG HUH?
PIP.
I'VE GOT AN ALL-NIGHTER AHEAD OF ME. SO, I'LL SEE YOU IN THE MORNING. SEE YA. ♡
W... WAIT ...
バタン
......
どーん

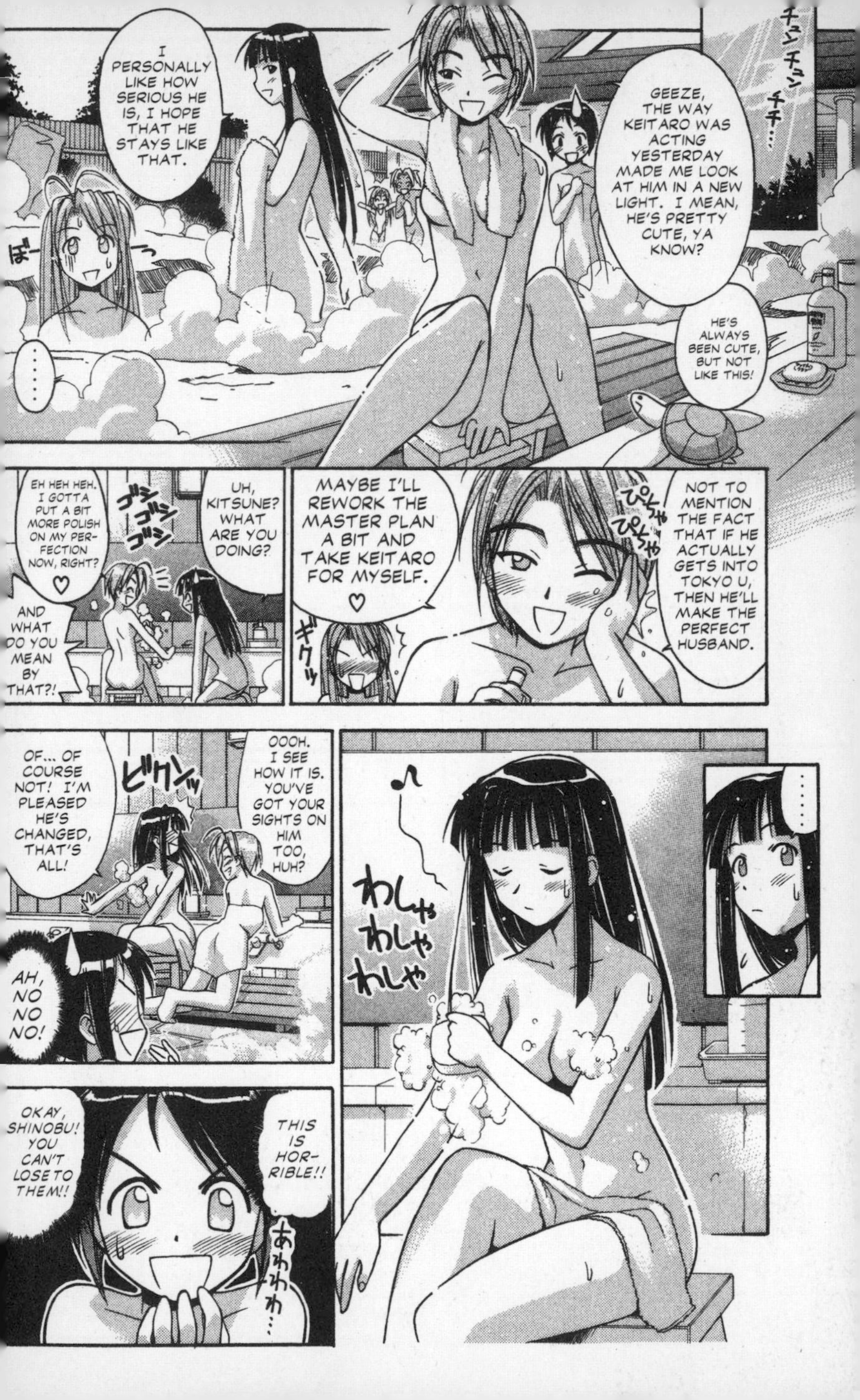

チュンチュン
チチ…
GEEZE, THE WAY KEITARO WAS ACTING YESTERDAY MADE ME LOOK AT HIM IN A NEW LIGHT. I MEAN, HE'S PRETTY CUTE, YA KNOW?
HE'S ALWAYS BEEN CUTE, BUT NOT LIKE THIS!
I PERSONALLY LIKE HOW SERIOUS HE IS, I HOPE THAT HE STAYS LIKE THAT.
ぼーっ
……
ぴちゃぴちゃ
NOT TO MENTION THE FACT THAT IF HE ACTUALLY GETS INTO TOKYO U, THEN HE'LL MAKE THE PERFECT HUSBAND.
MAYBE I'LL REWORK THE MASTER PLAN A BIT AND TAKE KEITARO FOR MYSELF. ♡
ギクッ
UH, KITSUNE? WHAT ARE YOU DOING?
ゴシゴシゴシ
EH HEH HEH. I GOTTA PUT A BIT MORE POLISH ON MY PERFECTION NOW, RIGHT? ♡
AND WHAT DO YOU MEAN BY THAT?!
……
♪
わしゃわしゃわしゃ
OOOH. I SEE HOW IT IS. YOU'VE GOT YOUR SIGHTS ON HIM TOO, HUH?
ビクンッ
OF... OF COURSE NOT! I'M PLEASED HE'S CHANGED, THAT'S ALL!
AH, NO NO NO!
THIS IS HOR-RIBLE!!
OKAY, SHINOBU! YOU CAN'T LOSE TO THEM!!
あわわわわ…

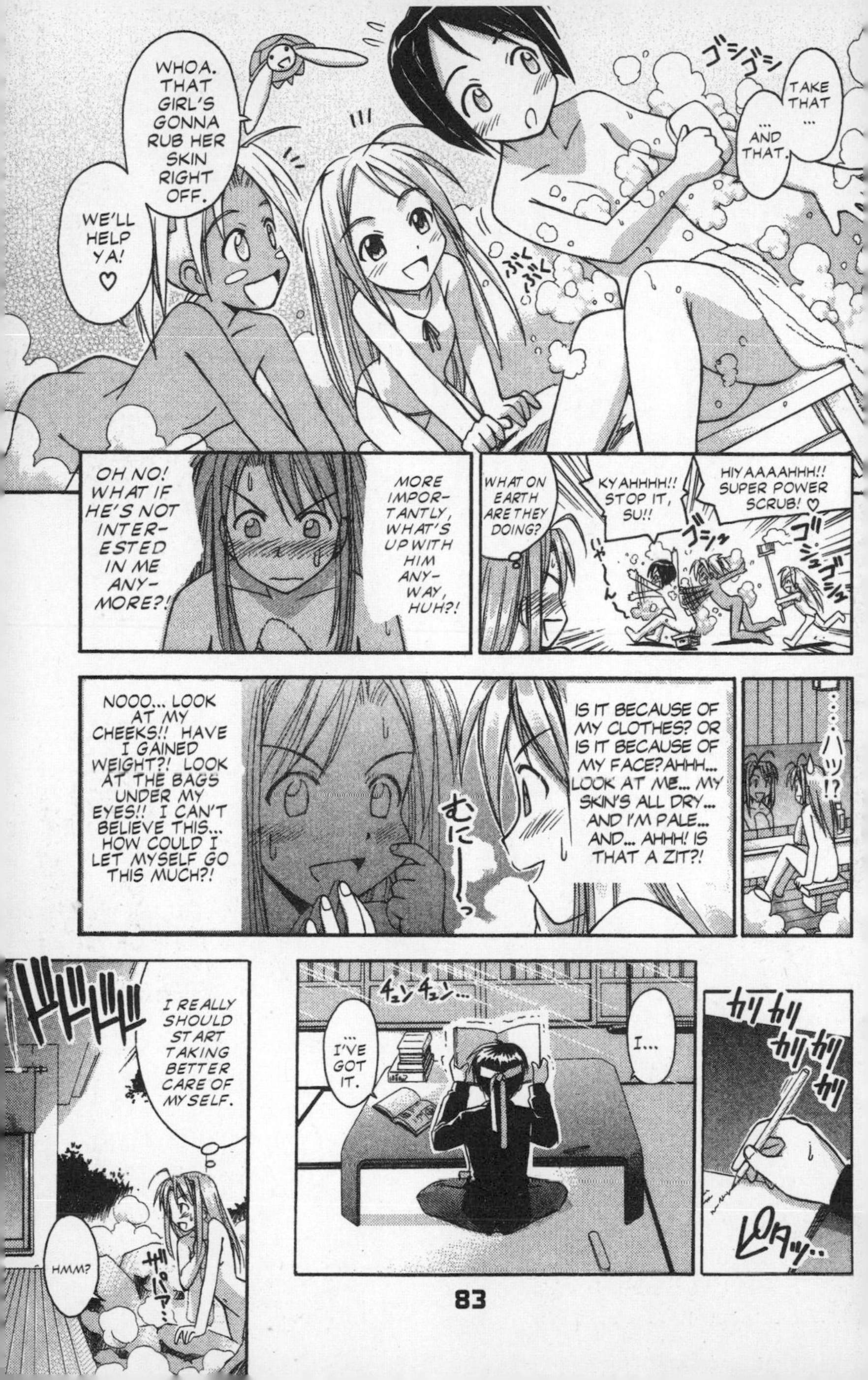
ゴシゴシ
TAKE THAT ... AND THAT.
WHOA. THAT GIRL'S GONNA RUB HER SKIN RIGHT OFF.
WE'LL HELP YA! ♡
HIYAAAAHHH!! SUPER POWER SCRUB! ♡
KYAHHHH!! STOP IT, SU!!
WHAT ON EARTH ARE THEY DOING?
MORE IMPORTANTLY, WHAT'S UP WITH HIM ANYWAY, HUH?!
OH NO! WHAT IF HE'S NOT INTERESTED IN ME ANYMORE?!
....ハッ!?
IS IT BECAUSE OF MY CLOTHES? OR IS IT BECAUSE OF MY FACE? AHHH... LOOK AT ME... MY SKIN'S ALL DRY... AND I'M PALE... AND... AHHH! IS THAT A ZIT?!
むにーっ
NOOO... LOOK AT MY CHEEKS!! HAVE I GAINED WEIGHT?! LOOK AT THE BAGS UNDER MY EYES!! I CAN'T BELIEVE THIS... HOW COULD I LET MYSELF GO THIS MUCH?!
カリカリカリカリカリ
ピタッ..
I...
... I'VE GOT IT.
I REALLY SHOULD START TAKING BETTER CARE OF MYSELF.
HMM?

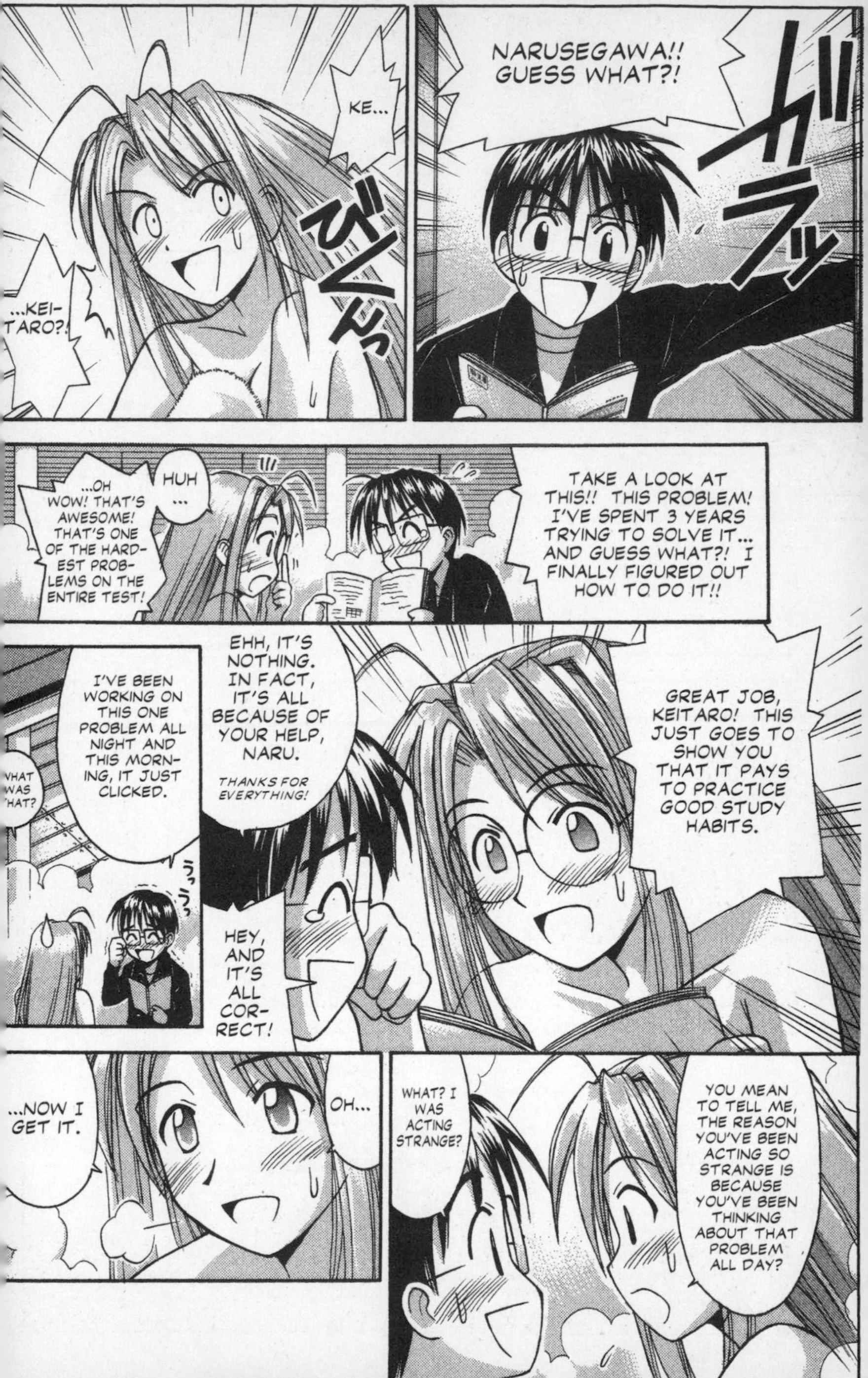
NARUSEGAWA!! GUESS WHAT?!
ガラッ
KE...
びくんっ
...KEI-TARO?!
TAKE A LOOK AT THIS!! THIS PROBLEM! I'VE SPENT 3 YEARS TRYING TO SOLVE IT... AND GUESS WHAT?! I FINALLY FIGURED OUT HOW TO DO IT!!
HUH...
...OH WOW! THAT'S AWESOME! THAT'S ONE OF THE HARD-EST PROB-LEMS ON THE ENTIRE TEST!
GREAT JOB, KEITARO! THIS JUST GOES TO SHOW YOU THAT IT PAYS TO PRACTICE GOOD STUDY HABITS.
EHH, IT'S NOTHING. IN FACT, IT'S ALL BECAUSE OF YOUR HELP, NARU.
THANKS FOR EVERYTHING!
HEY, AND IT'S ALL COR-RECT!
I'VE BEEN WORKING ON THIS ONE PROBLEM ALL NIGHT AND THIS MORN-ING, IT JUST CLICKED.
WHAT WAS THAT?
YOU MEAN TO TELL ME, THE REASON YOU'VE BEEN ACTING SO STRANGE IS BECAUSE YOU'VE BEEN THINKING ABOUT THAT PROBLEM ALL DAY?
WHAT? I WAS ACTING STRANGE?
OH...
...NOW I GET IT.

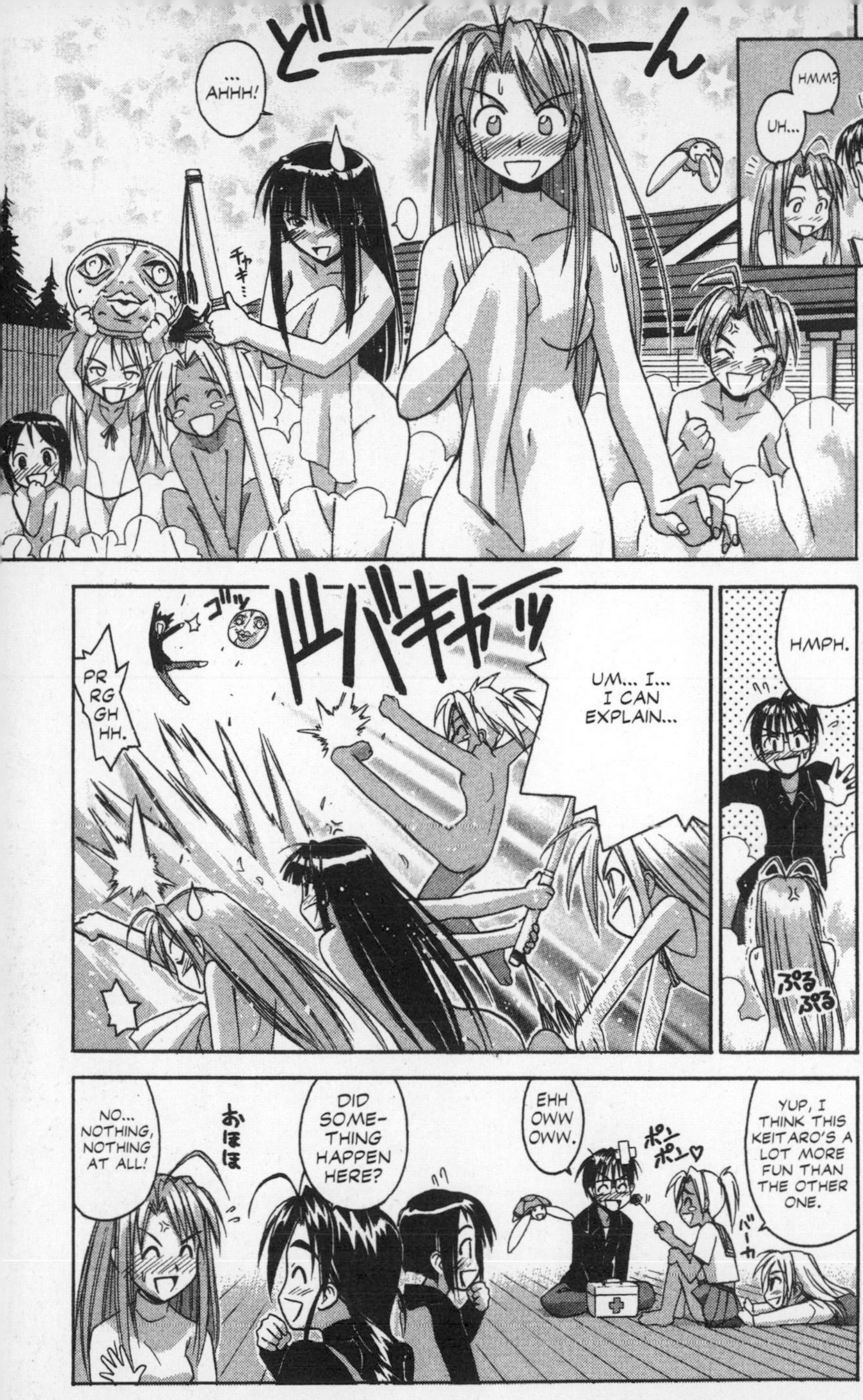
HMM?
UH...
どーーん
...AHHH!
チャキ
HMPH.
ぷるぷる
ドバキャッ
UM... I... I CAN EXPLAIN...
ゴッ
PR RG GH HH.
YUP, I THINK THIS KEITARO'S A LOT MORE FUN THAN THE OTHER ONE.
バーカ
ポンポン♡
EHH OWW OWW.
DID SOME-THING HAPPEN HERE?
おほほ
NO... NOTHING, NOTHING AT ALL!

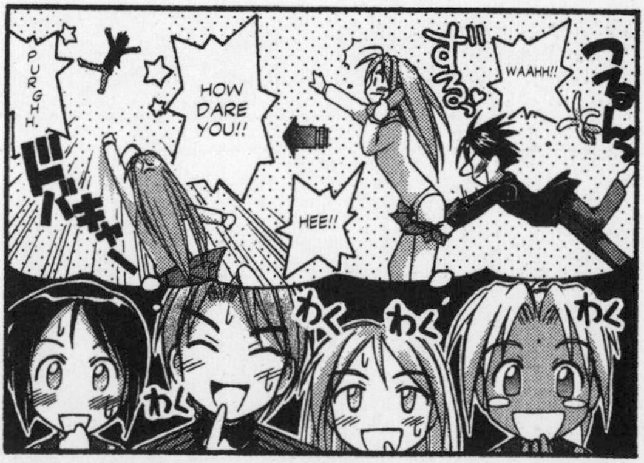
WAAHH!!
HEE!!
HOW DARE YOU!!
PURGH.
わく
わく
わく
わく

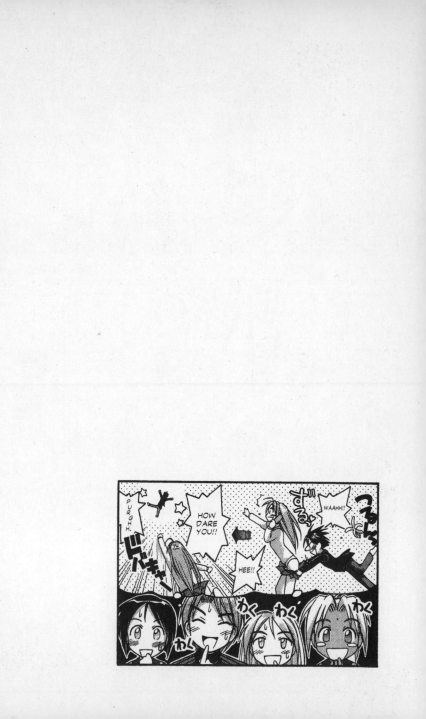

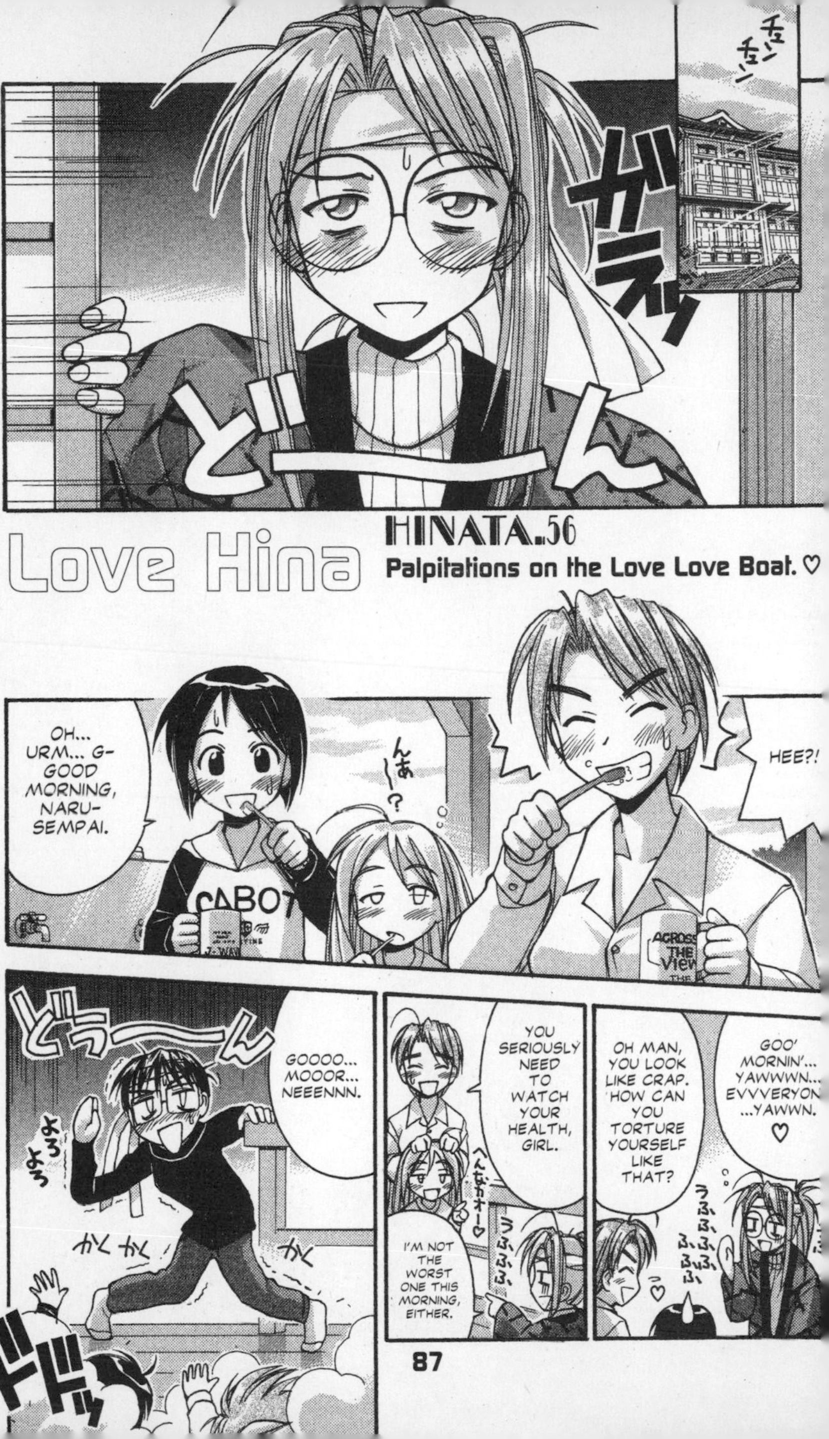
チュンチュン
ガラッ
どーーん
Love Hina
HINATA.56
Palpitations on the Love Love Boat. ♡
HEE?!
OH... URM... G-GOOD MORNING, NARU-SEMPAI.
GOO' MORNIN'... YAWWWN... EVVVERYON ...YAWWN. ♡
OH MAN, YOU LOOK LIKE CRAP. HOW CAN YOU TORTURE YOURSELF LIKE THAT?
うふふふふふふ
YOU SERIOUSLY NEED TO WATCH YOUR HEALTH, GIRL.
へんなカオー♡
うふふふ
I'M NOT THE WORST ONE THIS MORNING, EITHER.
GOOOO... MOOOR... NEEEENNN.
よろよろ
かくかく
かく

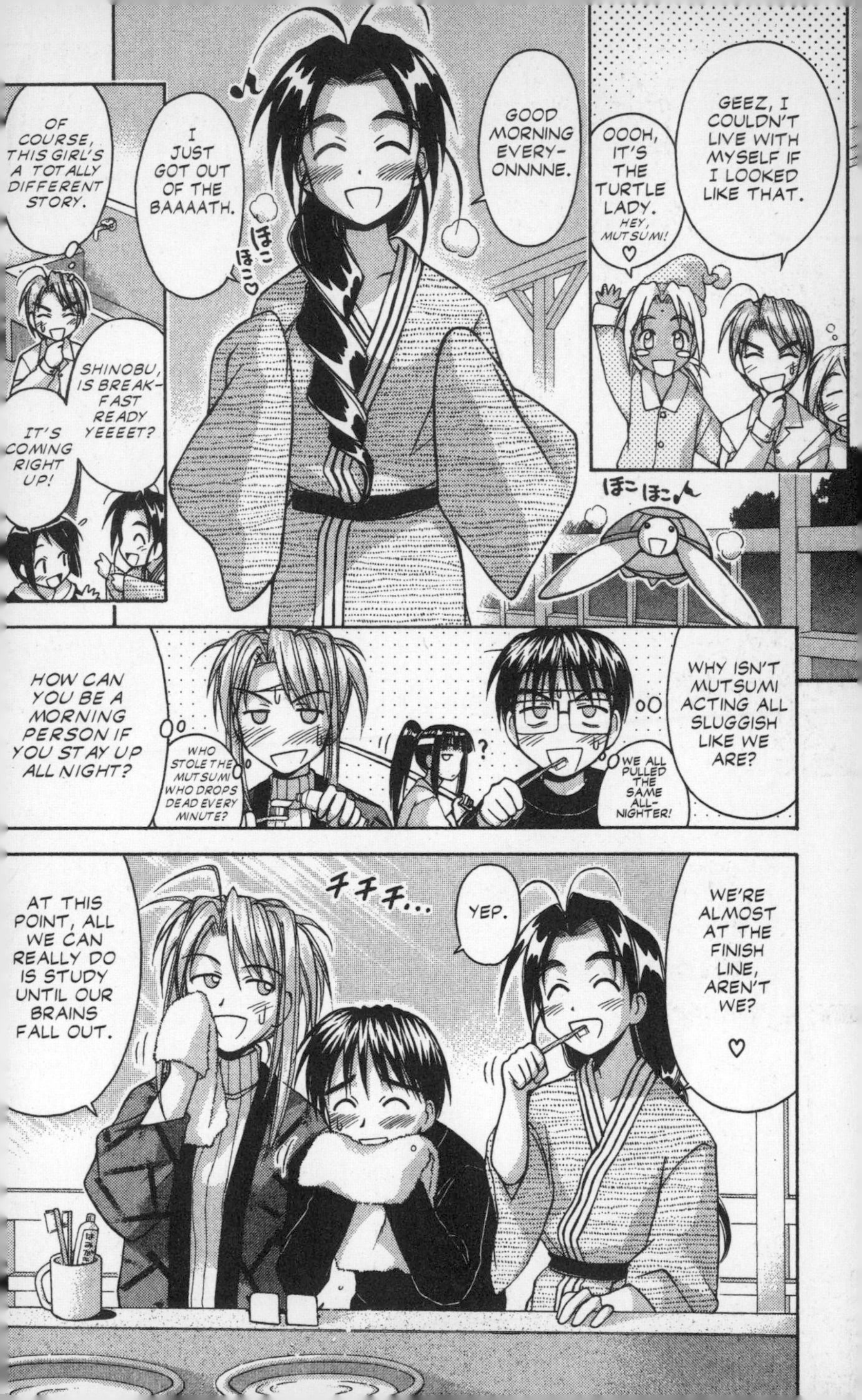
GEEZ, I COULDN'T LIVE WITH MYSELF IF I LOOKED LIKE THAT.
OOOH, IT'S THE TURTLE LADY.
HEY, MUTSUMI! ♡
GOOD MORNING EVERY-ONNNNE.
ほこほこ♡
I JUST GOT OUT OF THE BAAAATH.
ほこほこ♪
OF COURSE, THIS GIRL'S A TOTALLY DIFFERENT STORY.
SHINOBU, IS BREAKFAST READY YEEEET?
IT'S COMING RIGHT UP!
WHY ISN'T MUTSUMI ACTING ALL SLUGGISH LIKE WE ARE?
WE ALL PULLED THE SAME ALL-NIGHTER!
WHO STOLE THE MUTSUMI WHO DROPS DEAD EVERY MINUTE?
HOW CAN YOU BE A MORNING PERSON IF YOU STAY UP ALL NIGHT?
WE'RE ALMOST AT THE FINISH LINE, AREN'T WE? ♡
YEP.
チチチ...
AT THIS POINT, ALL WE CAN REALLY DO IS STUDY UNTIL OUR BRAINS FALL OUT.

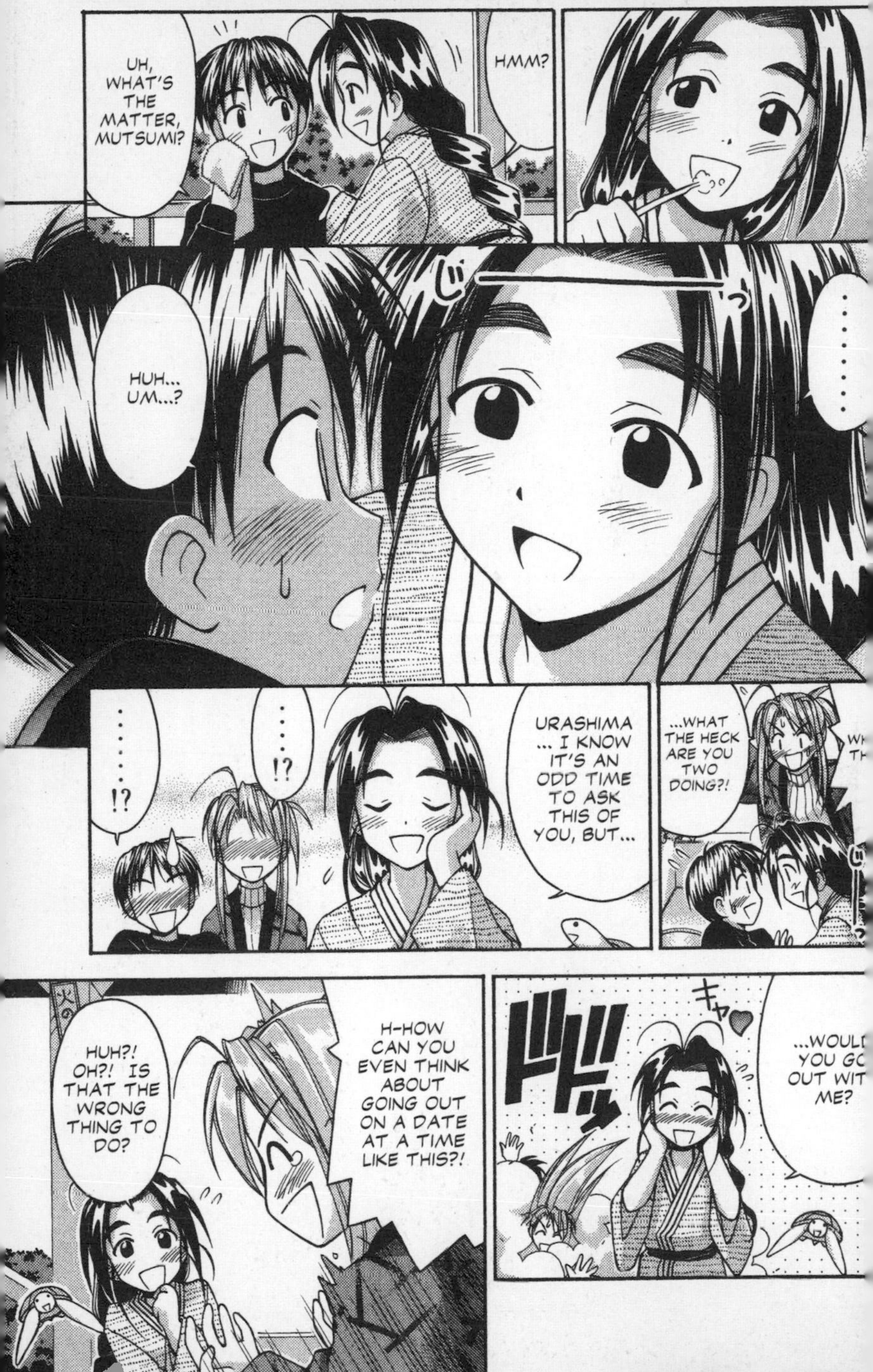
HMM?
UH, WHAT'S THE MATTER, MUTSUMI?
じーっ
......
HUH... UM...?
...WHAT THE HECK ARE YOU TWO DOING?!
URASHIMA ... I KNOW IT'S AN ODD TIME TO ASK THIS OF YOU, BUT...
......!?
......!?
キャ♥
...WOUL YOU G OUT WIT ME?
ドドドッ
H-HOW CAN YOU EVEN THINK ABOUT GOING OUT ON A DATE AT A TIME LIKE THIS?!
HUH?! OH?! IS THAT THE WRONG THING TO DO?
火の

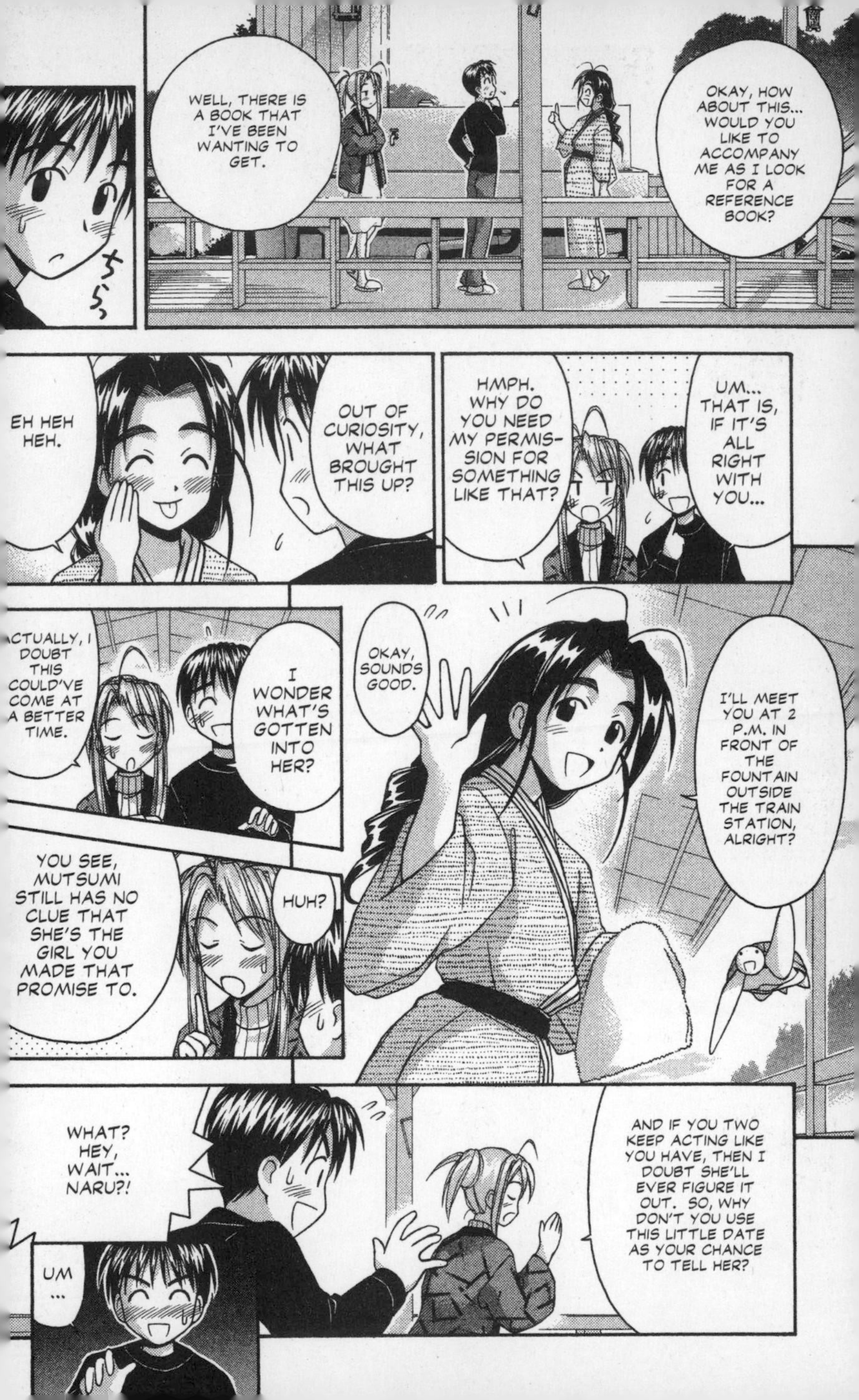
OKAY, HOW ABOUT THIS... WOULD YOU LIKE TO ACCOMPANY ME AS I LOOK FOR A REFERENCE BOOK?
WELL, THERE IS A BOOK THAT I'VE BEEN WANTING TO GET.
ちらっ
UM... THAT IS, IF IT'S ALL RIGHT WITH YOU...
HMPH. WHY DO YOU NEED MY PERMISSION FOR SOMETHING LIKE THAT?
OUT OF CURIOSITY, WHAT BROUGHT THIS UP?
EH HEH HEH.
I'LL MEET YOU AT 2 P.M. IN FRONT OF THE FOUNTAIN OUTSIDE THE TRAIN STATION, ALRIGHT?
OKAY, SOUNDS GOOD.
I WONDER WHAT'S GOTTEN INTO HER?
CTUALLY, I DOUBT THIS COULD'VE COME AT A BETTER TIME.
HUH?
YOU SEE, MUTSUMI STILL HAS NO CLUE THAT SHE'S THE GIRL YOU MADE THAT PROMISE TO.
AND IF YOU TWO KEEP ACTING LIKE YOU HAVE, THEN I DOUBT SHE'LL EVER FIGURE IT OUT. SO, WHY DON'T YOU USE THIS LITTLE DATE AS YOUR CHANCE TO TELL HER?
WHAT? HEY, WAIT... NARU?!
UM ...

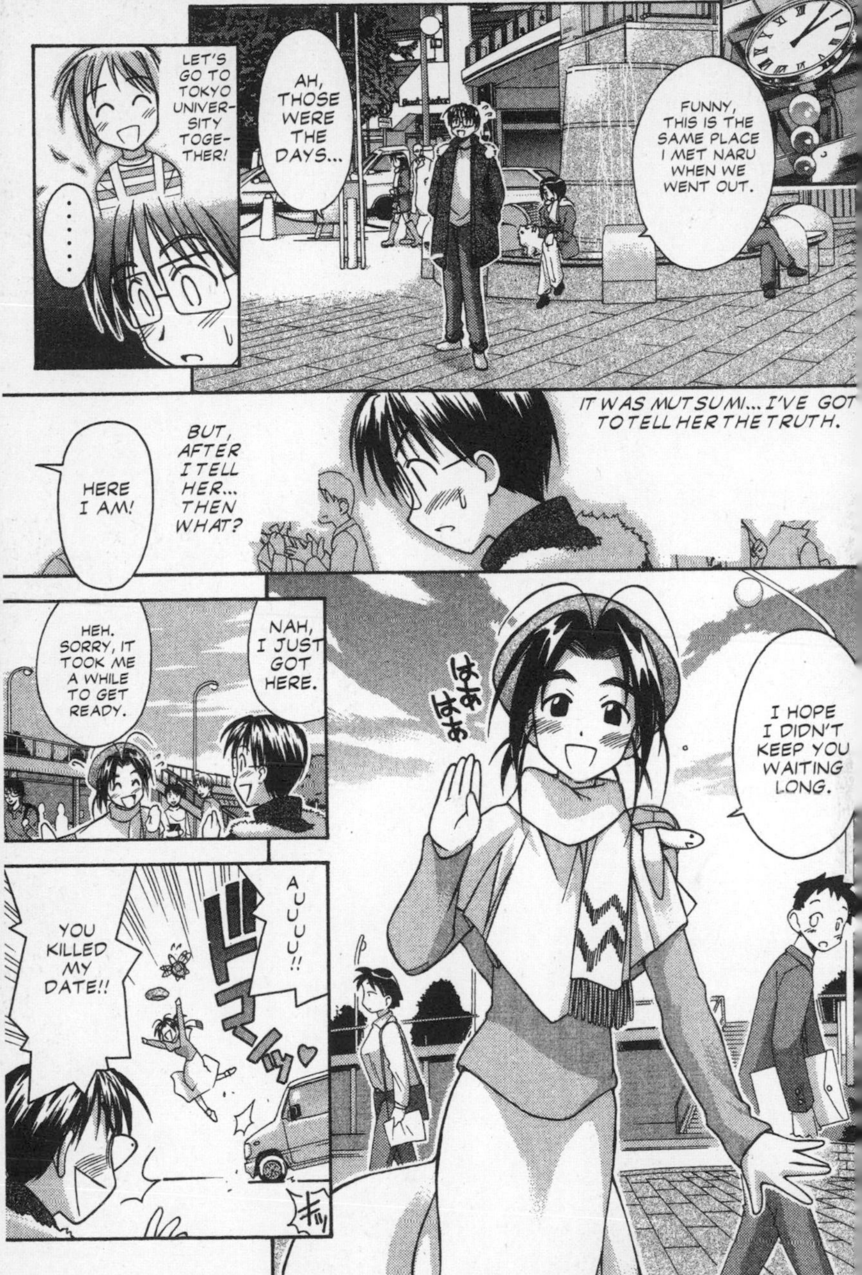
FUNNY, THIS IS THE SAME PLACE I MET NARU WHEN WE WENT OUT.
AH, THOSE WERE THE DAYS...
LET'S GO TO TOKYO UNIVERSITY TOGETHER!
......
IT WAS MUTSUMI... I'VE GOT TO TELL HER THE TRUTH.
BUT, AFTER I TELL HER... THEN WHAT?
HERE I AM!
I HOPE I DIDN'T KEEP YOU WAITING LONG.
はあ はあ
NAH, I JUST GOT HERE.
HEH. SORRY, IT TOOK ME A WHILE TO GET READY.
AUUUU!!
YOU KILLED MY DATE!!

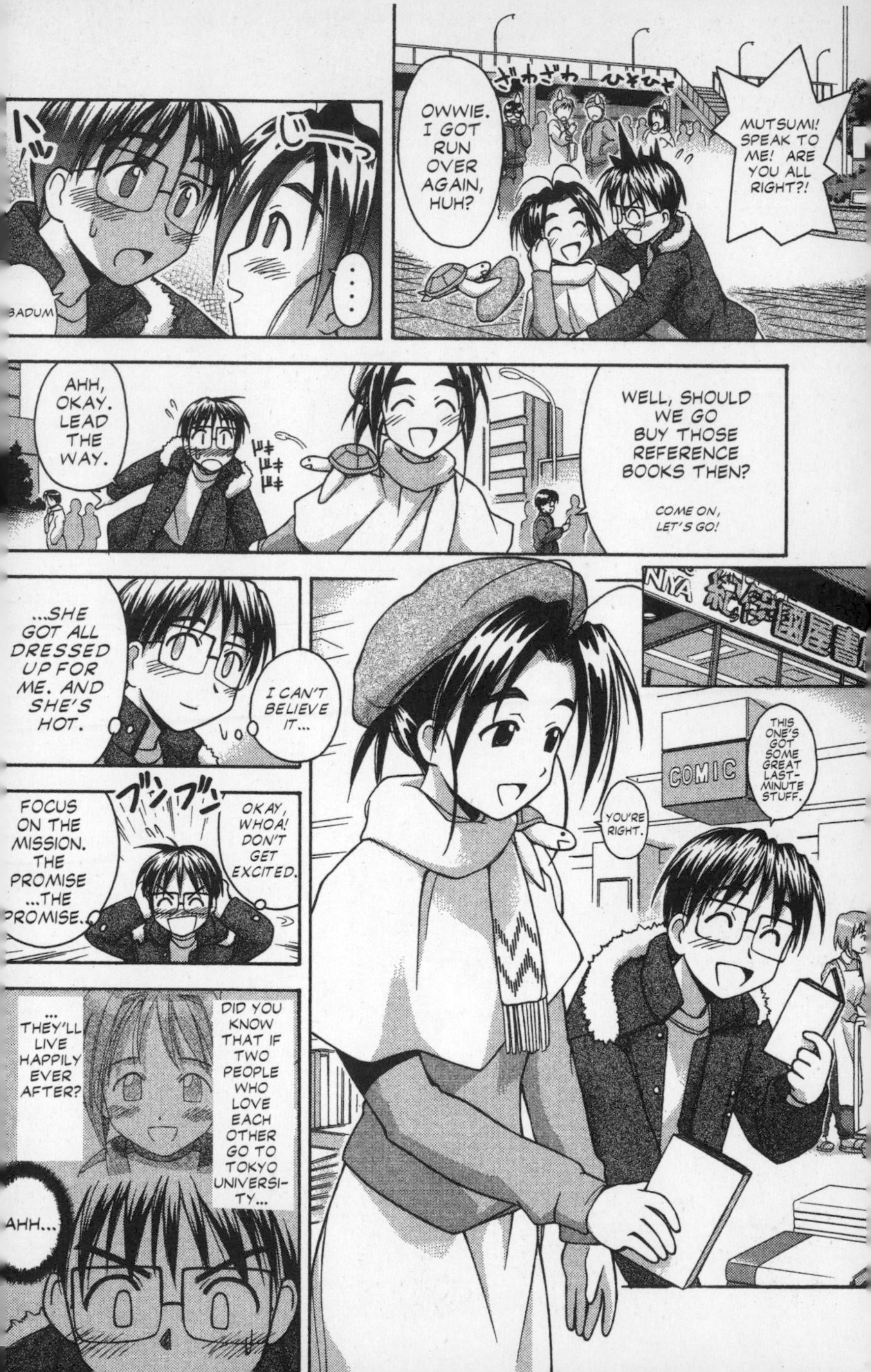

ざわざわ ひそひそ
MUTSUMI! SPEAK TO ME! ARE YOU ALL RIGHT?!
OWWIE. I GOT RUN OVER AGAIN, HUH?
ハッ!
...
BADUM
WELL, SHOULD WE GO BUY THOSE REFERENCE BOOKS THEN?
COME ON, LET'S GO!
AHH, OKAY. LEAD THE WAY.
NIYA
COMIC
THIS ONE'S GOT SOME GREAT LAST-MINUTE STUFF.
YOU'RE RIGHT.
...SHE GOT ALL DRESSED UP FOR ME. AND SHE'S HOT.
I CAN'T BELIEVE IT...
OKAY, WHOA! DON'T GET EXCITED.
FOCUS ON THE MISSION. THE PROMISE ...THE PROMISE...
DID YOU KNOW THAT IF TWO PEOPLE WHO LOVE EACH OTHER GO TO TOKYO UNIVERSITY...
...THEY'LL LIVE HAPPILY EVER AFTER?
AHH...

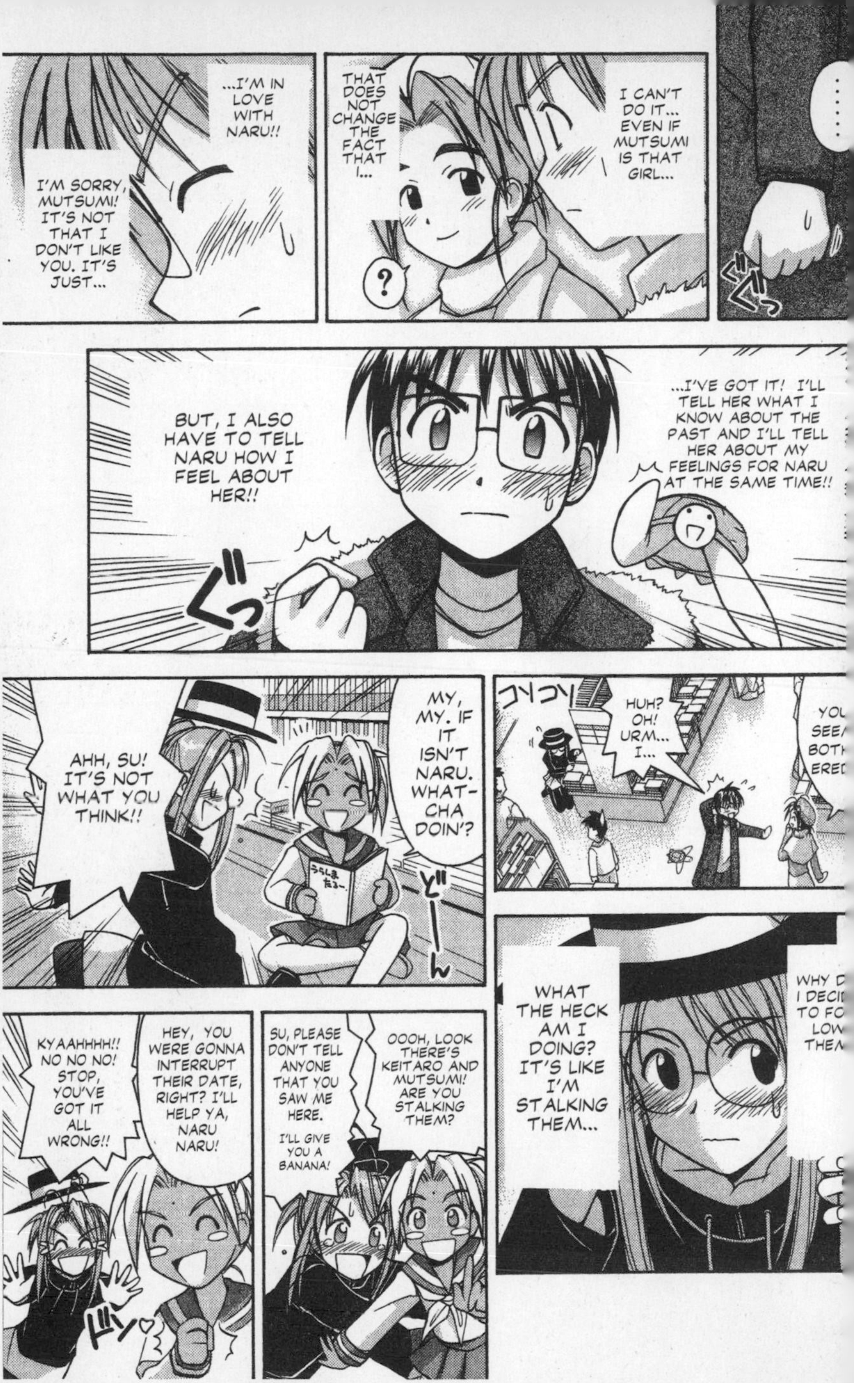
...
I CAN'T DO IT... EVEN IF MUTSUMI IS THAT GIRL...
THAT DOES NOT CHANGE THE FACT THAT I...
?
I'M SORRY, MUTSUMI! IT'S NOT THAT I DON'T LIKE YOU. IT'S JUST...
...I'M IN LOVE WITH NARU!!
...I'VE GOT IT! I'LL TELL HER WHAT I KNOW ABOUT THE PAST AND I'LL TELL HER ABOUT MY FEELINGS FOR NARU AT THE SAME TIME!!
BUT, I ALSO HAVE TO TELL NARU HOW I FEEL ABOUT HER!!
HUH? OH! URM... I...
WHAT THE HECK AM I DOING? IT'S LIKE I'M STALKING THEM...
MY, MY. IF IT ISN'T NARU. WHATCHA DOIN'?
AHH, SU! IT'S NOT WHAT YOU THINK!!
OOOH, LOOK THERE'S KEITARO AND MUTSUMI! ARE YOU STALKING THEM?
SU, PLEASE DON'T TELL ANYONE THAT YOU SAW ME HERE.
I'LL GIVE YOU A BANANA!
HEY, YOU WERE GONNA INTERRUPT THEIR DATE, RIGHT? I'LL HELP YA, NARU NARU!
KYAAHHHH!! NO NO NO! STOP, YOU'VE GOT IT ALL WRONG!!

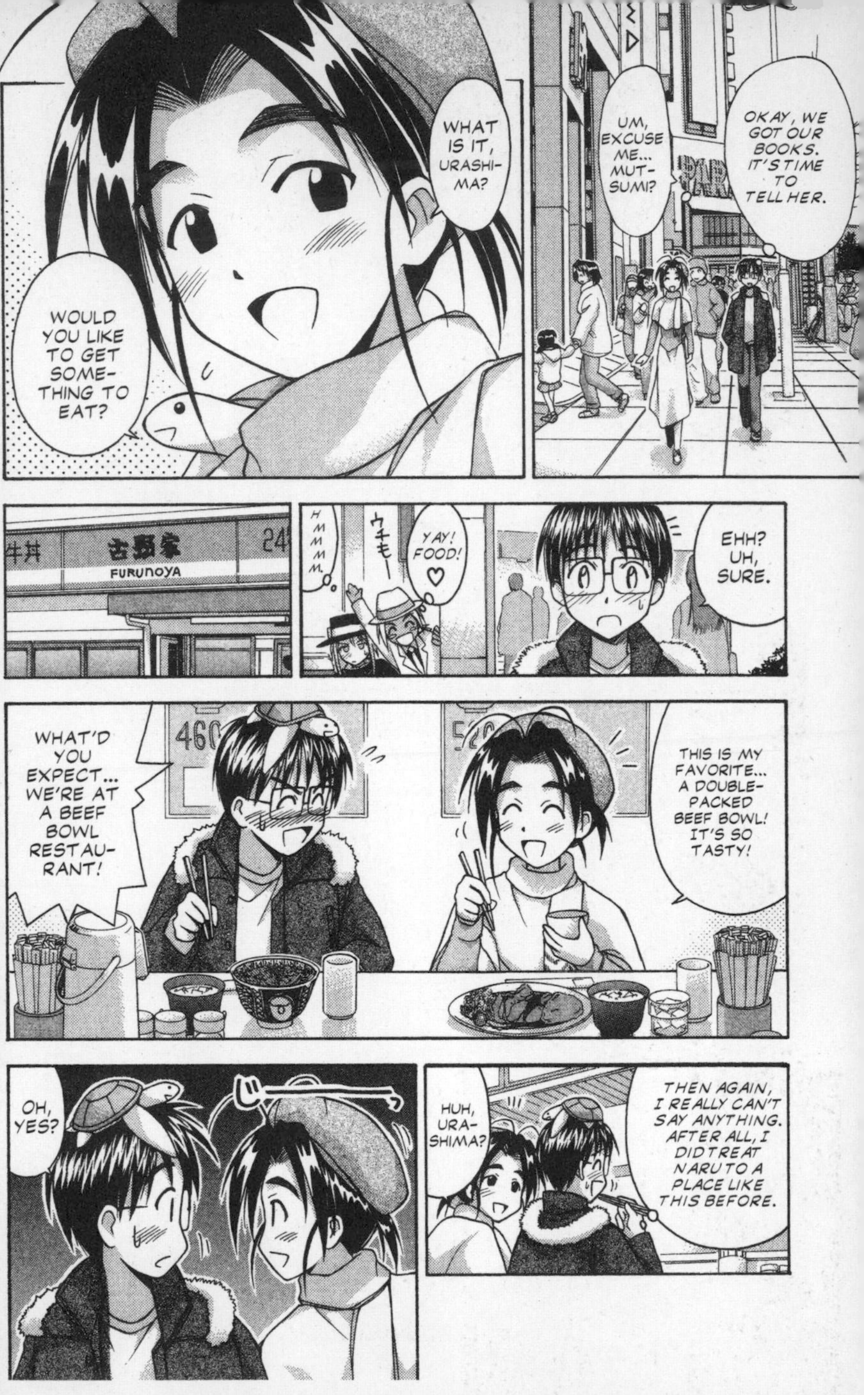
OKAY, WE GOT OUR BOOKS. IT'S TIME TO TELL HER.
UM, EXCUSE ME... MUT-SUMI?
WHAT IS IT, URASHI-MA?
WOULD YOU LIKE TO GET SOME-THING TO EAT?
EHH? UH, SURE.
YAY! FOOD! ♡
ウチもー
HMMMM.
牛丼
FURUNOYA
THIS IS MY FAVORITE... A DOUBLE-PACKED BEEF BOWL! IT'S SO TASTY!
WHAT'D YOU EXPECT... WE'RE AT A BEEF BOWL RESTAU-RANT!
THEN AGAIN, I REALLY CAN'T SAY ANYTHING. AFTER ALL, I DIDTREAT NARUTO A PLACE LIKE THIS BEFORE.
HUH, URA-SHIMA?
OH, YES?

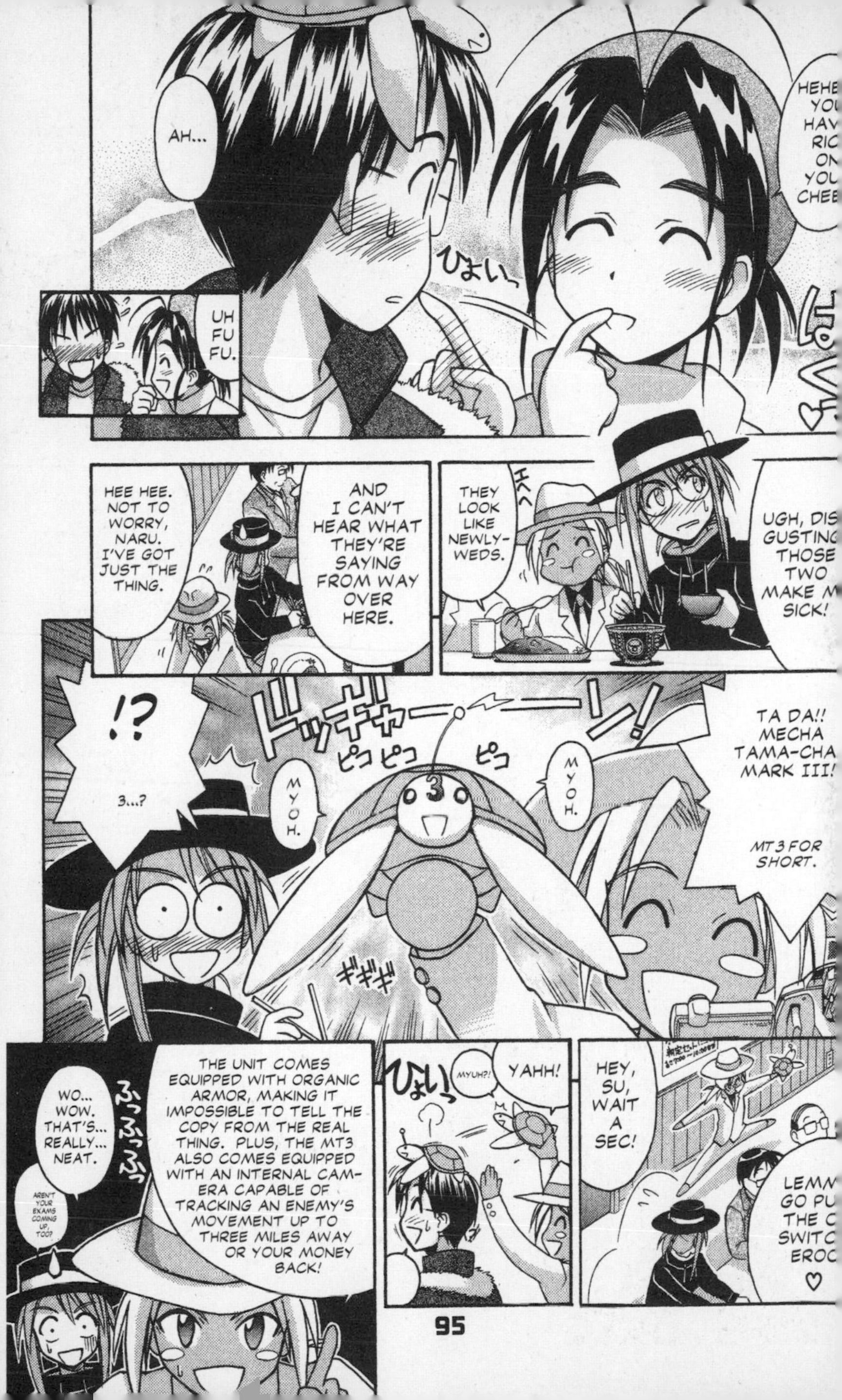
HEHE YOU HAV RIC ON YOU CHEE
ひょいっ
はぐっ♡
AH...
UH FU FU.
UGH, DIS GUSTING THOSE TWO MAKE M SICK!
エへへ
THEY LOOK LIKE NEWLY-WEDS.
AND I CAN'T HEAR WHAT THEY'RE SAYING FROM WAY OVER HERE.
HEE HEE. NOT TO WORRY, NARU. I'VE GOT JUST THE THING.
TA DA!! MECHA TAMA-CHA MARK III!
MT3 FOR SHORT.
ドッギャーーン!
ぴこ ぴこ ぴこ
MYOH.
MYOH.
!?
3...?
ギギギ
HEY, SU, WAIT A SEC!
LEMM GO PU THE C SWITC EROC ♡
YAHH!
MYUH?!
ひょいっ
THE UNIT COMES EQUIPPED WITH ORGANIC ARMOR, MAKING IT IMPOSSIBLE TO TELL THE COPY FROM THE REAL THING. PLUS, THE MT3 ALSO COMES EQUIPPED WITH AN INTERNAL CAM-ERA CAPABLE OF TRACKING AN ENEMY'S MOVEMENT UP TO THREE MILES AWAY OR YOUR MONEY BACK!
ふっふっふっ
WO... WOW. THAT'S... REALLY... NEAT.
AREN'T YOUR EXAMS COMING UP, TOO?

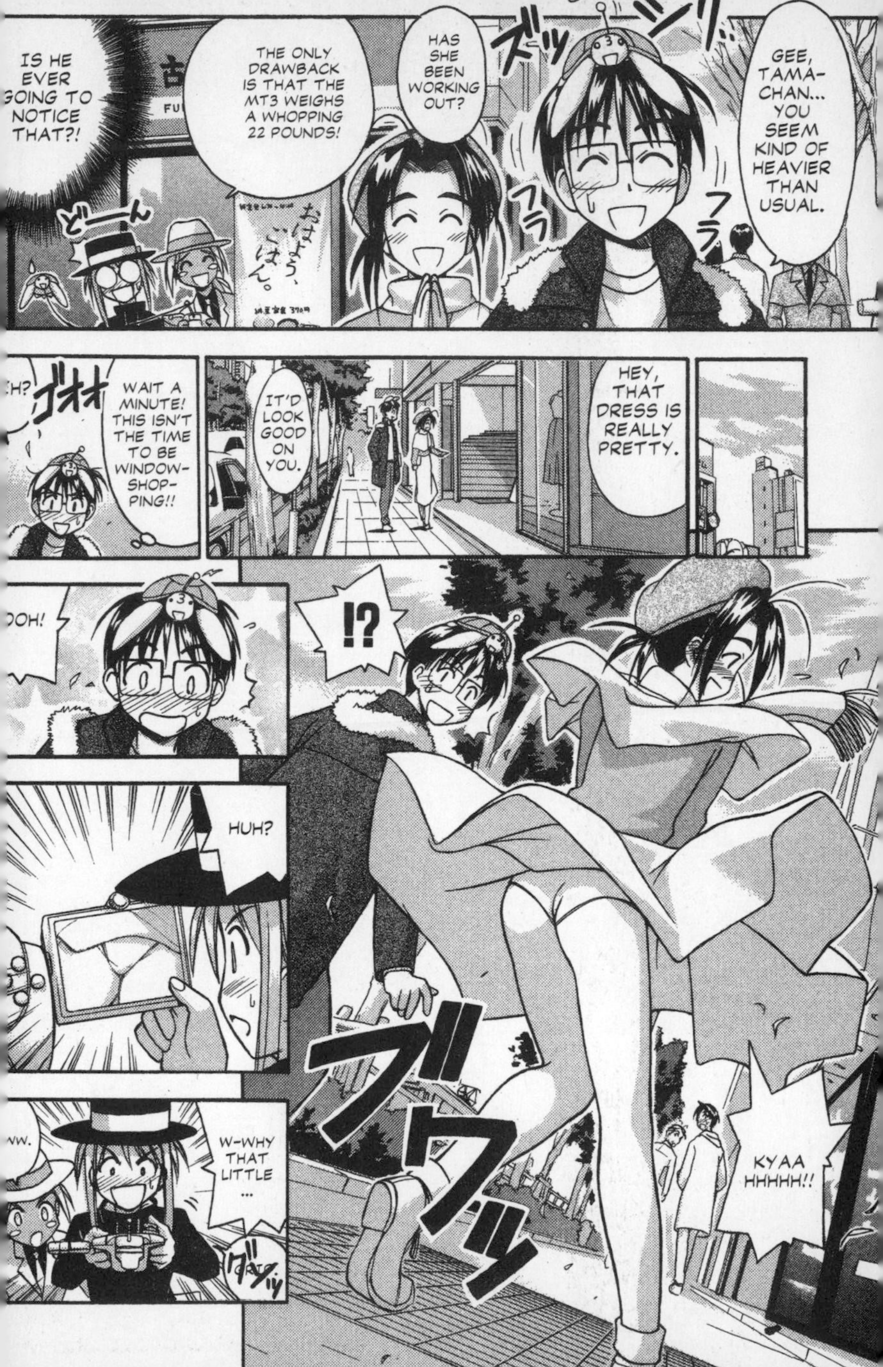
ピピピ
ズッシリ
GEE, TAMA-CHAN... YOU SEEM KIND OF HEAVIER THAN USUAL.
フラフラ
HAS SHE BEEN WORKING OUT?
THE ONLY DRAWBACK IS THAT THE MT3 WEIGHS A WHOPPING 22 POUNDS!
おはよう、ごはん。
IS HE EVER GOING TO NOTICE THAT?!
どーん
HEY, THAT DRESS IS REALLY PRETTY.
IT'D LOOK GOOD ON YOU.
ゴオオ
WAIT A MINUTE! THIS ISN'T THE TIME TO BE WINDOW-SHOPPING!!
!?
KYAA HHHHH!!
ブワッ
OOH!
HUH?
W-WHY THAT LITTLE ...

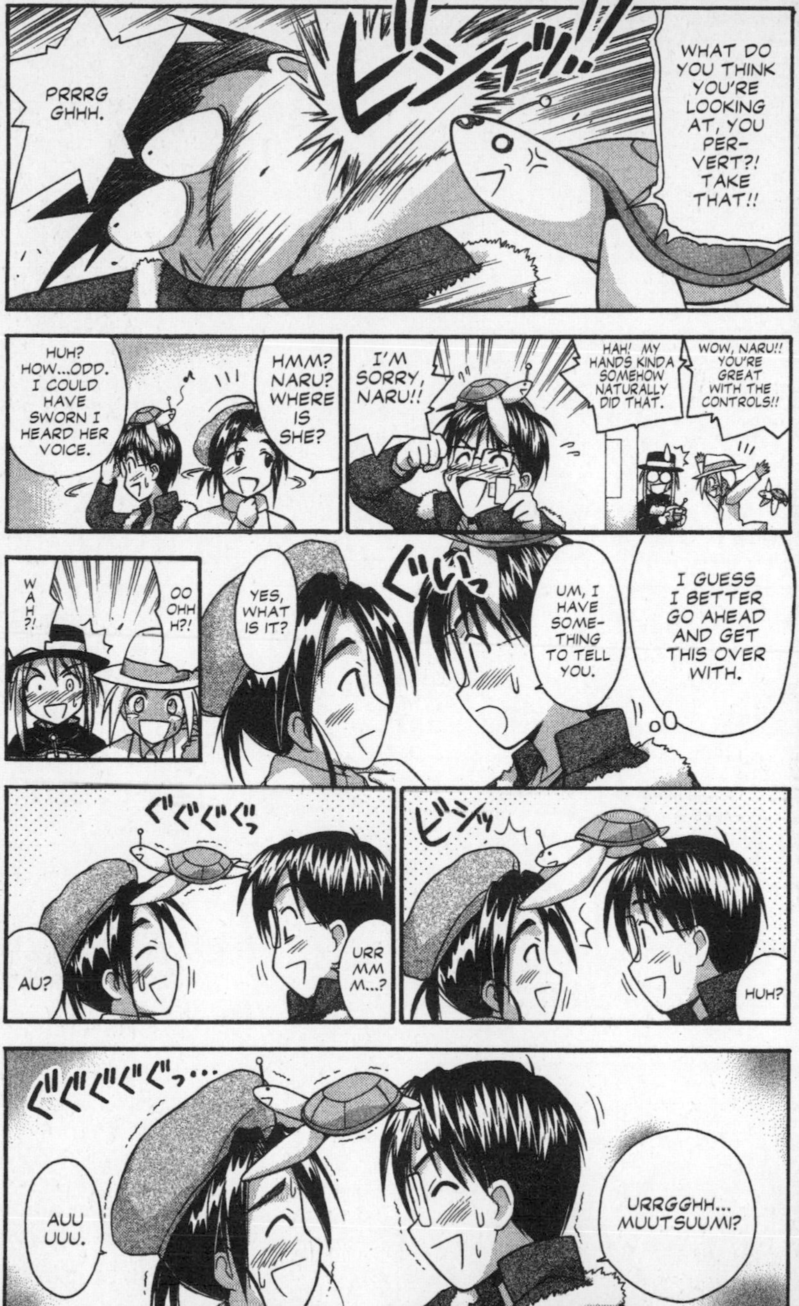
WHAT DO YOU THINK YOU'RE LOOKING AT, YOU PER-VERT?! TAKE THAT!!
PRRRG GHHH.
WOW, NARU!! YOU'RE GREAT WITH THE CONTROLS!!
HAH! MY HANDS KINDA SOMEHOW NATURALLY DID THAT.
I'M SORRY, NARU!!
HMM? NARU? WHERE IS SHE?
HUH? HOW...ODD. I COULD HAVE SWORN I HEARD HER VOICE.
I GUESS I BETTER GO AHEAD AND GET THIS OVER WITH.
UM, I HAVE SOME-THING TO TELL YOU.
YES, WHAT IS IT?
OO OHH H?!
WAH?!
HUH?
URR MM M...?
AU?
URRGGHH... MUUTSUUMI?
AUU UUU.

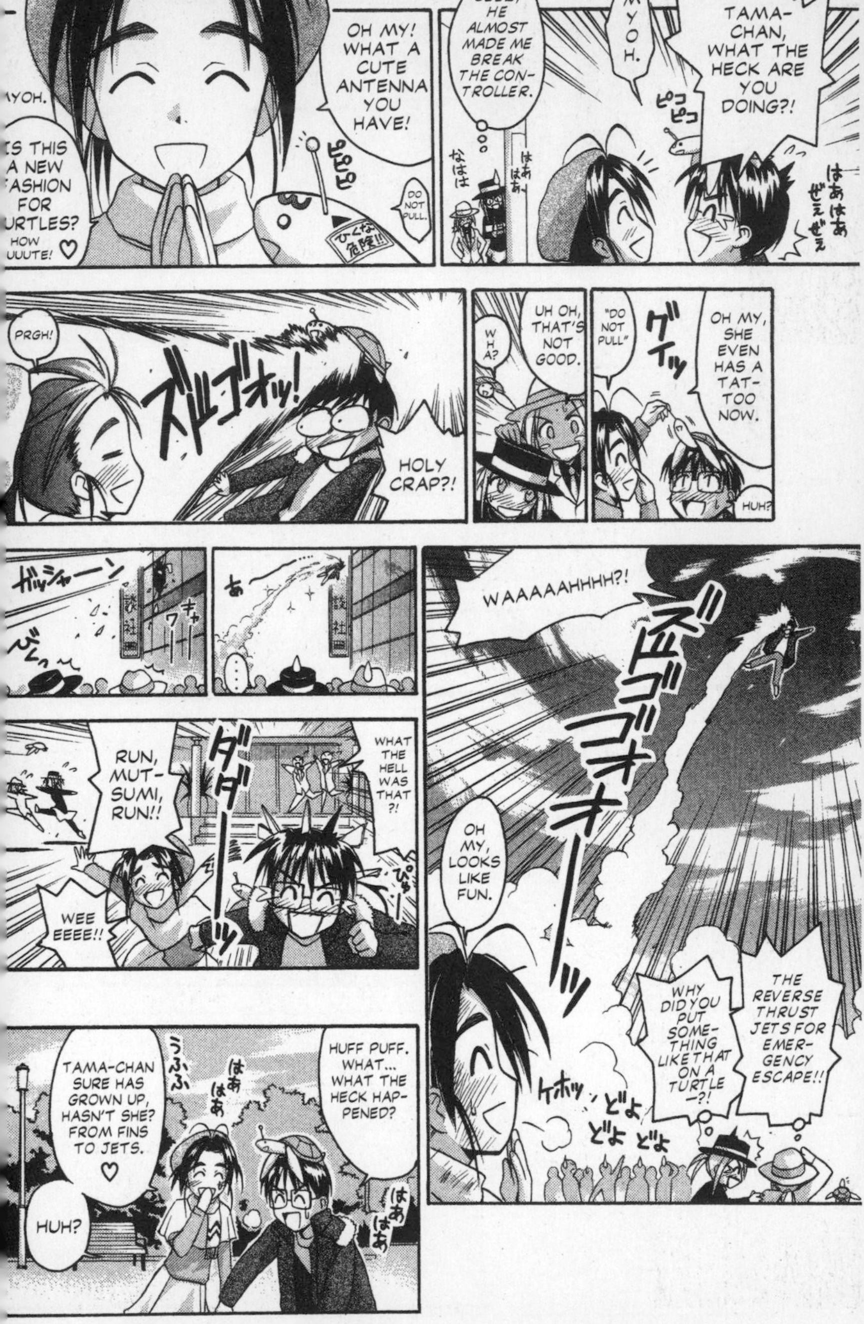
TAMA-CHAN, WHAT THE HECK ARE YOU DOING?!
はあはあ ぜえぜえ
ピコピコ
MYOH.
GEEZ, HE ALMOST MADE ME BREAK THE CONTROLLER.
はあはあ
なはは
OH MY! WHAT A CUTE ANTENNA YOU HAVE!
ピピピ
DO NOT PULL.
ひくな危険!!
MYOH.
IS THIS A NEW FASHION FOR TURTLES?
HOW CUUUTE! ♡
OH MY, SHE EVEN HAS A TAT-TOO NOW.
グイッ
"DO NOT PULL"
HUH?
UH OH, THAT'S NOT GOOD.
WHA?
PRGH!
ズドゴオッ!
HOLY CRAP?!
WAAAAAHHHH?!
ズドゴゴオオーーッ
OH MY, LOOKS LIKE FUN.
THE REVERSE THRUST JETS FOR EMERGENCY ESCAPE!!
WHY DID YOU PUT SOME-THING LIKE THAT ON A TURTLE-?!
ケホッ
どよ どよ どよ どよ
あ
ガッシャーン
キャーワー
びくっ
WHAT THE HELL WAS THAT?!
ダダーーッ
RUN, MUT-SUMI, RUN!!
WEE EEEE!!
HUFF PUFF. WHAT... WHAT THE HECK HAP-PENED?
はあはあ
うふふ
はあはあ
TAMA-CHAN SURE HAS GROWN UP, HASN'T SHE? FROM FINS TO JETS. ♡
HUH?

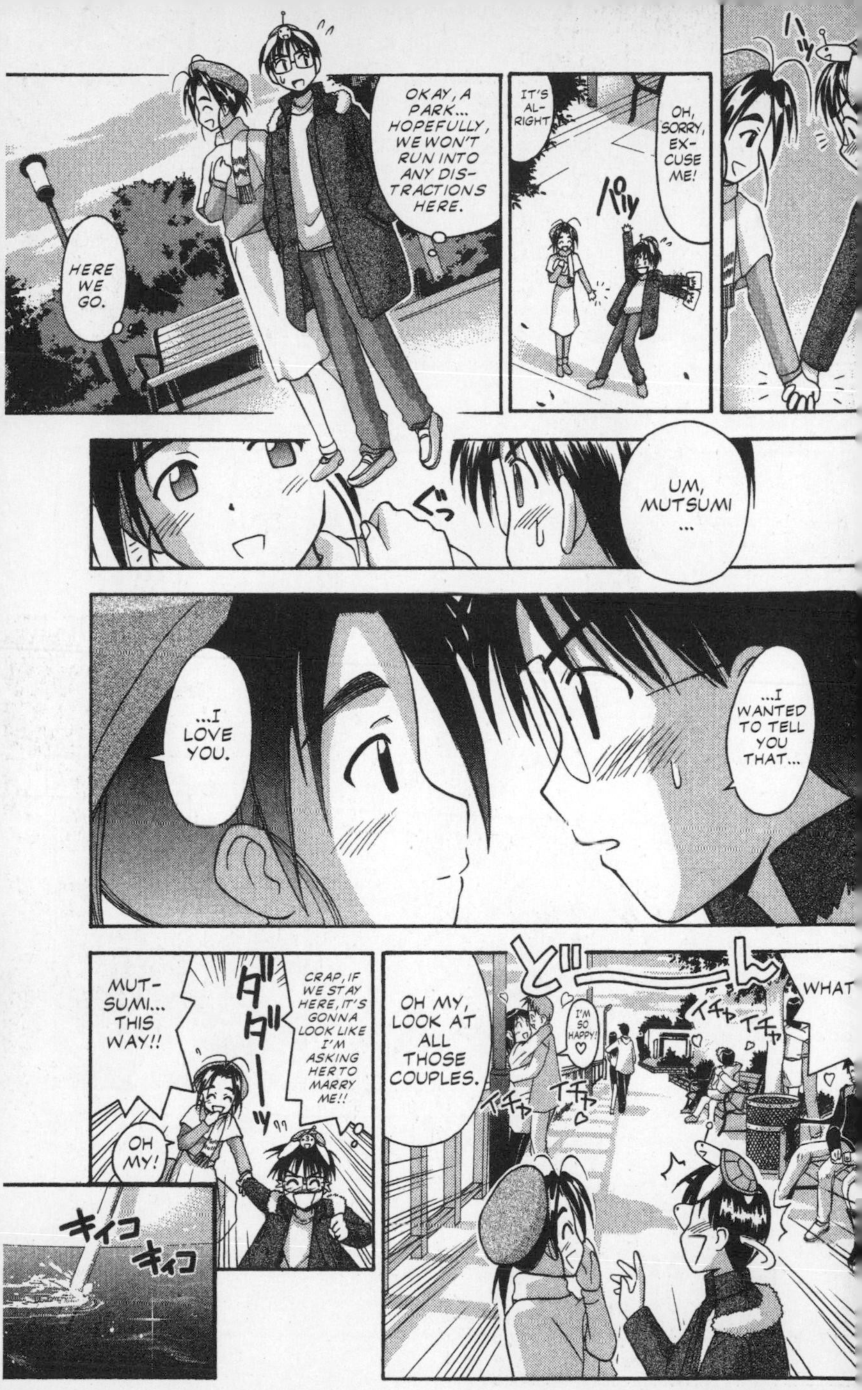
ハッ
OH, SORRY, EXCUSE ME!
IT'S ALRIGHT
パイ
OKAY, A PARK... HOPEFULLY, WE WON'T RUN INTO ANY DISTRACTIONS HERE.
HERE WE GO.
UM, MUTSUMI ...
ぐっ
...I WANTED TO TELL YOU THAT...
...I LOVE YOU.
どーーん
WHAT
OH MY, LOOK AT ALL THOSE COUPLES.
I'M SO HAPPY!
イチャ イチャ
イチャ イチャ
CRAP, IF WE STAY HERE, IT'S GONNA LOOK LIKE I'M ASKING HER TO MARRY ME!!
ダダーッ
MUT-SUMI... THIS WAY!!
OH MY!
キィコ キィコ

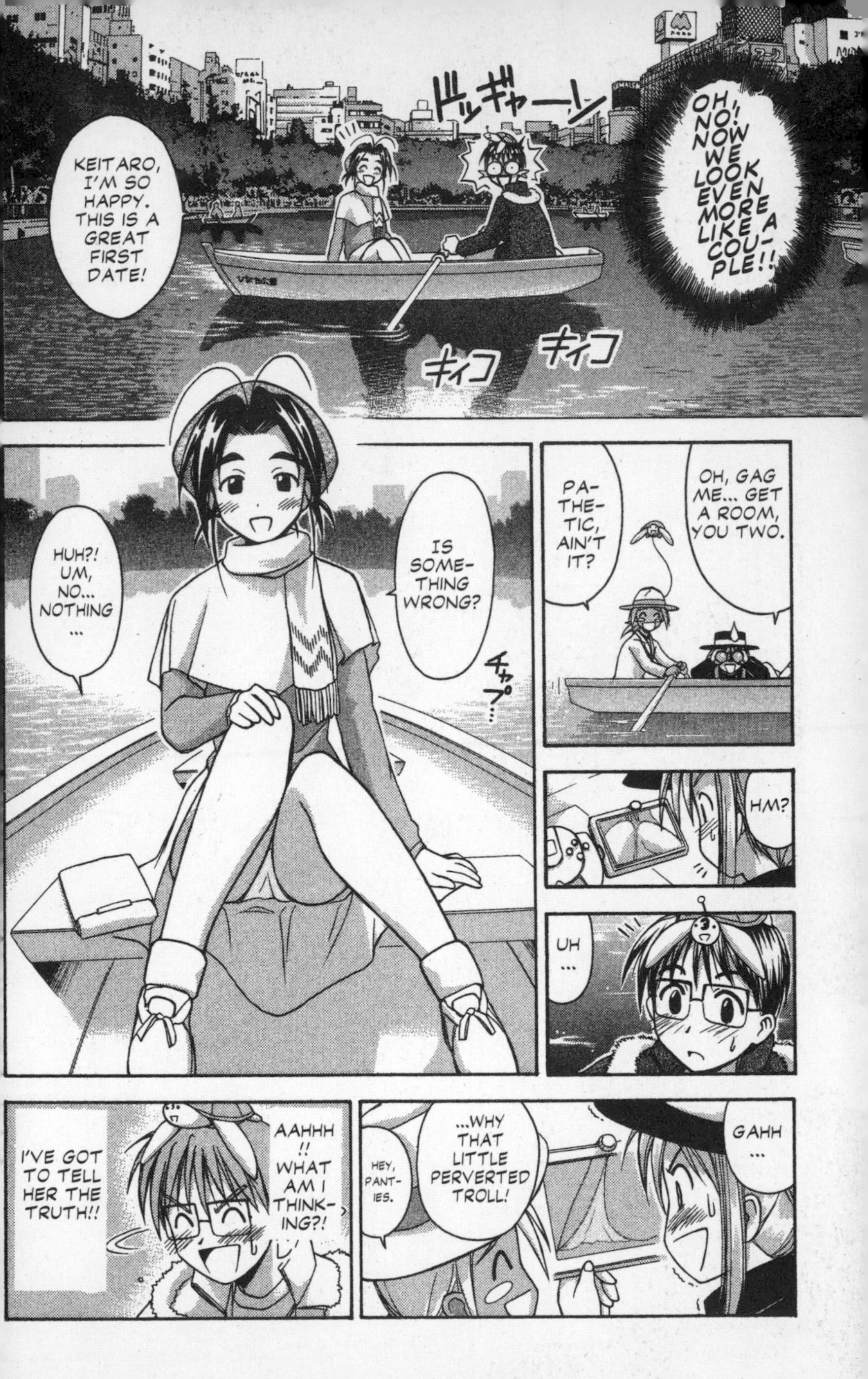
OH, NO! NOW WE LOOK EVEN MORE LIKE A COU-PLE!!
ドッギャーン
KEITARO, I'M SO HAPPY. THIS IS A GREAT FIRST DATE!
ギィコ
ギィコ
OH, GAG ME... GET A ROOM, YOU TWO.
PA-THE-TIC, AIN'T IT?
HM?
UH ...
IS SOME-THING WRONG?
HUH?! UM, NO... NOTHING ...
チャプ...
GAHH ...
...WHY THAT LITTLE PERVERTED TROLL!
HEY, PANT-IES.
AAHHH!! WHAT AM I THINK-ING?!
I'VE GOT TO TELL HER THE TRUTH!!

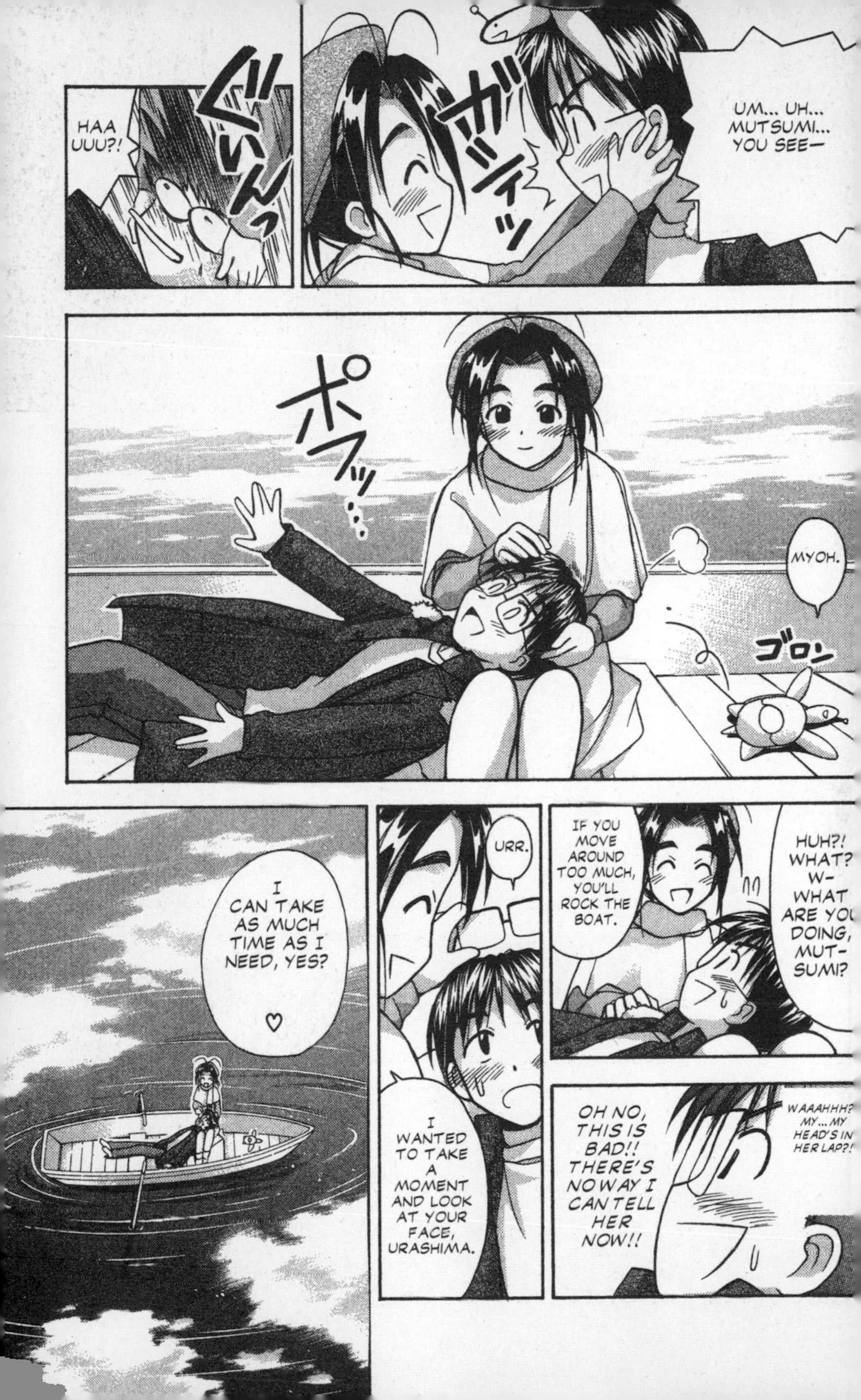
ガシッ
UM... UH... MUTSUMI... YOU SEE—
ぐいんっ
HAA UUU?!
ポフッ...
MYOH.
ゴロン
HUH?! WHAT? W-WHAT ARE YOU DOING, MUT-SUMI?
IF YOU MOVE AROUND TOO MUCH, YOU'LL ROCK THE BOAT.
WAAAHHH? MY... MY HEAD'S IN HER LAP?!
OH NO, THIS IS BAD!! THERE'S NO WAY I CAN TELL HER NOW!!
URR.
I WANTED TO TAKE A MOMENT AND LOOK AT YOUR FACE, URASHIMA.
I CAN TAKE AS MUCH TIME AS I NEED, YES? ♡

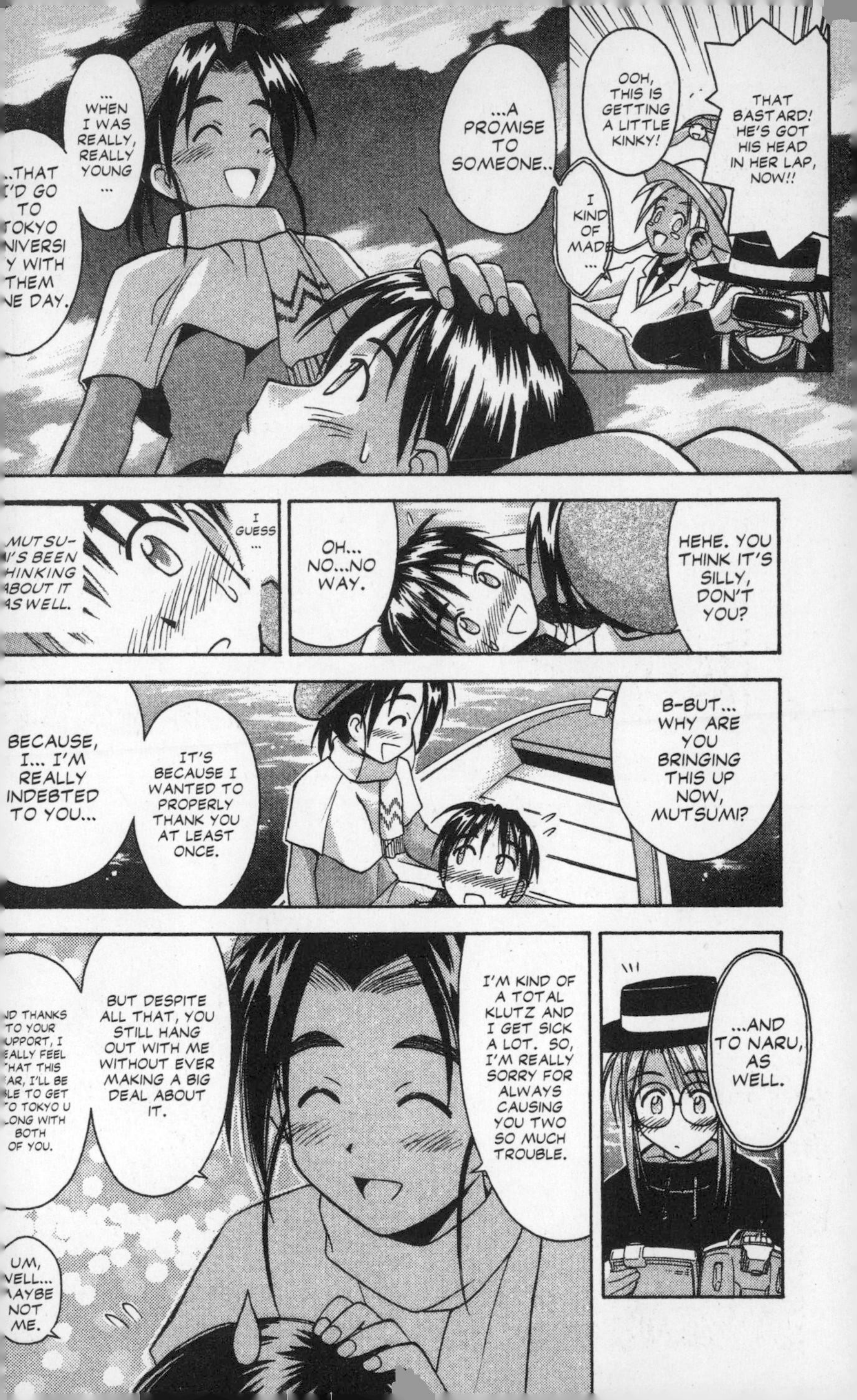
THAT BASTARD! HE'S GOT HIS HEAD IN HER LAP, NOW!!
OOH, THIS IS GETTING A LITTLE KINKY!
I KIND OF MADE...
...A PROMISE TO SOMEONE..
... WHEN I WAS REALLY, REALLY YOUNG ...
..THAT I'D GO TO TOKYO NIVERSI Y WITH THEM NE DAY.
HEHE. YOU THINK IT'S SILLY, DON'T YOU?
OH... NO...NO WAY.
I GUESS ...
MUTSU- I'S BEEN HINKING ABOUT IT AS WELL.
B-BUT... WHY ARE YOU BRINGING THIS UP NOW, MUTSUMI?
IT'S BECAUSE I WANTED TO PROPERLY THANK YOU AT LEAST ONCE.
BECAUSE, I... I'M REALLY INDEBTED TO YOU...
...AND TO NARU, AS WELL.
I'M KIND OF A TOTAL KLUTZ AND I GET SICK A LOT. SO, I'M REALLY SORRY FOR ALWAYS CAUSING YOU TWO SO MUCH TROUBLE.
BUT DESPITE ALL THAT, YOU STILL HANG OUT WITH ME WITHOUT EVER MAKING A BIG DEAL ABOUT IT.
ND THANKS TO YOUR UPPORT, I EALLY FEEL THAT THIS AR, I'LL BE LE TO GET O TOKYO U LONG WITH BOTH OF YOU.
UM, VELL... AAYBE NOT ME.

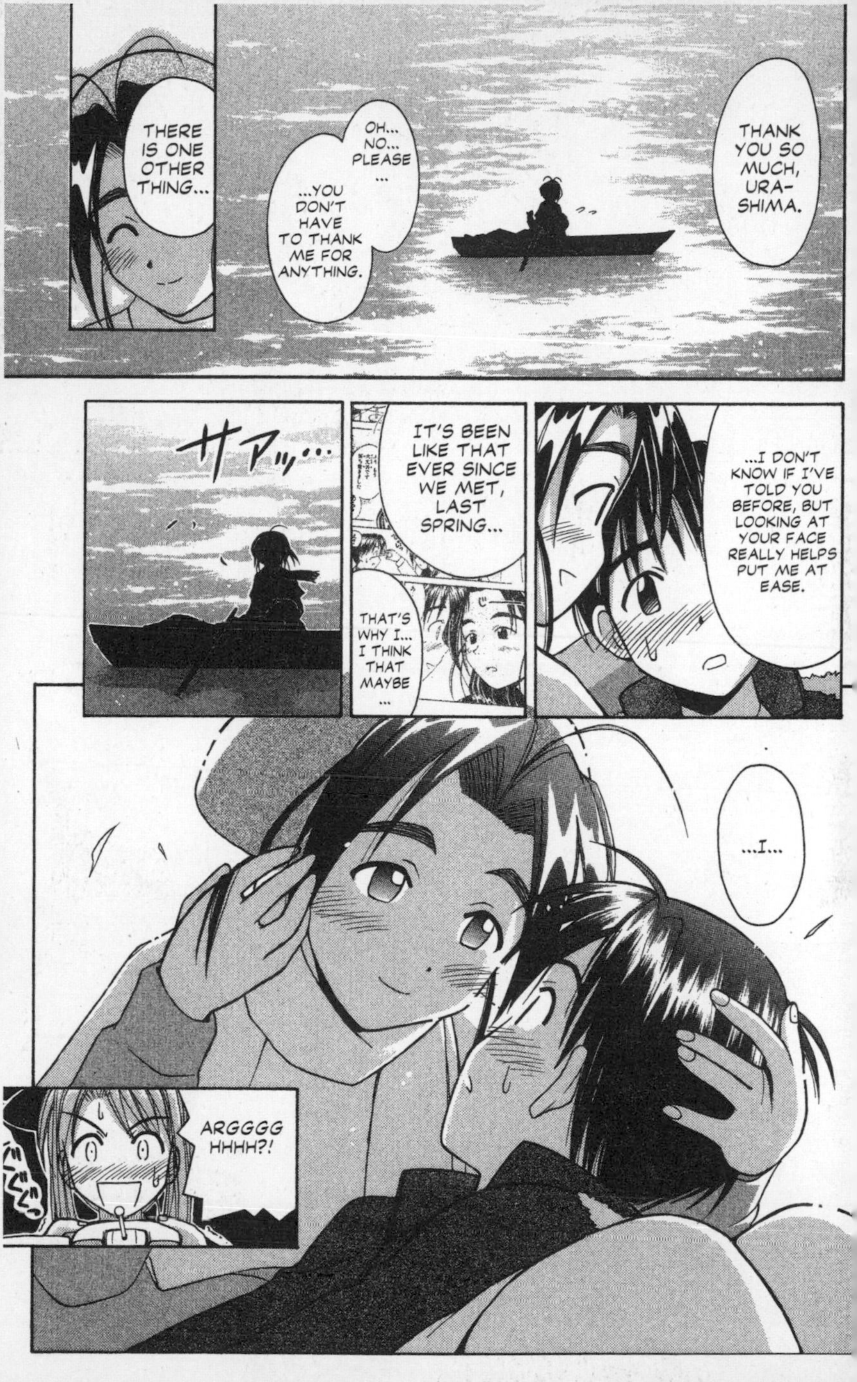
THANK YOU SO MUCH, URA-SHIMA.
OH... NO... PLEASE ...
...YOU DON'T HAVE TO THANK ME FOR ANYTHING.
THERE IS ONE OTHER THING...
...I DON'T KNOW IF I'VE TOLD YOU BEFORE, BUT LOOKING AT YOUR FACE REALLY HELPS PUT ME AT EASE.
IT'S BEEN LIKE THAT EVER SINCE WE MET, LAST SPRING...
THAT'S WHY I... I THINK THAT MAYBE ...
サアッ…
...I...
ARGGGG HHHH?!

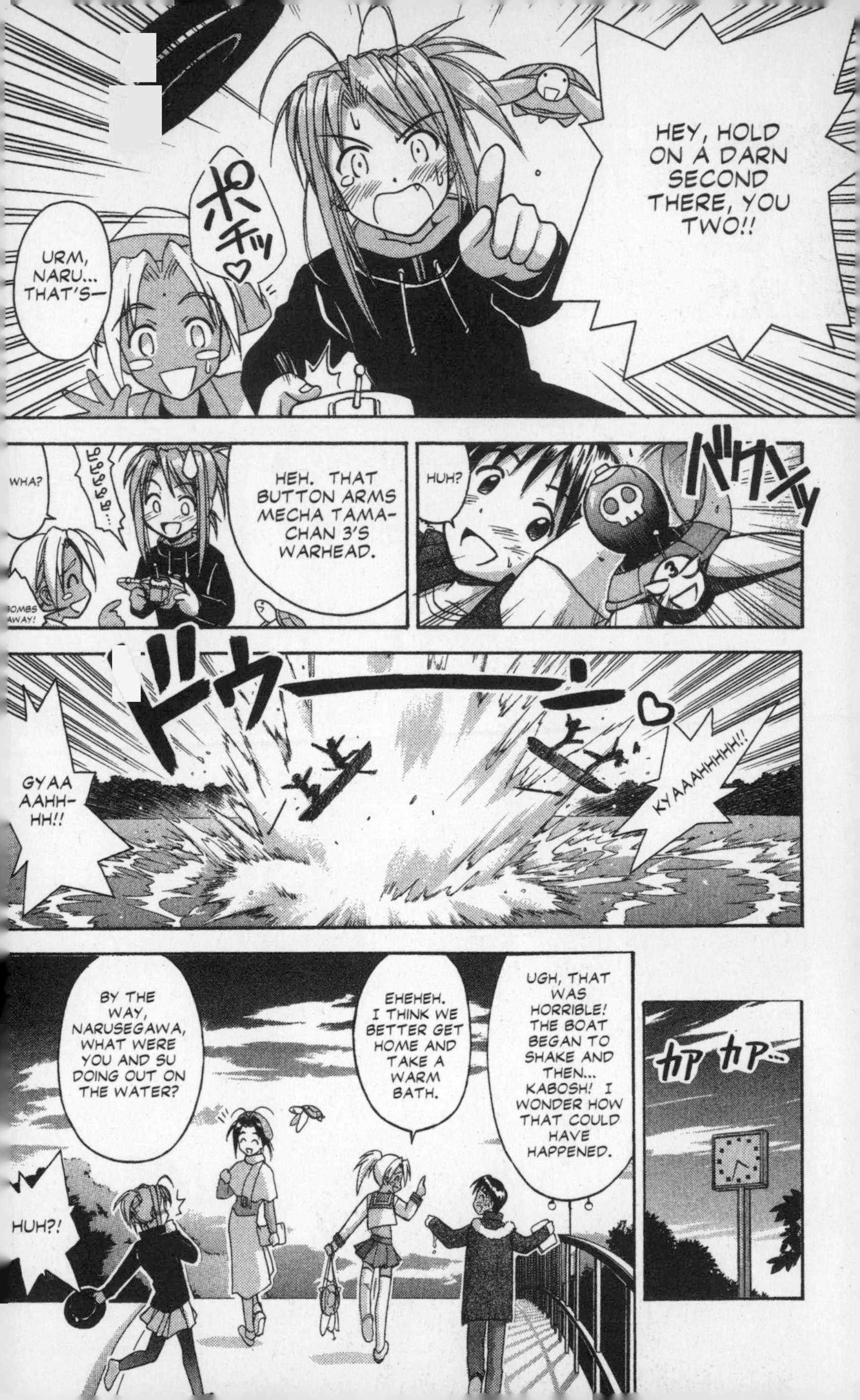
HEY, HOLD ON A DARN SECOND THERE, YOU TWO!!
ポチッ♡
URM, NARU... THAT'S—
バゴンッ
HUH?
HEH. THAT BUTTON ARMS MECHA TAMA-CHAN 3'S WARHEAD.
WHA?
BOMBS AWAY!
ドウーーン♡
KYAAAHHHHH!!
GYAA AAHH-HH!!
カア カア…
UGH, THAT WAS HORRIBLE! THE BOAT BEGAN TO SHAKE AND THEN... KABOSH! I WONDER HOW THAT COULD HAVE HAPPENED.
EHEHEH. I THINK WE BETTER GET HOME AND TAKE A WARM BATH.
BY THE WAY, NARUSEGAWA, WHAT WERE YOU AND SU DOING OUT ON THE WATER?
HUH?!

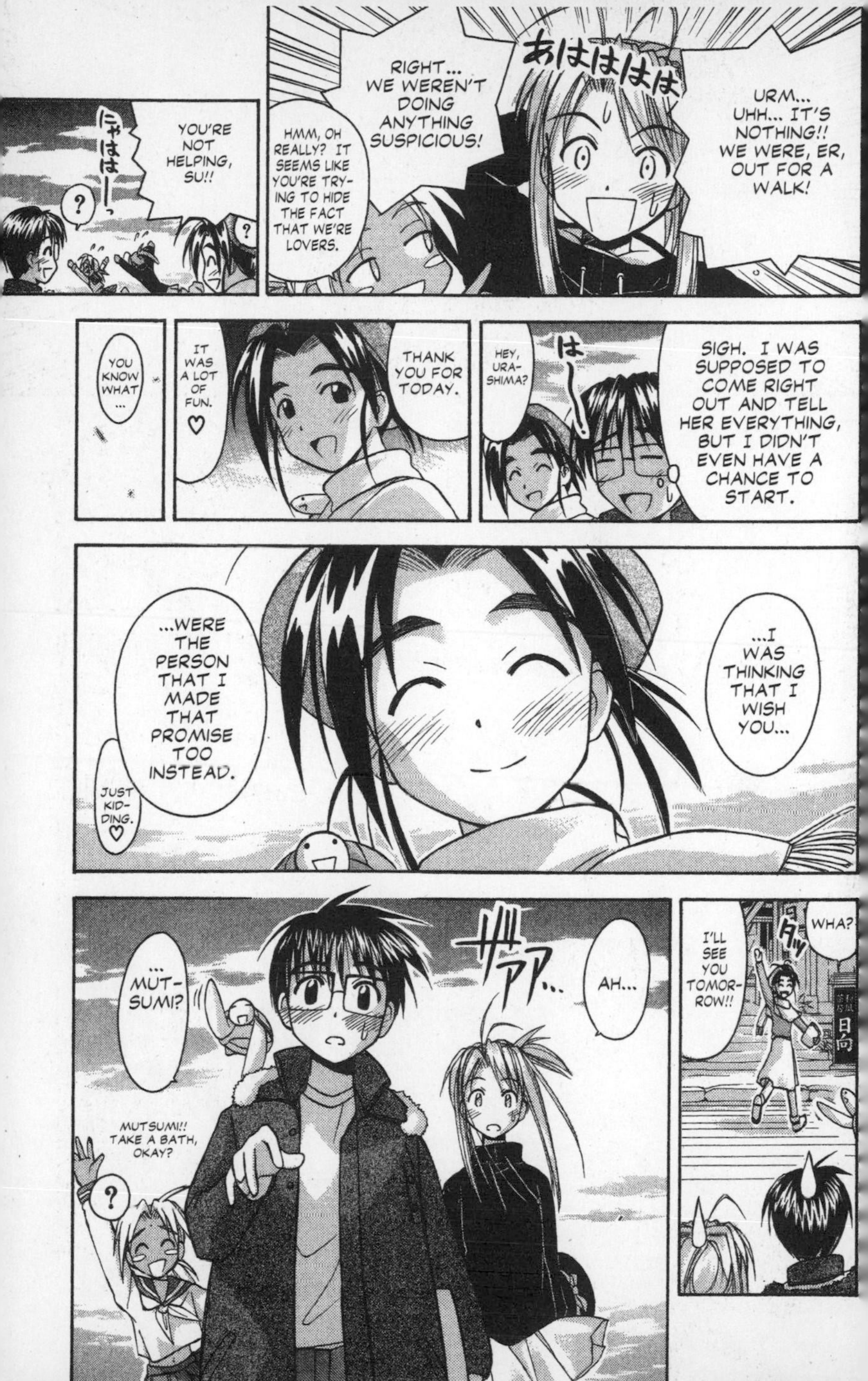
あははははは
URM... UHH... IT'S NOTHING!! WE WERE, ER, OUT FOR A WALK!
RIGHT... WE WEREN'T DOING ANYTHING SUSPICIOUS!
HMM, OH REALLY? IT SEEMS LIKE YOU'RE TRYING TO HIDE THE FACT THAT WE'RE LOVERS.
YOU'RE NOT HELPING, SU!!
にゃははーっ
?
?
SIGH. I WAS SUPPOSED TO COME RIGHT OUT AND TELL HER EVERYTHING, BUT I DIDN'T EVEN HAVE A CHANCE TO START.
は~
HEY, URASHIMA?
THANK YOU FOR TODAY.
IT WAS A LOT OF FUN. ♡
YOU KNOW WHAT...
...I WAS THINKING THAT I WISH YOU...
...WERE THE PERSON THAT I MADE THAT PROMISE TOO INSTEAD.
JUST KIDDING. ♡
WHA?
タッ
I'LL SEE YOU TOMORROW!!
日向
ザァア...
AH...
...MÜTSUMI?
MUTSUMI!! TAKE A BATH, OKAY?
?

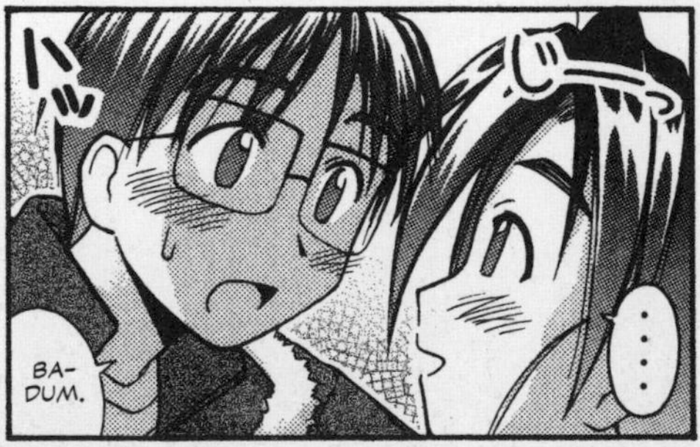

ハッ
....
BA-DUM.

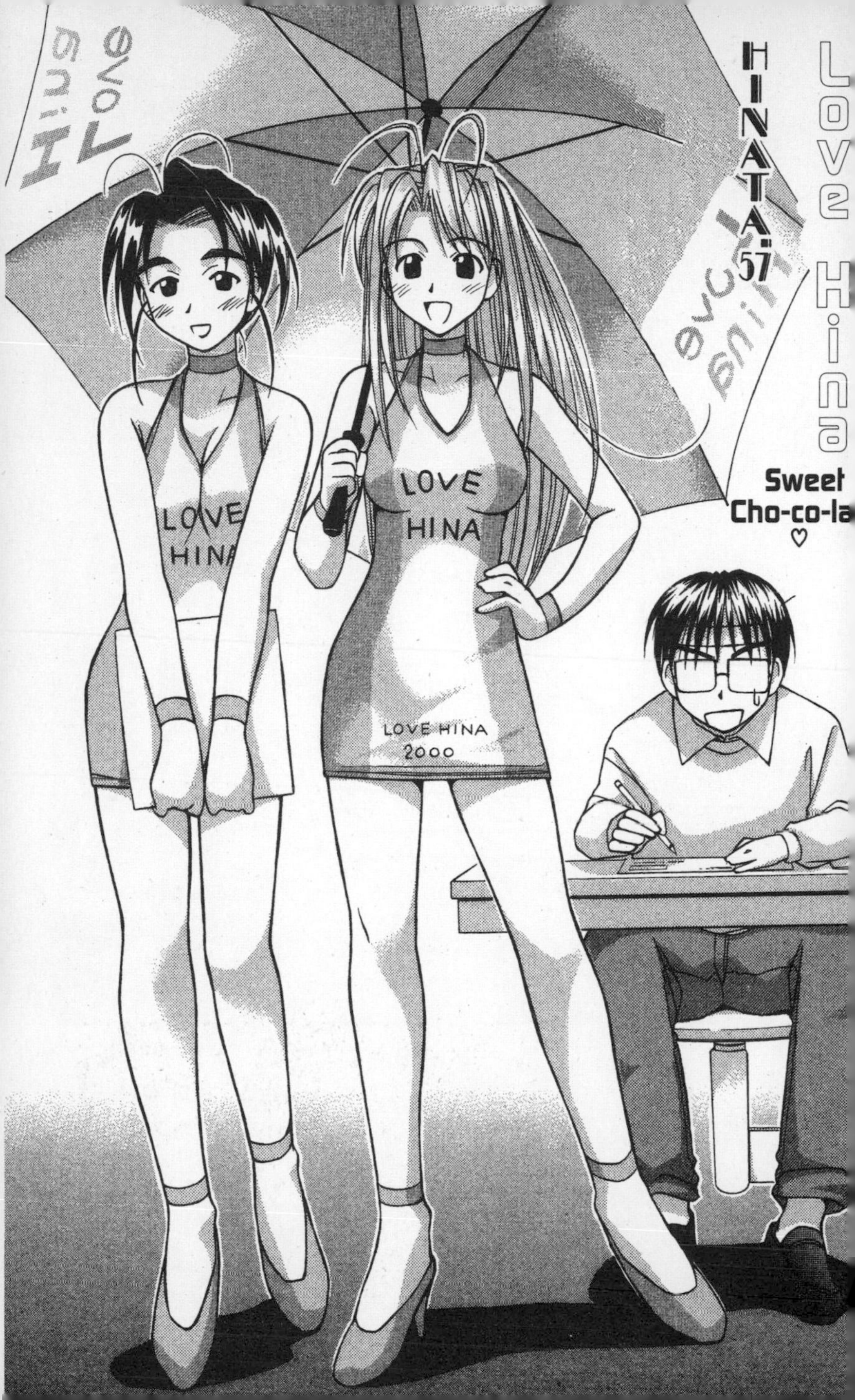
Love Hina
HINATA.57
Sweet Cho-co-la ♡
Love Hina
Love Hina
LOVE HINA
LOVE HINA
LOVE HINA 2000

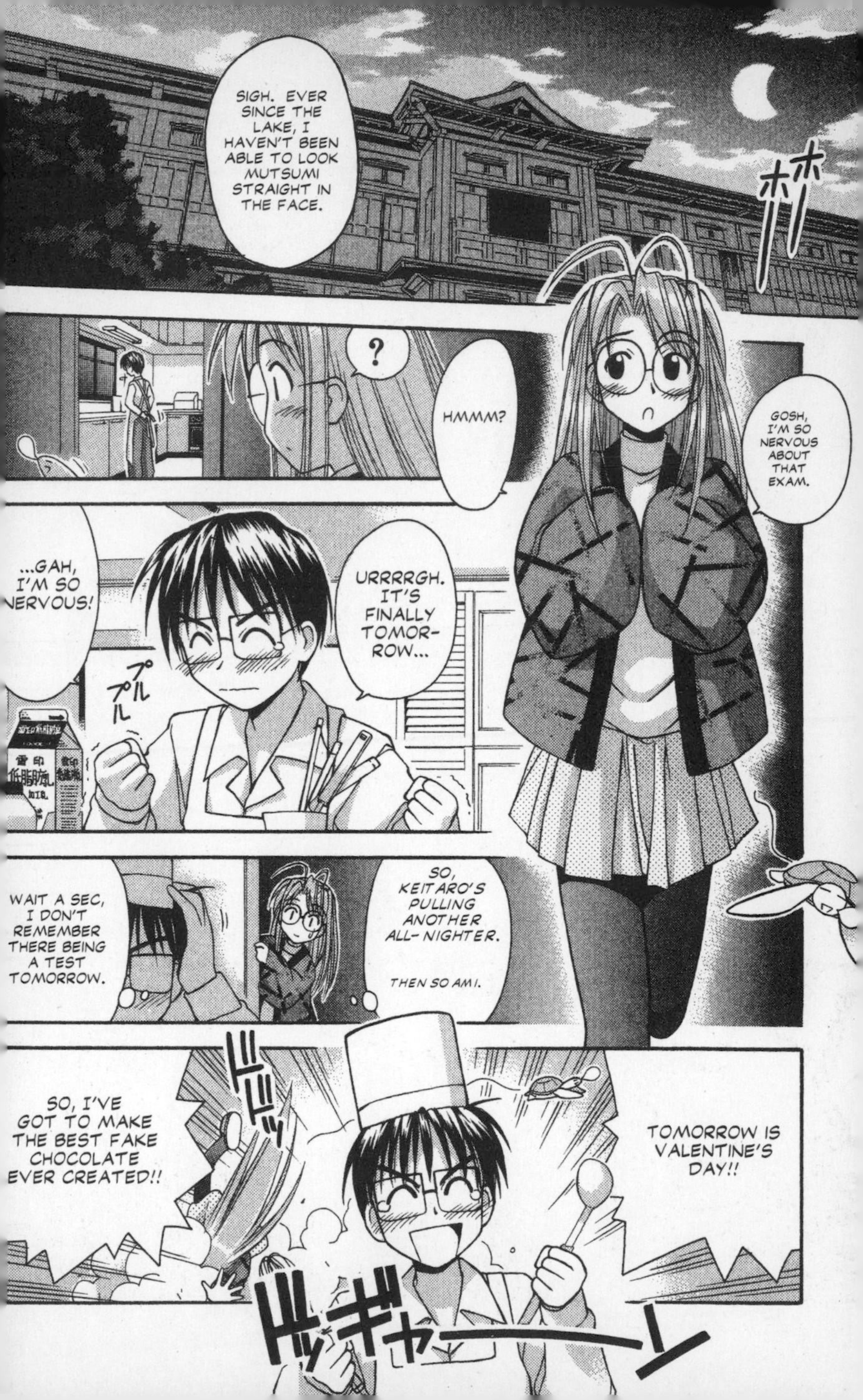

SIGH. EVER SINCE THE LAKE, I HAVEN'T BEEN ABLE TO LOOK MUTSUMI STRAIGHT IN THE FACE.
GOSH, I'M SO NERVOUS ABOUT THAT EXAM.
?
HMMM?
URRRRGH. IT'S FINALLY TOMOR-ROW...
...GAH, I'M SO NERVOUS!
プル
プル
SO, KEITARO'S PULLING ANOTHER ALL-NIGHTER.
THEN SO AM I.
WAIT A SEC, I DON'T REMEMBER THERE BEING A TEST TOMORROW.
TOMORROW IS VALENTINE'S DAY!!
SO, I'VE GOT TO MAKE THE BEST FAKE CHOCOLATE EVER CREATED!!
ドドドッ
ドッギャーーーン

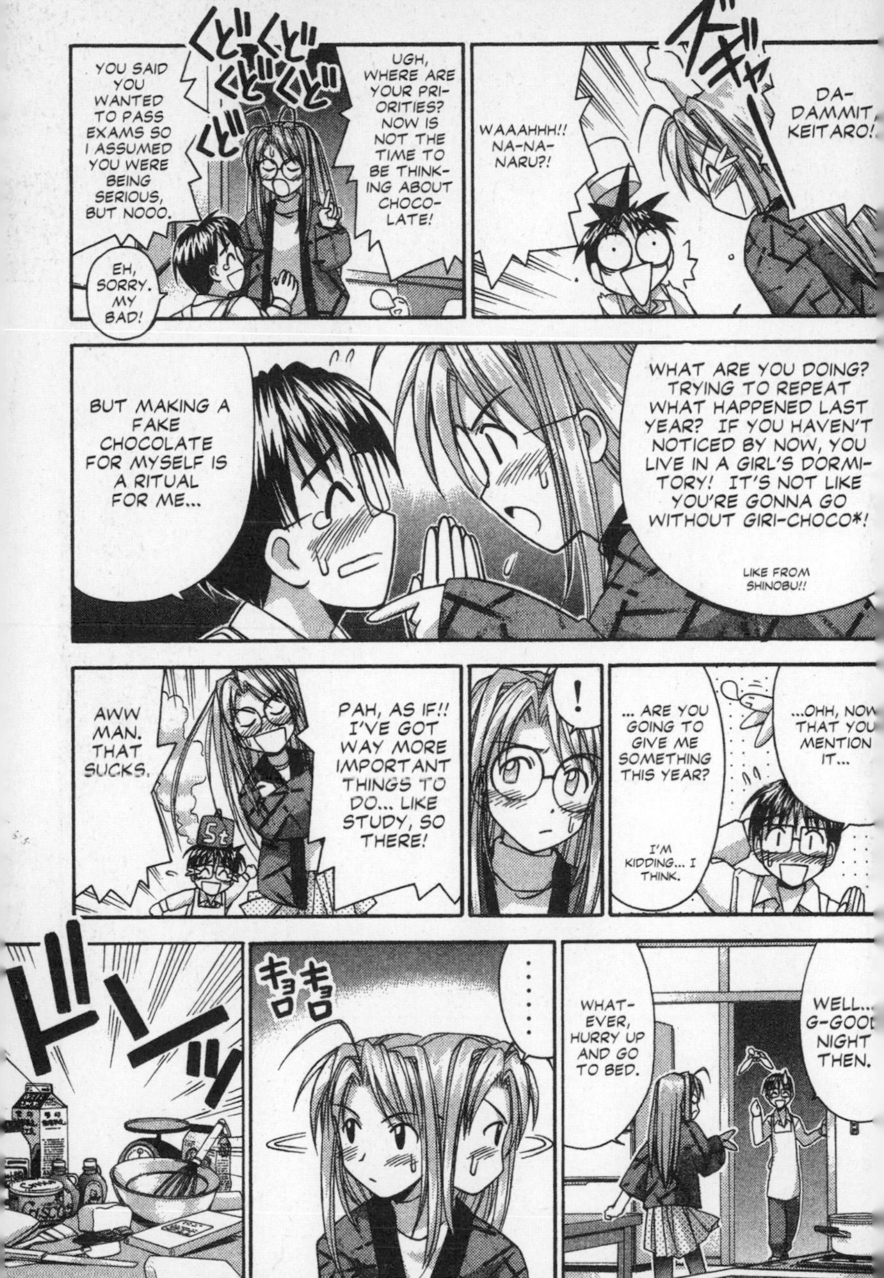
DA-DAMMIT, KEITARO!
WAAAHHH!! NA-NA-NARU?!
UGH, WHERE ARE YOUR PRI-ORITIES? NOW IS NOT THE TIME TO BE THINK-ING ABOUT CHOCO-LATE!
YOU SAID YOU WANTED TO PASS EXAMS SO I ASSUMED YOU WERE BEING SERIOUS, BUT NOOO.
EH, SORRY. MY BAD!
WHAT ARE YOU DOING? TRYING TO REPEAT WHAT HAPPENED LAST YEAR? IF YOU HAVEN'T NOTICED BY NOW, YOU LIVE IN A GIRL'S DORMI-TORY! IT'S NOT LIKE YOU'RE GONNA GO WITHOUT GIRI-CHOCO*!
LIKE FROM SHINOBU!!
BUT MAKING A FAKE CHOCOLATE FOR MYSELF IS A RITUAL FOR ME...
...OHH, NOW THAT YOU MENTION IT...
... ARE YOU GOING TO GIVE ME SOMETHING THIS YEAR?
I'M KIDDING... I THINK.
!
PAH, AS IF!! I'VE GOT WAY MORE IMPORTANT THINGS TO DO... LIKE STUDY, SO THERE!
AWW MAN. THAT SUCKS.
WELL... G-GOOD NIGHT THEN.
WHAT-EVER, HURRY UP AND GO TO BED.
......

* CHOCOLATE GIVEN TO FRIENDS AND ASSOCIATES IS KNOWN AS GIRI-CHOCO, WHILE CHOCOLATE GIVEN TO LOVERS AND PEOPLE YOU LIKE IS CALLED HONMEI-CHOCO.

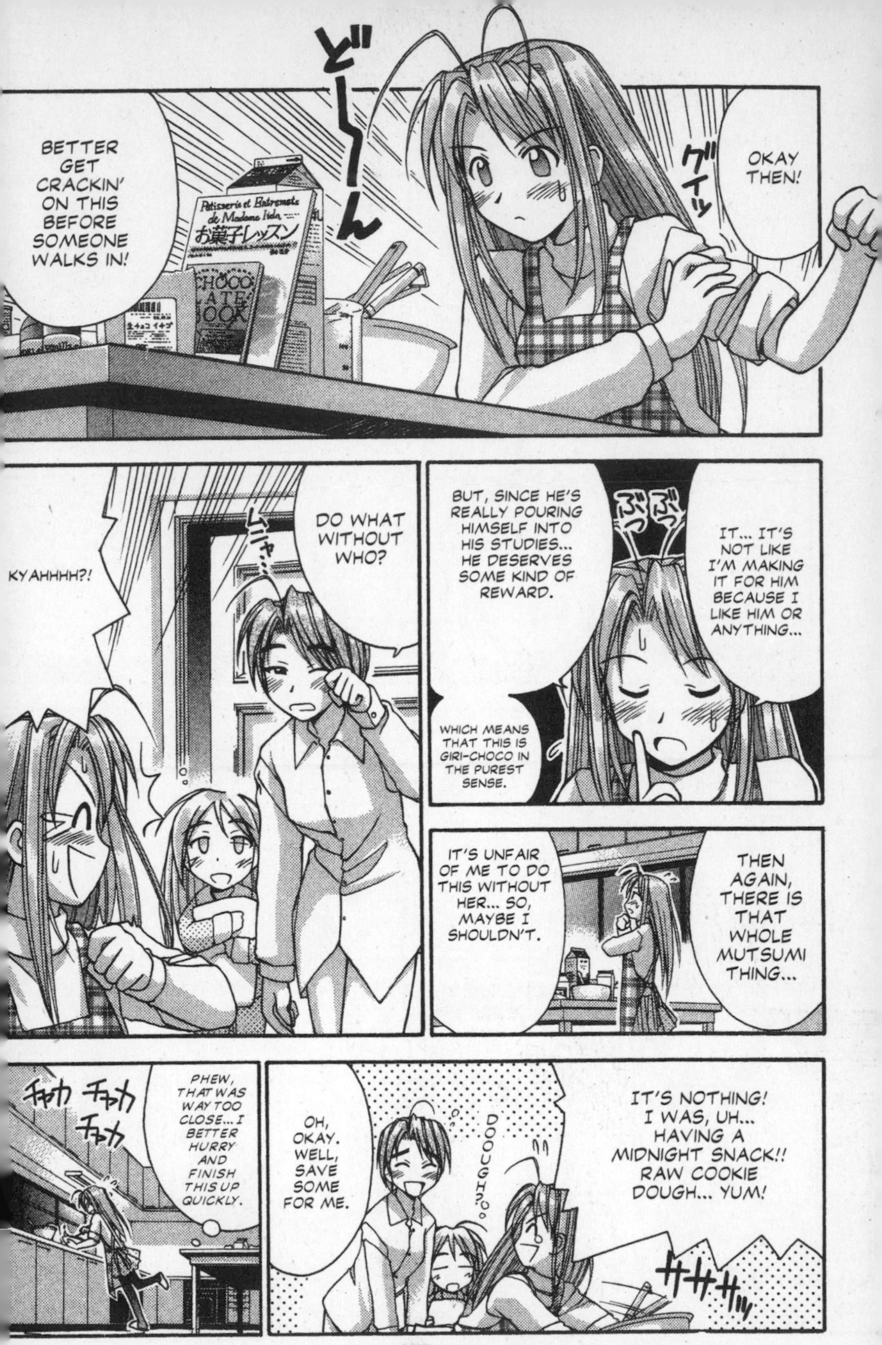
OKAY THEN!
グイッ
どーーん
BETTER GET CRACKIN' ON THIS BEFORE SOMEONE WALKS IN!
お菓子レッスン
IT... IT'S NOT LIKE I'M MAKING IT FOR HIM BECAUSE I LIKE HIM OR ANYTHING...
ぶつぶつ
BUT, SINCE HE'S REALLY POURING HIMSELF INTO HIS STUDIES... HE DESERVES SOME KIND OF REWARD.
WHICH MEANS THAT THIS IS GIRI-CHOCO IN THE PUREST SENSE.
THEN AGAIN, THERE IS THAT WHOLE MUTSUMI THING...
IT'S UNFAIR OF ME TO DO THIS WITHOUT HER... SO, MAYBE I SHOULDN'T.
DO WHAT WITHOUT WHO?
ムニャ...
KYAHHHH?!
IT'S NOTHING! I WAS, UH... HAVING A MIDNIGHT SNACK!! RAW COOKIE DOUGH... YUM!
サササッ
DOOUGH?
OH, OKAY. WELL, SAVE SOME FOR ME.
PHEW, THAT WAS WAY TOO CLOSE... I BETTER HURRY AND FINISH THIS UP QUICKLY.
チャカ チャカ チャカ

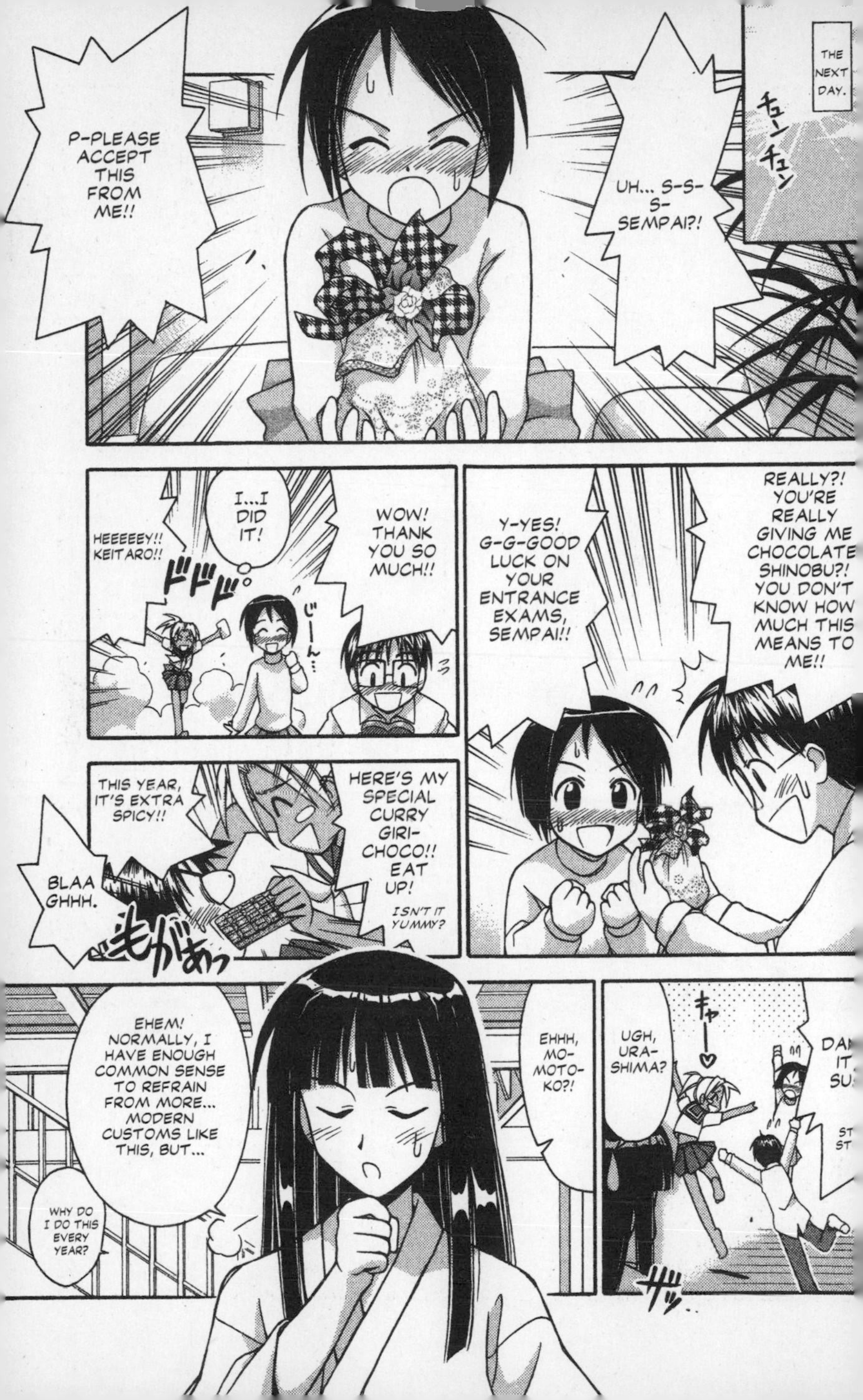
THE NEXT DAY.
チュンチュン
UH... S-S-S-SEMPAI?!
P-PLEASE ACCEPT THIS FROM ME!!
REALLY?! YOU'RE REALLY GIVING ME CHOCOLATE SHINOBU?! YOU DON'T KNOW HOW MUCH THIS MEANS TO ME!!
Y-YES! G-G-GOOD LUCK ON YOUR ENTRANCE EXAMS, SEMPAI!!
WOW! THANK YOU SO MUCH!!
I...I DID IT!
じーん…
HEEEEEY!! KEITARO!!
ドドド
HERE'S MY SPECIAL CURRY GIRI-CHOCO!! EAT UP!
ISN'T IT YUMMY?
THIS YEAR, IT'S EXTRA SPICY!!
BLAA GHHH.
もがあっ
キャー♥
UGH, URA-SHIMA?
EHHH, MO-MOTO-KO?!
ザッ..
EHEM! NORMALLY, I HAVE ENOUGH COMMON SENSE TO REFRAIN FROM MORE... MODERN CUSTOMS LIKE THIS, BUT...
WHY DO I DO THIS EVERY YEAR?

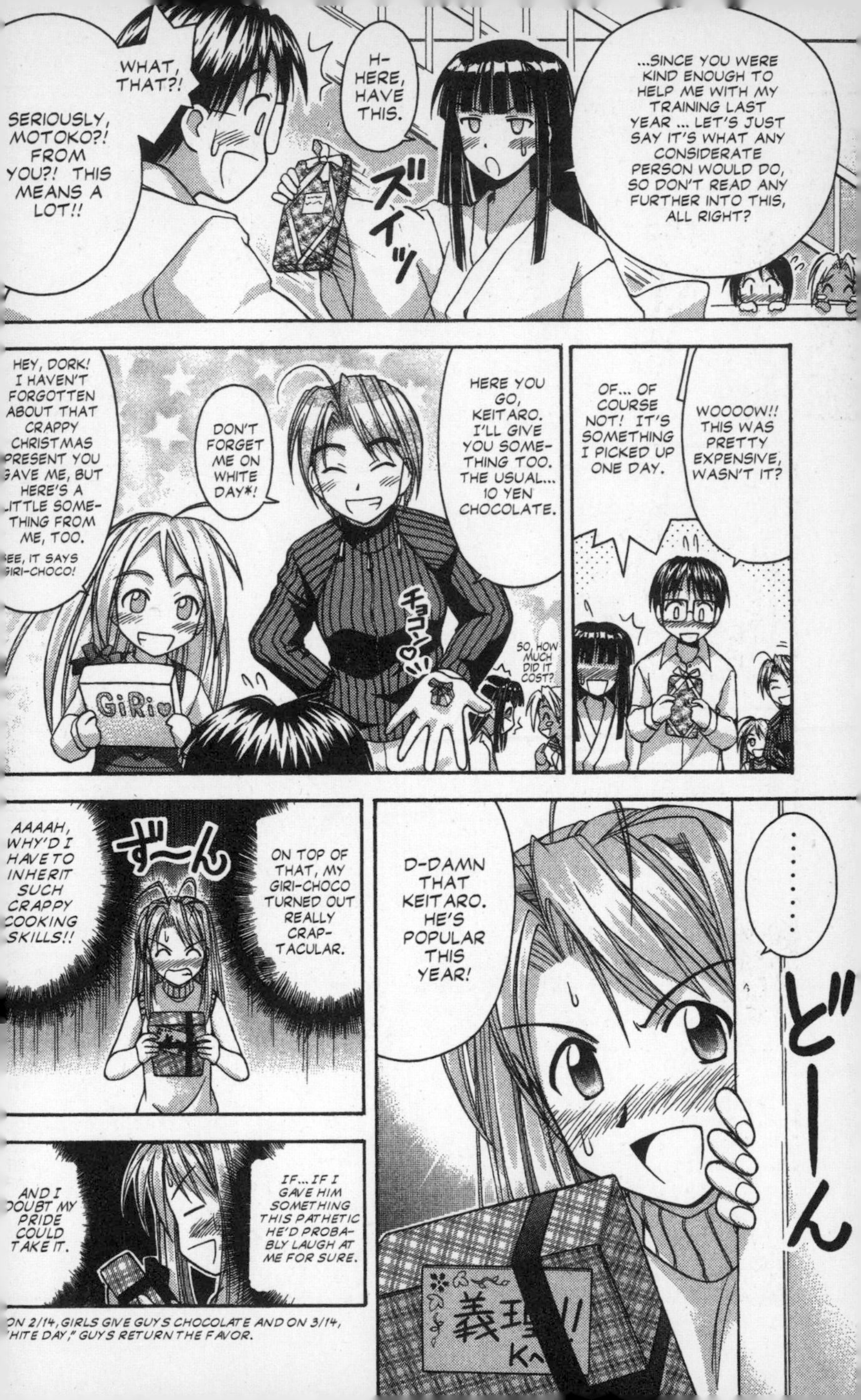
...SINCE YOU WERE KIND ENOUGH TO HELP ME WITH MY TRAINING LAST YEAR ... LET'S JUST SAY IT'S WHAT ANY CONSIDERATE PERSON WOULD DO, SO DON'T READ ANY FURTHER INTO THIS, ALL RIGHT?
H-HERE, HAVE THIS.
ズイッ
WHAT, THAT?!
SERIOUSLY, MOTOKO?! FROM YOU?! THIS MEANS A LOT!!
WOOOOW!! THIS WAS PRETTY EXPENSIVE, WASN'T IT?
OF... OF COURSE NOT! IT'S SOMETHING I PICKED UP ONE DAY.
HERE YOU GO, KEITARO. I'LL GIVE YOU SOMETHING TOO. THE USUAL... 10 YEN CHOCOLATE.
DON'T FORGET ME ON WHITE DAY*!
HEY, DORK! I HAVEN'T FORGOTTEN ABOUT THAT CRAPPY CHRISTMAS PRESENT YOU GAVE ME, BUT HERE'S A LITTLE SOMETHING FROM ME, TOO.
SEE, IT SAYS GIRI-CHOCO!
チョコン
SO, HOW MUCH DID IT COST?
GiRi
......
どーん
D-DAMN THAT KEITARO. HE'S POPULAR THIS YEAR!
義理
ON TOP OF THAT, MY GIRI-CHOCO TURNED OUT REALLY CRAP-TACULAR.
ずーん
AAAAH, WHY'D I HAVE TO INHERIT SUCH CRAPPY COOKING SKILLS!!
IF... IF I GAVE HIM SOMETHING THIS PATHETIC HE'D PROBABLY LAUGH AT ME FOR SURE.
AND I DOUBT MY PRIDE COULD TAKE IT.

*ON 2/14, GIRLS GIVE GUYS CHOCOLATE AND ON 3/14, "WHITE DAY," GUYS RETURN THE FAVOR.

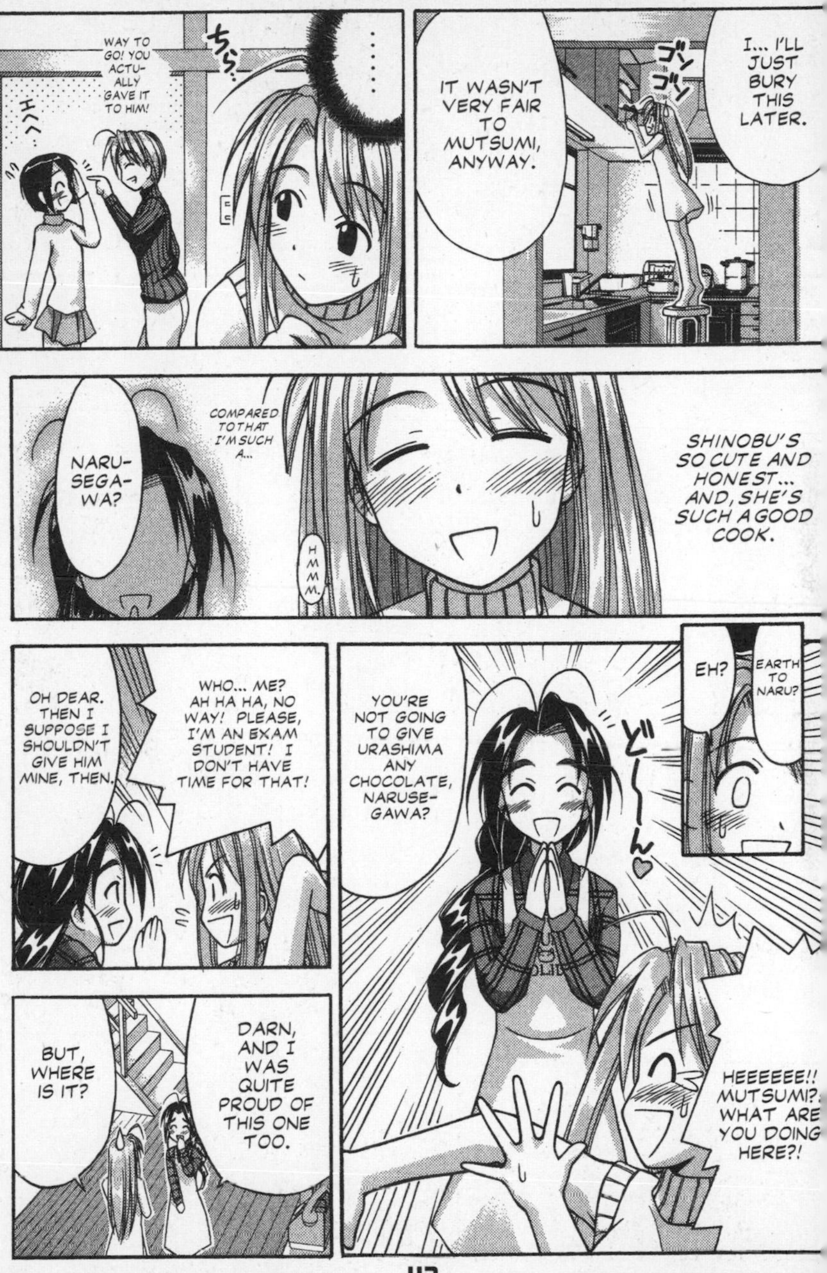
I... I'LL JUST BURY THIS LATER.
ゴンゴン
IT WASN'T VERY FAIR TO MUTSUMI, ANYWAY.
ちら
......
WAY TO GO! YOU ACTU-ALLY GAVE IT TO HIM!
エヘヘ
SHINOBU'S SO CUTE AND HONEST... AND, SHE'S SUCH A GOOD COOK.
COMPARED TO THAT I'M SUCH A...
HMMM.
NARU-SEGA-WA?
EARTH TO NARU?
EH?
HEEEEEE!! MUTSUMI?! WHAT ARE YOU DOING HERE?!
どーん
YOU'RE NOT GOING TO GIVE URASHIMA ANY CHOCOLATE, NARUSE-GAWA?
WHO... ME? AH HA HA, NO WAY! PLEASE, I'M AN EXAM STUDENT! I DON'T HAVE TIME FOR THAT!
OH DEAR. THEN I SUPPOSE I SHOULDN'T GIVE HIM MINE, THEN.
DARN, AND I WAS QUITE PROUD OF THIS ONE TOO.
BUT, WHERE IS IT?

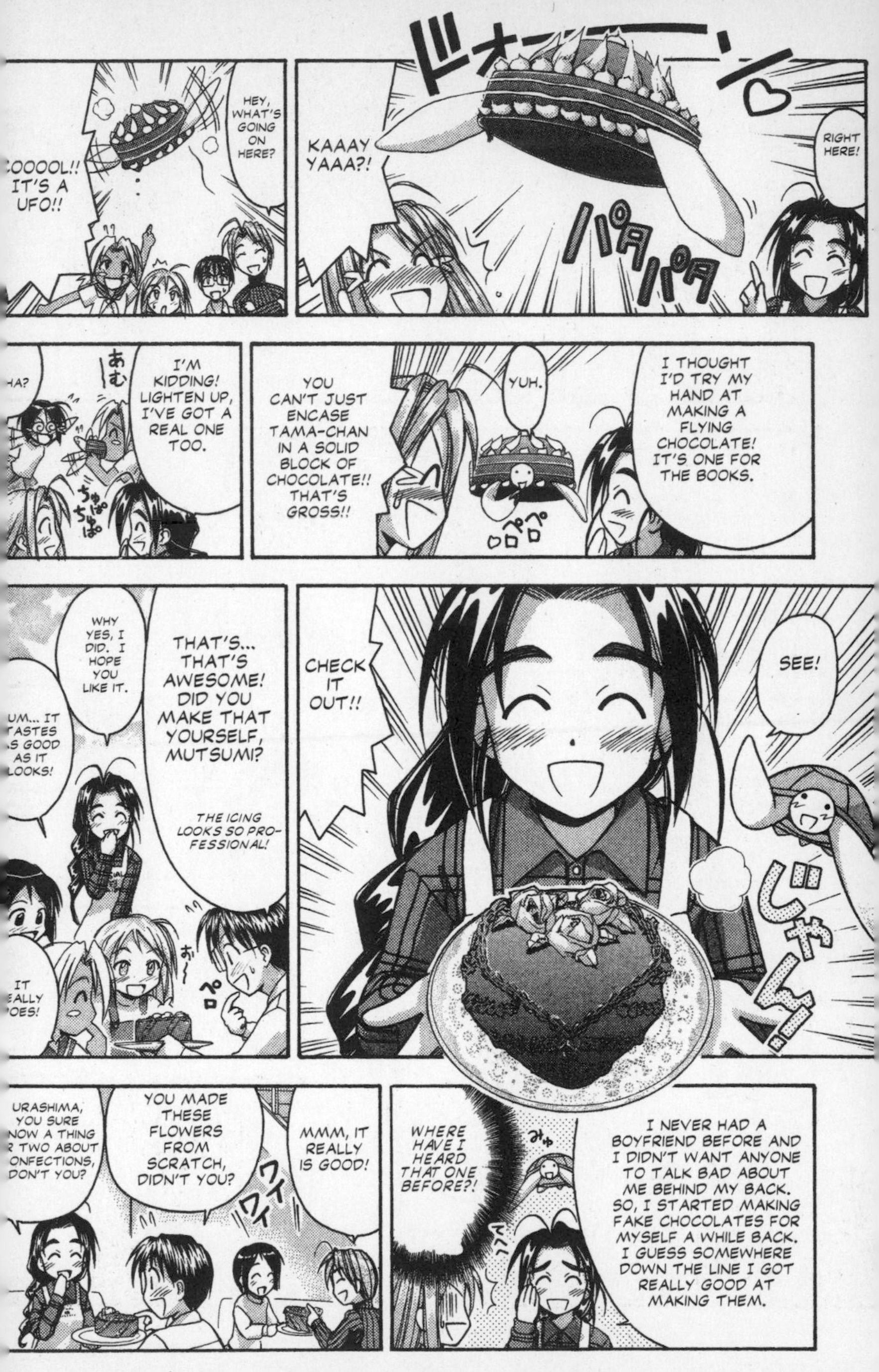
ドオーーーン
RIGHT HERE!
KAAAY YAAA?!
パタパタ
HEY, WHAT'S GOING ON HERE?
OOOOL!! IT'S A UFO!!
I THOUGHT I'D TRY MY HAND AT MAKING A FLYING CHOCOLATE! IT'S ONE FOR THE BOOKS.
YUH.
YOU CAN'T JUST ENCASE TAMA-CHAN IN A SOLID BLOCK OF CHOCOLATE!! THAT'S GROSS!!
ペロペロ
I'M KIDDING! LIGHTEN UP, I'VE GOT A REAL ONE TOO.
あむ
HA?
ちゅぱちゅぱ
SEE!
CHECK IT OUT!!
じゃ〜ん!
THAT'S... THAT'S AWESOME! DID YOU MAKE THAT YOURSELF, MUTSUMI?
WHY YES, I DID. I HOPE YOU LIKE IT.
THE ICING LOOKS SO PRO-FESSIONAL!
UM... IT TASTES GOOD AS IT LOOKS!
おー
ペロ
IT EALLY OES!
I NEVER HAD A BOYFRIEND BEFORE AND I DIDN'T WANT ANYONE TO TALK BAD ABOUT ME BEHIND MY BACK. SO, I STARTED MAKING FAKE CHOCOLATES FOR MYSELF A WHILE BACK. I GUESS SOMEWHERE DOWN THE LINE I GOT REALLY GOOD AT MAKING THEM.
みゅ
WHERE HAVE I HEARD THAT ONE BEFORE?!
MMM, IT REALLY IS GOOD!
ワイワイ
YOU MADE THESE FLOWERS FROM SCRATCH, DIDN'T YOU?
URASHIMA, YOU SURE NOW A THING R TWO ABOUT ONFECTIONS, DON'T YOU?

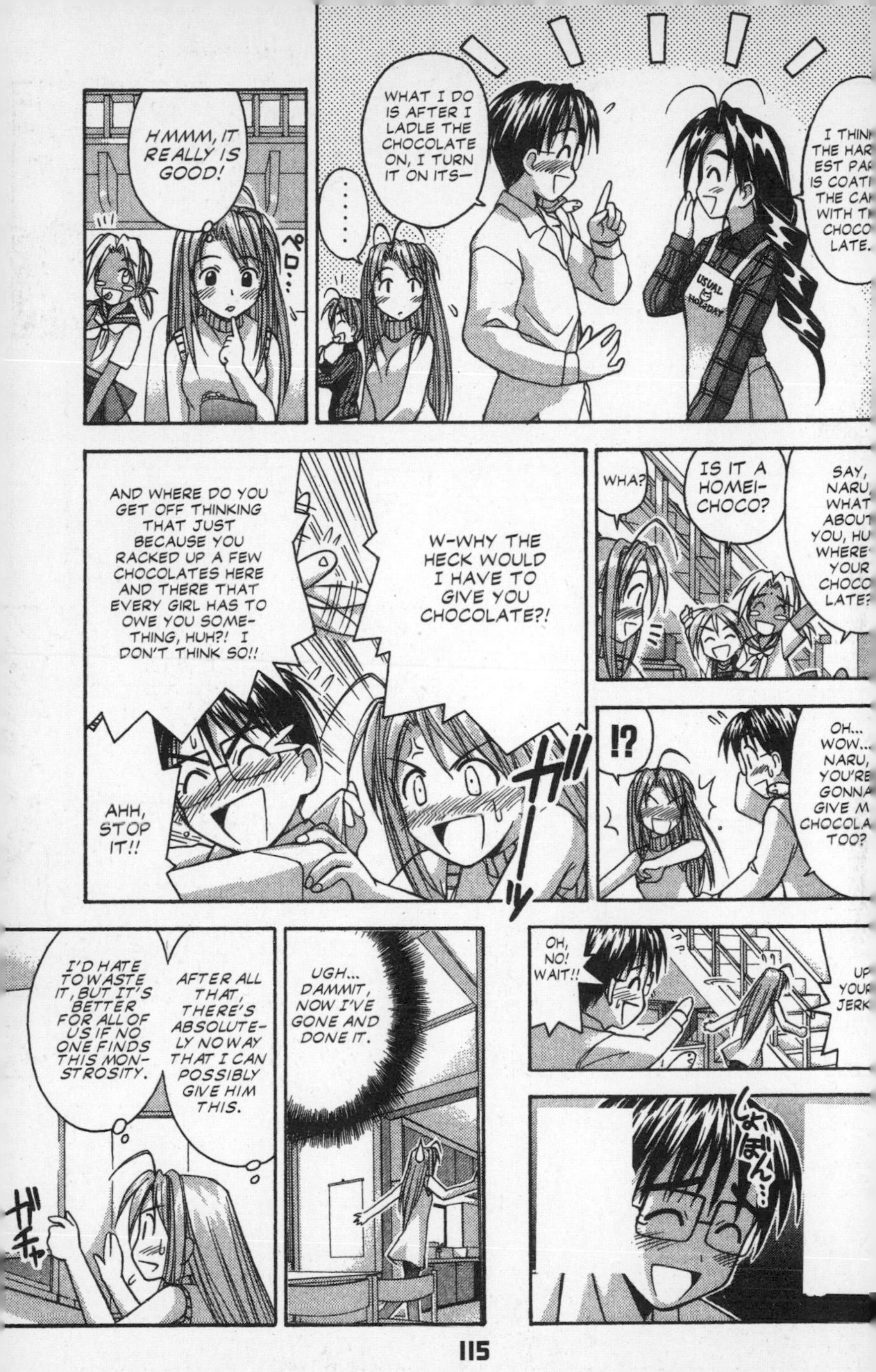
I THINI THE HAR EST PAR IS COATI THE CA WITH TH CHOCO LATE.
WHAT I DO IS AFTER I LADLE THE CHOCOLATE ON, I TURN IT ON ITS—
......
HMMM, IT REALLY IS GOOD!
ペロ...
SAY, NARU, WHAT ABOUT YOU, HU WHERE' YOUR CHOCO LATE?
IS IT A HOMEI-CHOCO?
WHA?
OH... WOW... NARU, YOU'RE GONNA GIVE M CHOCOLA TOO?
!?
W-WHY THE HECK WOULD I HAVE TO GIVE YOU CHOCOLATE?!
AND WHERE DO YOU GET OFF THINKING THAT JUST BECAUSE YOU RACKED UP A FEW CHOCOLATES HERE AND THERE THAT EVERY GIRL HAS TO OWE YOU SOMETHING, HUH?! I DON'T THINK SO!!
AHH, STOP IT!!
UP YOUR JERK
OH, NO! WAIT!!
しょぼん...
UGH... DAMMIT, NOW I'VE GONE AND DONE IT.
AFTER ALL THAT, THERE'S ABSOLUTELY NO WAY THAT I CAN POSSIBLY GIVE HIM THIS.
I'D HATE TO WASTE IT, BUT IT'S BETTER FOR ALL OF US IF NO ONE FINDS THIS MONSTROSITY.
ガチャ

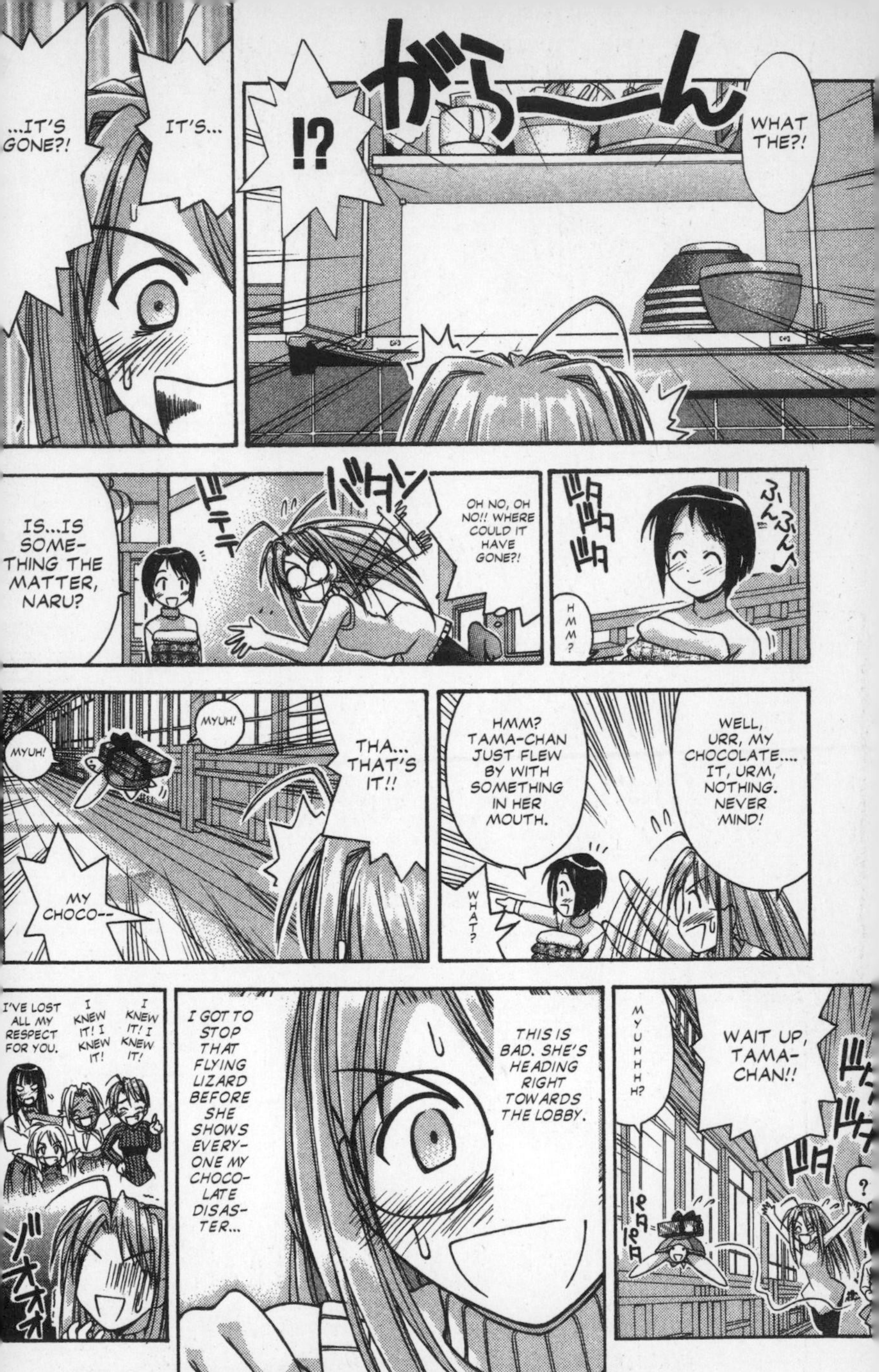
がら〜〜ん
WHAT THE?!
!?
IT'S...
...IT'S GONE?!
ふんふん♪
HMM?
バタン
OH NO, OH NO!! WHERE COULD IT HAVE GONE?!
IS...IS SOMETHING THE MATTER, NARU?
WELL, URR, MY CHOCOLATE.... IT, URM, NOTHING. NEVER MIND!
HMM? TAMA-CHAN JUST FLEW BY WITH SOMETHING IN HER MOUTH.
WHAT?
THA... THAT'S IT!!
MYUH!
MYUH!
MY CHOCO--
WAIT UP, TAMA-CHAN!!
MYUHHHH?
?
THIS IS BAD. SHE'S HEADING RIGHT TOWARDS THE LOBBY.
I GOT TO STOP THAT FLYING LIZARD BEFORE SHE SHOWS EVERYONE MY CHOCOLATE DISASTER...
I KNEW IT! I KNEW IT!
I KNEW IT! I KNEW IT!
I'VE LOST ALL MY RESPECT FOR YOU.

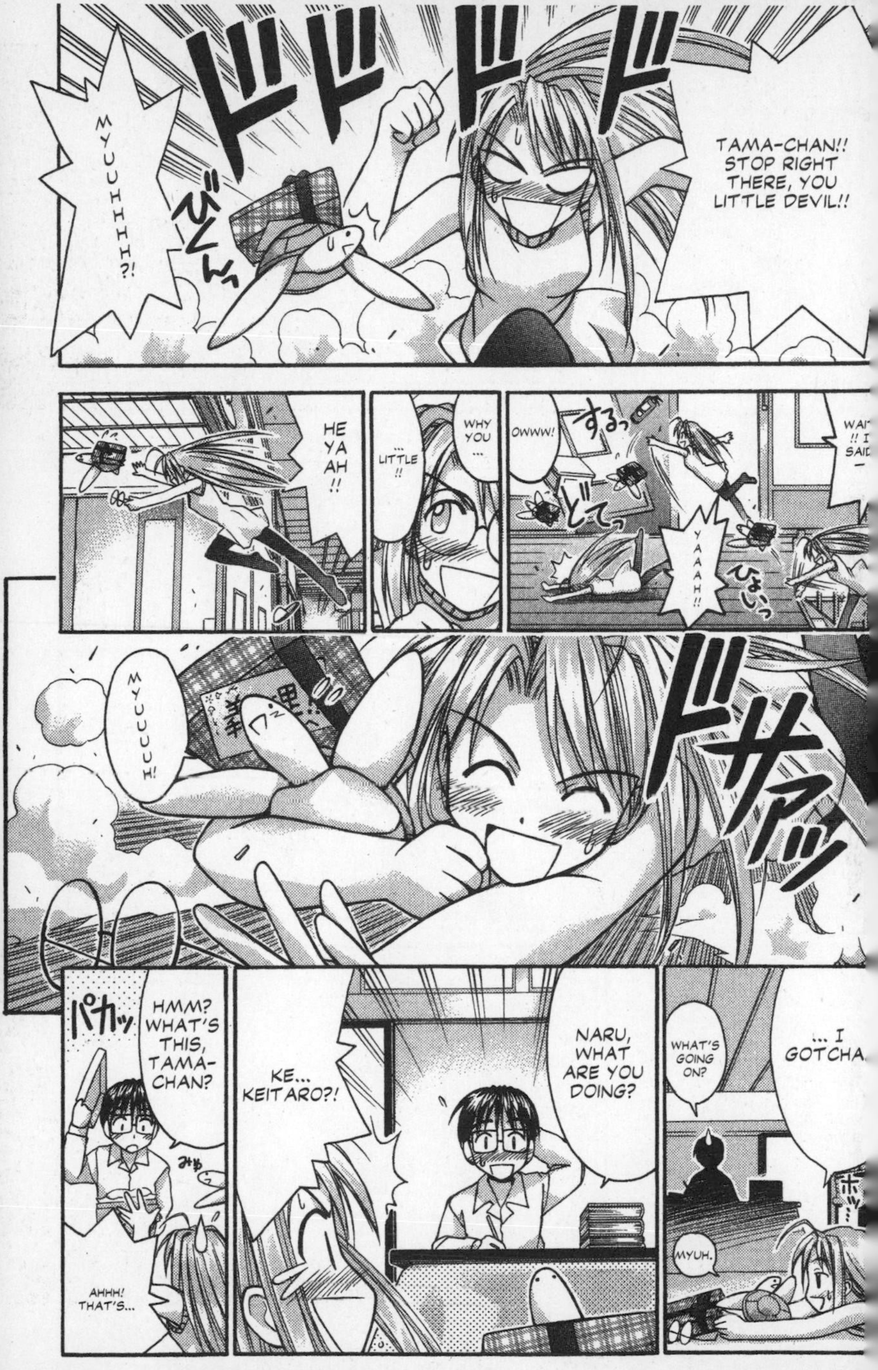

ドドドド
TAMA-CHAN!! STOP RIGHT THERE, YOU LITTLE DEVIL!!
びくんっ
MYUUHHHHH?!
WAIT!! I SAID—
するっ
OWWW!
どてっ
YAAAH!!
ひょいっ
WHY YOU ...
... LITTLE !!
HEYAAH!!
ドサアッ
MYUUUUH!
... I GOTCHA
WHAT'S GOING ON?
ホッ…
MYUH.
NARU, WHAT ARE YOU DOING?
KE... KEITARO?!
パカッ
HMM? WHAT'S THIS, TAMA-CHAN?
みゅ
AHHH! THAT'S...

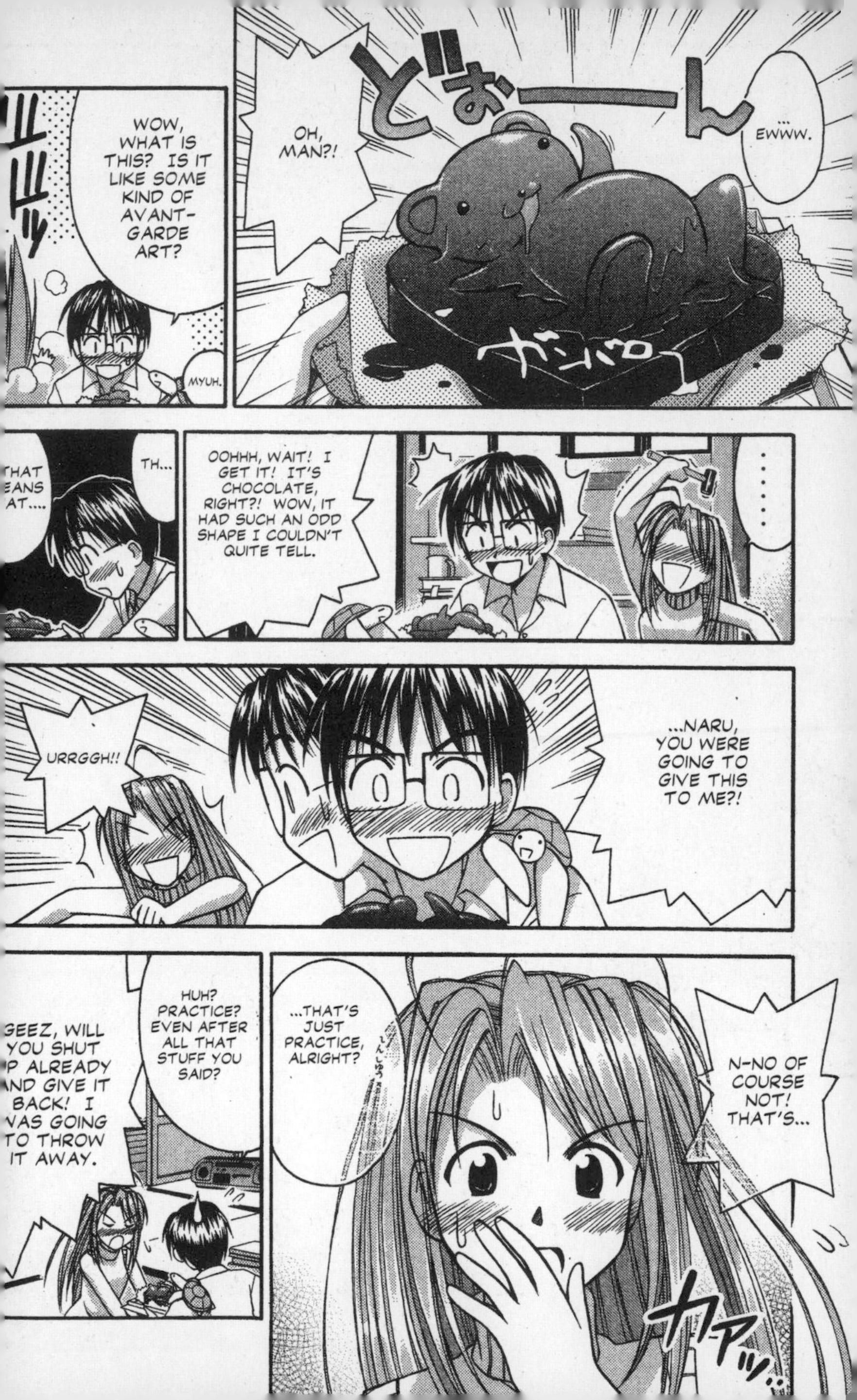
どぉーーん
...EWWW.
OH, MAN?!
WOW, WHAT IS THIS? IS IT LIKE SOME KIND OF AVANT-GARDE ART?
MYUH.
......
OOHHH, WAIT! I GET IT! IT'S CHOCOLATE, RIGHT?! WOW, IT HAD SUCH AN ODD SHAPE I COULDN'T QUITE TELL.
TH...
THAT EANS AT....
...NARU, YOU WERE GOING TO GIVE THIS TO ME?!
URRGGH!!
N-NO OF COURSE NOT! THAT'S...
...THAT'S JUST PRACTICE, ALRIGHT?
カアッ
HUH? PRACTICE? EVEN AFTER ALL THAT STUFF YOU SAID?
GEEZ, WILL YOU SHUT P ALREADY ND GIVE IT BACK! I VAS GOING TO THROW IT AWAY.

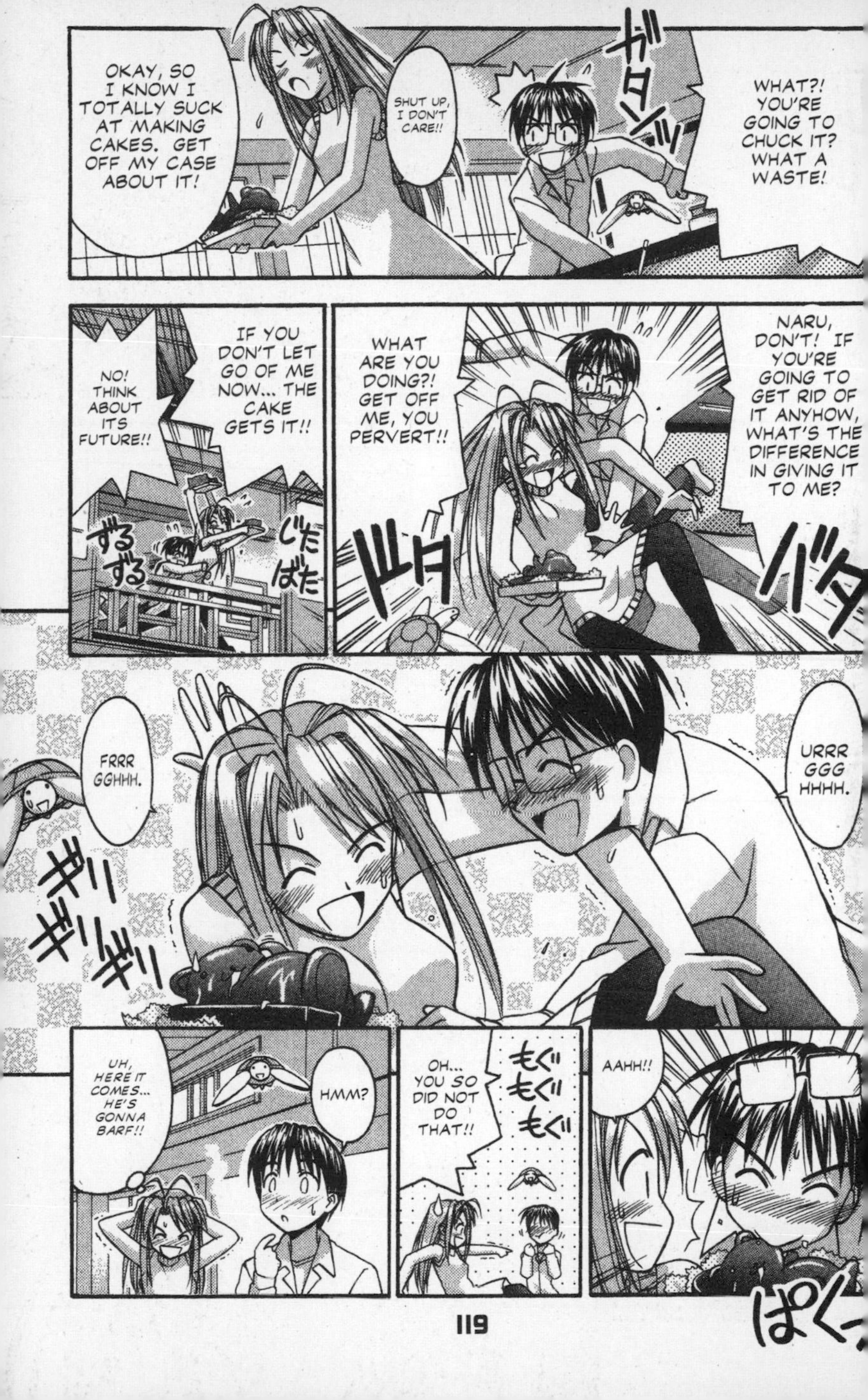

ガタンッ
WHAT?! YOU'RE GOING TO CHUCK IT? WHAT A WASTE!
SHUT UP, I DON'T CARE!!
OKAY, SO I KNOW I TOTALLY SUCK AT MAKING CAKES. GET OFF MY CASE ABOUT IT!
NARU, DON'T! IF YOU'RE GOING TO GET RID OF IT ANYHOW, WHAT'S THE DIFFERENCE IN GIVING IT TO ME?
バタ
WHAT ARE YOU DOING?! GET OFF ME, YOU PERVERT!!
ドタ
IF YOU DON'T LET GO OF ME NOW... THE CAKE GETS IT!!
NO! THINK ABOUT ITS FUTURE!!
じたばた
ずるずる
URRR GGG HHHH.
FRRR GGHHH.
ギリギリ
AAHH!!
ぱくっ
もぐもぐもぐ
OH... YOU SO DID NOT DO THAT!!
HMM?
UH, HERE IT COMES... HE'S GONNA BARF!!

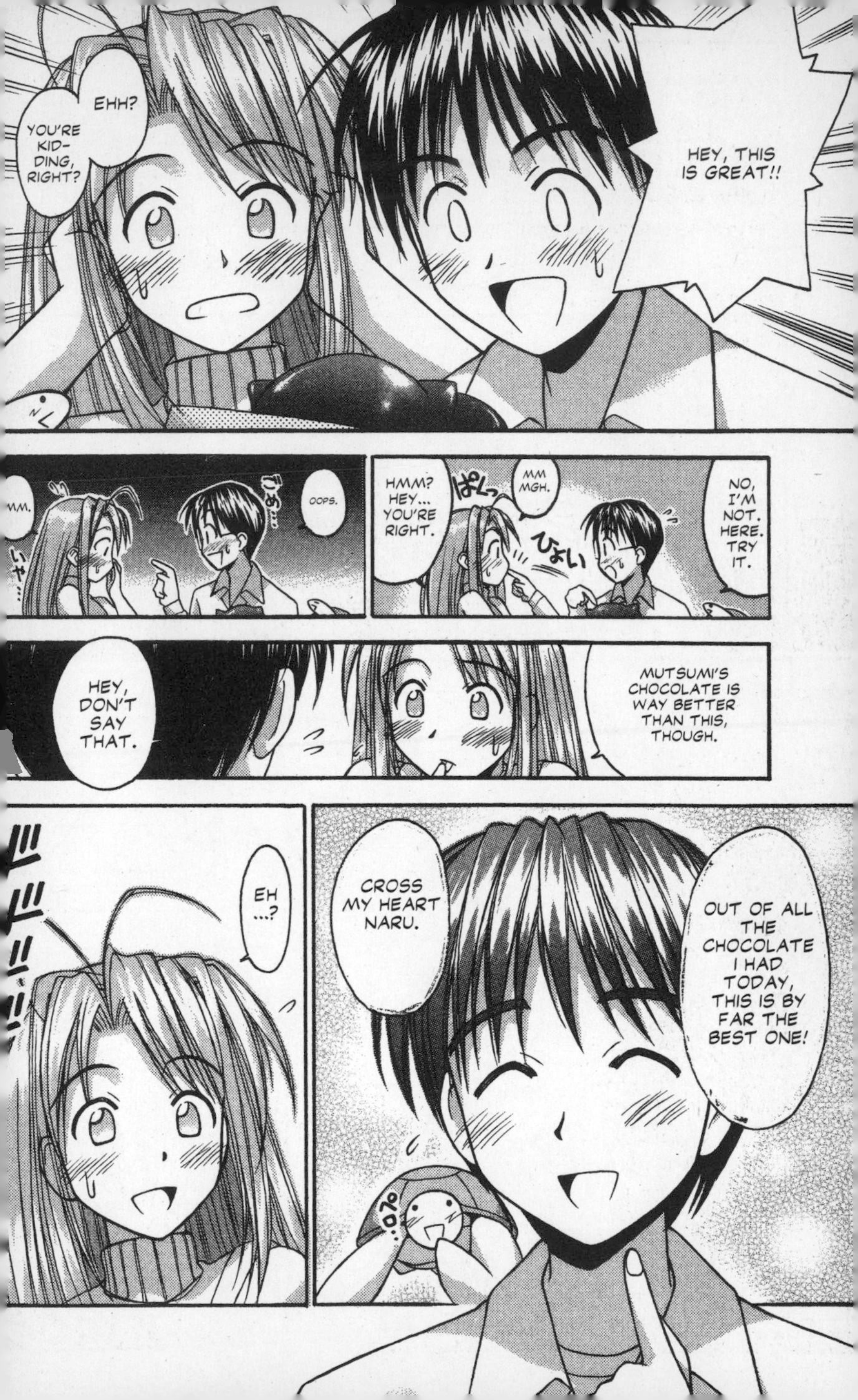
HEY, THIS IS GREAT!!
EHH? YOU'RE KID-DING, RIGHT?
NO, I'M NOT. HERE. TRY IT.
ひょい
MM MGH.
ぱくっ
HMM? HEY... YOU'RE RIGHT.
OOPS.
MM.
MUTSUMI'S CHOCOLATE IS WAY BETTER THAN THIS, THOUGH.
HEY, DON'T SAY THAT.
OUT OF ALL THE CHOCOLATE I HAD TODAY, THIS IS BY FAR THE BEST ONE!
CROSS MY HEART NARU.
EH ...?

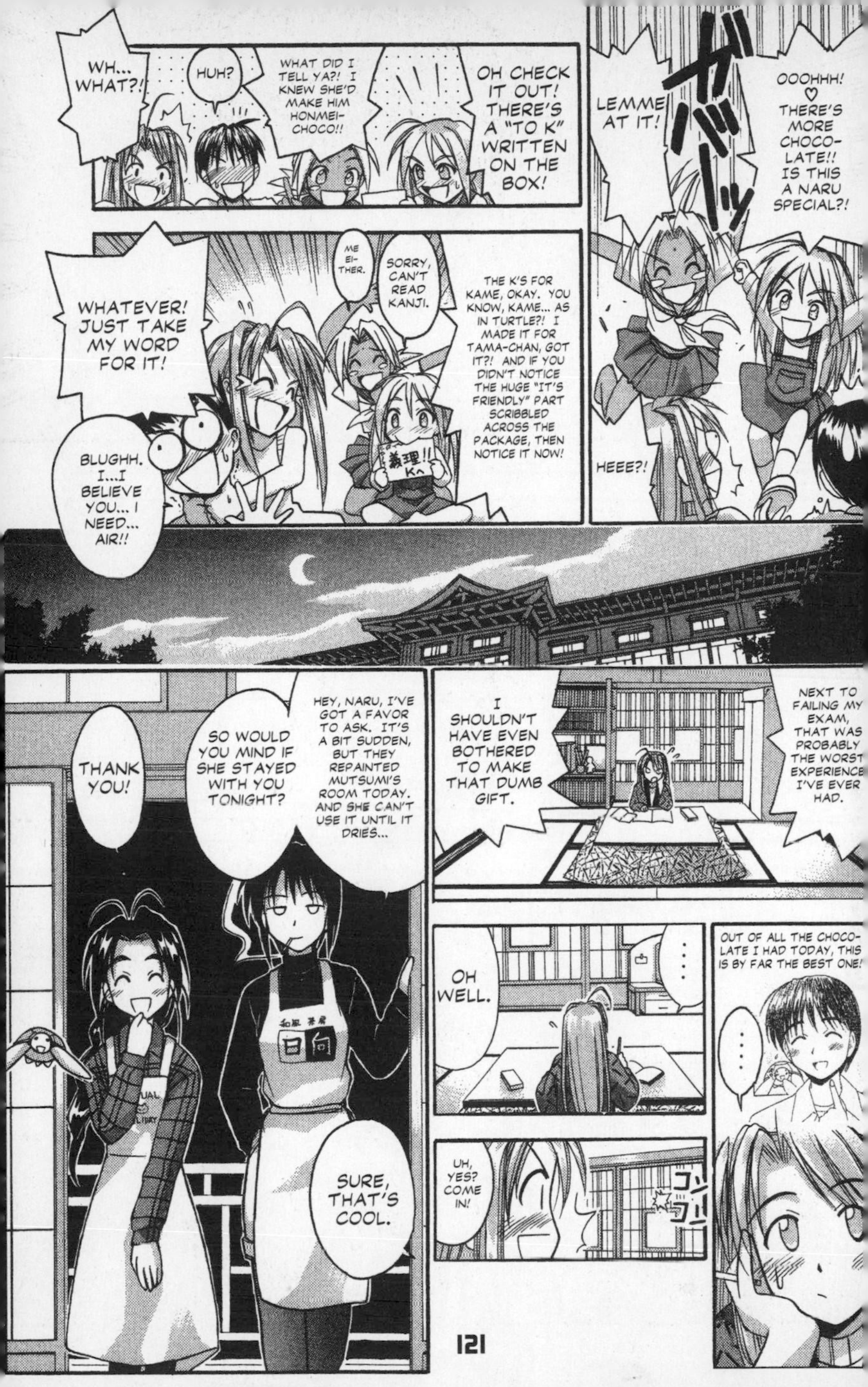
OOOHHH! ♡ THERE'S MORE CHOCO-LATE!! IS THIS A NARU SPECIAL?!
LEMME AT IT!
HEEE?!
OH CHECK IT OUT! THERE'S A "TO K" WRITTEN ON THE BOX!
WHAT DID I TELL YA?! I KNEW SHE'D MAKE HIM HONMEI-CHOCO!!
HUH?
WH... WHAT?!
THE K'S FOR KAME, OKAY. YOU KNOW, KAME... AS IN TURTLE?! I MADE IT FOR TAMA-CHAN, GOT IT?! AND IF YOU DIDN'T NOTICE THE HUGE "IT'S FRIENDLY" PART SCRIBBLED ACROSS THE PACKAGE, THEN NOTICE IT NOW!
SORRY, CAN'T READ KANJI.
ME EI-THER.
義理!!
WHATEVER! JUST TAKE MY WORD FOR IT!
BLUGHH. I...I BELIEVE YOU... I NEED... AIR!!
NEXT TO FAILING MY EXAM, THAT WAS PROBABLY THE WORST EXPERIENCE I'VE EVER HAD.
I SHOULDN'T HAVE EVEN BOTHERED TO MAKE THAT DUMB GIFT.
OUT OF ALL THE CHOCO-LATE I HAD TODAY, THIS IS BY FAR THE BEST ONE!
....
....
OH WELL.
UH, YES? COME IN!
HEY, NARU, I'VE GOT A FAVOR TO ASK. IT'S A BIT SUDDEN, BUT THEY REPAINTED MUTSUMI'S ROOM TODAY. AND SHE CAN'T USE IT UNTIL IT DRIES...
SO WOULD YOU MIND IF SHE STAYED WITH YOU TONIGHT?
THANK YOU!
SURE, THAT'S COOL.

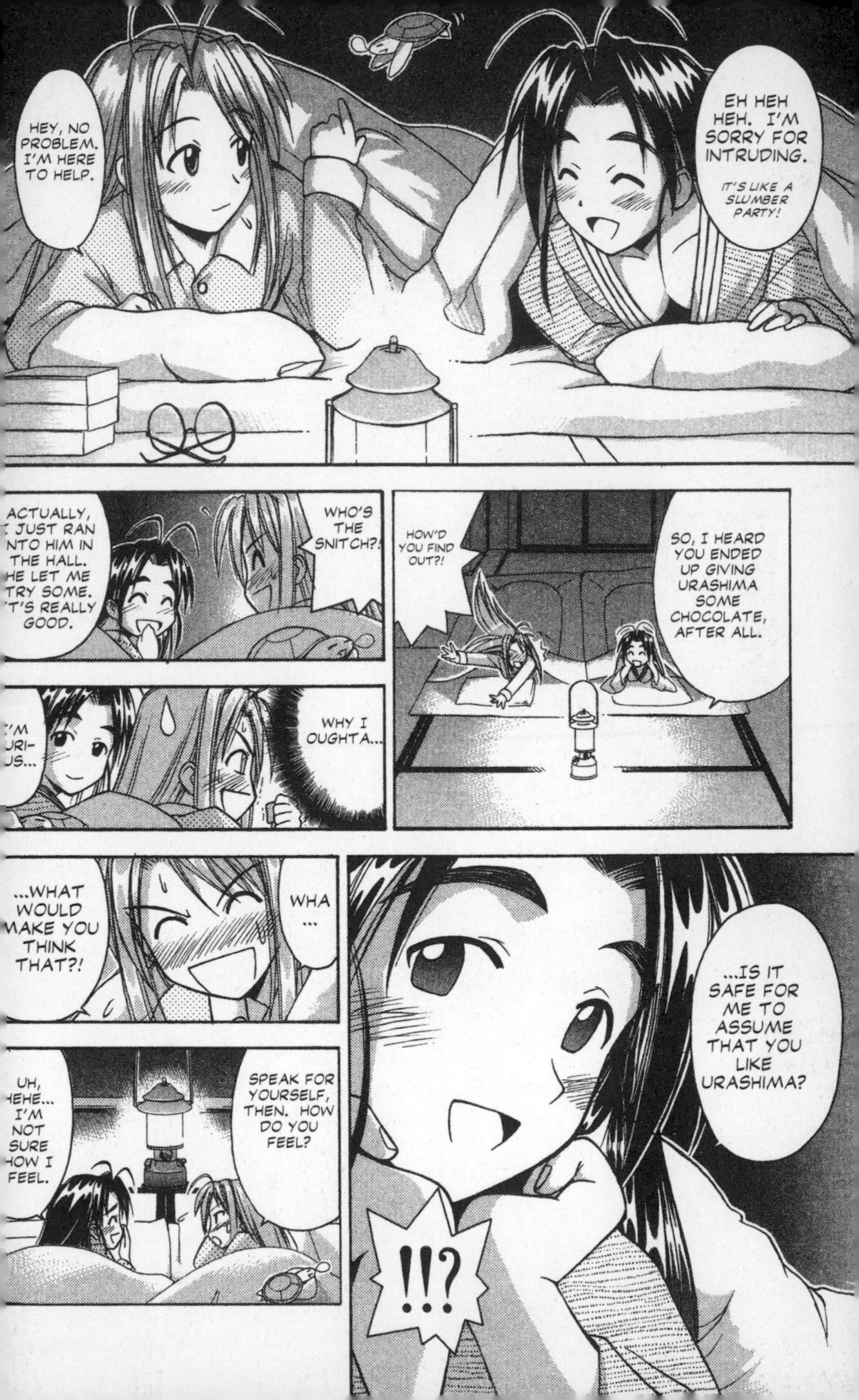

EH HEH HEH. I'M SORRY FOR INTRUDING.
IT'S LIKE A SLUMBER PARTY!
HEY, NO PROBLEM. I'M HERE TO HELP.
SO, I HEARD YOU ENDED UP GIVING URASHIMA SOME CHOCOLATE, AFTER ALL.
HOW'D YOU FIND OUT?!
WHO'S THE SNITCH?!
ACTUALLY, JUST RAN NTO HIM IN THE HALL. HE LET ME TRY SOME. T'S REALLY GOOD.
WHY I OUGHTA...
'M URI- US...
...IS IT SAFE FOR ME TO ASSUME THAT YOU LIKE URASHIMA?
!!?
WHA ...
...WHAT WOULD MAKE YOU THINK THAT?!
SPEAK FOR YOURSELF, THEN. HOW DO YOU FEEL?
UH, HEHE... I'M NOT SURE HOW I FEEL.

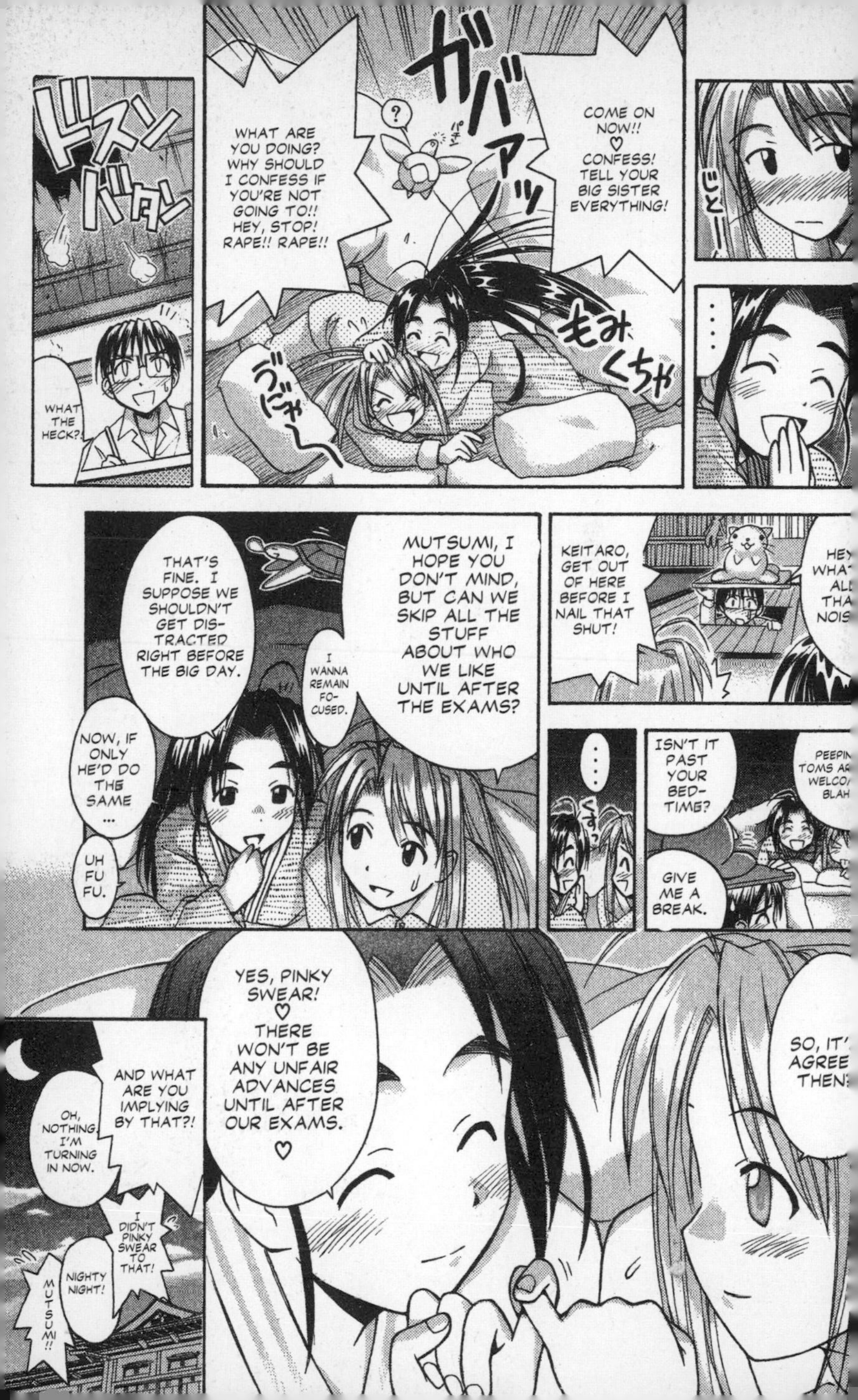
じとー
....
COME ON NOW!! ♡ CONFESS! TELL YOUR BIG SISTER EVERYTHING!
ガバァッ
WHAT ARE YOU DOING? WHY SHOULD I CONFESS IF YOU'RE NOT GOING TO!! HEY, STOP! RAPE!! RAPE!!
?
もみくちゃ
うにゃ~
ドスン
バタン
WHAT THE HECK?
HEY WHAT ALL THA NOIS
KEITARO, GET OUT OF HERE BEFORE I NAIL THAT SHUT!
PEEPIN TOMS AR WELCO BLAH
ISN'T IT PAST YOUR BED-TIME?
GIVE ME A BREAK.
....
くすっ
MUTSUMI, I HOPE YOU DON'T MIND, BUT CAN WE SKIP ALL THE STUFF ABOUT WHO WE LIKE UNTIL AFTER THE EXAMS?
I WANNA REMAIN FO-CUSED.
THAT'S FINE. I SUPPOSE WE SHOULDN'T GET DIS-TRACTED RIGHT BEFORE THE BIG DAY.
NOW, IF ONLY HE'D DO THE SAME ...
UH FU FU.
SO, IT' AGREE THEN?
YES, PINKY SWEAR! ♡ THERE WON'T BE ANY UNFAIR ADVANCES UNTIL AFTER OUR EXAMS. ♡
AND WHAT ARE YOU IMPLYING BY THAT?!
OH, NOTHING. I'M TURNING IN NOW.
I DIDN'T PINKY SWEAR TO THAT!
NIGHTY NIGHT!
MUTSUMI!!

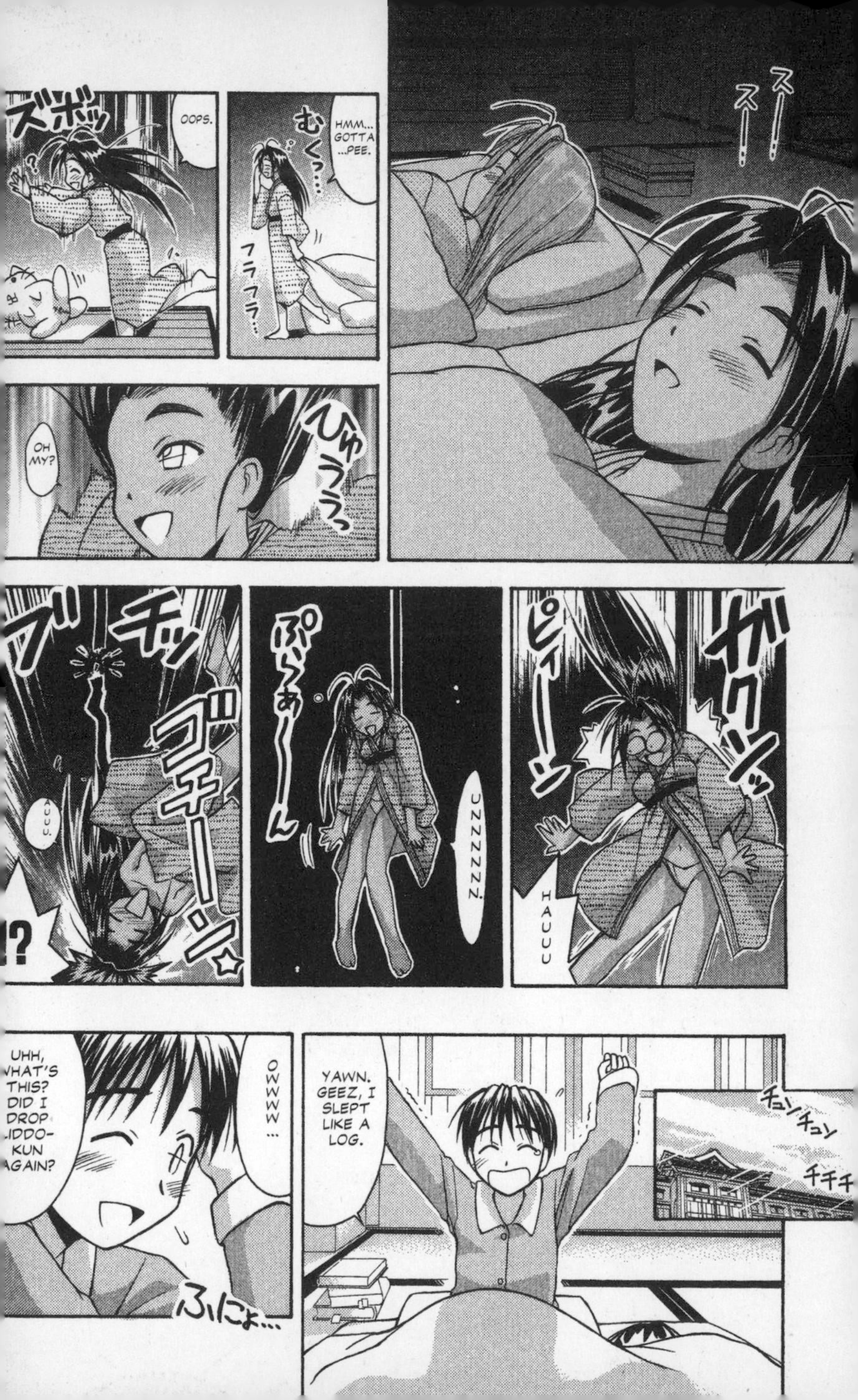
スースー
HMM... GOTTA ...PEE.
むくっ...
フラフラ...
ズボッ
OOPS.
OH MY?
ひゅううっ
ガクンッ
ピィィー
HAUUU
ぷらぁ〜ん
UNNNNNN.
ブチッ
ゴチーン
AUUU.
!?
チュンチュン
チチチ
YAWN. GEEZ, I SLEPT LIKE A LOG.
OWWWW...
UHH, WHAT'S THIS? DID I DROP IDDO-KUN AGAIN?
ふにょ...

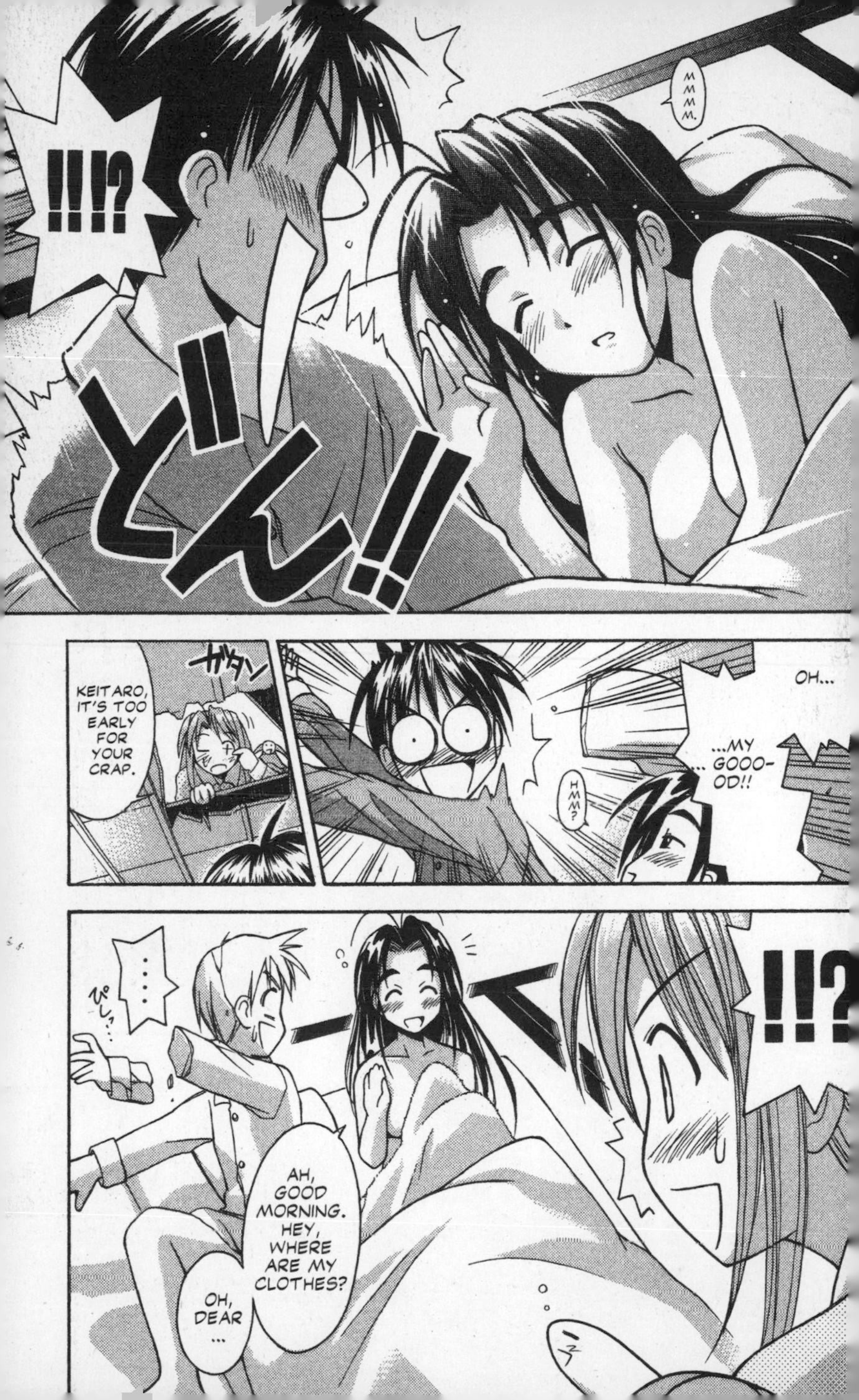
MMMM.
!!!?
どん!!
OH...
...MY GOOOO-OD!!
HMM?
ガタン
KEITARO, IT'S TOO EARLY FOR YOUR CRAP.
!!?
AH, GOOD MORNING. HEY, WHERE ARE MY CLOTHES?
....
OH, DEAR ...

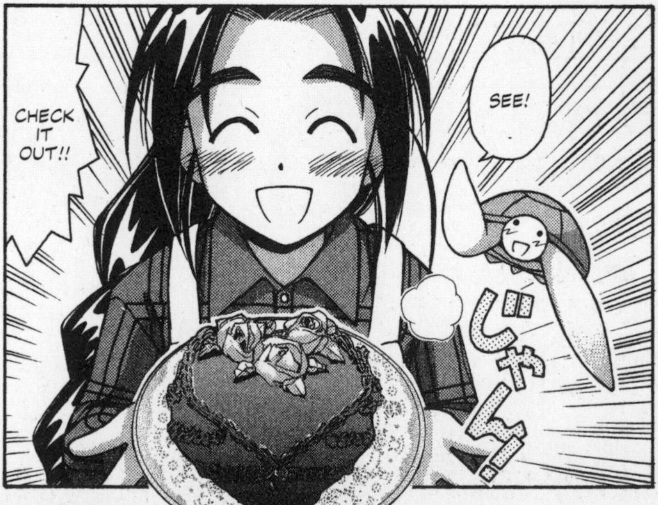
SEE!
CHECK IT OUT!!
じゃん!

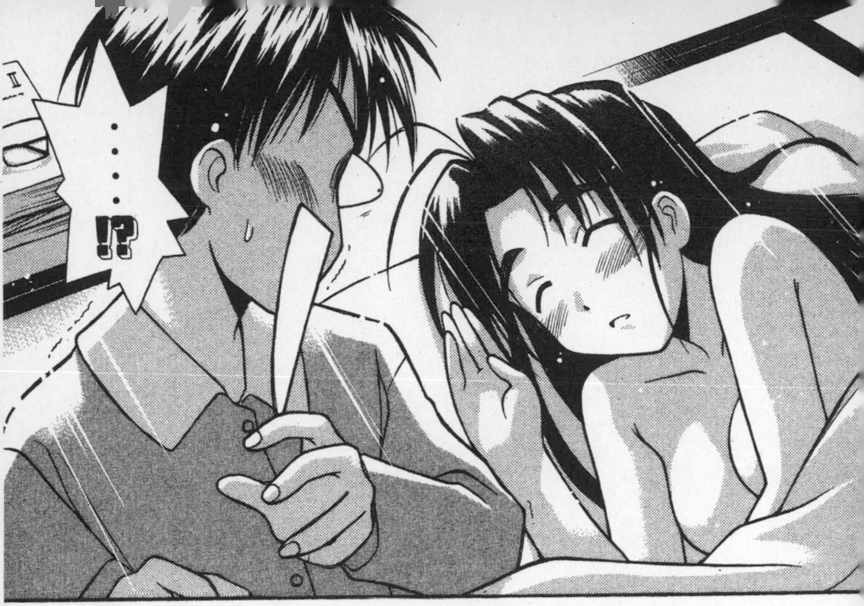
...
!?

# Love Hina

## Hinata.58 My Papa is a Ronin Stone?!

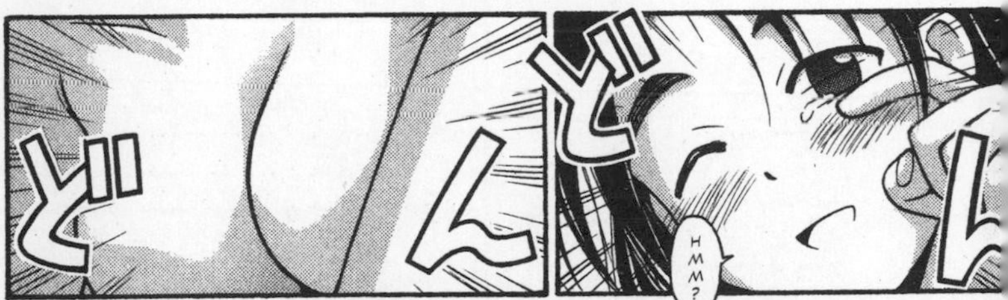
HMM?

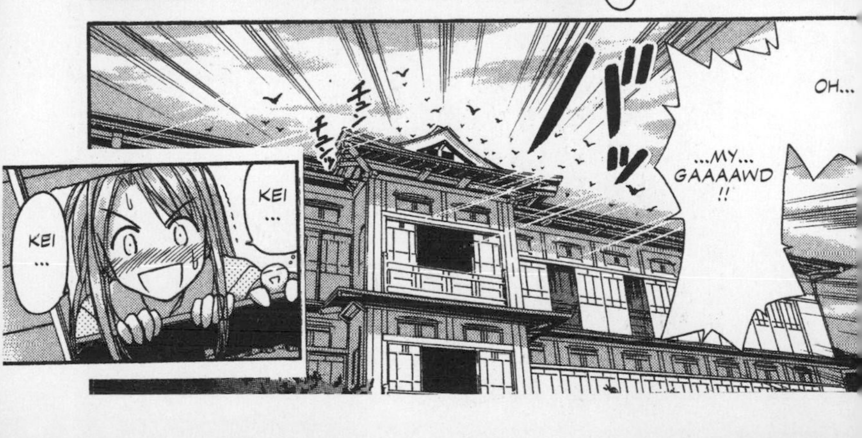
OH...
...MY... GAAAAWD !!
KEI ...
KEI ...

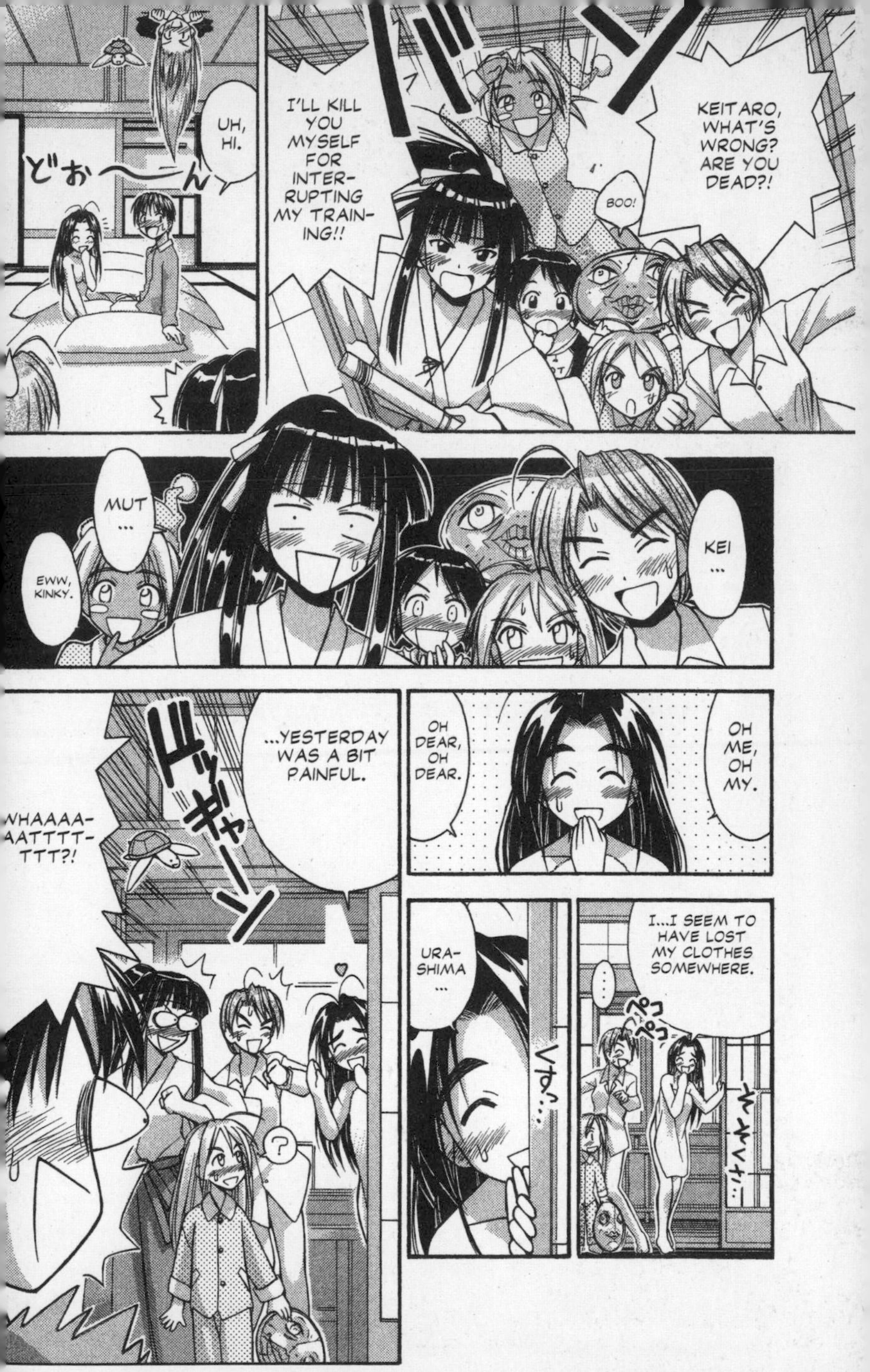
KEITARO, WHAT'S WRONG? ARE YOU DEAD?!
BOO!
I'LL KILL YOU MYSELF FOR INTER-RUPTING MY TRAIN-ING!!
UH, HI.
どおー～ん
KEI ...
MUT ...
EWW, KINKY.
OH ME, OH MY.
OH DEAR, OH DEAR.
I...I SEEM TO HAVE LOST MY CLOTHES SOMEWHERE.
...
ぺこぺこ
そそくさ...
URA-SHIMA ...
くすっ...
...YESTERDAY WAS A BIT PAINFUL.
ドッギャーン
WHAAAA-AATTTTT-TTT?!

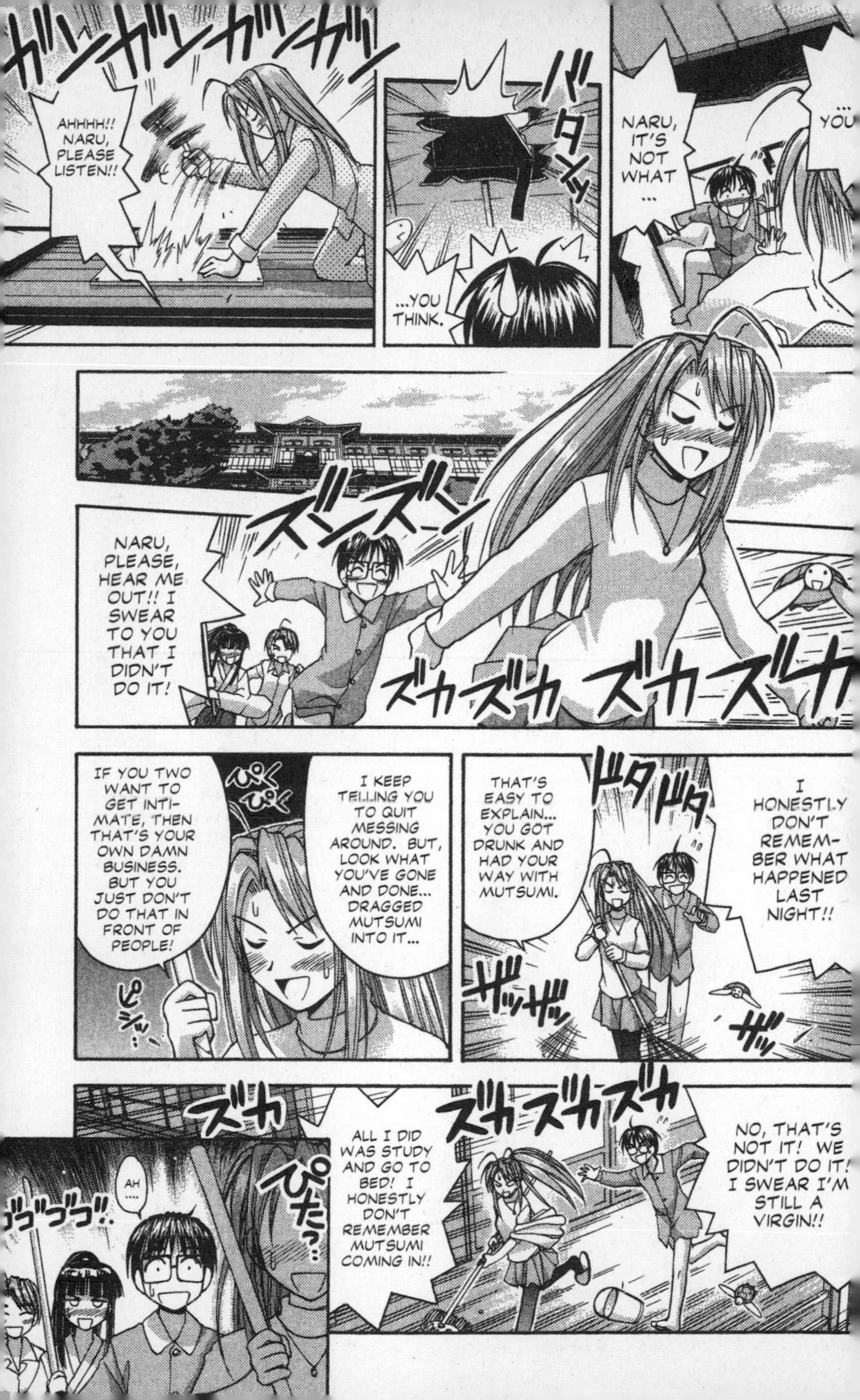
NARU, IT'S NOT WHAT ...
... YOU
...YOU THINK.
AHHHH!! NARU, PLEASE LISTEN!!
NARU, PLEASE, HEAR ME OUT!! I SWEAR TO YOU THAT I DIDN'T DO IT!
I HONESTLY DON'T REMEMBER WHAT HAPPENED LAST NIGHT!!
THAT'S EASY TO EXPLAIN... YOU GOT DRUNK AND HAD YOUR WAY WITH MUTSUMI.
I KEEP TELLING YOU TO QUIT MESSING AROUND. BUT, LOOK WHAT YOU'VE GONE AND DONE... DRAGGED MUTSUMI INTO IT...
IF YOU TWO WANT TO GET INTI-MATE, THEN THAT'S YOUR OWN DAMN BUSINESS. BUT YOU JUST DON'T DO THAT IN FRONT OF PEOPLE!
NO, THAT'S NOT IT! WE DIDN'T DO IT! I SWEAR I'M STILL A VIRGIN!!
ALL I DID WAS STUDY AND GO TO BED! I HONESTLY DON'T REMEMBER MUTSUMI COMING IN!!
AH ....

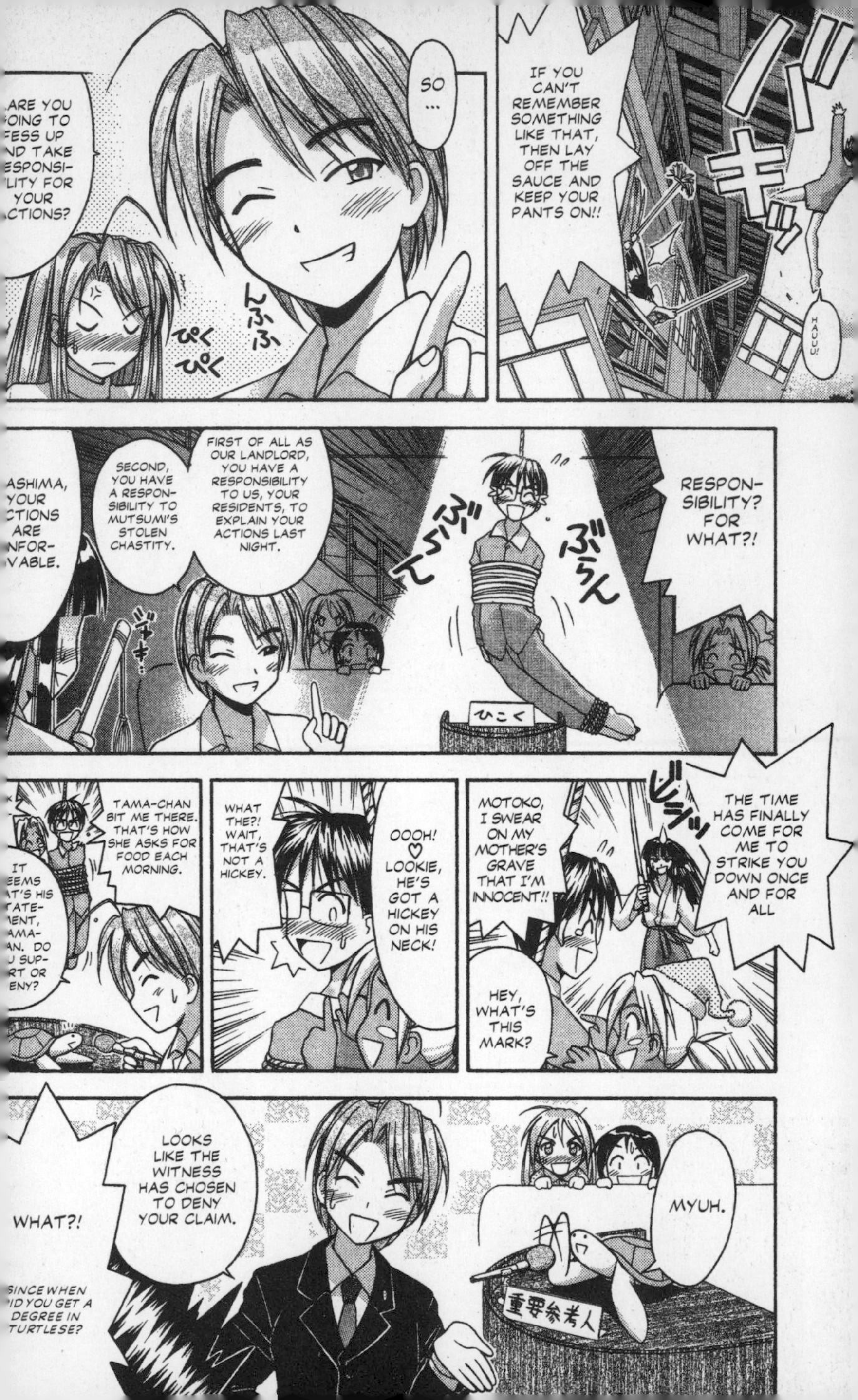
IF YOU CAN'T REMEMBER SOMETHING LIKE THAT, THEN LAY OFF THE SAUCE AND KEEP YOUR PANTS ON!!
HAUUU!
SO ...
ARE YOU OING TO ESS UP ND TAKE ESPONSI-ILITY FOR YOUR CTIONS?
んふふ
ぴくぴく
RESPON-SIBILITY? FOR WHAT?!
ぶらん
ぶらん
FIRST OF ALL AS OUR LANDLORD, YOU HAVE A RESPONSIBILITY TO US, YOUR RESIDENTS, TO EXPLAIN YOUR ACTIONS LAST NIGHT.
SECOND, YOU HAVE A RESPON-SIBILITY TO MUTSUMI'S STOLEN CHASTITY.
ASHIMA, YOUR CTIONS ARE NFOR-VABLE.
ひこく
THE TIME HAS FINALLY COME FOR ME TO STRIKE YOU DOWN ONCE AND FOR ALL
MOTOKO, I SWEAR ON MY MOTHER'S GRAVE THAT I'M INNOCENT!!
HEY, WHAT'S THIS MARK?
OOOH! ♡ LOOKIE, HE'S GOT A HICKEY ON HIS NECK!
WHAT THE?! WAIT, THAT'S NOT A HICKEY.
TAMA-CHAN BIT ME THERE. THAT'S HOW SHE ASKS FOR FOOD EACH MORNING.
IT EEMS AT'S HIS TATE-MENT, AMA-AN. DO U SUP-RT OR ENY?
MYUH.
重要参考人
LOOKS LIKE THE WITNESS HAS CHOSEN TO DENY YOUR CLAIM.
WHAT?!
SINCE WHEN ID YOU GET A DEGREE IN TURTLESE?

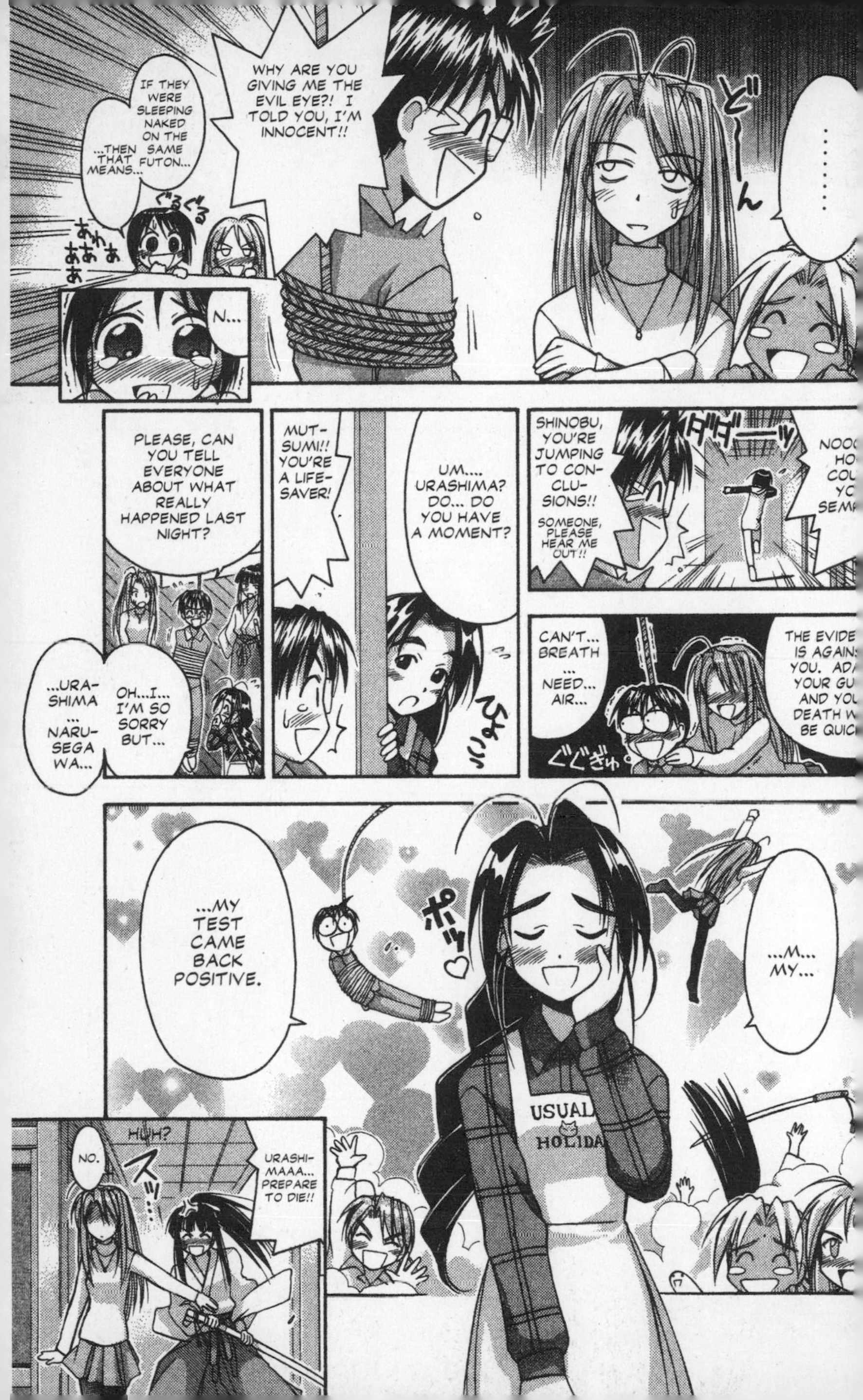
......
ど~ん
WHY ARE YOU GIVING ME THE EVIL EYE?! I TOLD YOU, I'M INNOCENT!!
IF THEY WERE SLEEPING NAKED ON THE SAME FUTON... ...THEN THAT MEANS...
ぐるぐる
N...
SHINOBU, YOU'RE JUMPING TO CONCLUSIONS!!
SOMEONE, PLEASE HEAR ME OUT!!
CAN'T... BREATH ... NEED... AIR...
UM.... URASHIMA? DO... DO YOU HAVE A MOMENT?
MUT-SUMI!! YOU'RE A LIFE-SAVER!
PLEASE, CAN YOU TELL EVERYONE ABOUT WHAT REALLY HAPPENED LAST NIGHT?
OH...I... I'M SO SORRY BUT...
...URA-SHIMA ... NARU-SEGA WA...
...M... MY...
...MY TEST CAME BACK POSITIVE.
URASHI-MAAA... PREPARE TO DIE!!
HUH?
NO.

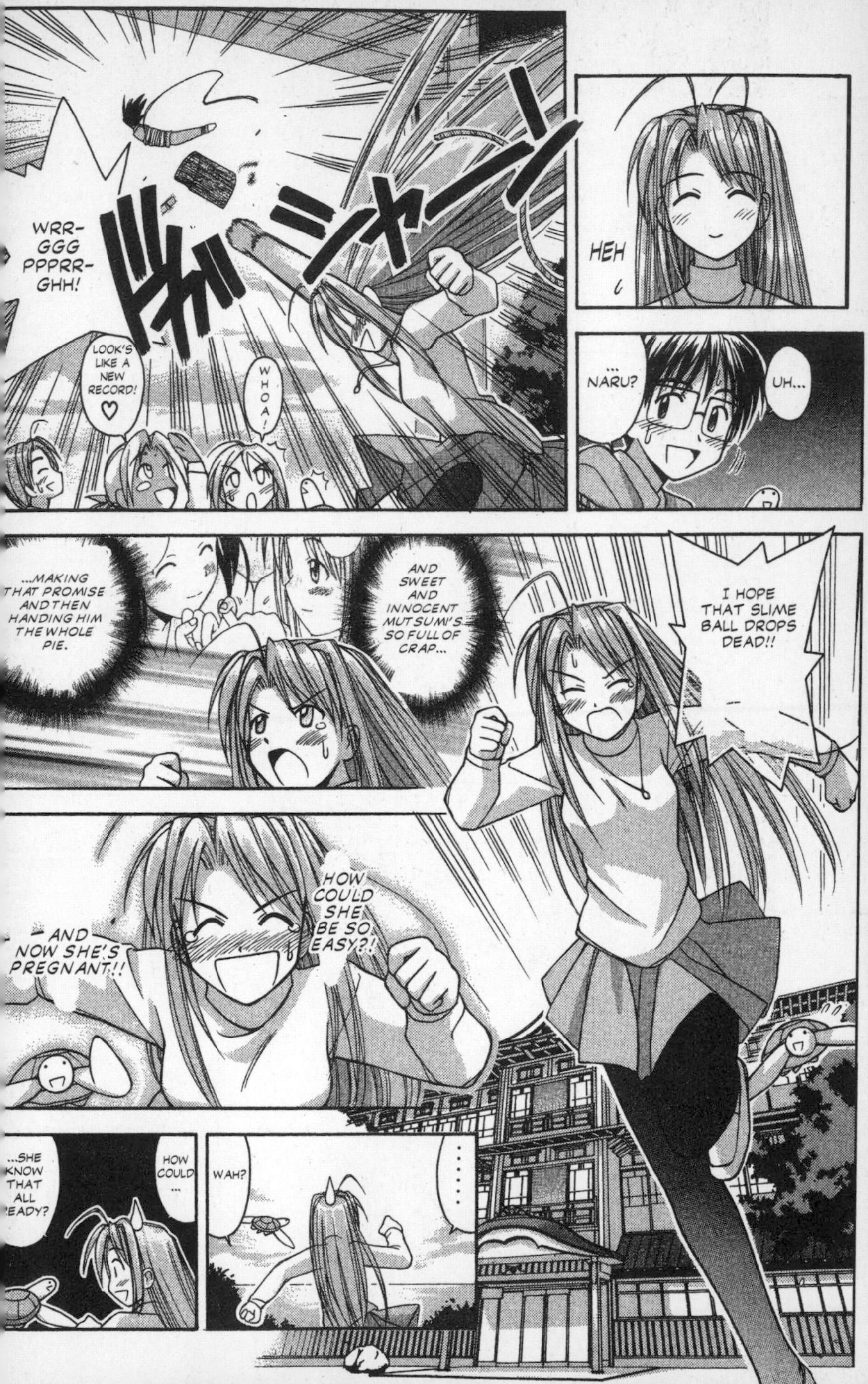
HEH
UH...
...NARU?
WHOA!
LOOK'S LIKE A NEW RECORD! ♡
WRR-GGG PPPRR-GHH!
I HOPE THAT SLIME BALL DROPS DEAD!!
AND SWEET AND INNOCENT MUTSUMI'S SO FULL OF CRAP...
...MAKING THAT PROMISE AND THEN HANDING HIM THE WHOLE PIE.
HOW COULD SHE BE SO EASY?!
–AND NOW SHE'S PREGNANT!!
......
WAH?
HOW COULD ...
...SHE KNOW THAT ALL EADY?

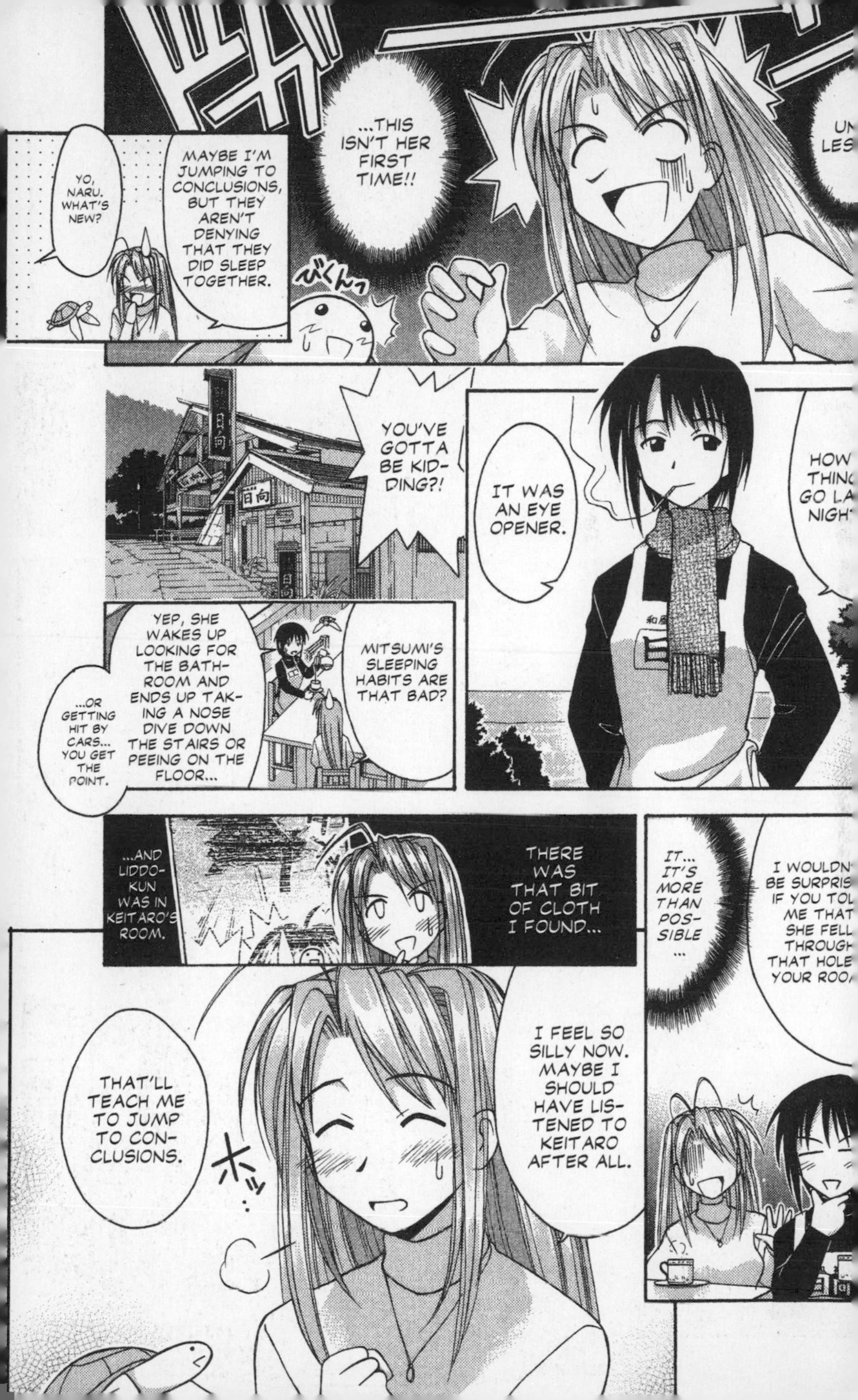
UN
LES
...THIS ISN'T HER FIRST TIME!!
びくんっ
MAYBE I'M JUMPING TO CONCLUSIONS, BUT THEY AREN'T DENYING THAT THEY DID SLEEP TOGETHER.
YO, NARU. WHAT'S NEW?
HOW THING GO LA NIGHT
IT WAS AN EYE OPENER.
YOU'VE GOTTA BE KID-DING?!
MITSUMI'S SLEEPING HABITS ARE THAT BAD?
YEP, SHE WAKES UP LOOKING FOR THE BATH-ROOM AND ENDS UP TAK-ING A NOSE DIVE DOWN THE STAIRS OR PEEING ON THE FLOOR...
...OR GETTING HIT BY CARS... YOU GET THE POINT.
I WOULDN BE SURPRIS IF YOU TOL ME THAT SHE FELL THROUGH THAT HOLE YOUR ROO
IT... IT'S MORE THAN POS-SIBLE ...
THERE WAS THAT BIT OF CLOTH I FOUND...
...AND LIDDO-KUN WAS IN KEITARO'S ROOM.
I FEEL SO SILLY NOW. MAYBE I SHOULD HAVE LIS-TENED TO KEITARO AFTER ALL.
THAT'LL TEACH ME TO JUMP TO CON-CLUSIONS.
ホッ

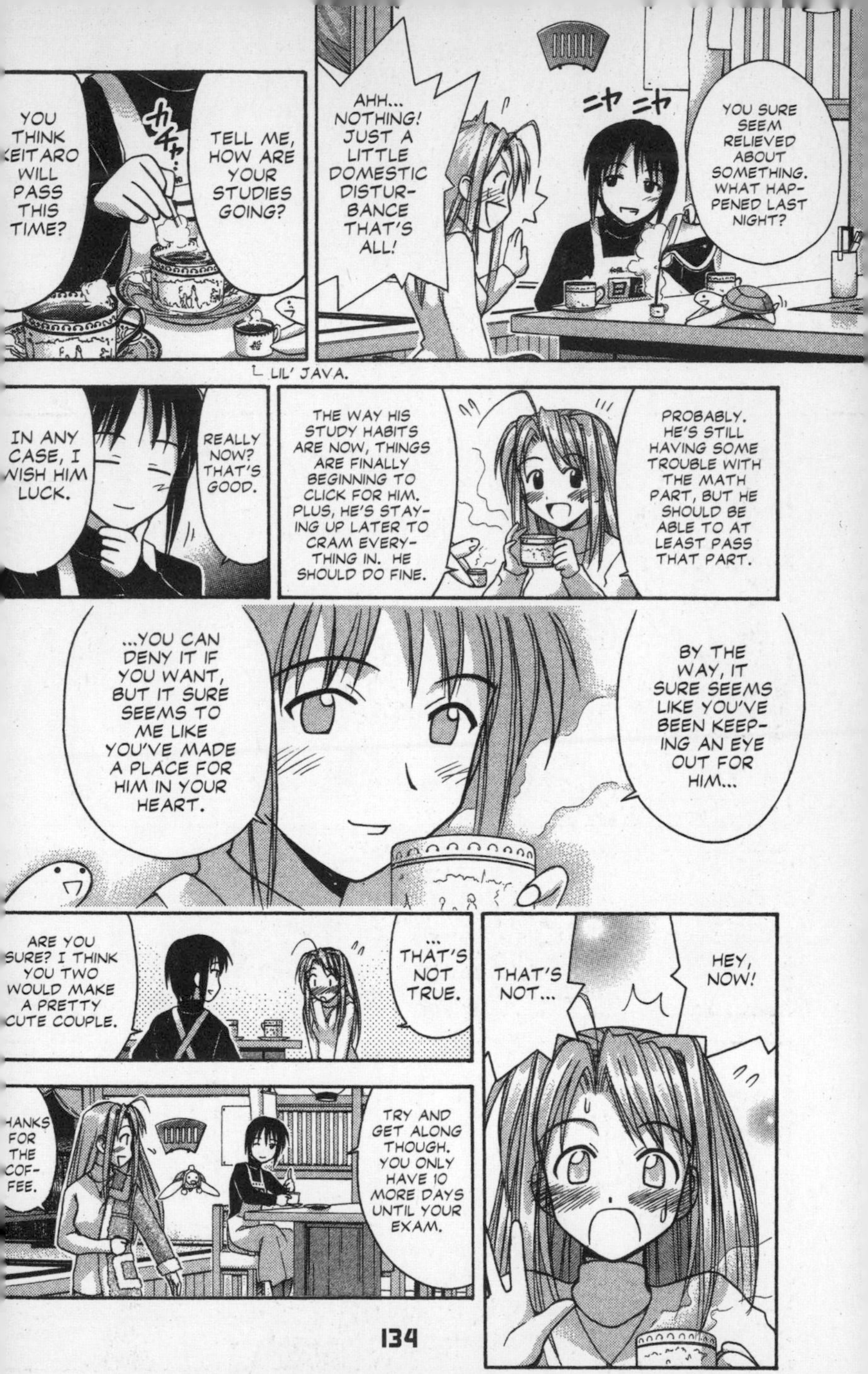

YOU SURE SEEM RELIEVED ABOUT SOMETHING. WHAT HAPPENED LAST NIGHT?
ニヤ ニヤ
AHH... NOTHING! JUST A LITTLE DOMESTIC DISTURBANCE THAT'S ALL!
TELL ME, HOW ARE YOUR STUDIES GOING?
カチャ…
YOU THINK KEITARO WILL PASS THIS TIME?
LIL' JAVA.
PROBABLY. HE'S STILL HAVING SOME TROUBLE WITH THE MATH PART, BUT HE SHOULD BE ABLE TO AT LEAST PASS THAT PART.
THE WAY HIS STUDY HABITS ARE NOW, THINGS ARE FINALLY BEGINNING TO CLICK FOR HIM. PLUS, HE'S STAYING UP LATER TO CRAM EVERYTHING IN. HE SHOULD DO FINE.
REALLY NOW? THAT'S GOOD.
IN ANY CASE, I WISH HIM LUCK.
BY THE WAY, IT SURE SEEMS LIKE YOU'VE BEEN KEEPING AN EYE OUT FOR HIM...
...YOU CAN DENY IT IF YOU WANT, BUT IT SURE SEEMS TO ME LIKE YOU'VE MADE A PLACE FOR HIM IN YOUR HEART.
HEY, NOW!
THAT'S NOT...
... THAT'S NOT TRUE.
ARE YOU SURE? I THINK YOU TWO WOULD MAKE A PRETTY CUTE COUPLE.
TRY AND GET ALONG THOUGH. YOU ONLY HAVE 10 MORE DAYS UNTIL YOUR EXAM.
THANKS FOR THE COFFEE.

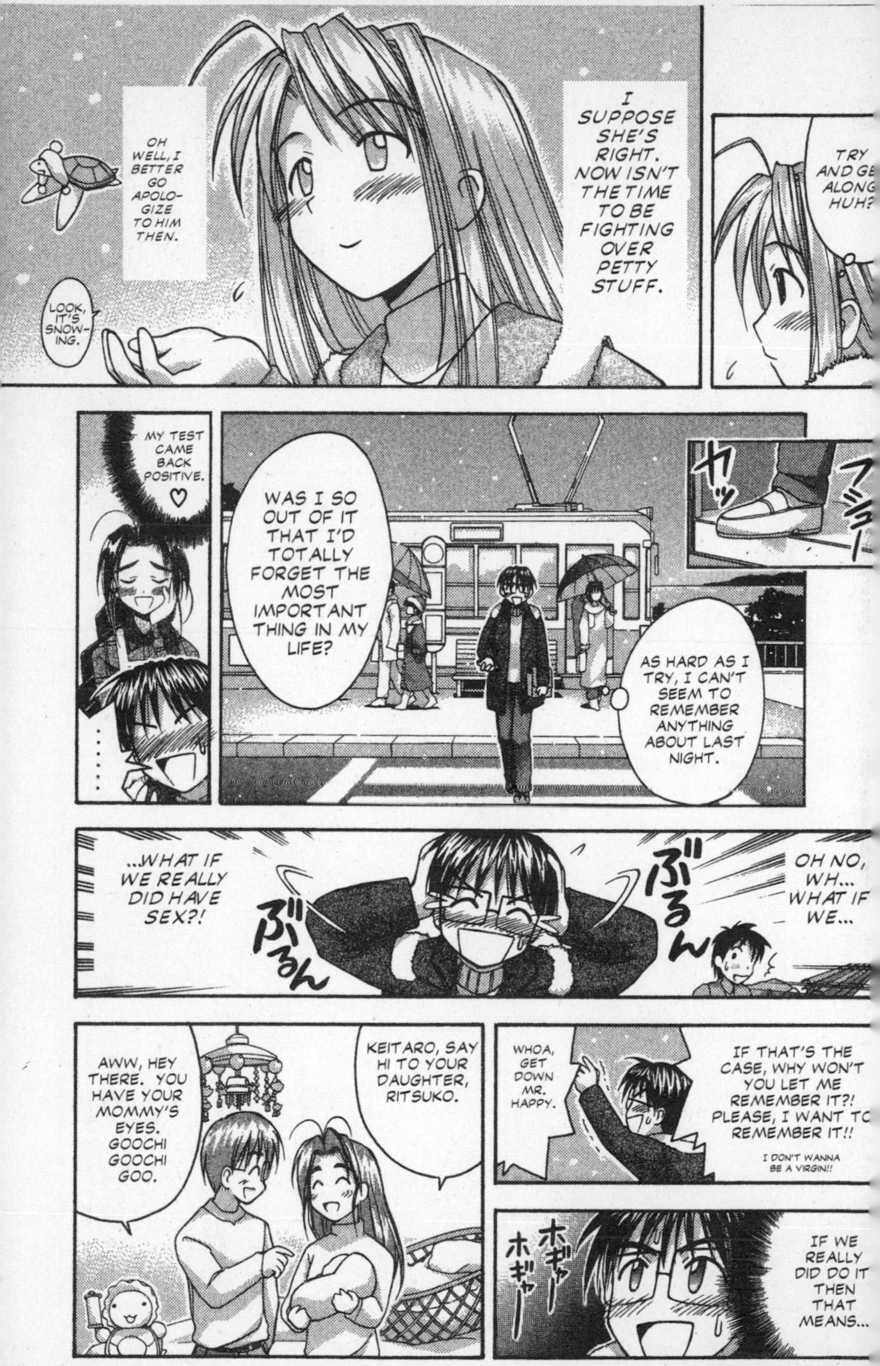
TRY AND GE ALONG HUH?
I SUPPOSE SHE'S RIGHT. NOW ISN'T THE TIME TO BE FIGHTING OVER PETTY STUFF.
OH WELL, I BETTER GO APOLOGIZE TO HIM THEN.
LOOK, IT'S SNOWING.
ヤッ
WAS I SO OUT OF IT THAT I'D TOTALLY FORGET THE MOST IMPORTANT THING IN MY LIFE?
AS HARD AS I TRY, I CAN'T SEEM TO REMEMBER ANYTHING ABOUT LAST NIGHT.
MY TEST CAME BACK POSITIVE. ♡
......
OH NO, WH... WHAT IF WE...
ぶるん
ぶるん
...WHAT IF WE REALLY DID HAVE SEX?!
IF THAT'S THE CASE, WHY WON'T YOU LET ME REMEMBER IT?! PLEASE, I WANT T REMEMBER IT!!
I DON'T WANNA BE A VIRGIN!!
WHOA, GET DOWN MR. HAPPY.
IF WE REALLY DID DO IT THEN THAT MEANS...
ホギャー
ホギャー
KEITARO, SAY HI TO YOUR DAUGHTER, RITSUKO.
AWW, HEY THERE. YOU HAVE YOUR MOMMY'S EYES. GOOCHI GOOCHI GOO.

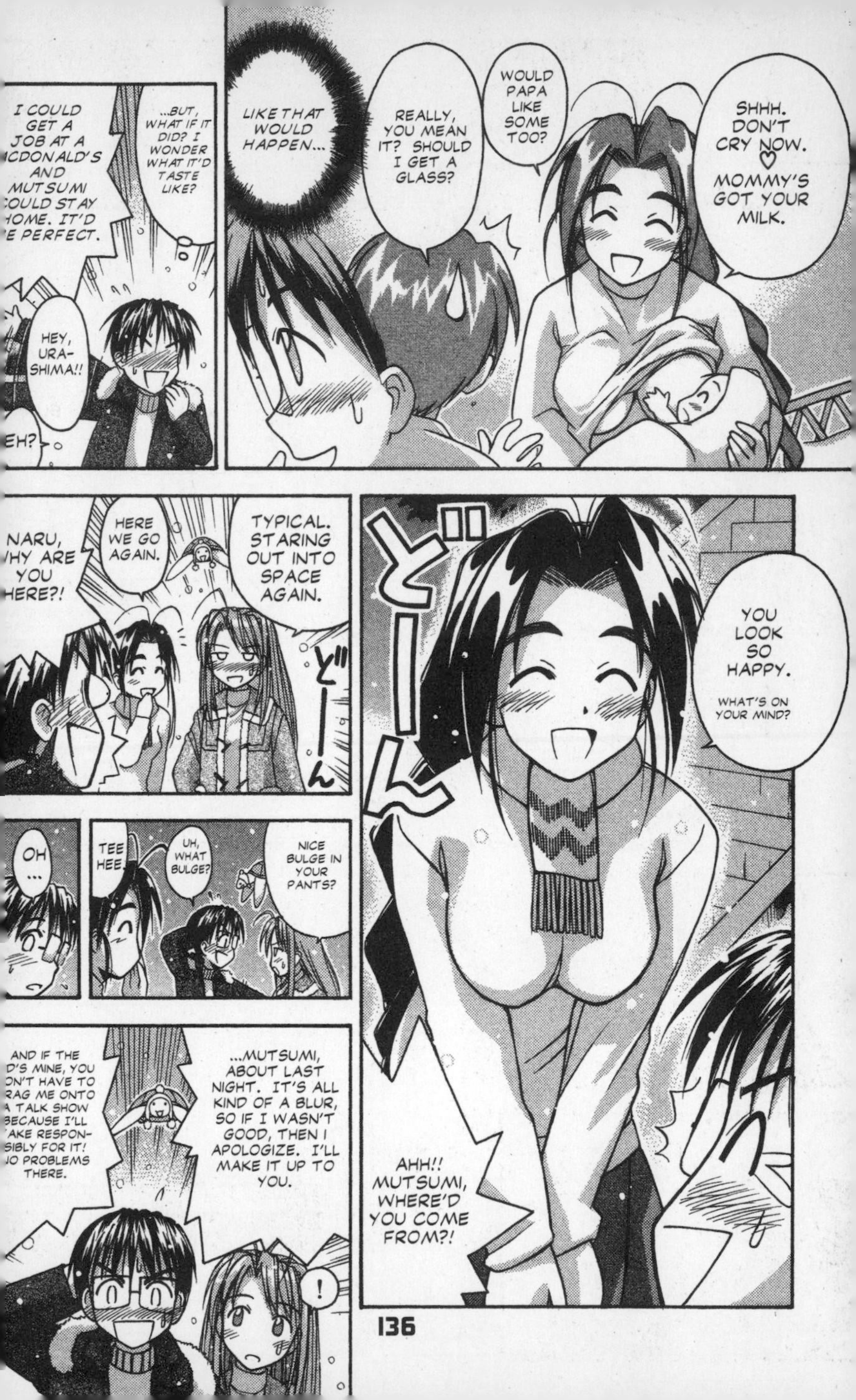
SHHH. DON'T CRY NOW. ♡ MOMMY'S GOT YOUR MILK.
WOULD PAPA LIKE SOME TOO?
REALLY, YOU MEAN IT? SHOULD I GET A GLASS?
LIKE THAT WOULD HAPPEN...
...BUT, WHAT IF IT DID? I WONDER WHAT IT'D TASTE LIKE?
I COULD GET A JOB AT A CDONALD'S AND MUTSUMI COULD STAY HOME. IT'D E PERFECT.
HEY, URA-SHIMA!!
EH?
YOU LOOK SO HAPPY.
WHAT'S ON YOUR MIND?
どーーん
AHH!! MUTSUMI, WHERE'D YOU COME FROM?!
TYPICAL. STARING OUT INTO SPACE AGAIN.
HERE WE GO AGAIN.
NARU, HY ARE YOU HERE?!
どーん
NICE BULGE IN YOUR PANTS?
UH, WHAT BULGE?
TEE HEE.
OH ...
...MUTSUMI, ABOUT LAST NIGHT. IT'S ALL KIND OF A BLUR, SO IF I WASN'T GOOD, THEN I APOLOGIZE. I'LL MAKE IT UP TO YOU.
AND IF THE D'S MINE, YOU ON'T HAVE TO RAG ME ONTO A TALK SHOW BECAUSE I'LL AKE RESPON-SIBLY FOR IT! O PROBLEMS THERE.
!

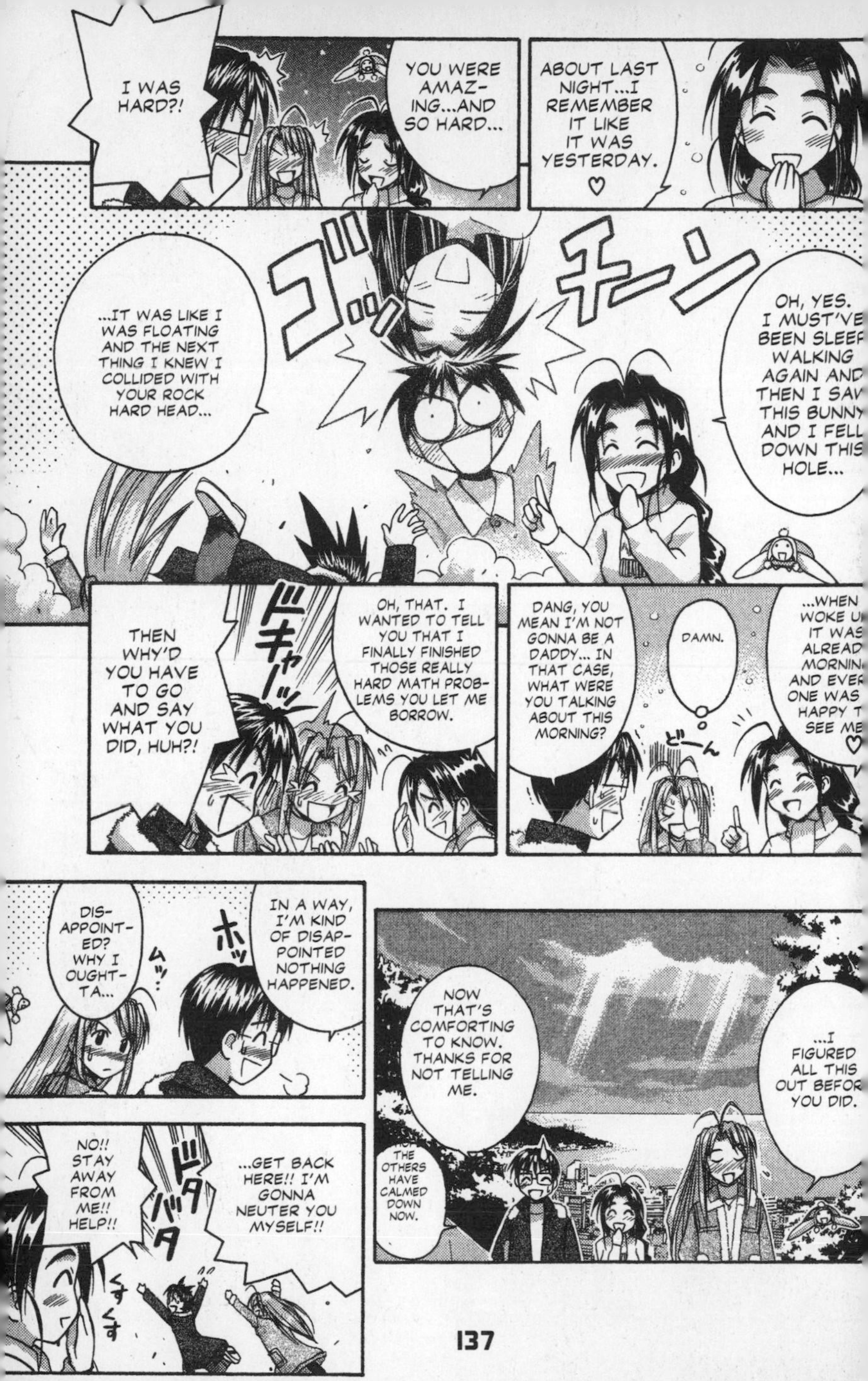

ABOUT LAST NIGHT...I REMEMBER IT LIKE IT WAS YESTERDAY. ♡
YOU WERE AMAZ-ING...AND SO HARD...
I WAS HARD?!
ゴッ
チーン
OH, YES. I MUST'VE BEEN SLEEP WALKING AGAIN AND THEN I SAW THIS BUNNY AND I FELL DOWN THIS HOLE...
...IT WAS LIKE I WAS FLOATING AND THE NEXT THING I KNEW I COLLIDED WITH YOUR ROCK HARD HEAD...
...WHEN I WOKE UP IT WAS ALREADY MORNING AND EVERYONE WAS HAPPY TO SEE ME ♡
DAMN.
DANG, YOU MEAN I'M NOT GONNA BE A DADDY... IN THAT CASE, WHAT WERE YOU TALKING ABOUT THIS MORNING?
どーん
OH, THAT. I WANTED TO TELL YOU THAT I FINALLY FINISHED THOSE REALLY HARD MATH PROB-LEMS YOU LET ME BORROW.
ドギャッ
THEN WHY'D YOU HAVE TO GO AND SAY WHAT YOU DID, HUH?!
...I FIGURED ALL THIS OUT BEFORE YOU DID.
NOW THAT'S COMFORTING TO KNOW. THANKS FOR NOT TELLING ME.
THE OTHERS HAVE CALMED DOWN NOW.
IN A WAY, I'M KIND OF DISAP-POINTED NOTHING HAPPENED.
ホッ
ムッ
DIS-APPOINT-ED? WHY I OUGHT-TA...
...GET BACK HERE!! I'M GONNA NEUTER YOU MYSELF!!
ドタバタ
NO!! STAY AWAY FROM ME!! HELP!!
くすくす

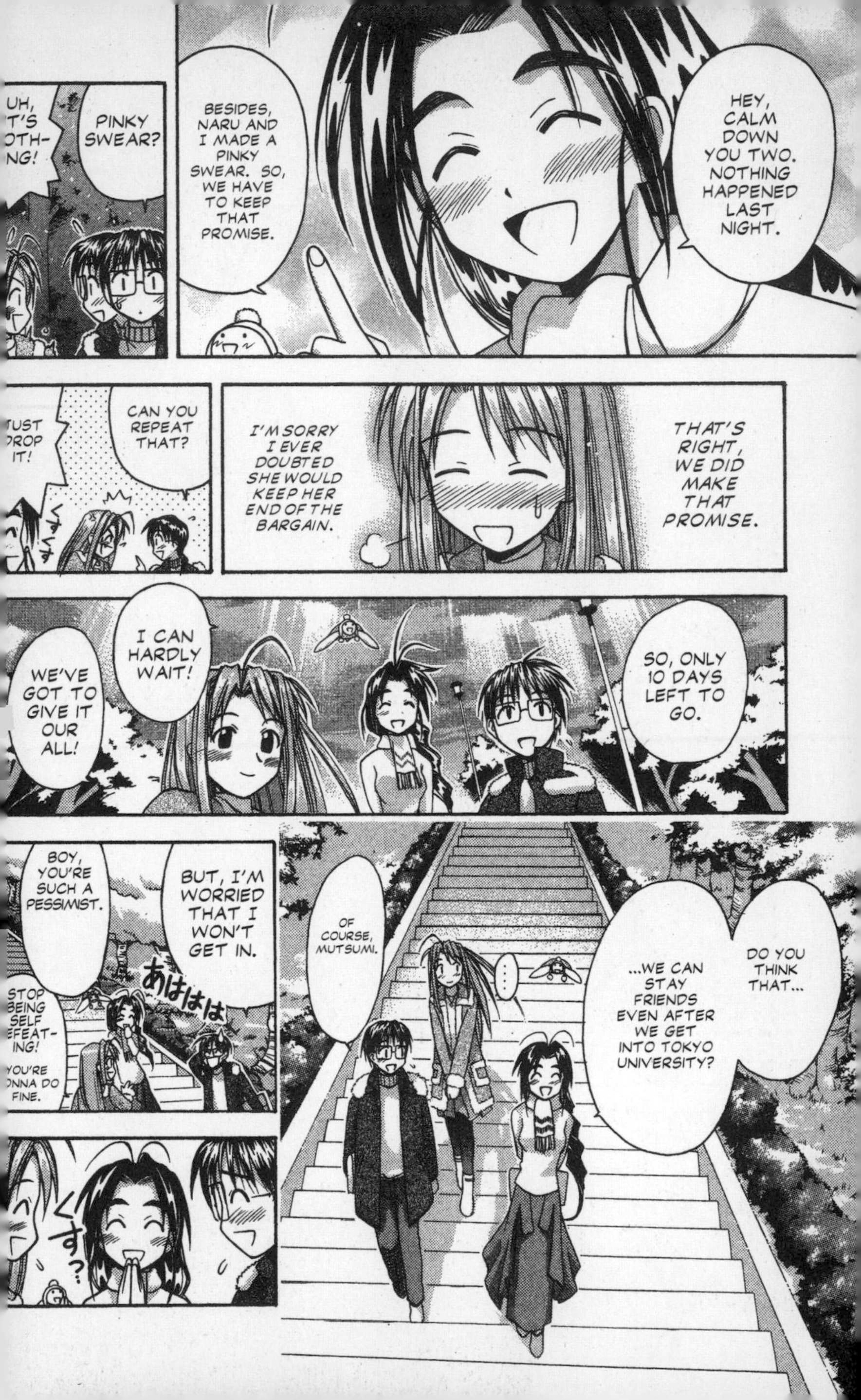
HEY, CALM DOWN YOU TWO. NOTHING HAPPENED LAST NIGHT.
BESIDES, NARU AND I MADE A PINKY SWEAR. SO, WE HAVE TO KEEP THAT PROMISE.
PINKY SWEAR?
UH, T'S OTH- NG!
THAT'S RIGHT, WE DID MAKE THAT PROMISE.
I'M SORRY I EVER DOUBTED SHE WOULD KEEP HER END OF THE BARGAIN.
CAN YOU REPEAT THAT?
TUST ROP IT!
くすくす
SO, ONLY 10 DAYS LEFT TO GO.
I CAN HARDLY WAIT!
WE'VE GOT TO GIVE IT OUR ALL!
DO YOU THINK THAT...
...WE CAN STAY FRIENDS EVEN AFTER WE GET INTO TOKYO UNIVERSITY?
...
OF COURSE, MUTSUMI.
BUT, I'M WORRIED THAT I WON'T GET IN.
BOY, YOU'RE SUCH A PESSIMIST.
あははは
STOP BEING SELF EFEAT- ING!
YOU'RE ONNA DO FINE.
くすっ

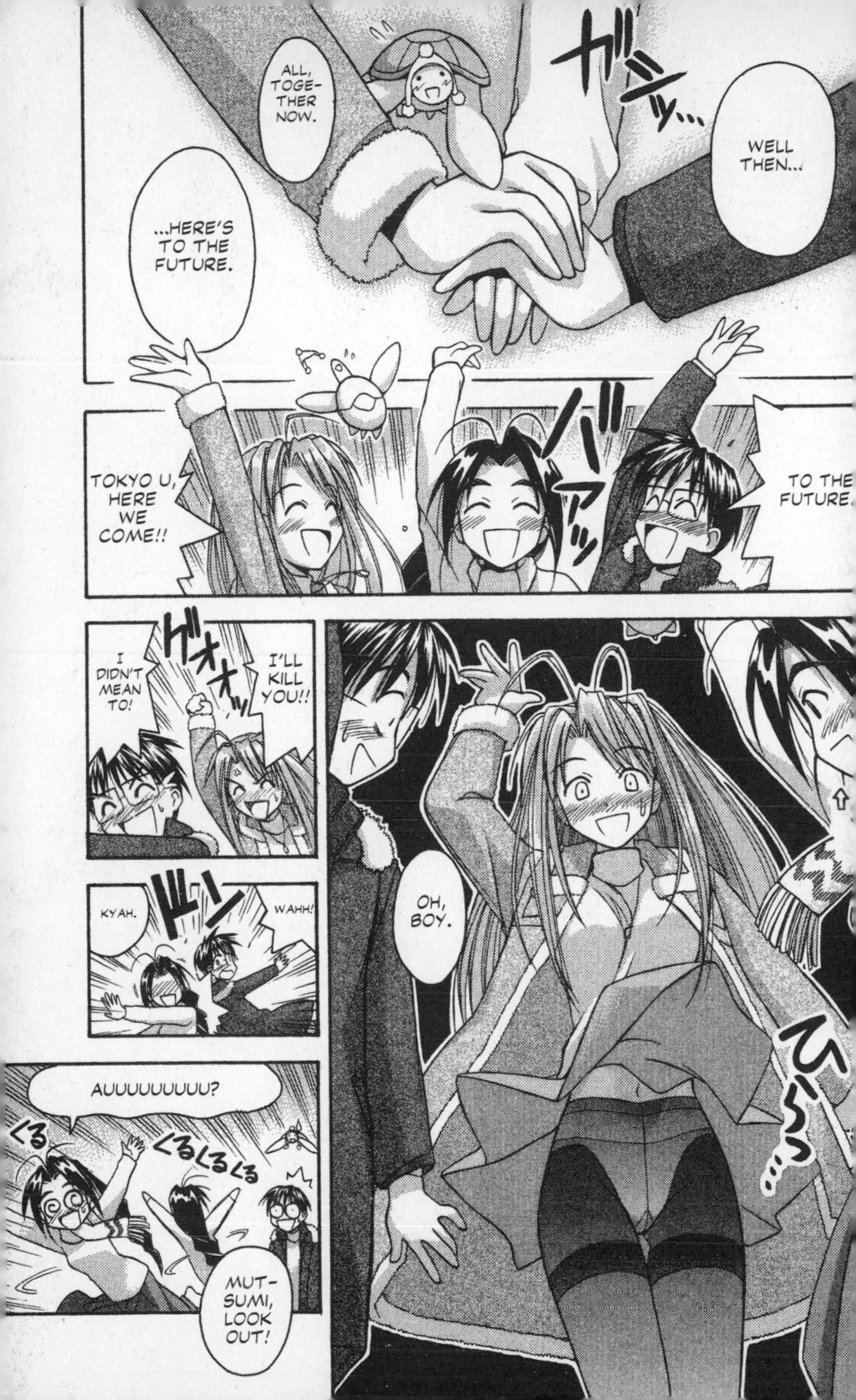

WELL THEN...
ガシッ...
ALL, TOGETHER NOW.
...HERE'S TO THE FUTURE.
TO THE FUTURE.
バアッ
TOKYO U, HERE WE COME!!
OH, BOY.
I'LL KILL YOU!!
I DIDN'T MEAN TO!
WAHH!
ドン
KYAH.
AUUUUUUUUU?
くるくるくるくる
MUT-SUMI, LOOK OUT!

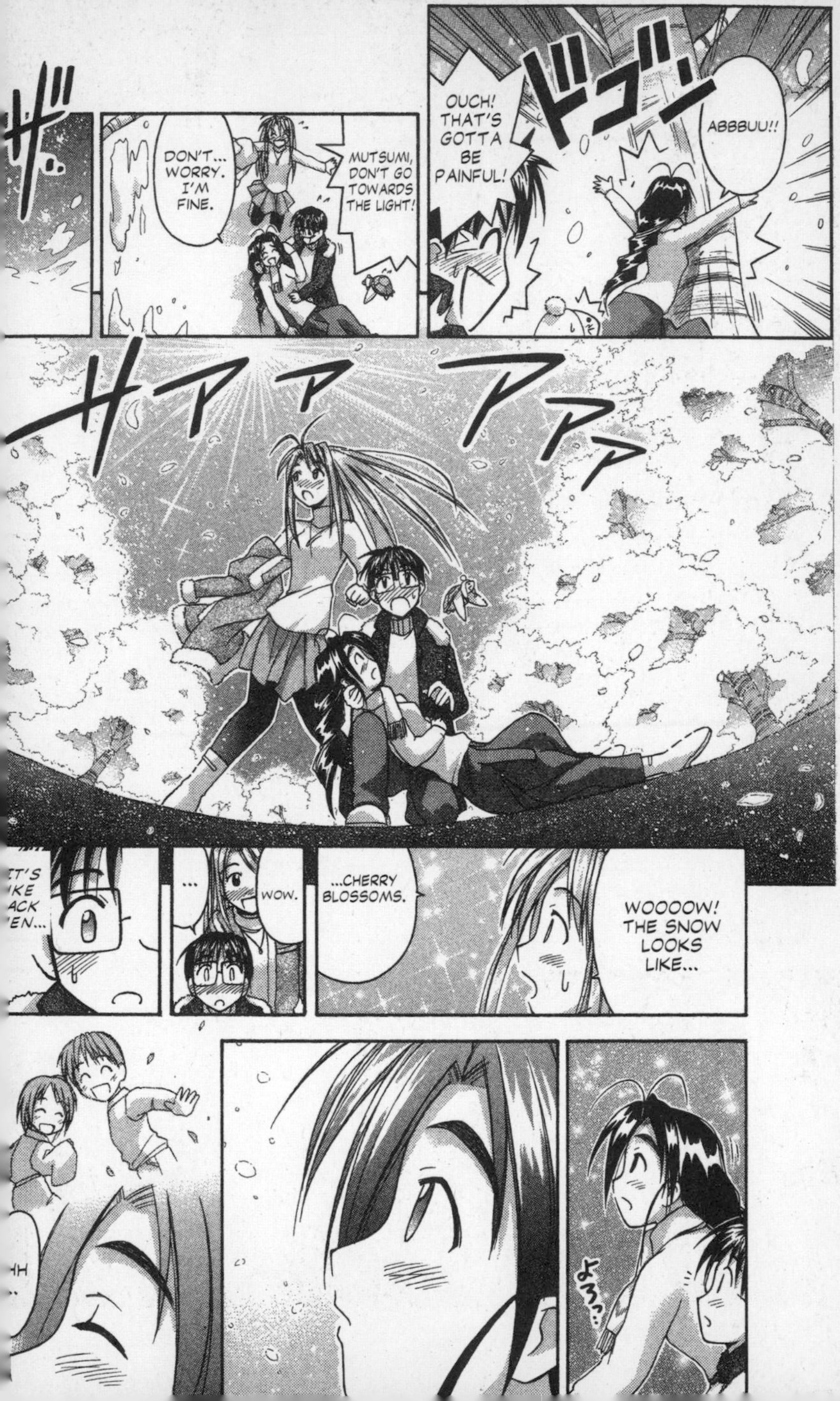
ドゴン
ABBBUU!!
OUCH! THAT'S GOTTA BE PAINFUL!
MUTSUMI, DON'T GO TOWARDS THE LIGHT!
DON'T... WORRY. I'M FINE.
ザ
サァァァァ
WOOOOW! THE SNOW LOOKS LIKE...
...CHERRY BLOSSOMS.
WOW.
...
よろっ...

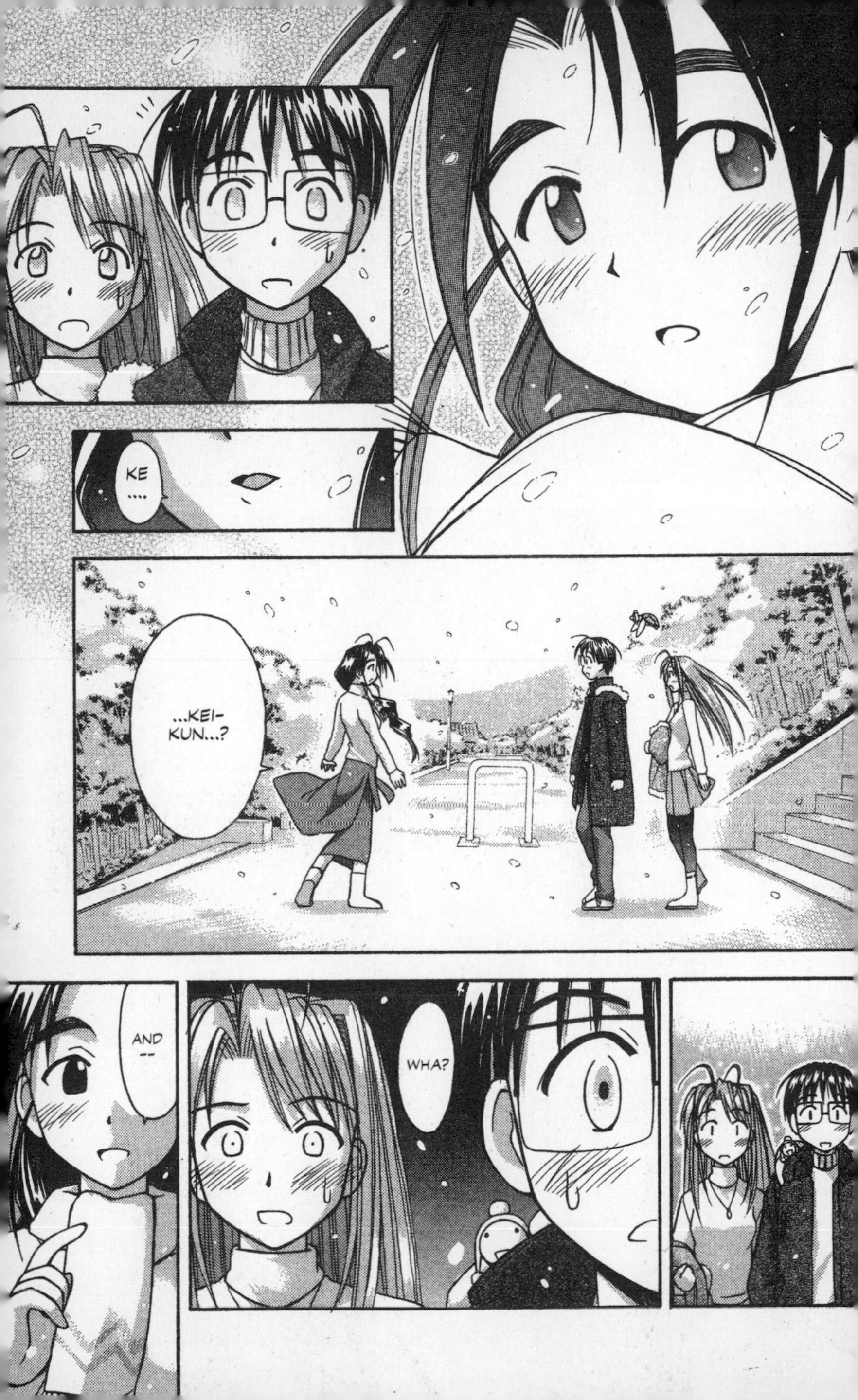
KE ....
...KEI-KUN...?
WHA?
AND --

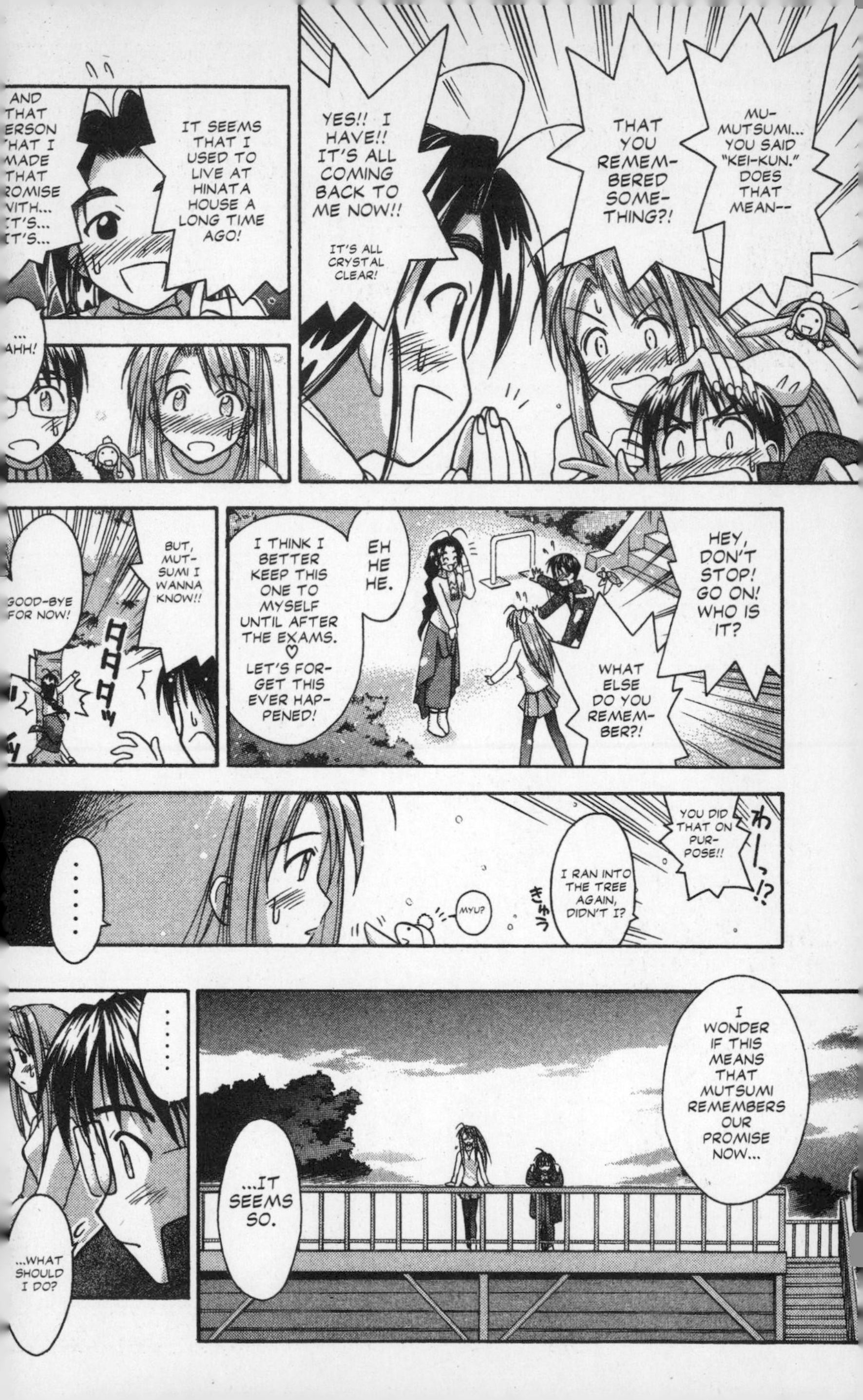
MU-MUTSUMI... YOU SAID "KEI-KUN." DOES THAT MEAN--
THAT YOU REMEMBERED SOMETHING?!
YES!! I HAVE!! IT'S ALL COMING BACK TO ME NOW!!
IT'S ALL CRYSTAL CLEAR!
IT SEEMS THAT I USED TO LIVE AT HINATA HOUSE A LONG TIME AGO!
AND THAT ERSON THAT I MADE THAT ROMISE WITH... T'S... T'S...
... AHH!
HEY, DON'T STOP! GO ON! WHO IS IT?
WHAT ELSE DO YOU REMEMBER?!
EH HE HE.
I THINK I BETTER KEEP THIS ONE TO MYSELF UNTIL AFTER THE EXAMS. ♡ LET'S FORGET THIS EVER HAPPENED!
BUT, MUTSUMI I WANNA KNOW!!
GOOD-BYE FOR NOW!
タタタッ
YOU DID THAT ON PURPOSE!!
わーっ!?
I RAN INTO THE TREE AGAIN, DIDN'T I?
きゅう
MYU?
......
I WONDER IF THIS MEANS THAT MUTSUMI REMEMBERS OUR PROMISE NOW...
...IT SEEMS SO.
......
...WHAT SHOULD I DO?

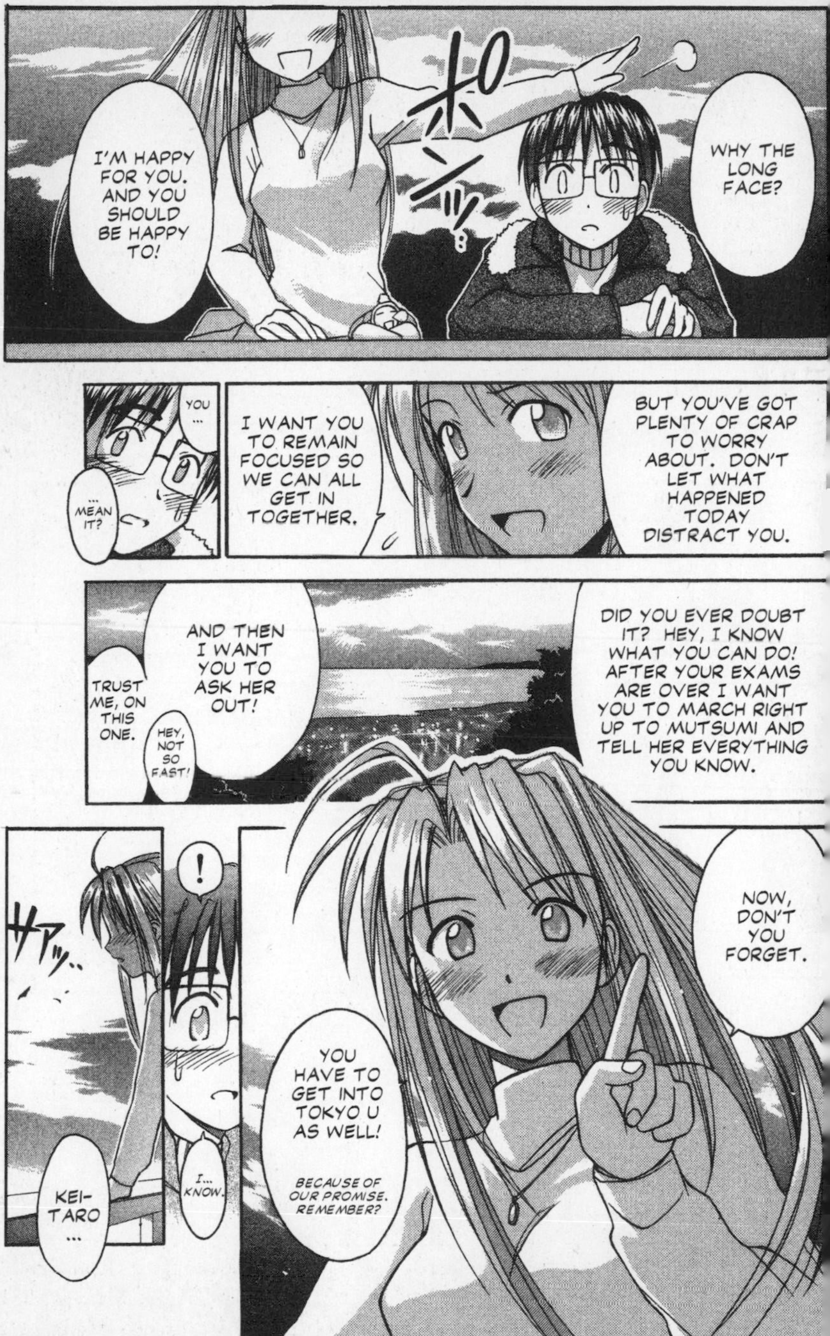
WHY THE LONG FACE?
I'M HAPPY FOR YOU. AND YOU SHOULD BE HAPPY TO!
BUT YOU'VE GOT PLENTY OF CRAP TO WORRY ABOUT. DON'T LET WHAT HAPPENED TODAY DISTRACT YOU.
I WANT YOU TO REMAIN FOCUSED SO WE CAN ALL GET IN TOGETHER.
YOU ...
... MEAN IT?
DID YOU EVER DOUBT IT? HEY, I KNOW WHAT YOU CAN DO! AFTER YOUR EXAMS ARE OVER I WANT YOU TO MARCH RIGHT UP TO MUTSUMI AND TELL HER EVERYTHING YOU KNOW.
AND THEN I WANT YOU TO ASK HER OUT!
HEY, NOT SO FAST!
TRUST ME, ON THIS ONE.
NOW, DON'T YOU FORGET.
YOU HAVE TO GET INTO TOKYO U AS WELL!
BECAUSE OF OUR PROMISE. REMEMBER?
!
I... KNOW.
KEI-TARO ...

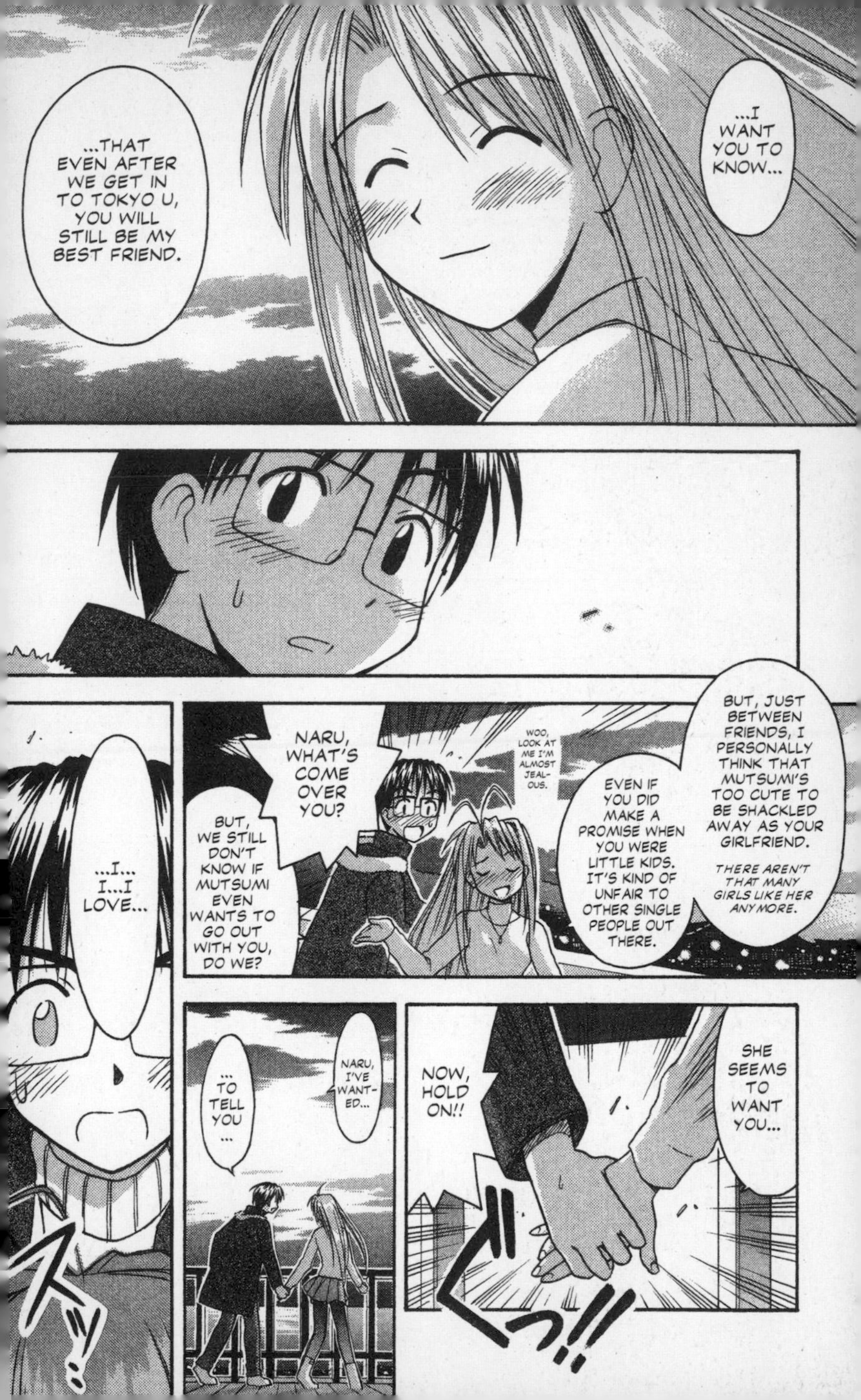
...I WANT YOU TO KNOW...
...THAT EVEN AFTER WE GET IN TO TOKYO U, YOU WILL STILL BE MY BEST FRIEND.
BUT, JUST BETWEEN FRIENDS, I PERSONALLY THINK THAT MUTSUMI'S TOO CUTE TO BE SHACKLED AWAY AS YOUR GIRLFRIEND.
THERE AREN'T THAT MANY GIRLS LIKE HER ANYMORE.
EVEN IF YOU DID MAKE A PROMISE WHEN YOU WERE LITTLE KIDS. IT'S KIND OF UNFAIR TO OTHER SINGLE PEOPLE OUT THERE.
WOO, LOOK AT ME I'M ALMOST JEAL-OUS.
NARU, WHAT'S COME OVER YOU?
BUT, WE STILL DON'T KNOW IF MUTSUMI EVEN WANTS TO GO OUT WITH YOU, DO WE?
SHE SEEMS TO WANT YOU...
NOW, HOLD ON!!
NARU, I'VE WANT-ED...
...TO TELL YOU...
...I... I...I LOVE...

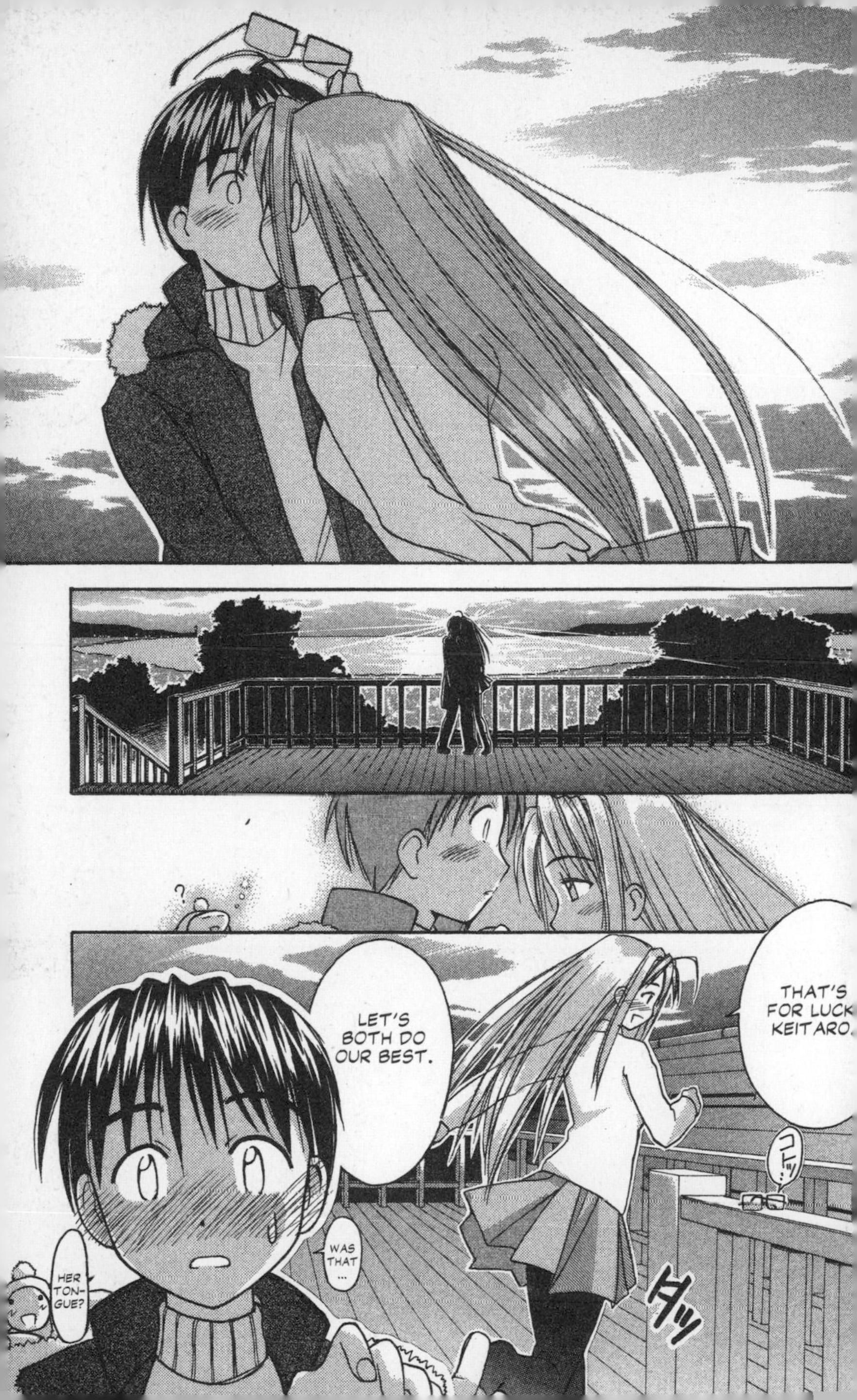
THAT'S FOR LUCK KEITARO.
LET'S BOTH DO OUR BEST.
コトッ
ダッ
WAS THAT ...
HER TONGUE?

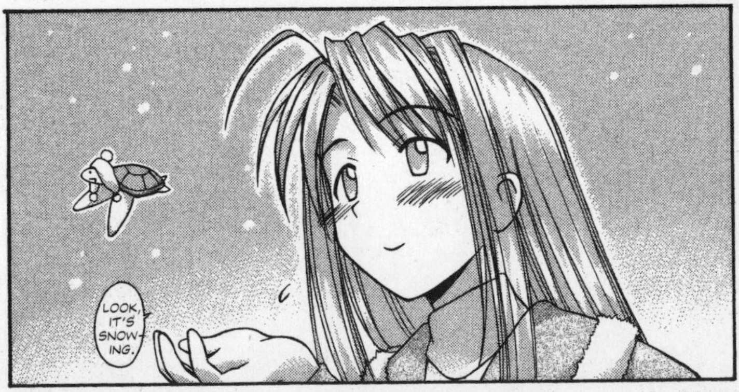
LOOK, IT'S SNOW-ING.

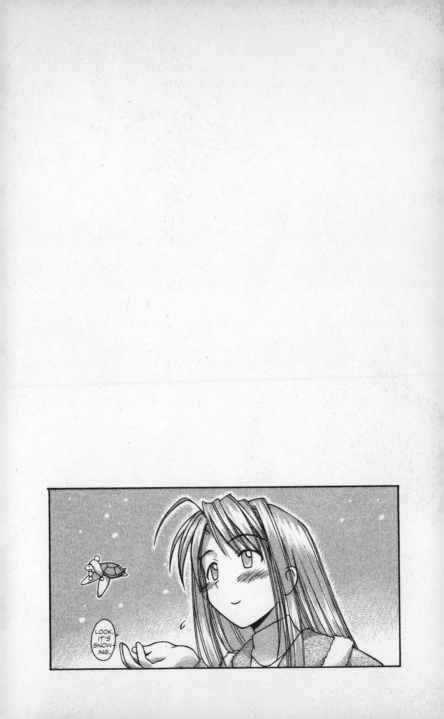

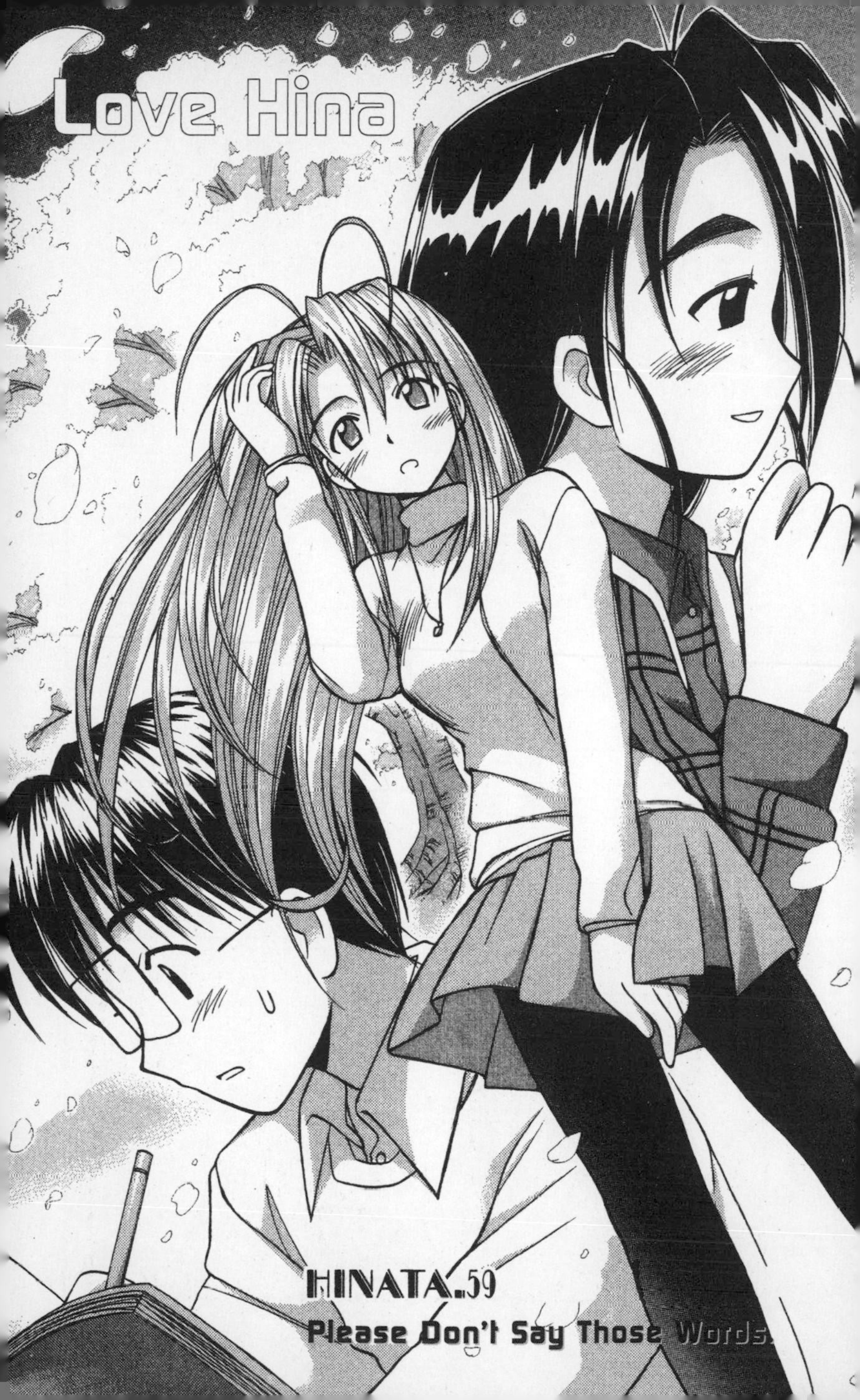
Love Hina
HINATA.59
Please Don't Say Those Words

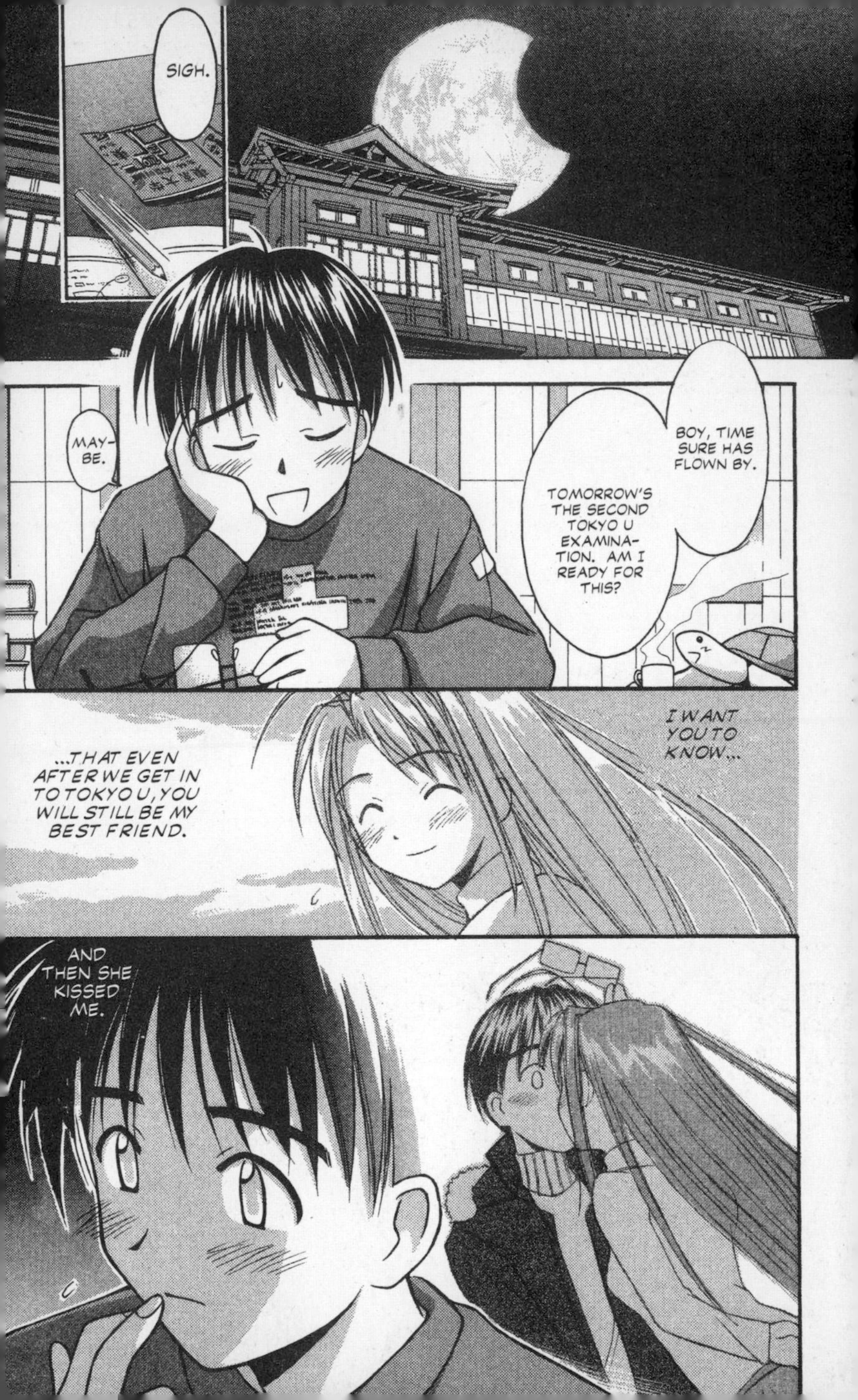
SIGH.
BOY, TIME SURE HAS FLOWN BY.
TOMORROW'S THE SECOND TOKYO U EXAMINATION. AM I READY FOR THIS?
MAY-BE.
I WANT YOU TO KNOW...
...THAT EVEN AFTER WE GET IN TO TOKYO U, YOU WILL STILL BE MY BEST FRIEND.
AND THEN SHE KISSED ME.

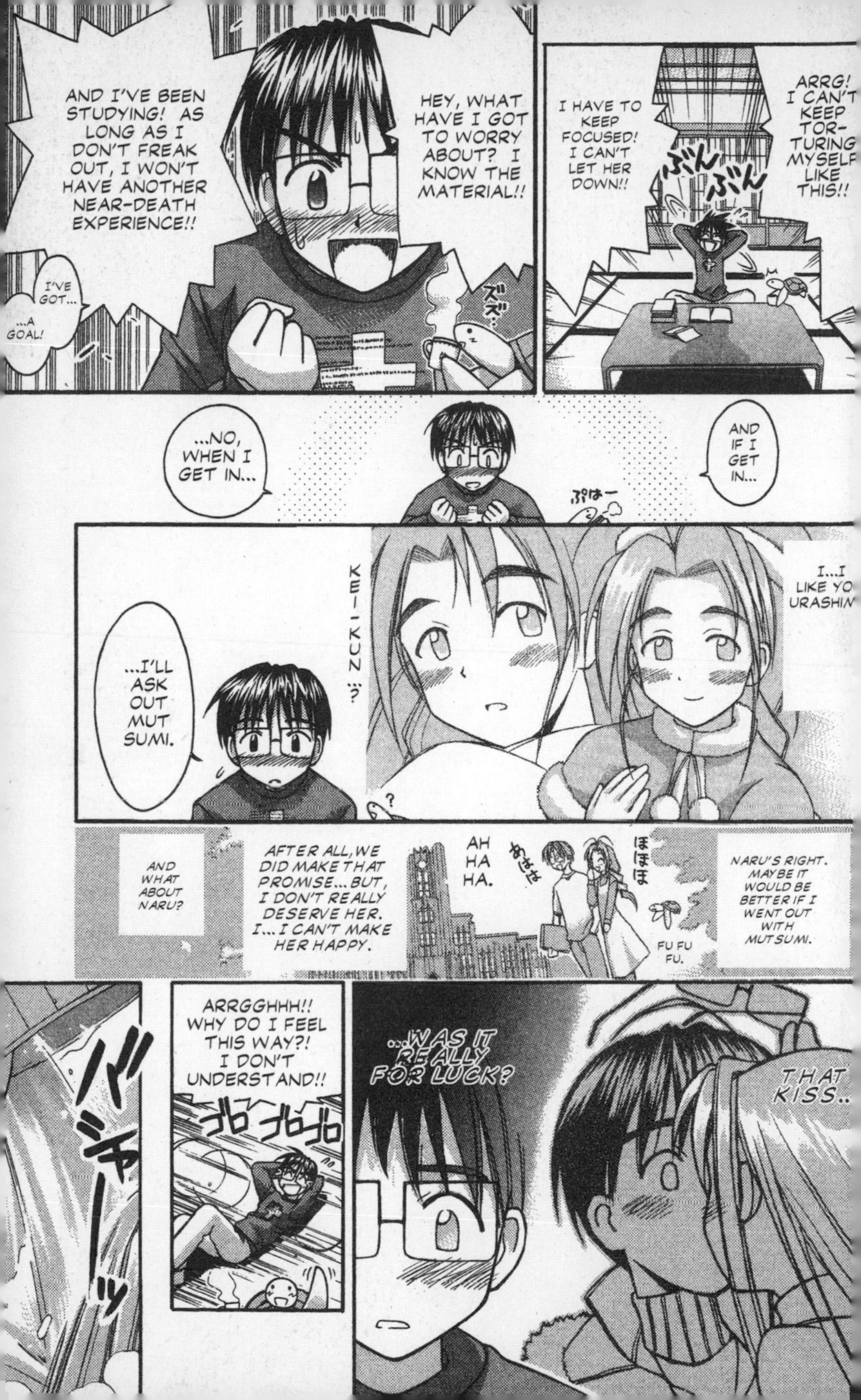
ARRG! I CAN'T KEEP TOR-TURING MYSELF LIKE THIS!!
ぶんぶん
I HAVE TO KEEP FOCUSED! I CAN'T LET HER DOWN!!
HEY, WHAT HAVE I GOT TO WORRY ABOUT? I KNOW THE MATERIAL!!
ズズ…
AND I'VE BEEN STUDYING! AS LONG AS I DON'T FREAK OUT, I WON'T HAVE ANOTHER NEAR-DEATH EXPERIENCE!!
I'VE GOT...
...A GOAL!
AND IF I GET IN...
ぷはー
...NO, WHEN I GET IN...
I...I LIKE YO URASHIM
KEI-KUN...?
...I'LL ASK OUT MUT SUMI.
NARU'S RIGHT. MAYBE IT WOULD BE BETTER IF I WENT OUT WITH MUTSUMI.
ほほほ
FU FU FU.
あはは
AH HA HA.
AFTER ALL, WE DID MAKE THAT PROMISE... BUT, I DON'T REALLY DESERVE HER. I...I CAN'T MAKE HER HAPPY.
AND WHAT ABOUT NARU?
THAT KISS..
...WAS IT REALLY FOR LUCK?
ARRGGHHH!! WHY DO I FEEL THIS WAY?! I DON'T UNDERSTAND!!
ゴロゴロゴロ
バシャーーッ

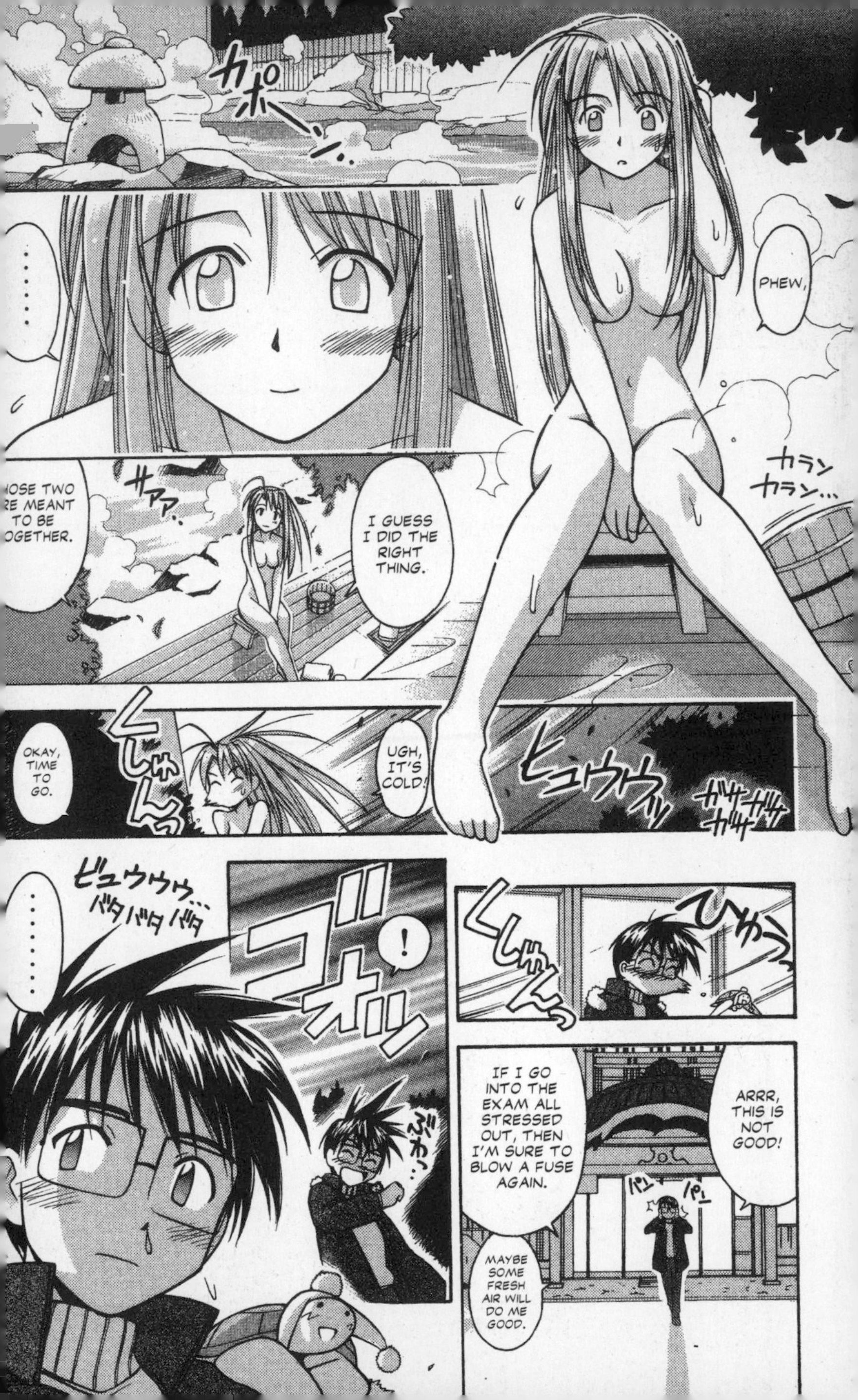
PHEW,
カラン
カラン…
カポーン…
……
サァァ…
I GUESS I DID THE RIGHT THING.
HOSE TWO RE MEANT TO BE OGETHER.
ヒュウウゥッ
ガサガサ
ガサ
UGH, IT'S COLD!
くしゅんっ
OKAY, TIME TO GO.
くしゅんっ
ひゅうっ
ARRR, THIS IS NOT GOOD!
IF I GO INTO THE EXAM ALL STRESSED OUT, THEN I'M SURE TO BLOW A FUSE AGAIN.
パン
パン
MAYBE SOME FRESH AIR WILL DO ME GOOD.
ビュウウウ…
バタバタバタ
……
ゴオッ
!
ぶわっ…

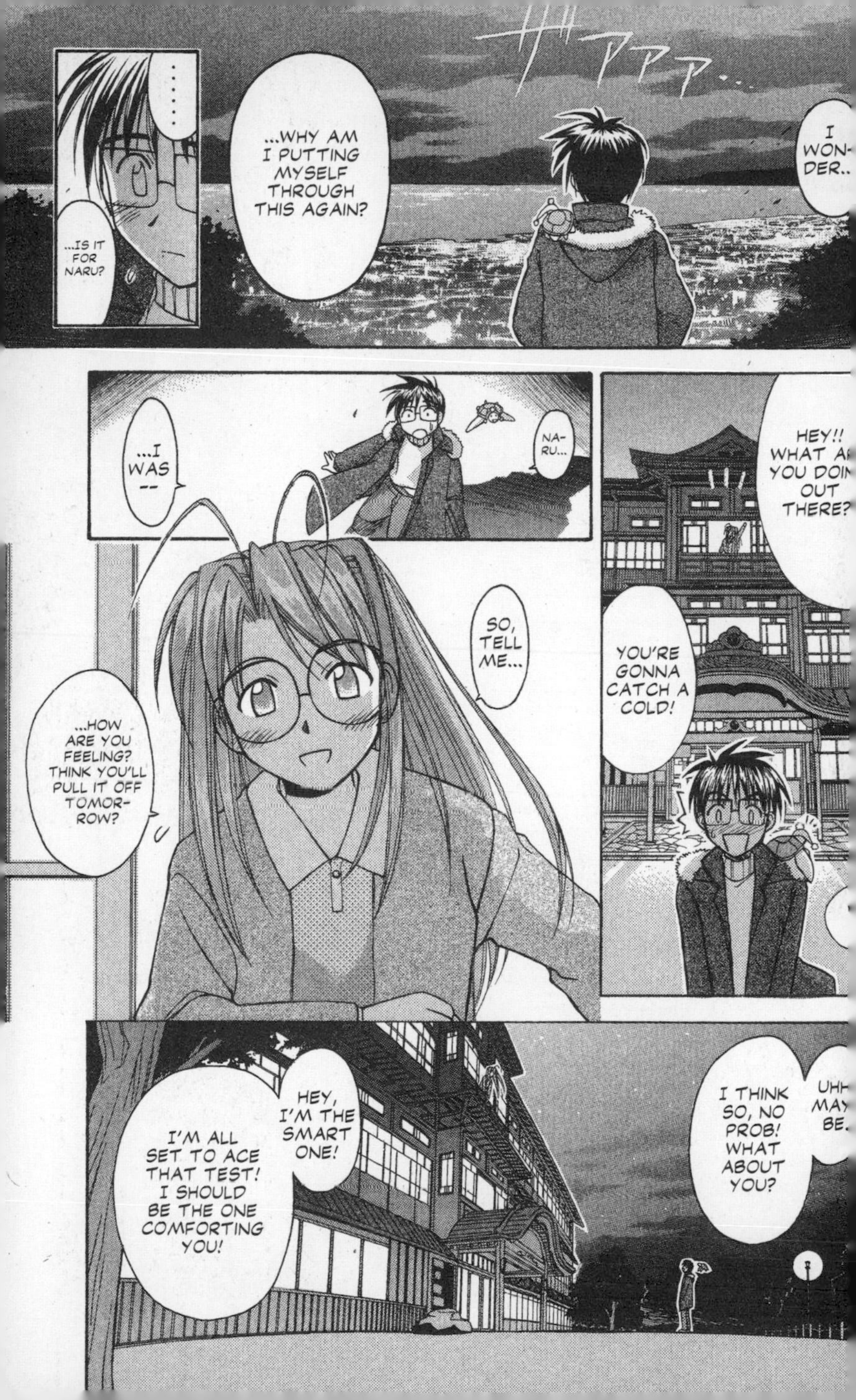
ザァァァ...
I WONDER..
...WHY AM I PUTTING MYSELF THROUGH THIS AGAIN?
......
...IS IT FOR NARU?
HEY!! WHAT A YOU DOIN OUT THERE?
YOU'RE GONNA CATCH A COLD!
NARU...
...I WAS --
SO, TELL ME...
...HOW ARE YOU FEELING? THINK YOU'LL PULL IT OFF TOMORROW?
UHH MAYBE.
I THINK SO, NO PROB! WHAT ABOUT YOU?
HEY, I'M THE SMART ONE!
I'M ALL SET TO ACE THAT TEST! I SHOULD BE THE ONE COMFORTING YOU!

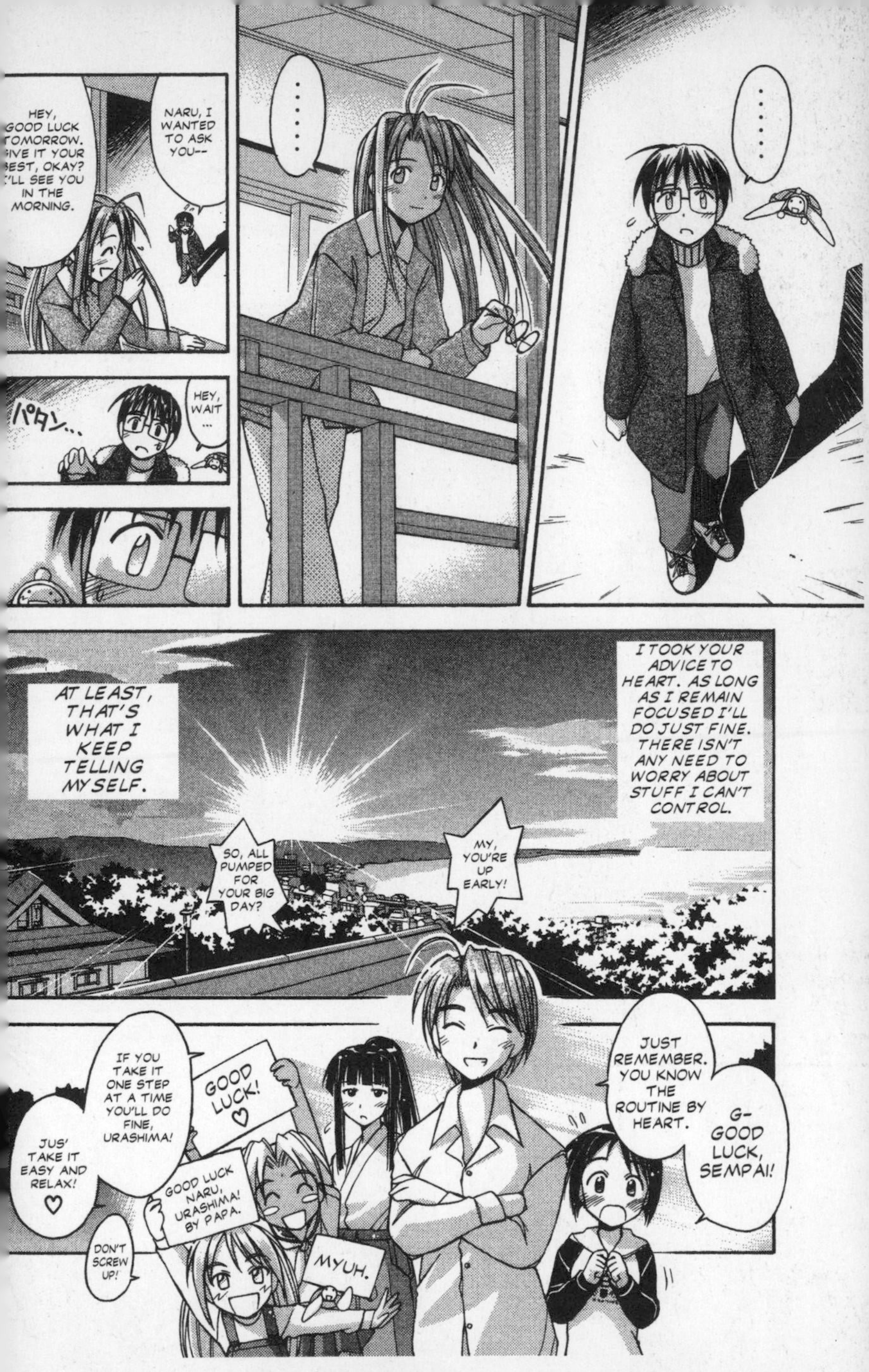

......
......
NARU, I WANTED TO ASK YOU--
HEY, GOOD LUCK TOMORROW. GIVE IT YOUR BEST, OKAY? I'LL SEE YOU IN THE MORNING.
HEY, WAIT ...
パタン...
I TOOK YOUR ADVICE TO HEART. AS LONG AS I REMAIN FOCUSED I'LL DO JUST FINE. THERE ISN'T ANY NEED TO WORRY ABOUT STUFF I CAN'T CONTROL.
AT LEAST, THAT'S WHAT I KEEP TELLING MYSELF.
MY, YOU'RE UP EARLY!
SO, ALL PUMPED FOR YOUR BIG DAY?
G-GOOD LUCK, SEMPAI!
JUST REMEMBER. YOU KNOW THE ROUTINE BY HEART.
GOOD LUCK! ♡
IF YOU TAKE IT ONE STEP AT A TIME YOU'LL DO FINE, URASHIMA!
GOOD LUCK NARU, URASHIMA! BY PAPA.
JUS' TAKE IT EASY AND RELAX! ♡
MYUH.
DON'T SCREW UP!

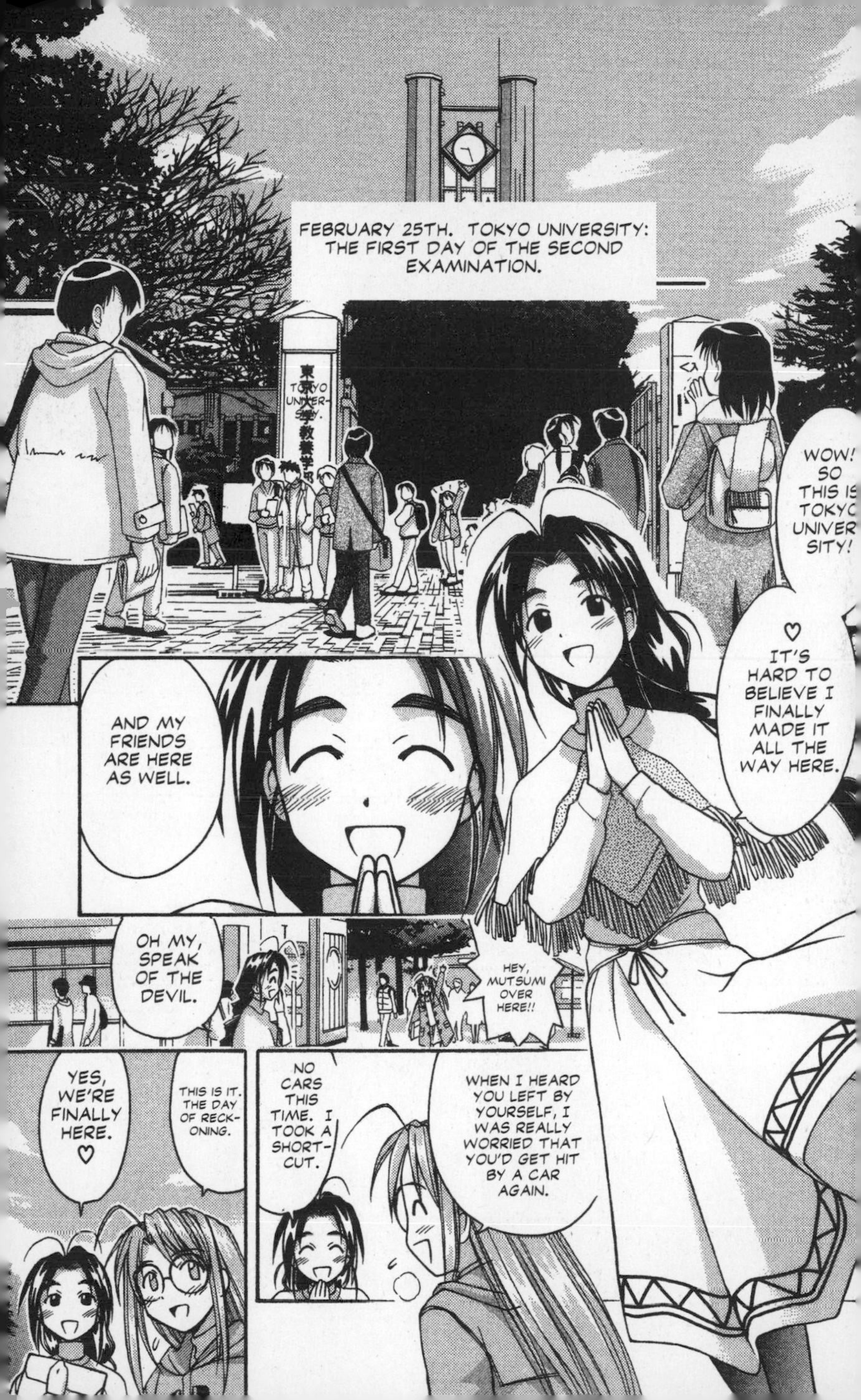
FEBRUARY 25TH. TOKYO UNIVERSITY: THE FIRST DAY OF THE SECOND EXAMINATION.
TOKYO UNIVERSITY.
WOW! SO THIS IS TOKYO UNIVERSITY!
♡ IT'S HARD TO BELIEVE I FINALLY MADE IT ALL THE WAY HERE.
AND MY FRIENDS ARE HERE AS WELL.
HEY, MUTSUMI OVER HERE!!
OH MY, SPEAK OF THE DEVIL.
WHEN I HEARD YOU LEFT BY YOURSELF, I WAS REALLY WORRIED THAT YOU'D GET HIT BY A CAR AGAIN.
NO CARS THIS TIME. I TOOK A SHORT-CUT.
THIS IS IT. THE DAY OF RECK-ONING.
YES, WE'RE FINALLY HERE. ♡

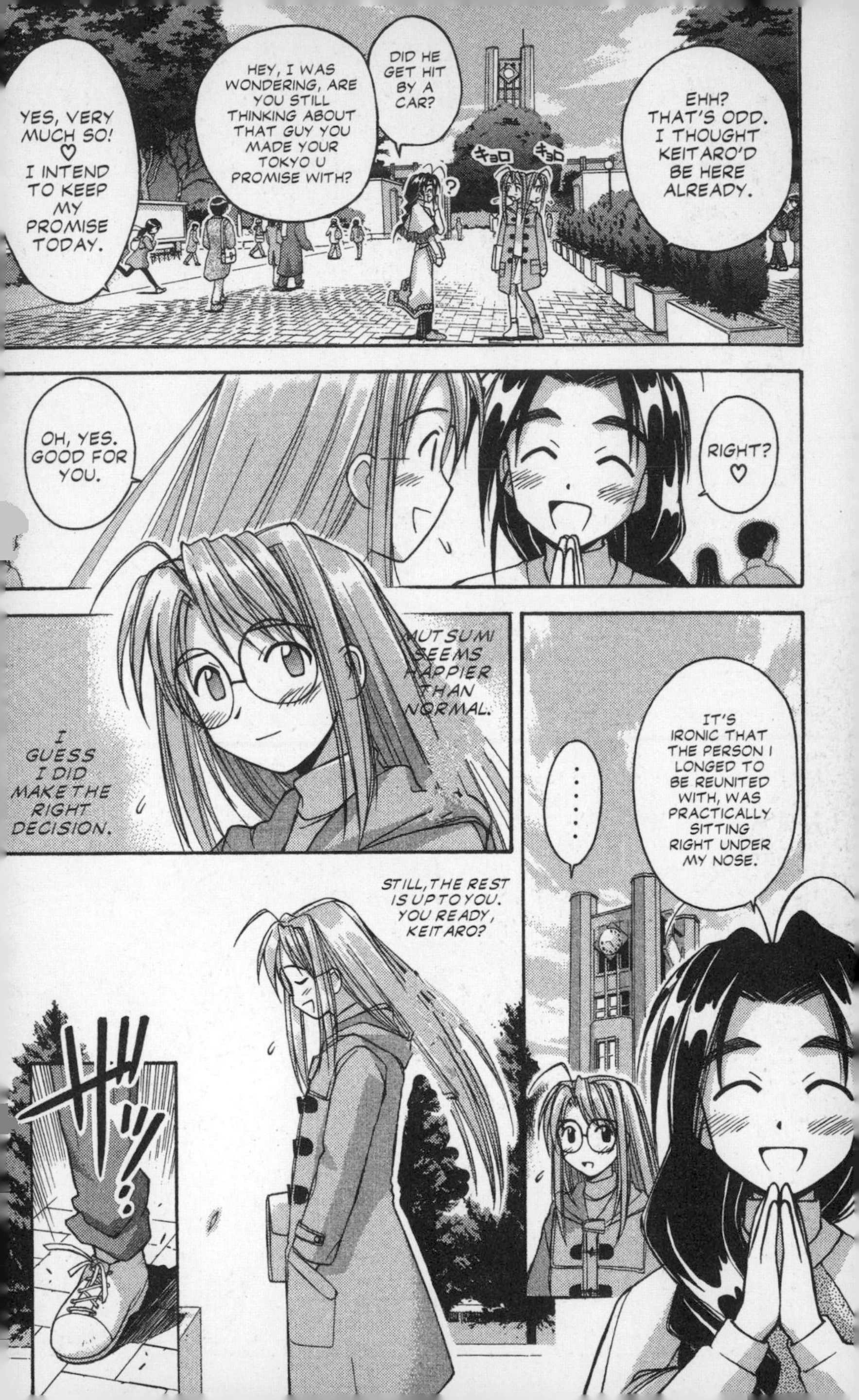
EHH? THAT'S ODD. I THOUGHT KEITARO'D BE HERE ALREADY.
キョロ
キョロ
DID HE GET HIT BY A CAR?
HEY, I WAS WONDERING, ARE YOU STILL THINKING ABOUT THAT GUY YOU MADE YOUR TOKYO U PROMISE WITH?
YES, VERY MUCH SO! ♡ I INTEND TO KEEP MY PROMISE TODAY.
RIGHT? ♡
OH, YES. GOOD FOR YOU.
IT'S IRONIC THAT THE PERSON I LONGED TO BE REUNITED WITH, WAS PRACTICALLY SITTING RIGHT UNDER MY NOSE.
......
MUTSUMI SEEMS HAPPIER THAN NORMAL.
I GUESS I DID MAKE THE RIGHT DECISION.
STILL, THE REST IS UP TO YOU. YOU READY, KEITARO?
ザッ

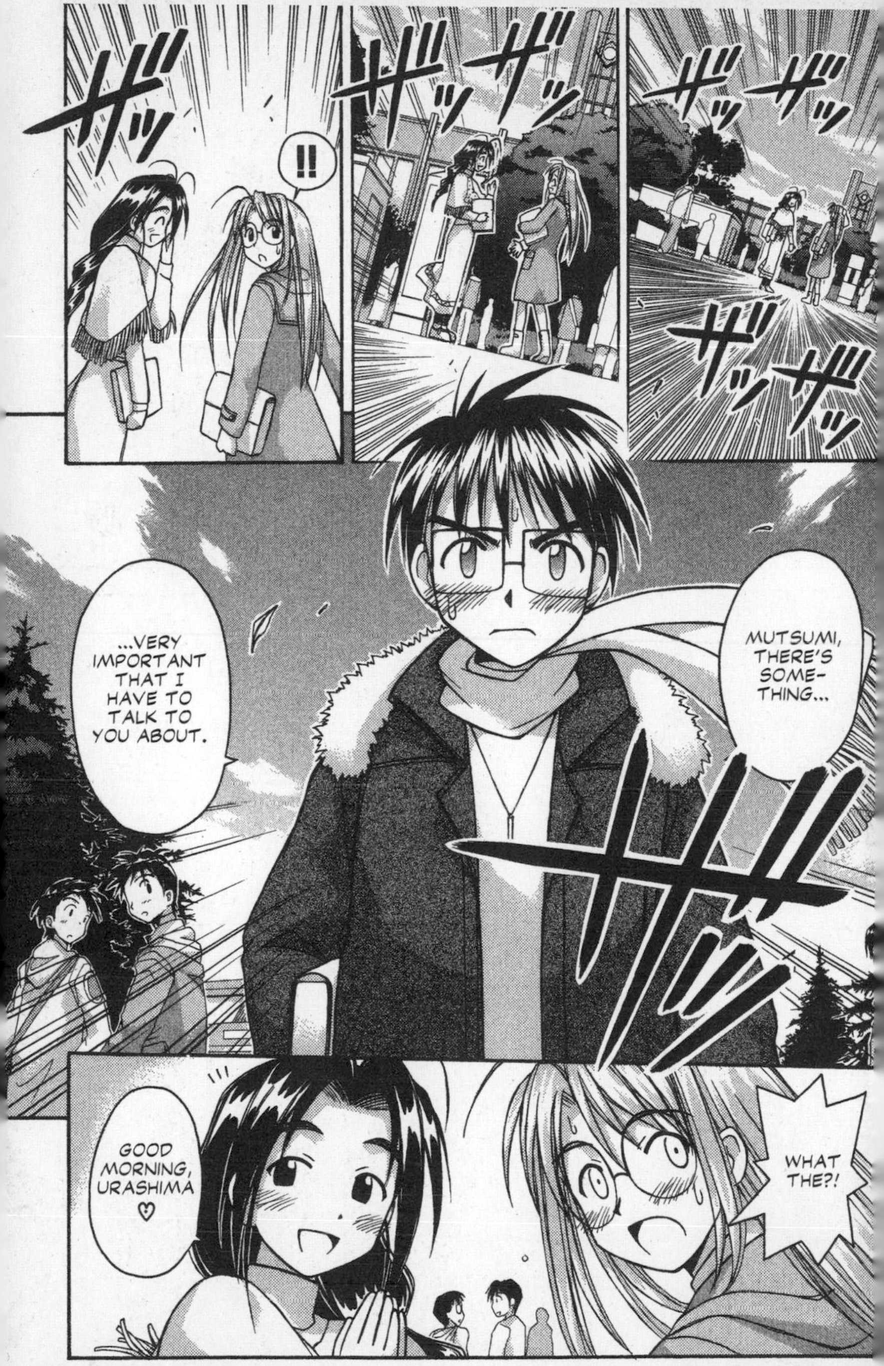
ザッ ザッ
ザッ ザッ
ザッ ザッ
ザッ
!!
MUTSUMI, THERE'S SOME-THING...
...VERY IMPORTANT THAT I HAVE TO TALK TO YOU ABOUT.
ザッ
WHAT THE?!
GOOD MORNING, URASHIMA ♡

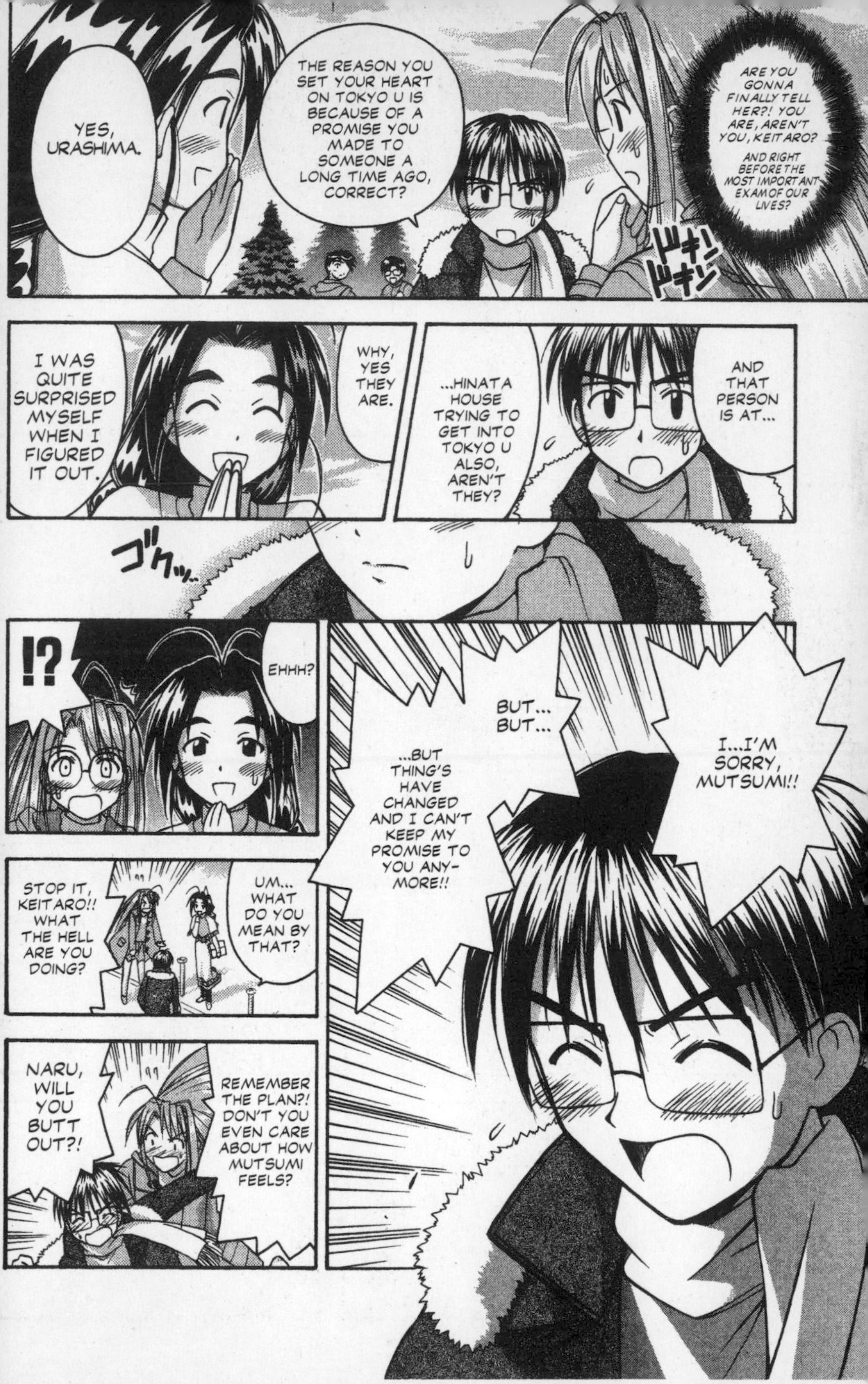
ARE YOU GONNA FINALLY TELL HER?! YOU ARE, AREN'T YOU, KEITARO?
AND RIGHT BEFORE THE MOST IMPORTANT EXAM OF OUR LIVES?
ドキン ドキン
THE REASON YOU SET YOUR HEART ON TOKYO U IS BECAUSE OF A PROMISE YOU MADE TO SOMEONE A LONG TIME AGO, CORRECT?
YES, URASHIMA.
AND THAT PERSON IS AT...
...HINATA HOUSE TRYING TO GET INTO TOKYO U ALSO, AREN'T THEY?
WHY, YES THEY ARE.
I WAS QUITE SURPRISED MYSELF WHEN I FIGURED IT OUT.
ゴクッ
I...I'M SORRY, MUTSUMI!!
BUT... BUT...
...BUT THING'S HAVE CHANGED AND I CAN'T KEEP MY PROMISE TO YOU ANY-MORE!!
!?
EHHH?
UM... WHAT DO YOU MEAN BY THAT?
STOP IT, KEITARO!! WHAT THE HELL ARE YOU DOING?
REMEMBER THE PLAN?! DON'T YOU EVEN CARE ABOUT HOW MUTSUMI FEELS?
NARU, WILL YOU BUTT OUT?!

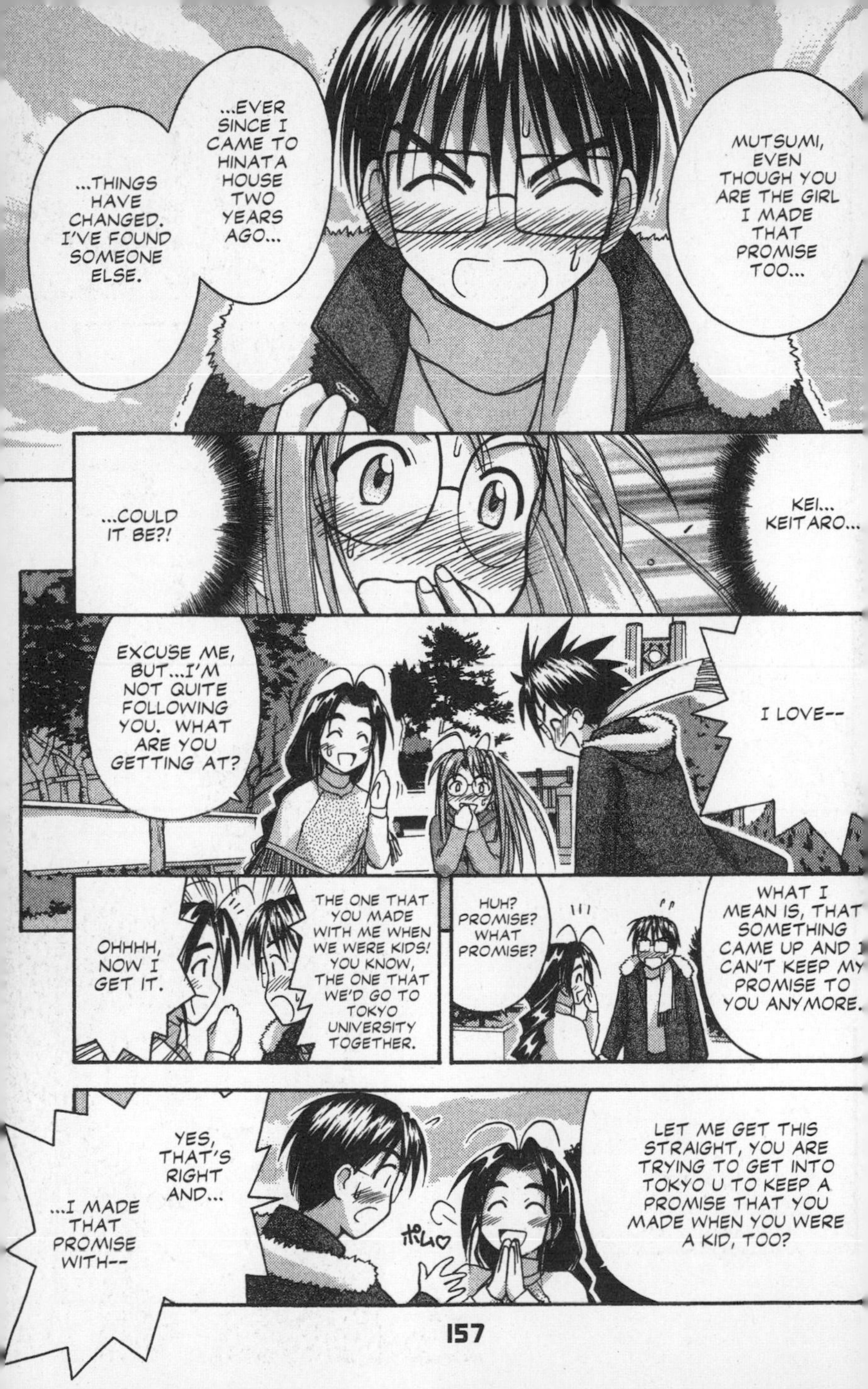
MUTSUMI, EVEN THOUGH YOU ARE THE GIRL I MADE THAT PROMISE TOO...
...EVER SINCE I CAME TO HINATA HOUSE TWO YEARS AGO...
...THINGS HAVE CHANGED. I'VE FOUND SOMEONE ELSE.
KEI... KEITARO...
...COULD IT BE?!
I LOVE--
EXCUSE ME, BUT...I'M NOT QUITE FOLLOWING YOU. WHAT ARE YOU GETTING AT?
WHAT I MEAN IS, THAT SOMETHING CAME UP AND I CAN'T KEEP MY PROMISE TO YOU ANYMORE.
HUH? PROMISE? WHAT PROMISE?
THE ONE THAT YOU MADE WITH ME WHEN WE WERE KIDS! YOU KNOW, THE ONE THAT WE'D GO TO TOKYO UNIVERSITY TOGETHER.
OHHHH, NOW I GET IT.
LET ME GET THIS STRAIGHT, YOU ARE TRYING TO GET INTO TOKYO U TO KEEP A PROMISE THAT YOU MADE WHEN YOU WERE A KID, TOO?
YES, THAT'S RIGHT AND...
...I MADE THAT PROMISE WITH--

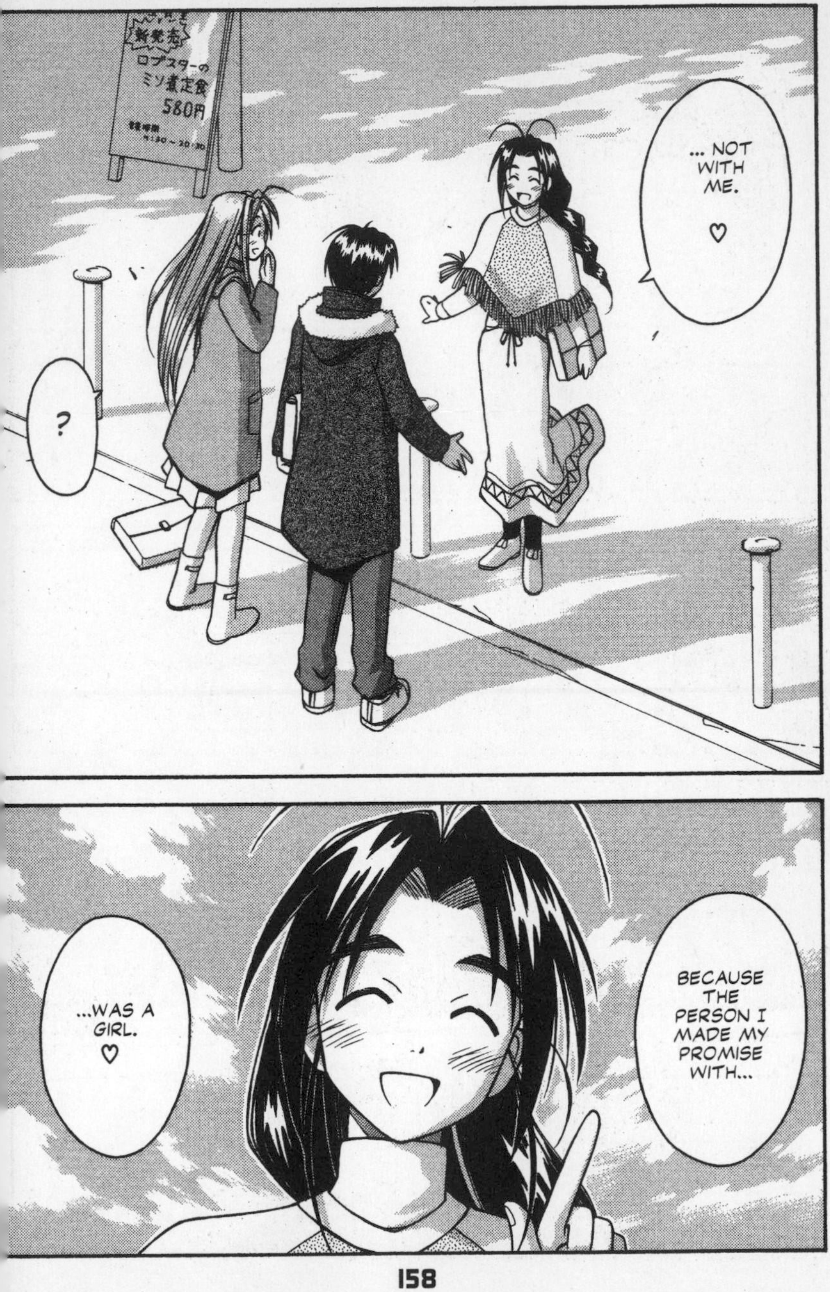
... NOT WITH ME. ♡
新発売
ロブスターの
ミソ煮定食
580円
?
BECAUSE THE PERSON I MADE MY PROMISE WITH...
...WAS A GIRL. ♡

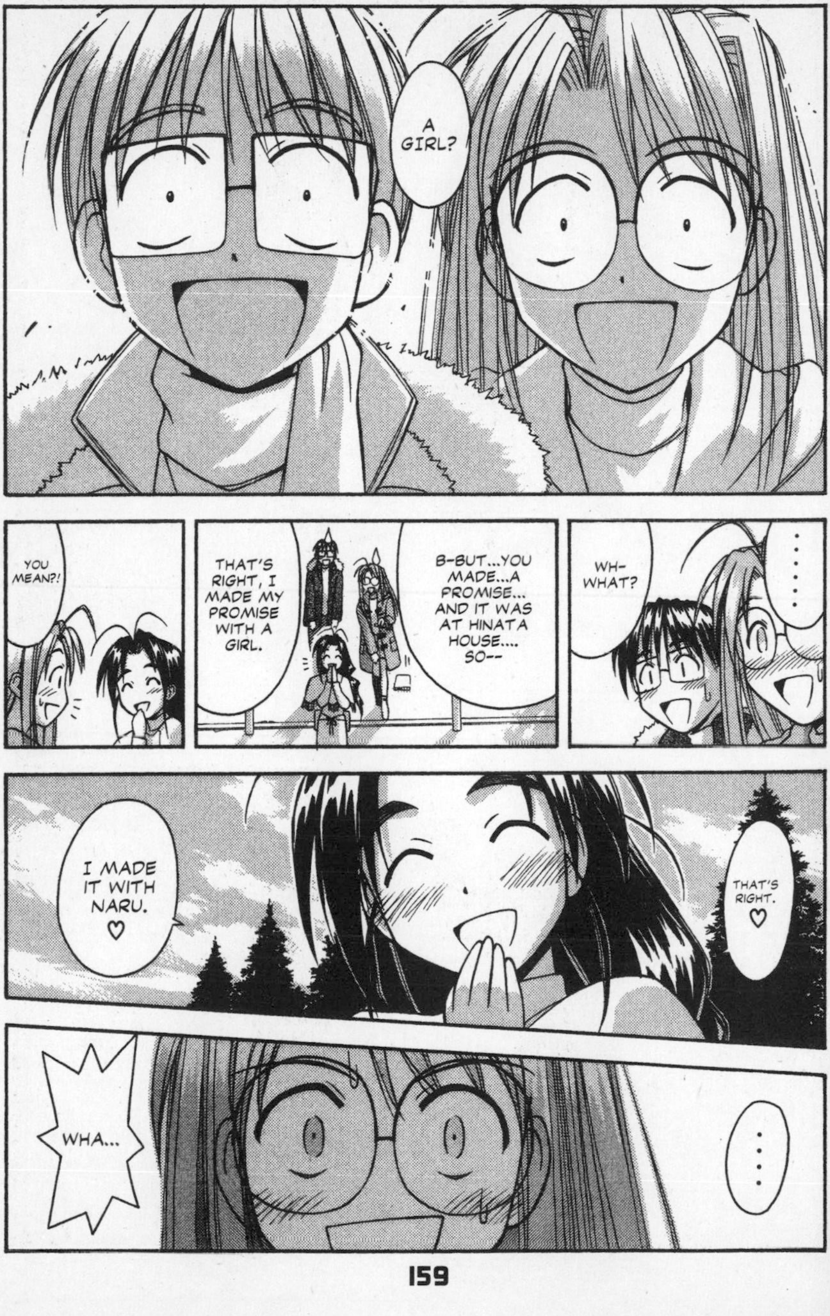
A GIRL?
......
WH- WHAT?
B-BUT...YOU MADE...A PROMISE... AND IT WAS AT HINATA HOUSE.... SO--
THAT'S RIGHT, I MADE MY PROMISE WITH A GIRL.
YOU MEAN?!
THAT'S RIGHT. ♡
I MADE IT WITH NARU. ♡
.....
WHA...

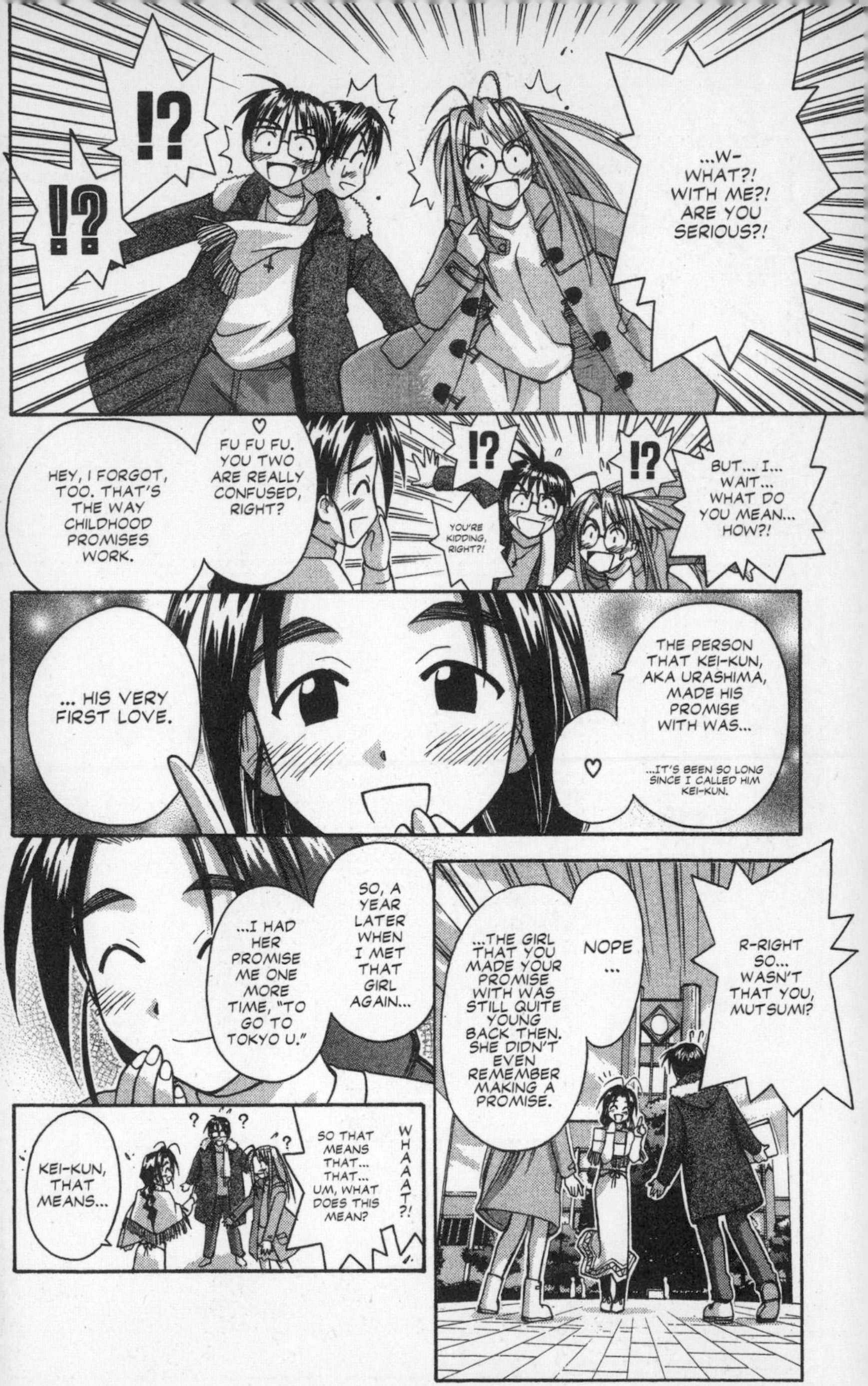
...W- WHAT?! WITH ME?! ARE YOU SERIOUS?!
!?
!?
BUT... I... WAIT... WHAT DO YOU MEAN... HOW?!
!?
!?
YOU'RE KIDDING, RIGHT?!
FU FU FU. YOU TWO ARE REALLY CONFUSED, RIGHT?
HEY, I FORGOT, TOO. THAT'S THE WAY CHILDHOOD PROMISES WORK.
THE PERSON THAT KEI-KUN, AKA URASHIMA, MADE HIS PROMISE WITH WAS...
...IT'S BEEN SO LONG SINCE I CALLED HIM KEI-KUN.
... HIS VERY FIRST LOVE.
R-RIGHT SO... WASN'T THAT YOU, MUTSUMI?
NOPE ...
...THE GIRL THAT YOU MADE YOUR PROMISE WITH WAS STILL QUITE YOUNG BACK THEN. SHE DIDN'T EVEN REMEMBER MAKING A PROMISE.
SO, A YEAR LATER WHEN I MET THAT GIRL AGAIN...
...I HAD HER PROMISE ME ONE MORE TIME, "TO GO TO TOKYO U."
WHAAAAT?!
SO THAT MEANS THAT... THAT... UM, WHAT DOES THIS MEAN?
KEI-KUN, THAT MEANS...

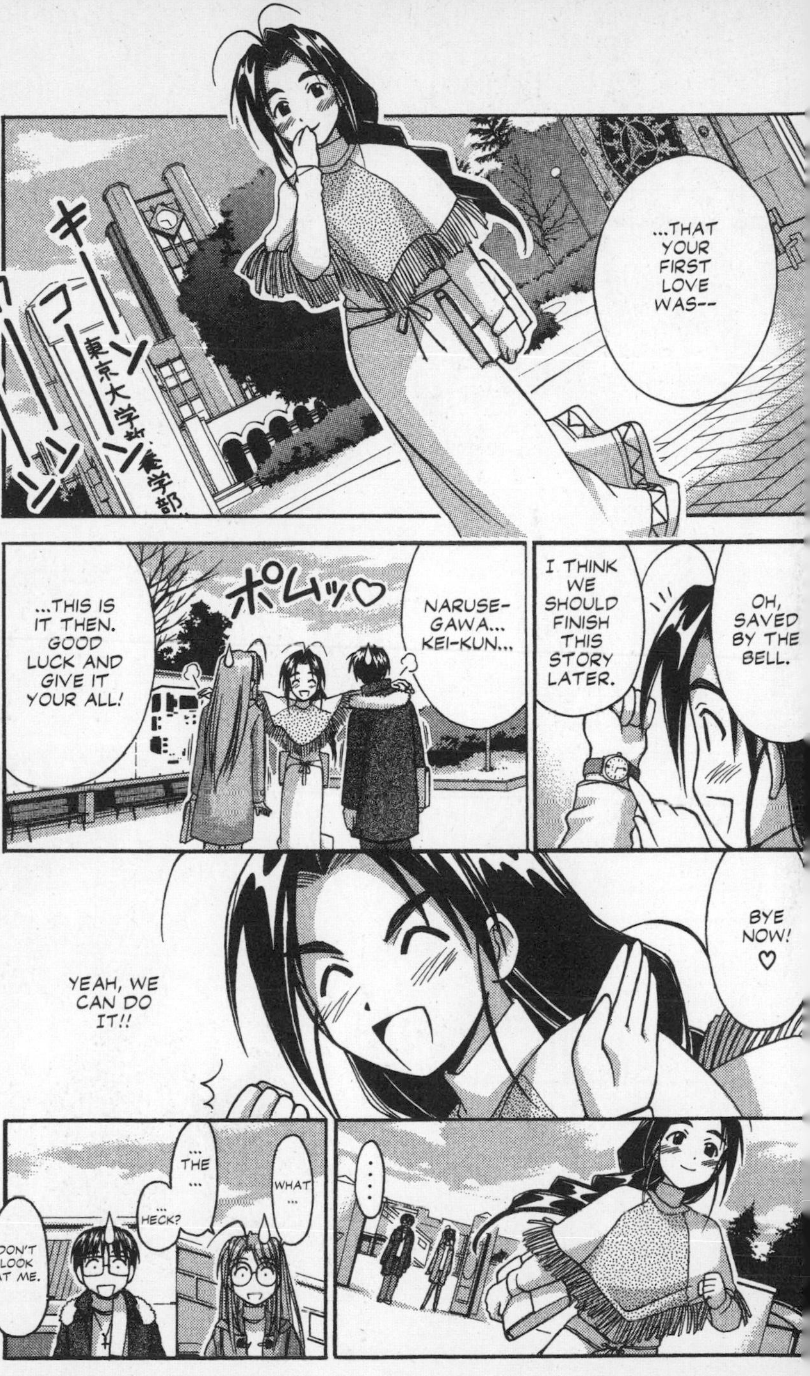
...THAT YOUR FIRST LOVE WAS--
キーンコーン
カーンコーン
東京大学教養学部
OH, SAVED BY THE BELL.
I THINK WE SHOULD FINISH THIS STORY LATER.
NARUSE-GAWA... KEI-KUN...
ポムッ♡
...THIS IS IT THEN. GOOD LUCK AND GIVE IT YOUR ALL!
BYE NOW! ♡
YEAH, WE CAN DO IT!!
....
WHAT ...
... THE ...
... HECK?
DON'T LOOK AT ME.

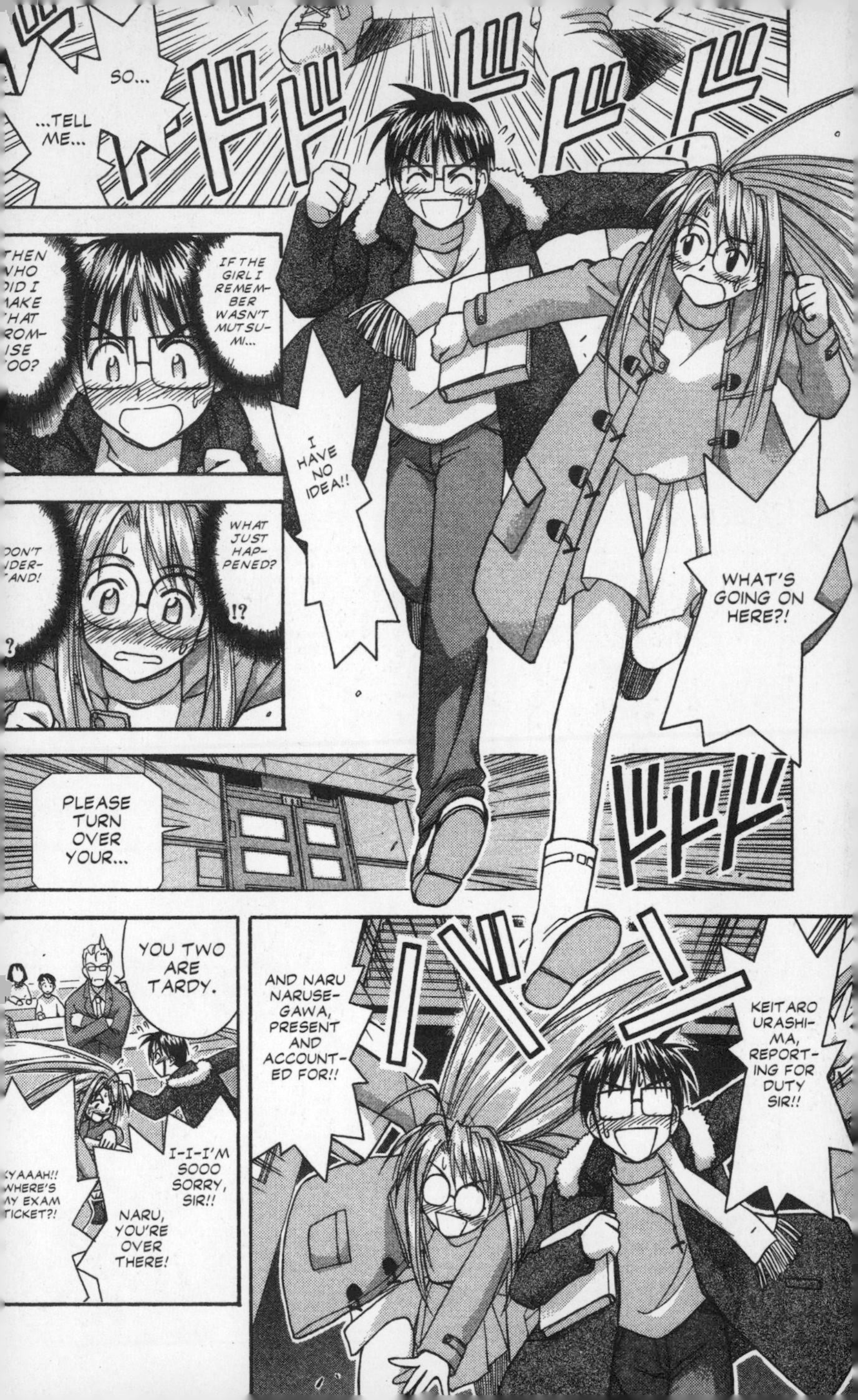
SO...
...TELL ME...
I HAVE NO IDEA!!
WHAT'S GOING ON HERE?!
IF THE GIRL I REMEMBER WASN'T MUTSUMI...
THEN WHO DID I MAKE THAT PROMISE TOO?
WHAT JUST HAPPENED?
!?
DON'T UNDERSTAND!
?
PLEASE TURN OVER YOUR...
KEITARO URASHIMA, REPORTING FOR DUTY SIR!!
AND NARU NARUSEGAWA, PRESENT AND ACCOUNTED FOR!!
YOU TWO ARE TARDY.
I-I-I'M SOOO SORRY, SIR!!
NARU, YOU'RE OVER THERE!
KYAAAH!! WHERE'S MY EXAM TICKET?!

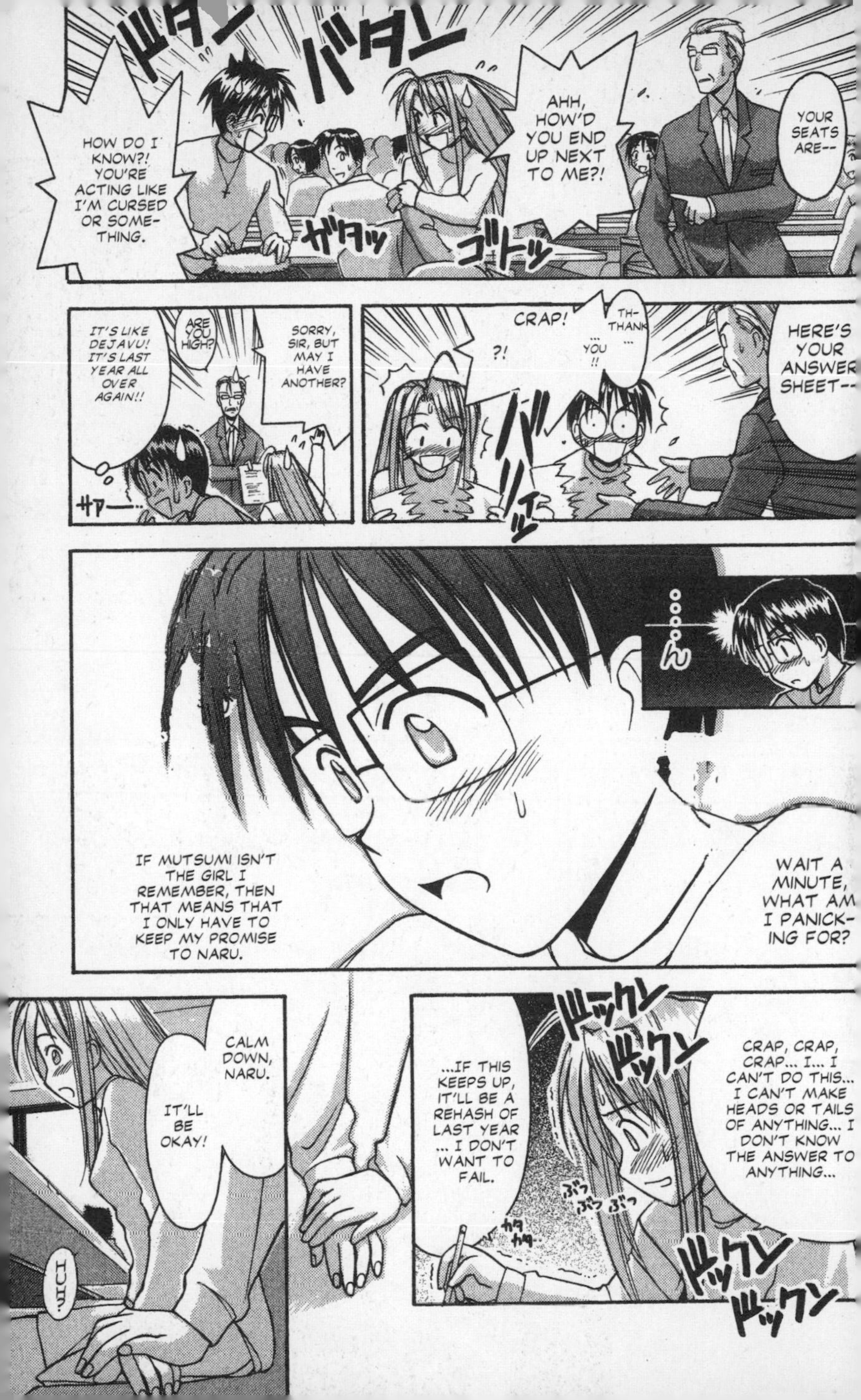
YOUR SEATS ARE--
バタン
AHH, HOW'D YOU END UP NEXT TO ME?!
ドタン
HOW DO I KNOW?! YOU'RE ACTING LIKE I'M CURSED OR SOME-THING.
ゴトッ
ガタッ
HERE'S YOUR ANSWER SHEET--
TH-THANK... YOU!!
CRAP!
?!
SORRY, SIR, BUT MAY I HAVE ANOTHER?
ARE YOU HIGH?
IT'S LIKE DEJAVU! IT'S LAST YEAR ALL OVER AGAIN!!
サァー…
WAIT A MINUTE, WHAT AM I PANICK-ING FOR?
IF MUTSUMI ISN'T THE GIRL I REMEMBER, THEN THAT MEANS THAT I ONLY HAVE TO KEEP MY PROMISE TO NARU.
CRAP, CRAP, CRAP... I... I CAN'T DO THIS... I CAN'T MAKE HEADS OR TAILS OF ANYTHING... I DON'T KNOW THE ANSWER TO ANYTHING...
ドックン ドックン
...IF THIS KEEPS UP, IT'LL BE A REHASH OF LAST YEAR ... I DON'T WANT TO FAIL.
ぶつ ぶつ ぶつ
ドックン ドックン
CALM DOWN, NARU.
IT'LL BE OKAY!
HUH?

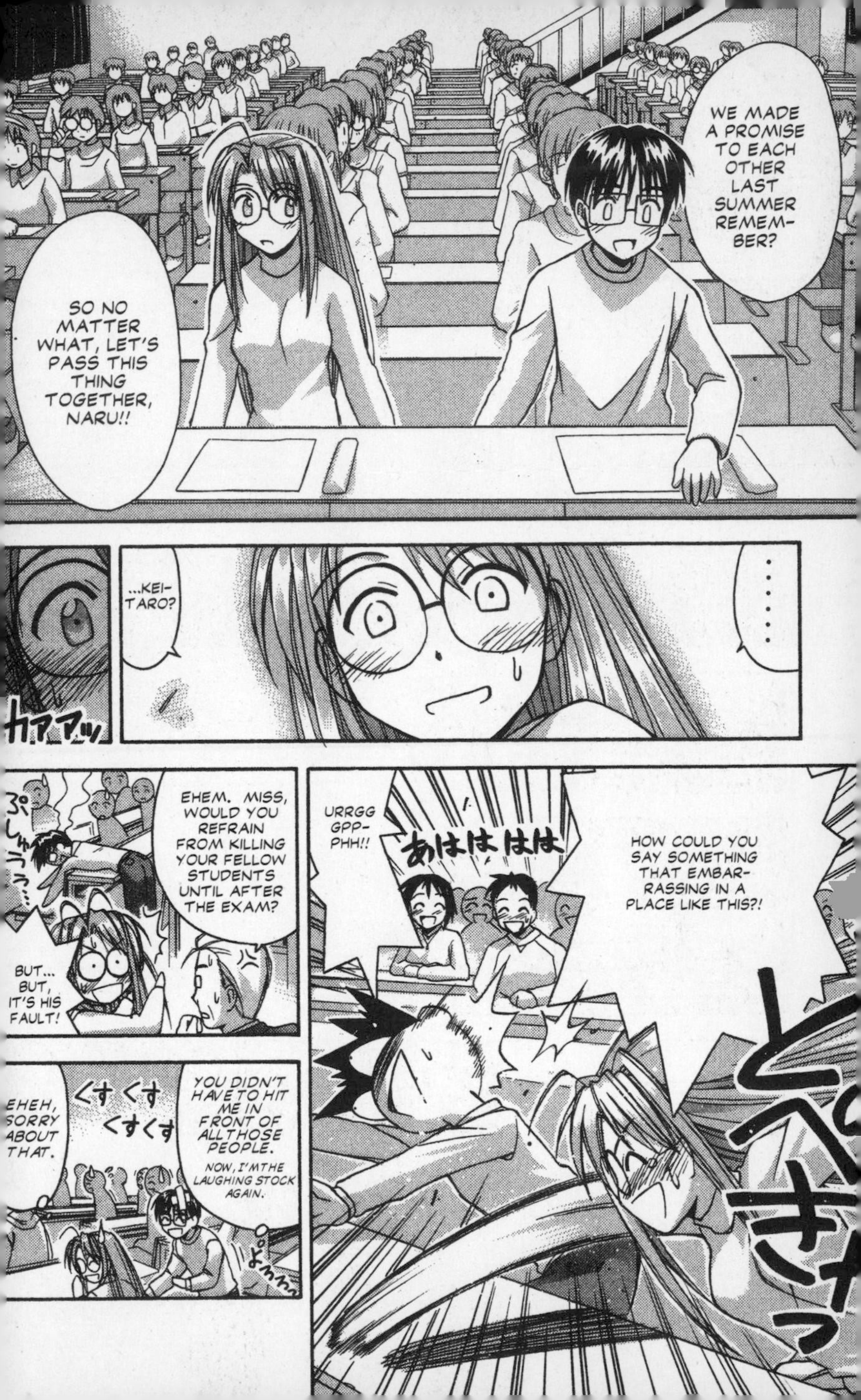
WE MADE A PROMISE TO EACH OTHER LAST SUMMER REMEMBER?
SO NO MATTER WHAT, LET'S PASS THIS THING TOGETHER, NARU!!
......
...KEI-TARO?
カアアッ
HOW COULD YOU SAY SOMETHING THAT EMBARRASSING IN A PLACE LIKE THIS?!
あははははは
URRGG GPP-PHH!!
EHEM. MISS, WOULD YOU REFRAIN FROM KILLING YOUR FELLOW STUDENTS UNTIL AFTER THE EXAM?
BUT... BUT, IT'S HIS FAULT!
YOU DIDN'T HAVE TO HIT ME IN FRONT OF ALL THOSE PEOPLE.
NOW, I'M THE LAUGHING STOCK AGAIN.
くすくす
くすくす
EHEH, SORRY ABOUT THAT.

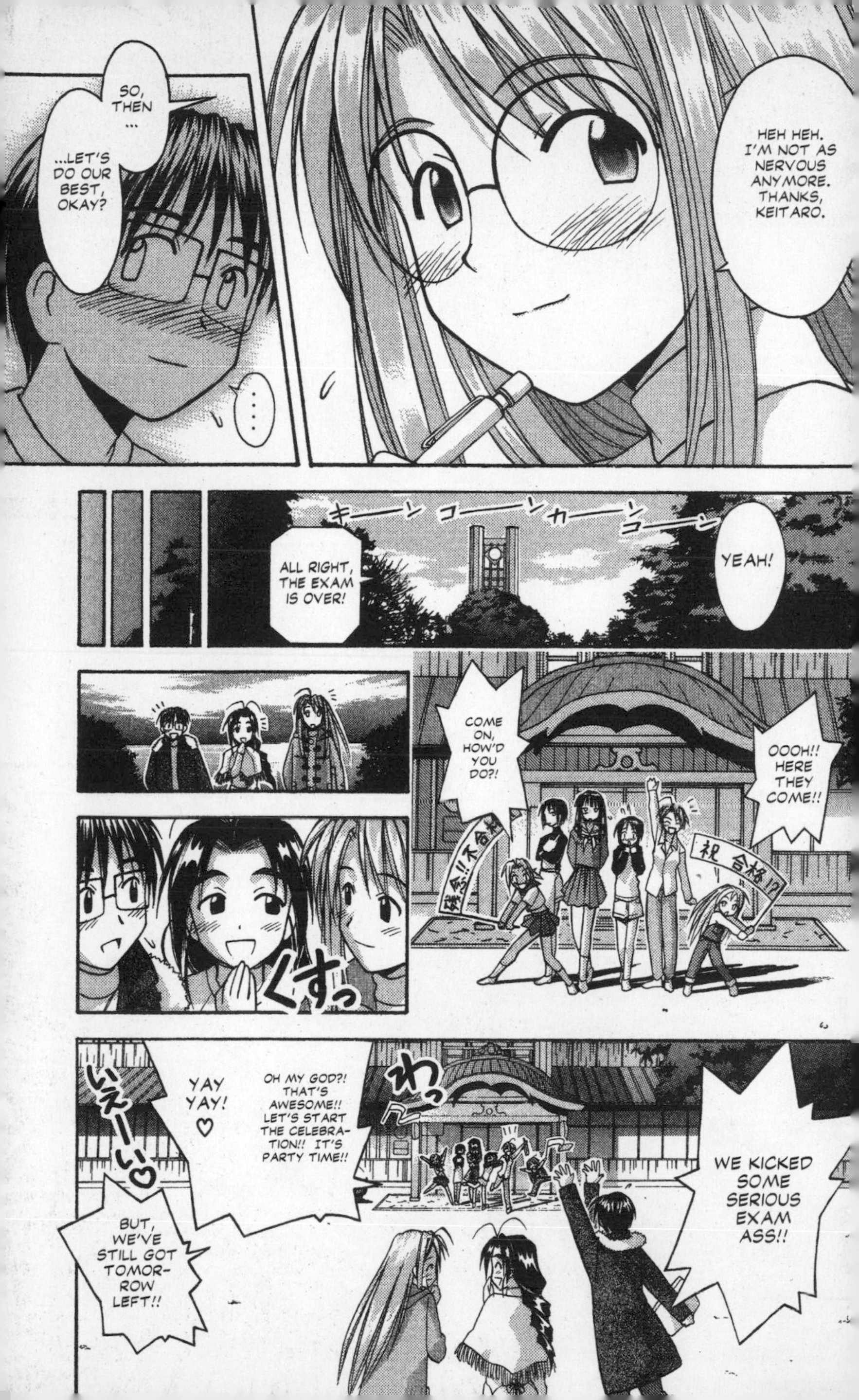
HEH HEH. I'M NOT AS NERVOUS ANYMORE. THANKS, KEITARO.
SO, THEN ...
...LET'S DO OUR BEST, OKAY?
......
キーンコーンカーン
コーン
ALL RIGHT, THE EXAM IS OVER!
YEAH!
OOOH!! HERE THEY COME!!
COME ON, HOW'D YOU DO?!
祝 合格!!
残念!!不合格
くすっ
WE KICKED SOME SERIOUS EXAM ASS!!
わっ
OH MY GOD?! THAT'S AWESOME!! LET'S START THE CELEBRATION!! IT'S PARTY TIME!!
YAY YAY! ♡
いえーい♡
BUT, WE'VE STILL GOT TOMORROW LEFT!!

Finally, here it is! Sorry for keeping you waiting!

# It's the results for the Love Hina Character Popularity Poll---------!!

As to be expected, coming in t number 1 is none other than ur heroine, Naru! Way to go! (Well, that's not the only eason.) The number of votes he raked in only cements the strength of her popularity. In econd place we have Shinobu. She's got a lot of hardcore fans, so this seems to be just the right standing for her.

And in third, who else but MOTOKO! Surprisingly only 50 votes away from capturing Shinobu's second place spot! What a battle! Now Ken "I Love Motoko" Akamatsu can sleep easy (Laugh). At this point, Mutsumi came in fourth. But as her role and importance continue to increase, who can say how high she'll climb when we do this again------

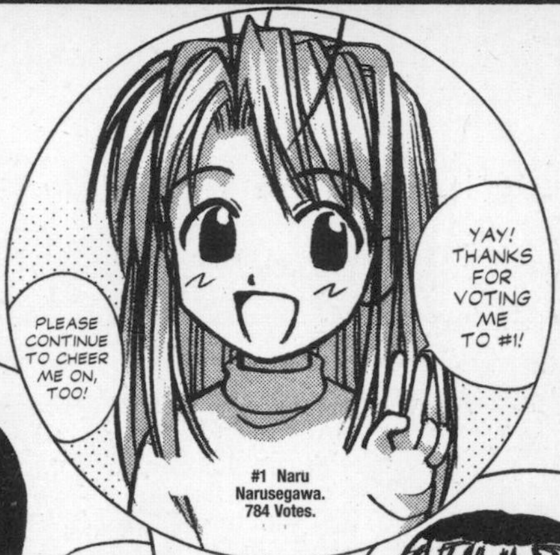
YAY! THANKS FOR VOTING ME TO #1!
PLEASE CONTINUE TO CHEER ME ON, TOO!
#1 Naru Narusegawa. 784 Votes.

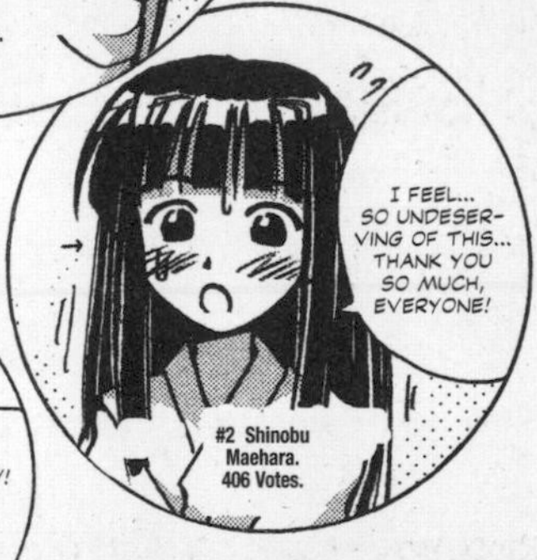
I FEEL... SO UNDESERVING OF THIS... THANK YOU SO MUCH, EVERYONE!
#2 Shinobu Maehara. 406 Votes.

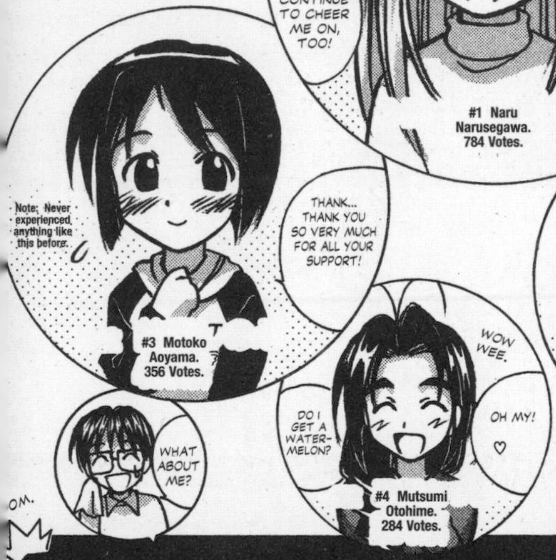
THANK... THANK YOU SO VERY MUCH FOR ALL YOUR SUPPORT!
Note: Never experienced anything like this before.
#3 Motoko Aoyama. 356 Votes.
WOW WEE.
OH MY!
DO I GET A WATER-MELON?
#4 Mutsumi Otohime. 284 Votes.
WHAT ABOUT ME?

It's ironic how Akamatsu's assistant Magii ranked higher than him. (Laugh.) Then again, he's always naked so maybe that drew some sympathy votes?

#5. Keitaro Urashima. 154 Votes.
#6. Tama-chan. 112 Votes.
Tama-chan: Myuh!
#7. Kaolla Su. 106 Votes.
Su: I'll beat you next time!!
#8. Kitsune: 100 Votes.
#9. Haruka Urashima. 58 Votes.
#10. Sarah. 33 Votes.
#11. Liddo-kun. 29 Votes.
#12. Seta. 20 Votes.

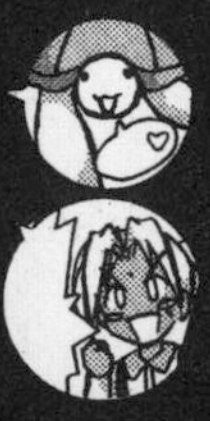

#13. Mutsumi's uncle. 10 Votes.
#14. Grandma Hinata. 6 Votes.
#15. Magii. Female Tokyo U Student (Hinata 32). 5 Votes.
#16. Krishna. Ken Akamatsu. Shirai. Haitani. 4 Votes.
#17. Mecha Tama-chan. Motoko's sister. The Yakuza on the Shinkansen. (Hinata 18). The Innkeeper (Hinata 20). 3 Votes.
#18. The guy that pushed Mutsumi over (Hinata 47). The bar owner. 2 Votes.
#19. The girl from Keitaro's memories. Keitaro when he was 5. Pochi. Kana-chan. Ooboke. Shankara-kun. 1 Vote.

And that was it! We received a total of 2506 votes. Thanks all for your participation.

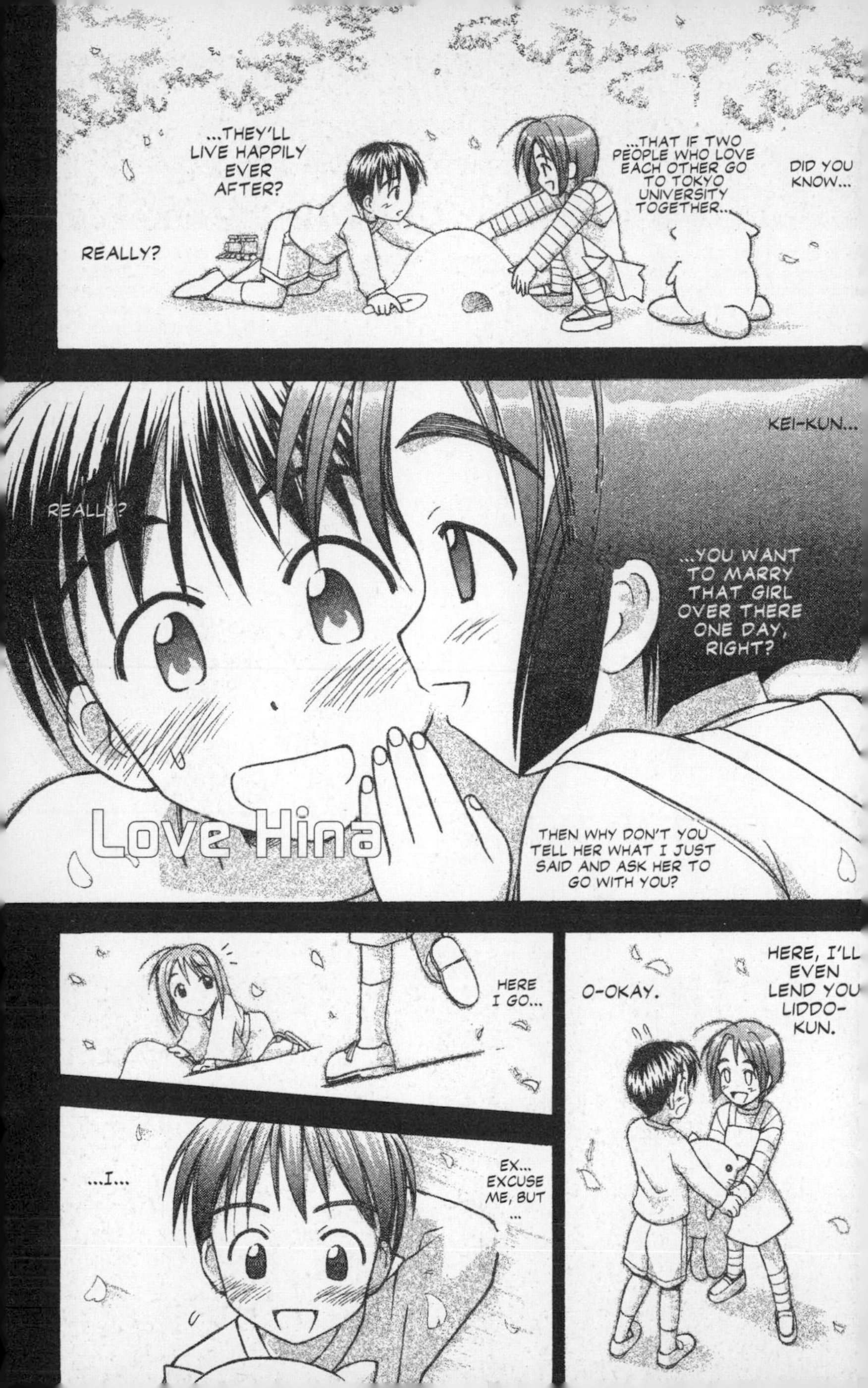
DID YOU KNOW...
...THAT IF TWO PEOPLE WHO LOVE EACH OTHER GO TO TOKYO UNIVERSITY TOGETHER...
...THEY'LL LIVE HAPPILY EVER AFTER?
REALLY?
KEI-KUN...
...YOU WANT TO MARRY THAT GIRL OVER THERE ONE DAY, RIGHT?
REALLY?
THEN WHY DON'T YOU TELL HER WHAT I JUST SAID AND ASK HER TO GO WITH YOU?
Love Hina
HERE, I'LL EVEN LEND YOU LIDDO-KUN.
O-OKAY.
HERE I GO...
EX... EXCUSE ME, BUT ...
...I...

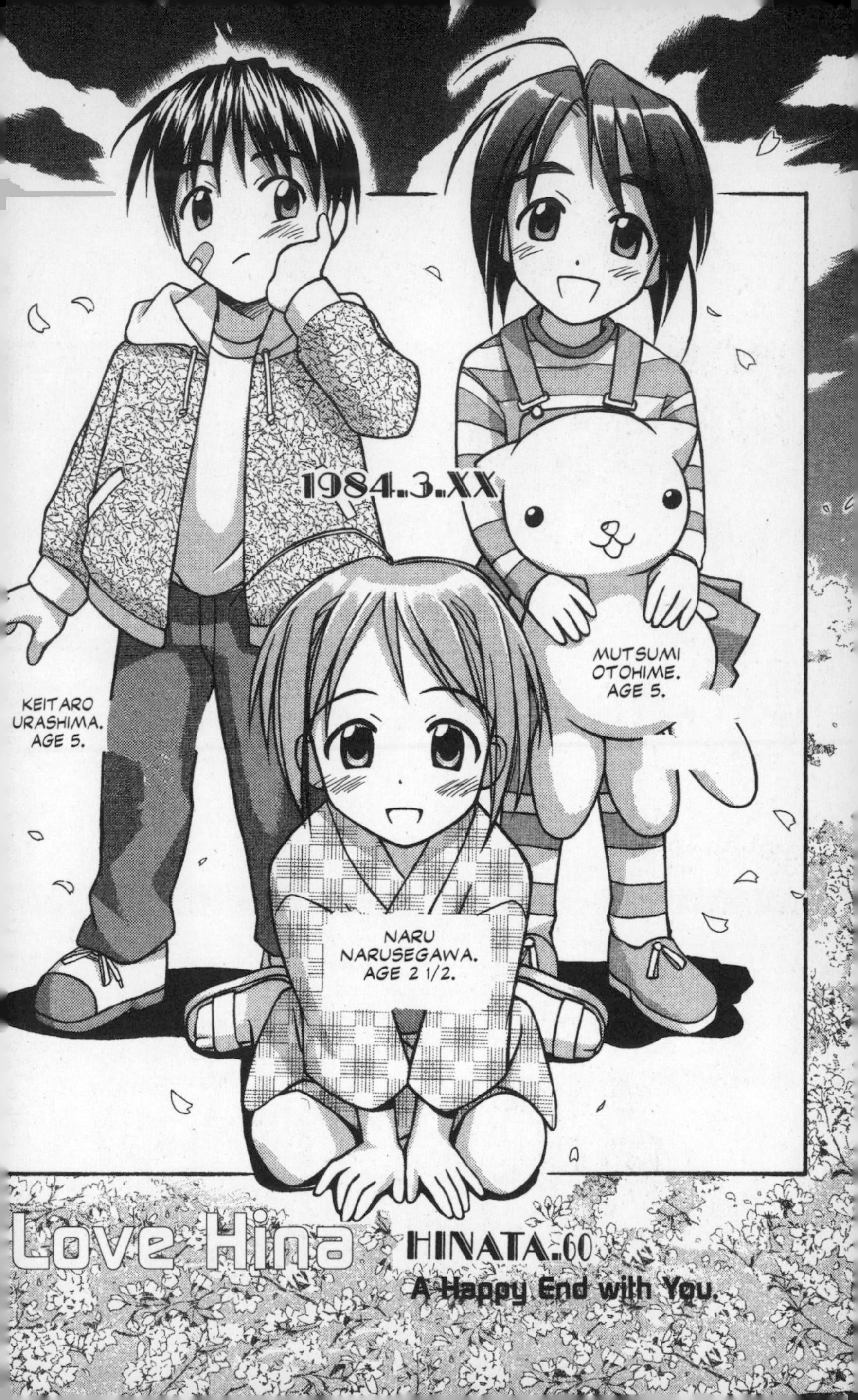
1984.3.XX
MUTSUMI OTOHIME. AGE 5.
KEITARO URASHIMA. AGE 5.
NARU NARUSEGAWA. AGE 2 1/2.
Love Hina
HINATA.60
A Happy End with You.

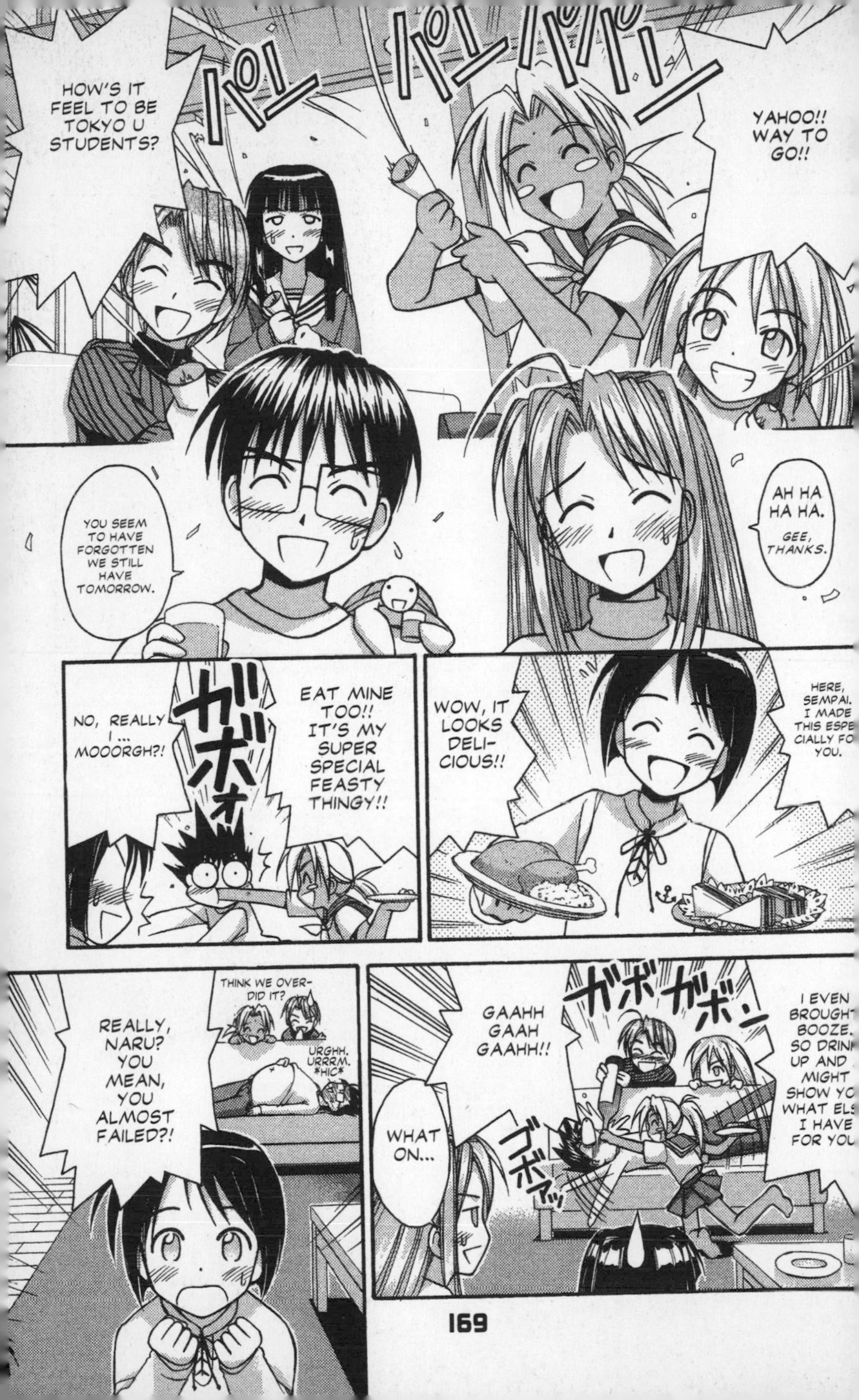
YAHOO!! WAY TO GO!!
パン パン パパ
HOW'S IT FEEL TO BE TOKYO U STUDENTS?
AH HA HA HA. GEE, THANKS.
YOU SEEM TO HAVE FORGOTTEN WE STILL HAVE TOMORROW.
HERE, SEMPAI. I MADE THIS ESPE CIALLY FO YOU.
WOW, IT LOOKS DELI-CIOUS!!
EAT MINE TOO!! IT'S MY SUPER SPECIAL FEASTY THINGY!!
ガボォ
NO, REALLY I... MOOORGH?!
I EVEN BROUGHT BOOZE. SO DRIN UP AND MIGHT SHOW YO WHAT ELS I HAVE FOR YOU
ガボガボン
GAAHH GAAH GAAHH!!
ゴボァッ
WHAT ON...
THINK WE OVER-DID IT?
URGHH. URRRM. *HIC*
REALLY, NARU? YOU MEAN, YOU ALMOST FAILED?!

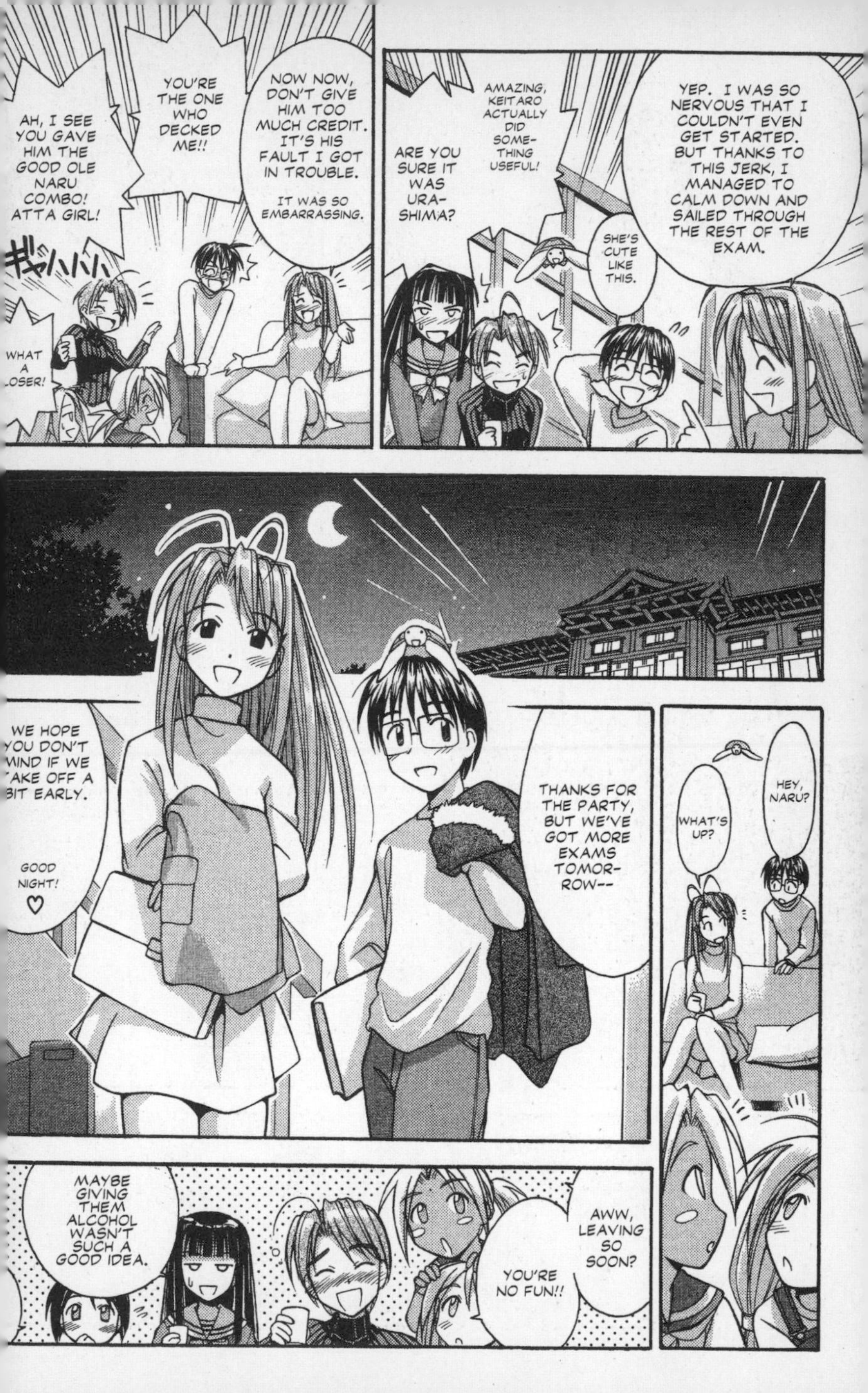
YEP. I WAS SO NERVOUS THAT I COULDN'T EVEN GET STARTED. BUT THANKS TO THIS JERK, I MANAGED TO CALM DOWN AND SAILED THROUGH THE REST OF THE EXAM.
SHE'S CUTE LIKE THIS.
AMAZING, KEITARO ACTUALLY DID SOME-THING USEFUL!
ARE YOU SURE IT WAS URA-SHIMA?
NOW NOW, DON'T GIVE HIM TOO MUCH CREDIT. IT'S HIS FAULT I GOT IN TROUBLE.
IT WAS SO EMBARRASSING.
YOU'RE THE ONE WHO DECKED ME!!
AH, I SEE YOU GAVE HIM THE GOOD OLE NARU COMBO! ATTA GIRL!
ギャハハハ
WHAT A LOSER!
THANKS FOR THE PARTY, BUT WE'VE GOT MORE EXAMS TOMOR-ROW--
WE HOPE YOU DON'T MIND IF WE TAKE OFF A BIT EARLY.
GOOD NIGHT! ♡
HEY, NARU?
WHAT'S UP?
AWW, LEAVING SO SOON?
YOU'RE NO FUN!!
MAYBE GIVING THEM ALCOHOL WASN'T SUCH A GOOD IDEA.

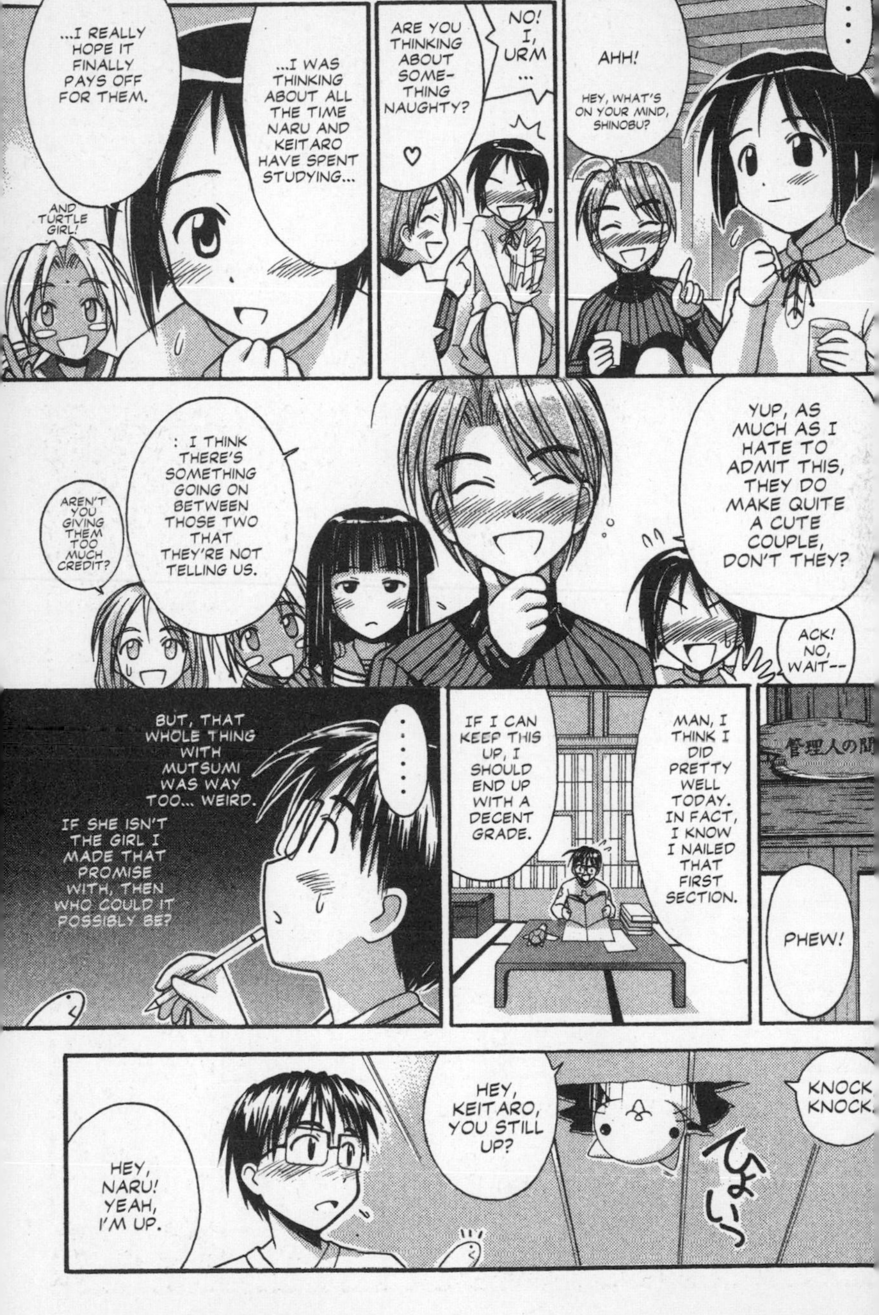
. . . . .
AHH!
HEY, WHAT'S ON YOUR MIND, SHINOBU?
ARE YOU THINKING ABOUT SOME-THING NAUGHTY? ♡
NO! I, URM ...
...I WAS THINKING ABOUT ALL THE TIME NARU AND KEITARO HAVE SPENT STUDYING...
...I REALLY HOPE IT FINALLY PAYS OFF FOR THEM.
AND TURTLE GIRL!
YUP, AS MUCH AS I HATE TO ADMIT THIS, THEY DO MAKE QUITE A CUTE COUPLE, DON'T THEY?
ACK! NO, WAIT--
: I THINK THERE'S SOMETHING GOING ON BETWEEN THOSE TWO THAT THEY'RE NOT TELLING US.
AREN'T YOU GIVING THEM TOO MUCH CREDIT?
管理人の
PHEW!
MAN, I THINK I DID PRETTY WELL TODAY. IN FACT, I KNOW I NAILED THAT FIRST SECTION.
IF I CAN KEEP THIS UP, I SHOULD END UP WITH A DECENT GRADE.
. . . . . .
BUT, THAT WHOLE THING WITH MUTSUMI WAS WAY TOO... WEIRD.
IF SHE ISN'T THE GIRL I MADE THAT PROMISE WITH, THEN WHO COULD IT POSSIBLY BE?
KNOCK KNOCK.
HEY, KEITARO, YOU STILL UP?
HEY, NARU! YEAH, I'M UP.

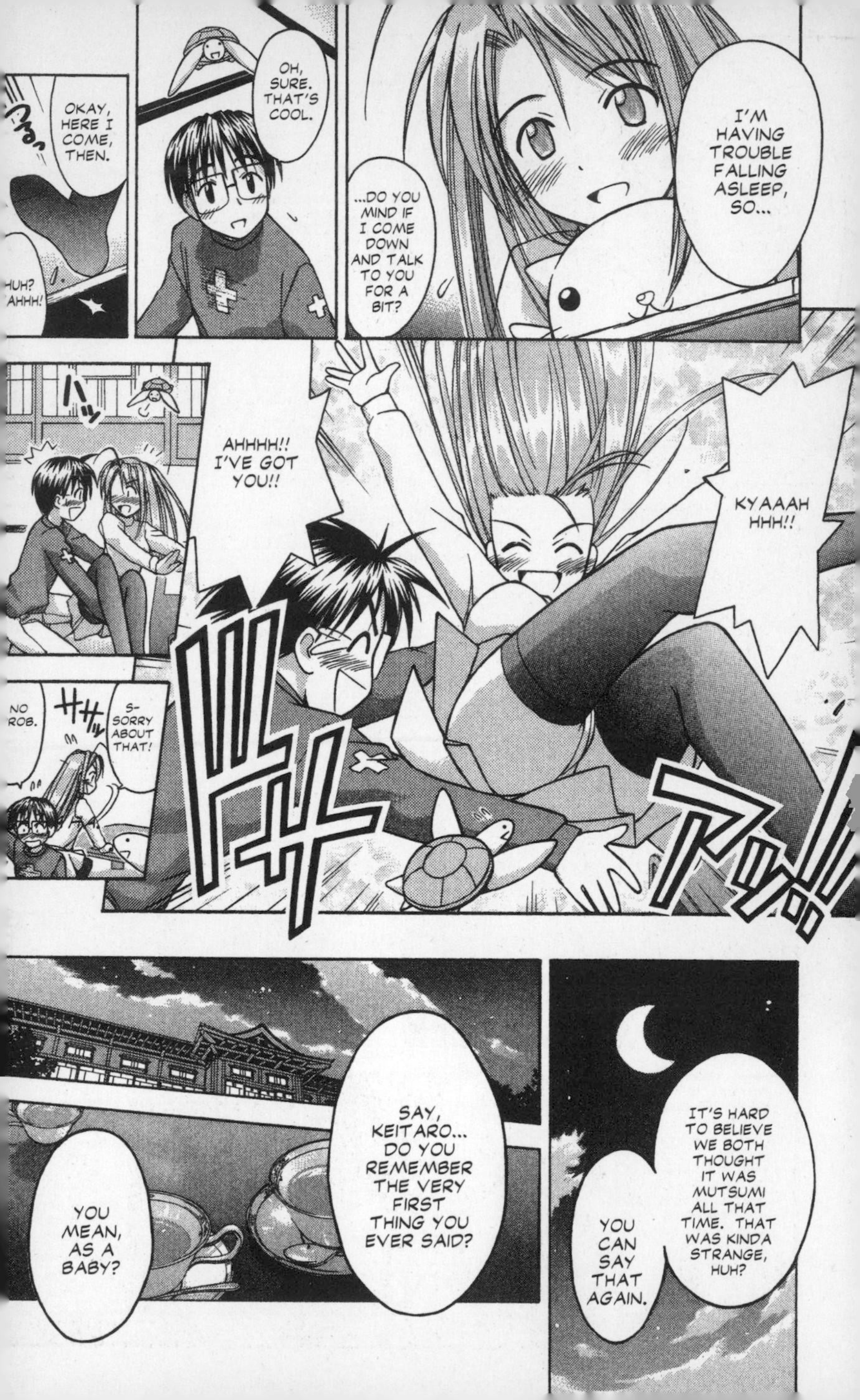
I'M HAVING TROUBLE FALLING ASLEEP, SO...
...DO YOU MIND IF I COME DOWN AND TALK TO YOU FOR A BIT?
OH, SURE. THAT'S COOL.
OKAY, HERE I COME, THEN.
HUH? AHHH!
KYAAAH HHH!!
AHHHH!! I'VE GOT YOU!!
S-SORRY ABOUT THAT!
NO ROB.
IT'S HARD TO BELIEVE WE BOTH THOUGHT IT WAS MUTSUMI ALL THAT TIME. THAT WAS KINDA STRANGE, HUH?
YOU CAN SAY THAT AGAIN.
SAY, KEITARO... DO YOU REMEMBER THE VERY FIRST THING YOU EVER SAID?
YOU MEAN, AS A BABY?

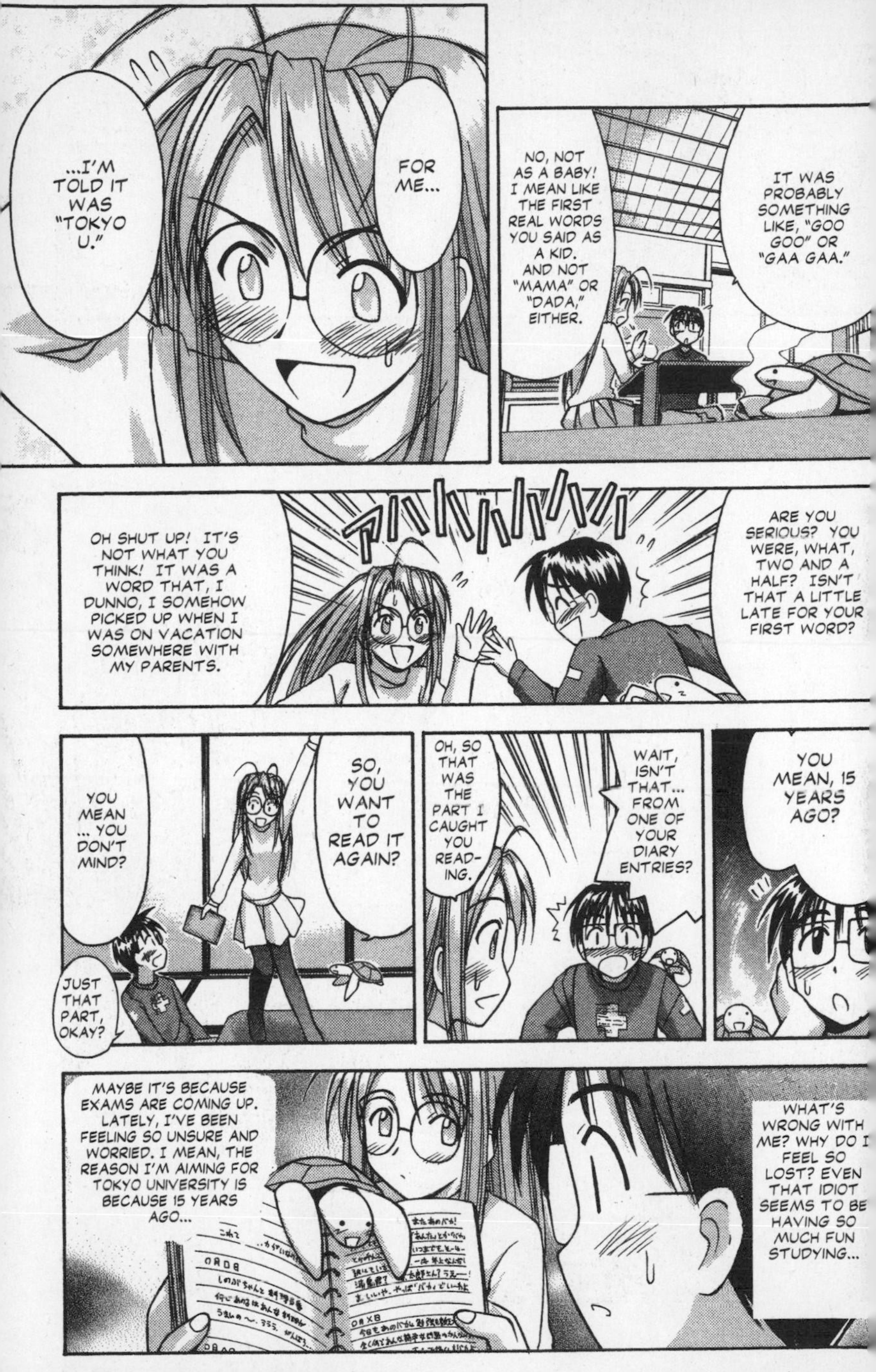
IT WAS PROBABLY SOMETHING LIKE, "GOO GOO" OR "GAA GAA."
NO, NOT AS A BABY! I MEAN LIKE THE FIRST REAL WORDS YOU SAID AS A KID. AND NOT "MAMA" OR "DADA," EITHER.
FOR ME...
...I'M TOLD IT WAS "TOKYO U."
ARE YOU SERIOUS? YOU WERE, WHAT, TWO AND A HALF? ISN'T THAT A LITTLE LATE FOR YOUR FIRST WORD?
OH SHUT UP! IT'S NOT WHAT YOU THINK! IT WAS A WORD THAT, I DUNNO, I SOMEHOW PICKED UP WHEN I WAS ON VACATION SOMEWHERE WITH MY PARENTS.
YOU MEAN, 15 YEARS AGO?
WAIT, ISN'T THAT... FROM ONE OF YOUR DIARY ENTRIES?
OH, SO THAT WAS THE PART I CAUGHT YOU READ-ING.
SO, YOU WANT TO READ IT AGAIN?
YOU MEAN ... YOU DON'T MIND?
JUST THAT PART, OKAY?
WHAT'S WRONG WITH ME? WHY DO I FEEL SO LOST? EVEN THAT IDIOT SEEMS TO BE HAVING SO MUCH FUN STUDYING...
MAYBE IT'S BECAUSE EXAMS ARE COMING UP. LATELY, I'VE BEEN FEELING SO UNSURE AND WORRIED. I MEAN, THE REASON I'M AIMING FOR TOKYO UNIVERSITY IS BECAUSE 15 YEARS AGO...

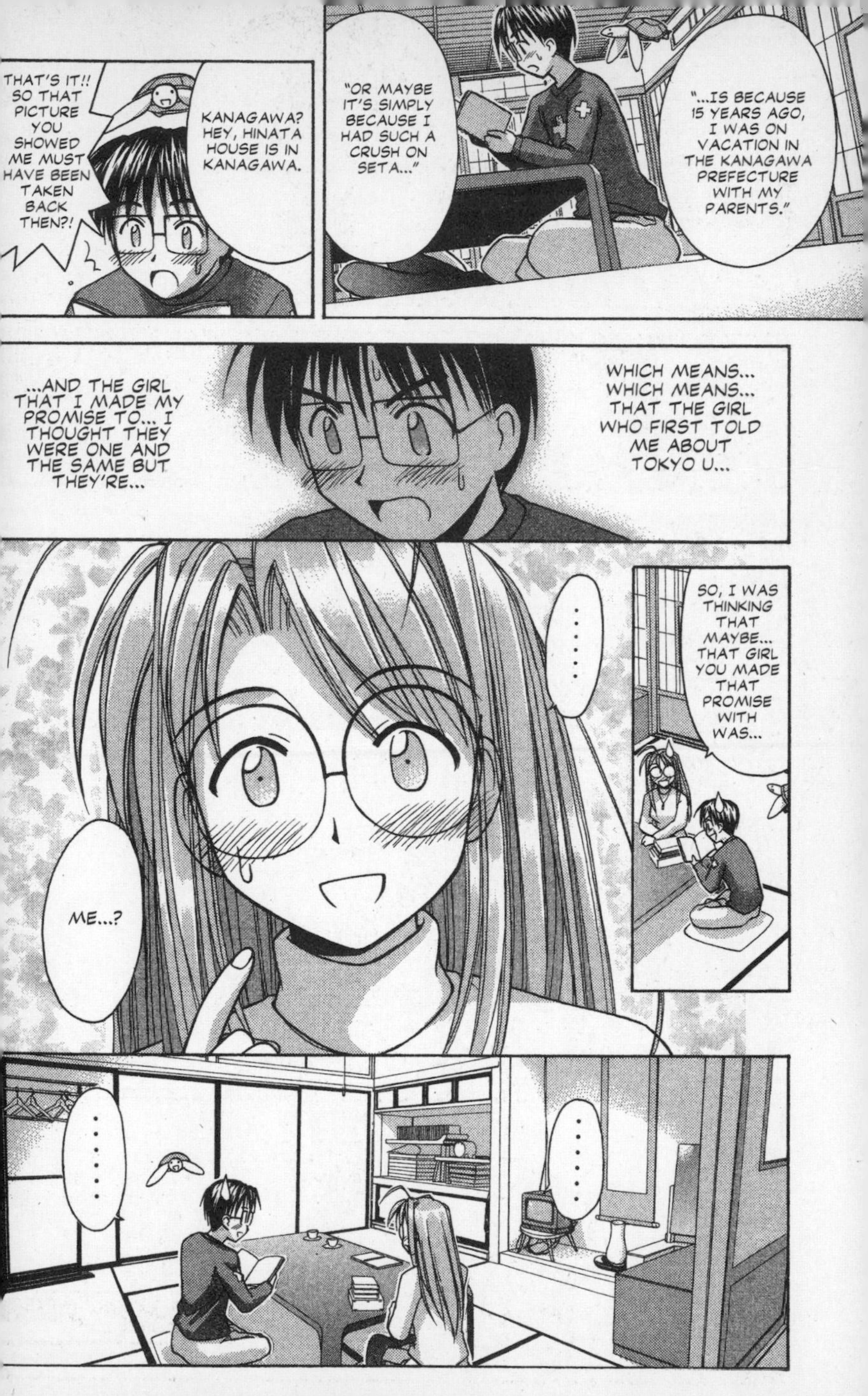
"...IS BECAUSE 15 YEARS AGO, I WAS ON VACATION IN THE KANAGAWA PREFECTURE WITH MY PARENTS."
"OR MAYBE IT'S SIMPLY BECAUSE I HAD SUCH A CRUSH ON SETA..."
KANAGAWA? HEY, HINATA HOUSE IS IN KANAGAWA.
THAT'S IT!! SO THAT PICTURE YOU SHOWED ME MUST HAVE BEEN TAKEN BACK THEN?!
WHICH MEANS... WHICH MEANS... THAT THE GIRL WHO FIRST TOLD ME ABOUT TOKYO U...
...AND THE GIRL THAT I MADE MY PROMISE TO... I THOUGHT THEY WERE ONE AND THE SAME BUT THEY'RE...
SO, I WAS THINKING THAT MAYBE... THAT GIRL YOU MADE THAT PROMISE WITH WAS...
......
ME...?
......
......

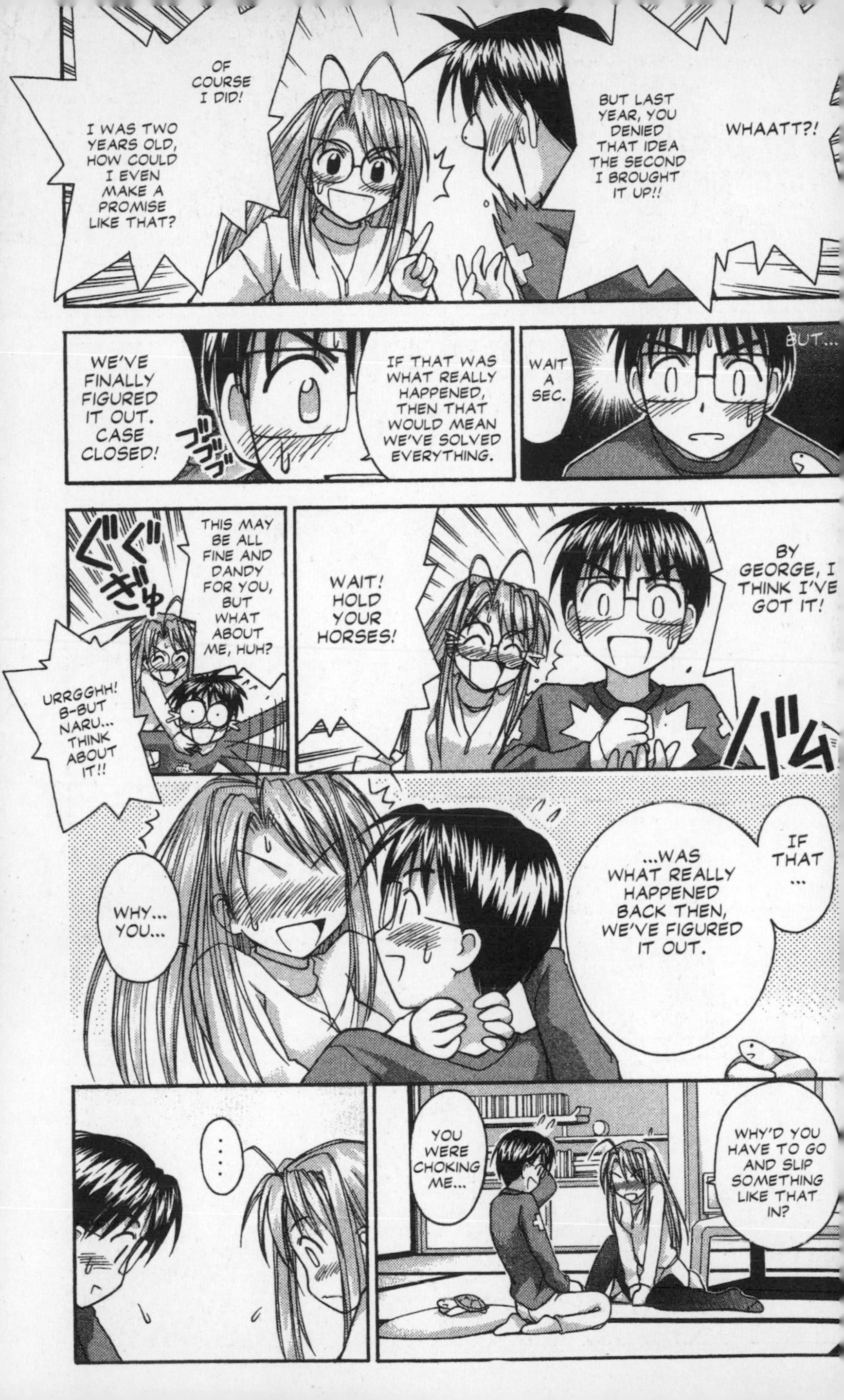
WHAATT?!
BUT LAST YEAR, YOU DENIED THAT IDEA THE SECOND I BROUGHT IT UP!!
OF COURSE I DID!
I WAS TWO YEARS OLD, HOW COULD I EVEN MAKE A PROMISE LIKE THAT?
BUT...
WAIT A SEC.
IF THAT WAS WHAT REALLY HAPPENED, THEN THAT WOULD MEAN WE'VE SOLVED EVERYTHING.
WE'VE FINALLY FIGURED IT OUT. CASE CLOSED!
BY GEORGE, I THINK I'VE GOT IT!
WAIT! HOLD YOUR HORSES!
THIS MAY BE ALL FINE AND DANDY FOR YOU, BUT WHAT ABOUT ME, HUH?
URRGGHH! B-BUT NARU... THINK ABOUT IT!!
IF THAT...
...WAS WHAT REALLY HAPPENED BACK THEN, WE'VE FIGURED IT OUT.
WHY... YOU...
WHY'D YOU HAVE TO GO AND SLIP SOMETHING LIKE THAT IN?
YOU WERE CHOKING ME...
....

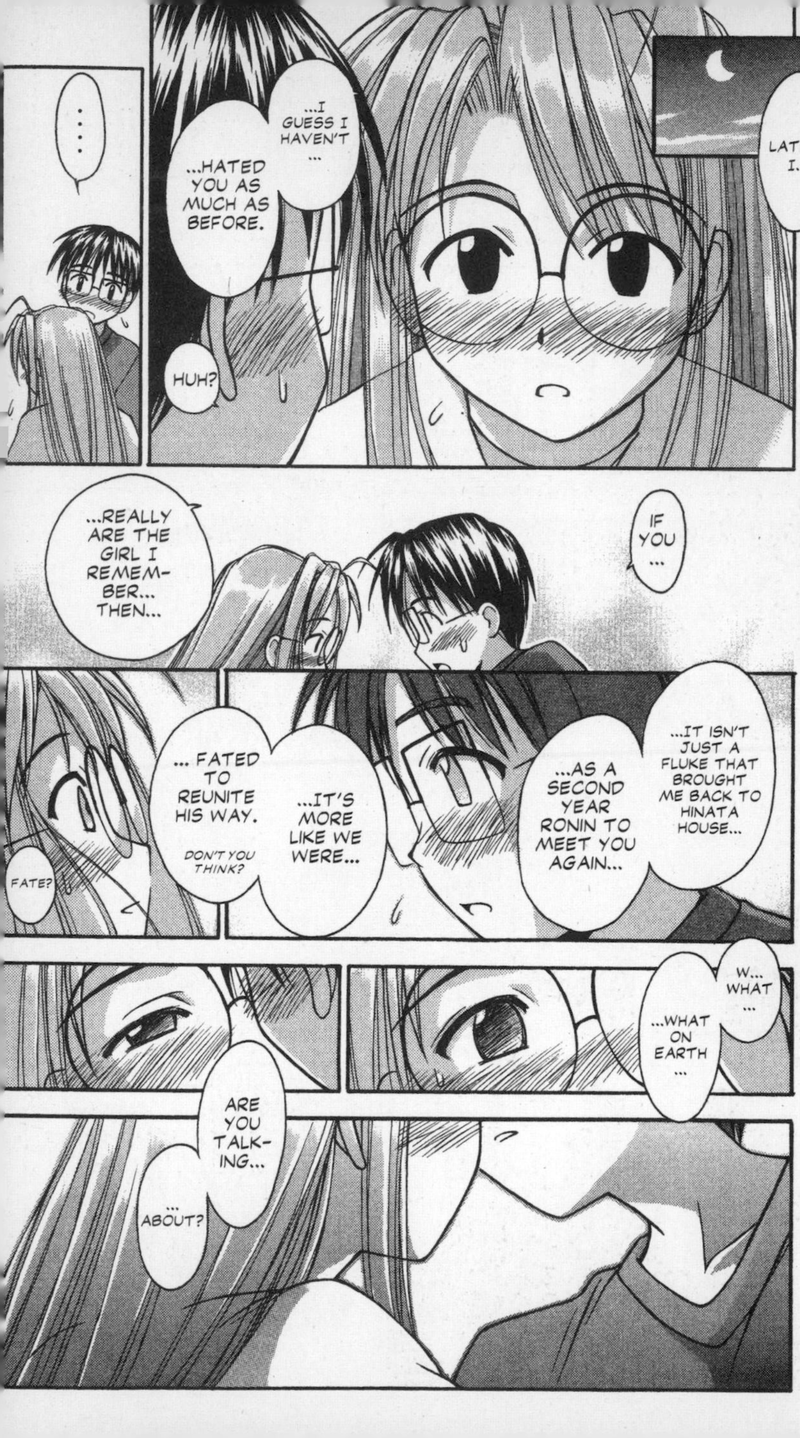
LATELY I...
...I GUESS I HAVEN'T ...
...HATED YOU AS MUCH AS BEFORE.
HUH?
....
IF YOU ...
...REALLY ARE THE GIRL I REMEMBER... THEN...
...IT ISN'T JUST A FLUKE THAT BROUGHT ME BACK TO HINATA HOUSE...
...AS A SECOND YEAR RONIN TO MEET YOU AGAIN...
...IT'S MORE LIKE WE WERE...
... FATED TO REUNITE HIS WAY.
DON'T YOU THINK?
FATE?
W... WHAT ...
...WHAT ON EARTH ...
ARE YOU TALKING...
... ABOUT?

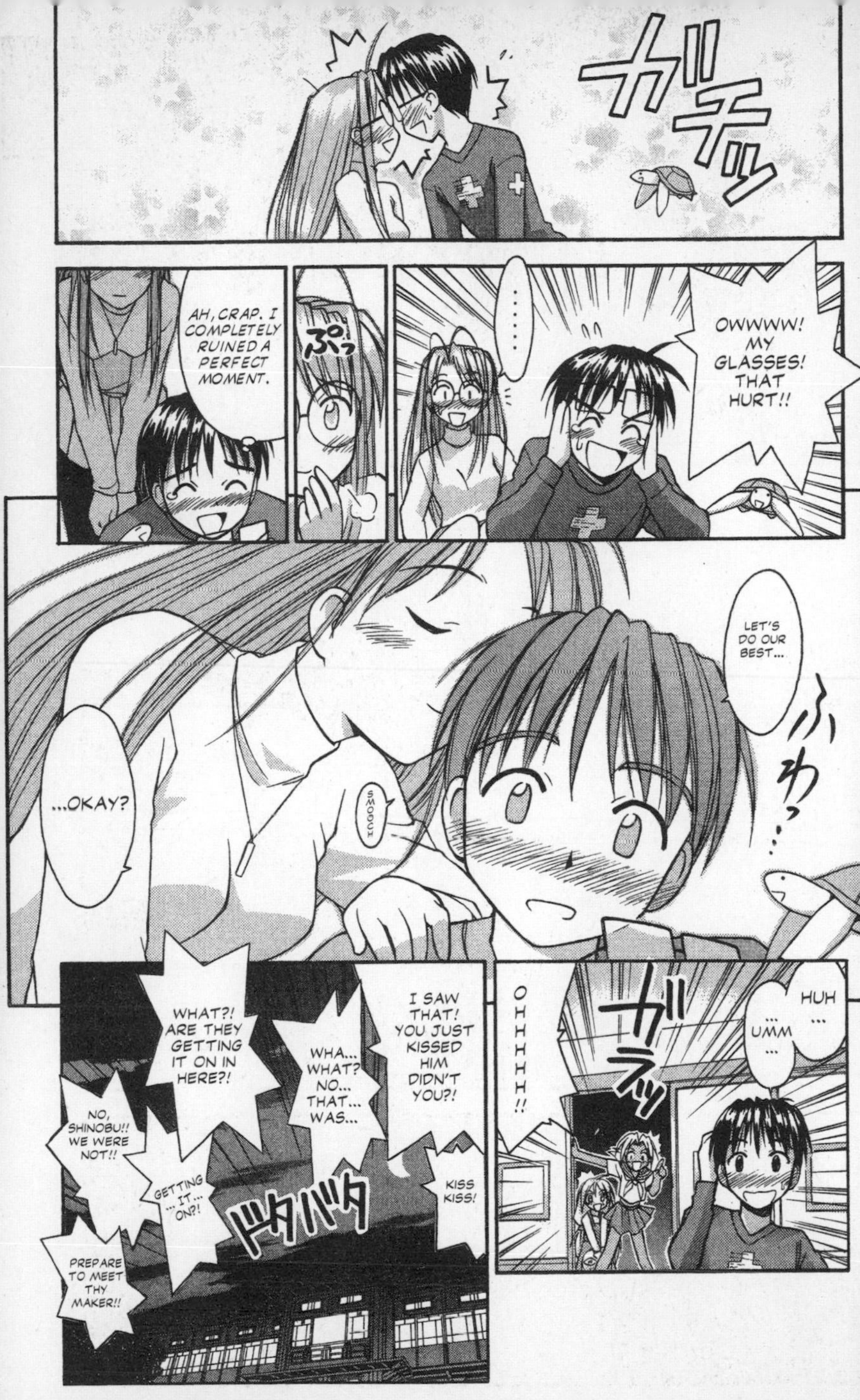
ガチッ
OWWWW! MY GLASSES! THAT HURT!!
......
ぷっ
AH, CRAP. I COMPLETELY RUINED A PERFECT MOMENT.
LET'S DO OUR BEST...
ふわっ...
SMOOCH
...OKAY?
HUH ... UMM ...
ガラッ
OHHHHH!!
I SAW THAT! YOU JUST KISSED HIM DIDN'T YOU?!
WHAT?! ARE THEY GETTING IT ON IN HERE?!
WHA... WHAT? NO... THAT... WAS...
KISS KISS!
NO, SHINOBU!! WE WERE NOT!!
GETTING ... IT ... ON?!
ドタバタ
PREPARE TO MEET THY MAKER!!

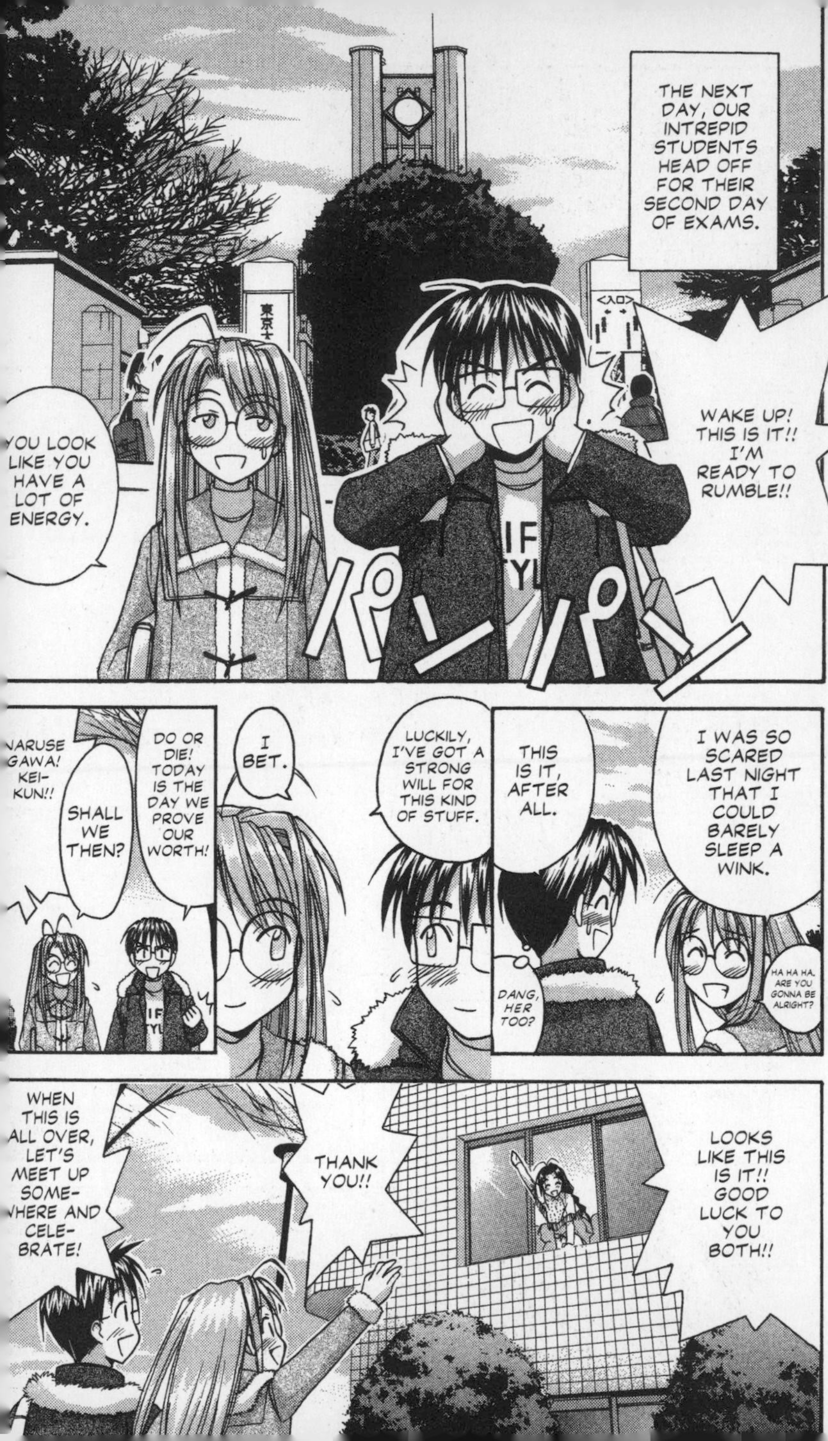
THE NEXT DAY, OUR INTREPID STUDENTS HEAD OFF FOR THEIR SECOND DAY OF EXAMS.
WAKE UP! THIS IS IT!! I'M READY TO RUMBLE!!
YOU LOOK LIKE YOU HAVE A LOT OF ENERGY.
I WAS SO SCARED LAST NIGHT THAT I COULD BARELY SLEEP A WINK.
HA HA HA. ARE YOU GONNA BE ALRIGHT?
THIS IS IT, AFTER ALL.
DANG, HER TOO?
LUCKILY, I'VE GOT A STRONG WILL FOR THIS KIND OF STUFF.
I BET.
DO OR DIE! TODAY IS THE DAY WE PROVE OUR WORTH!
SHALL WE THEN?
NARUSE GAWA! KEI-KUN!!
LOOKS LIKE THIS IS IT!! GOOD LUCK TO YOU BOTH!!
THANK YOU!!
WHEN THIS IS ALL OVER, LET'S MEET UP SOME-WHERE AND CELE-BRATE!

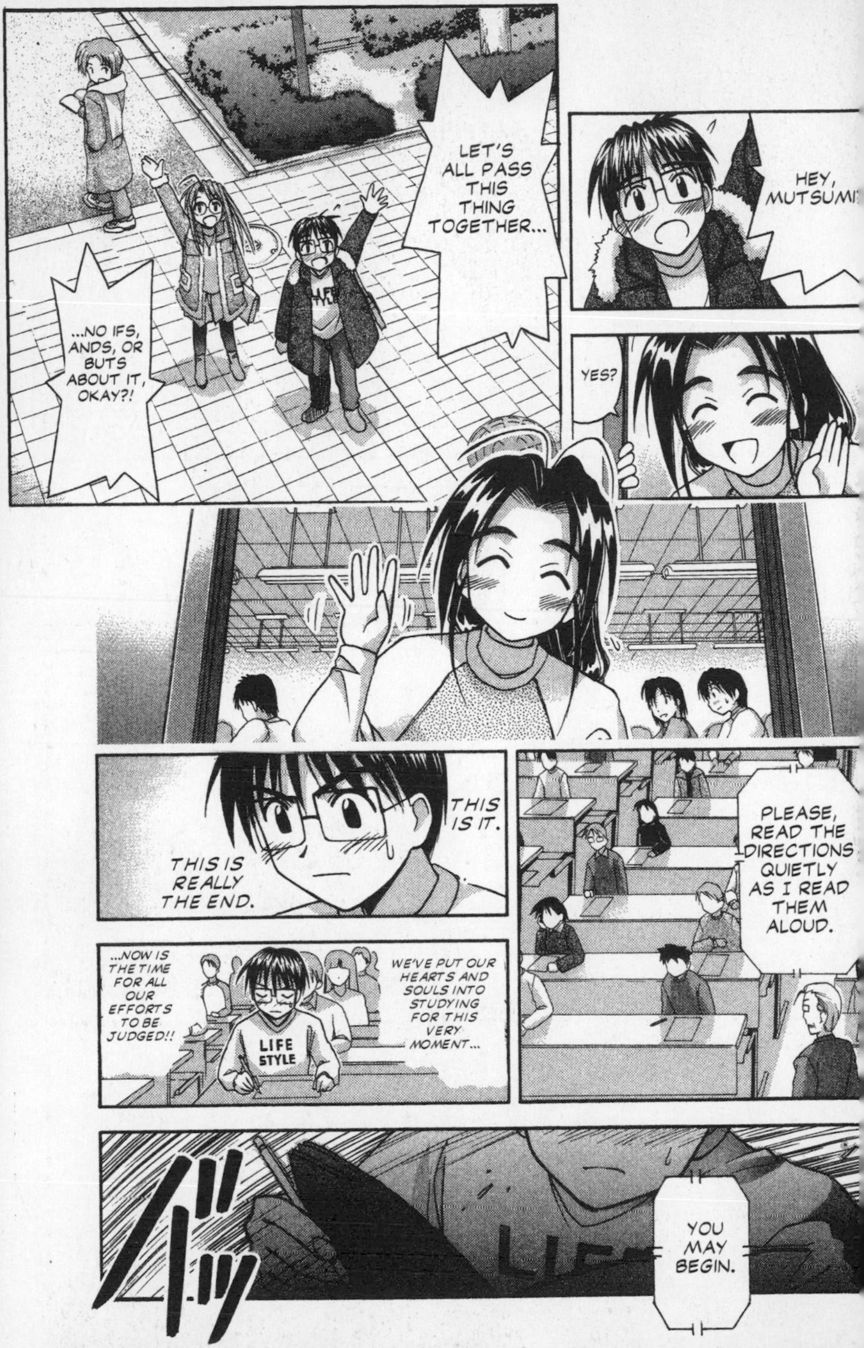

HEY, MUTSUMI
YES?
LET'S ALL PASS THIS THING TOGETHER...
...NO IFS, ANDS, OR BUTS ABOUT IT, OKAY?!
PLEASE, READ THE DIRECTIONS QUIETLY AS I READ THEM ALOUD.
THIS IS IT.
THIS IS REALLY THE END.
WE'VE PUT OUR HEARTS AND SOULS INTO STUDYING FOR THIS VERY MOMENT...
...NOW IS THE TIME FOR ALL OUR EFFORTS TO BE JUDGED!!
YOU MAY BEGIN.
バッ

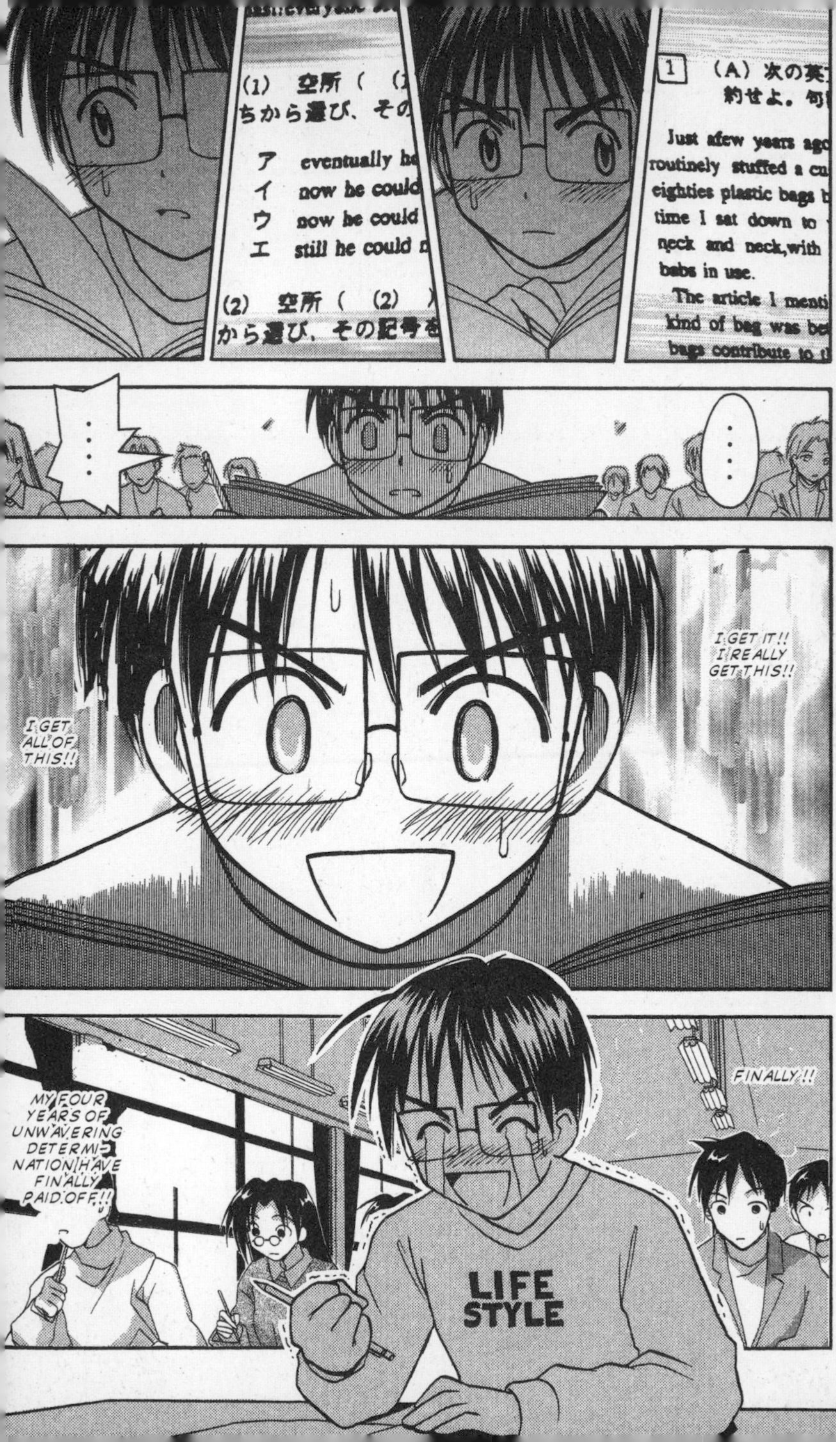
1 （A）次の英
約せよ。句
Just afew years ago
routinely stuffed a cu
eighties plastic bags b
time I sat down to
neck and neck,with
babs in use.
The article I menti
kind of bag was be
bags contribute to t
(1) 空所（ (1
ちから選び、その
ア eventually he
イ now he could
ウ now he could
エ still he could
(2) 空所（ (2)
から選び、その記号を
...
...
I GET IT!! I REALLY GET THIS!!
I GET ALL OF THIS!!
FINALLY!!
MY FOUR YEARS OF UNWAVERING DETERMINATION HAVE FINALLY PAID OFF!!
LIFE STYLE

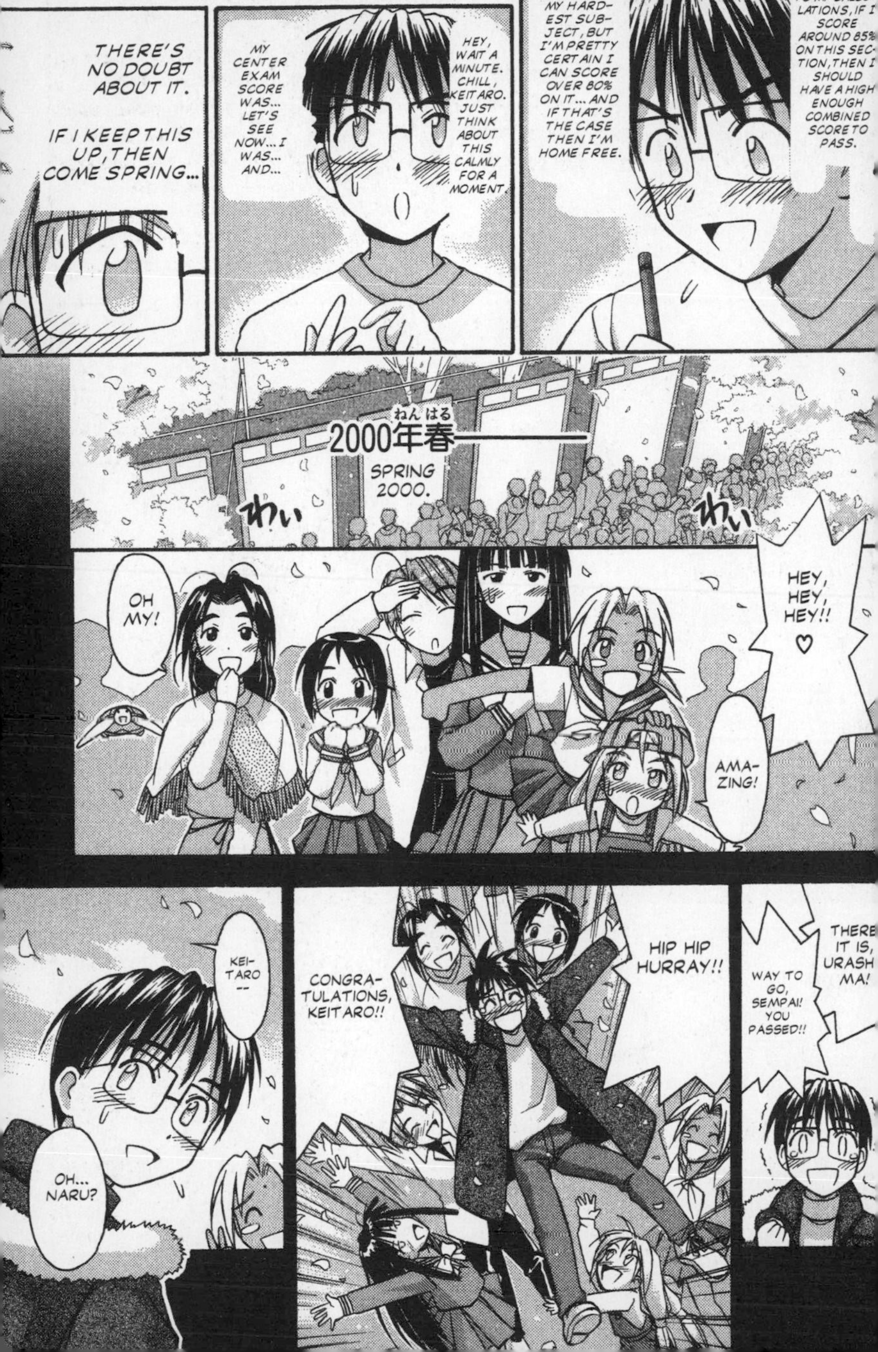
ACCORDING TO MY CALCULATIONS, IF I SCORE AROUND 85% ON THIS SECTION, THEN I SHOULD HAVE A HIGH ENOUGH COMBINED SCORE TO PASS.
ENGLISH IS MY HARDEST SUBJECT, BUT I'M PRETTY CERTAIN I CAN SCORE OVER 80% ON IT... AND IF THAT'S THE CASE THEN I'M HOME FREE.
HEY, WAIT A MINUTE. CHILL, KEITARO. JUST THINK ABOUT THIS CALMLY FOR A MOMENT.
MY CENTER EXAM SCORE WAS... LET'S SEE NOW... I WAS... AND...
THERE'S NO DOUBT ABOUT IT.
IF I KEEP THIS UP, THEN COME SPRING...
わい
2000年春(ねんはる)——
SPRING 2000.
わい
HEY, HEY, HEY!! ♡
AMAZING!
OH MY!
THERE IT IS, URASHIMA!
WAY TO GO, SEMPAI! YOU PASSED!!
HIP HIP HURRAY!!
CONGRATULATIONS, KEITARO!!
KEITARO--
OH... NARU?

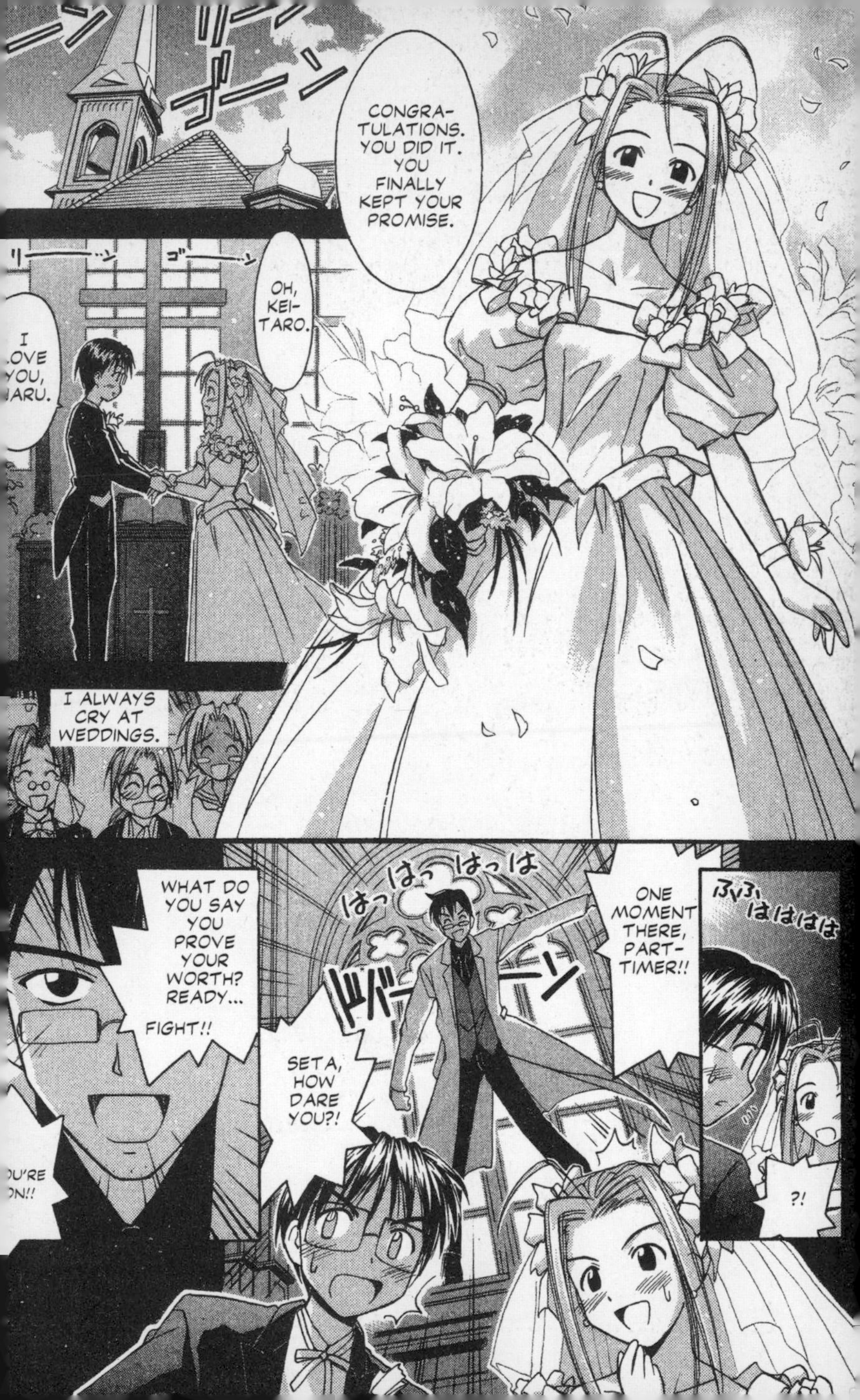

CONGRATULATIONS. YOU DID IT. YOU FINALLY KEPT YOUR PROMISE.
リーン
ゴーン
リーン
ゴーン
OH, KEI-TARO.
I OVE YOU, ARU.
I ALWAYS CRY AT WEDDINGS.
ふふ ははははは
?!
はっ はっ はっ は
ONE MOMENT THERE, PART-TIMER!!
ドバーン
SETA, HOW DARE YOU?!
WHAT DO YOU SAY YOU PROVE YOUR WORTH? READY...
FIGHT!!
OU'RE ON!!

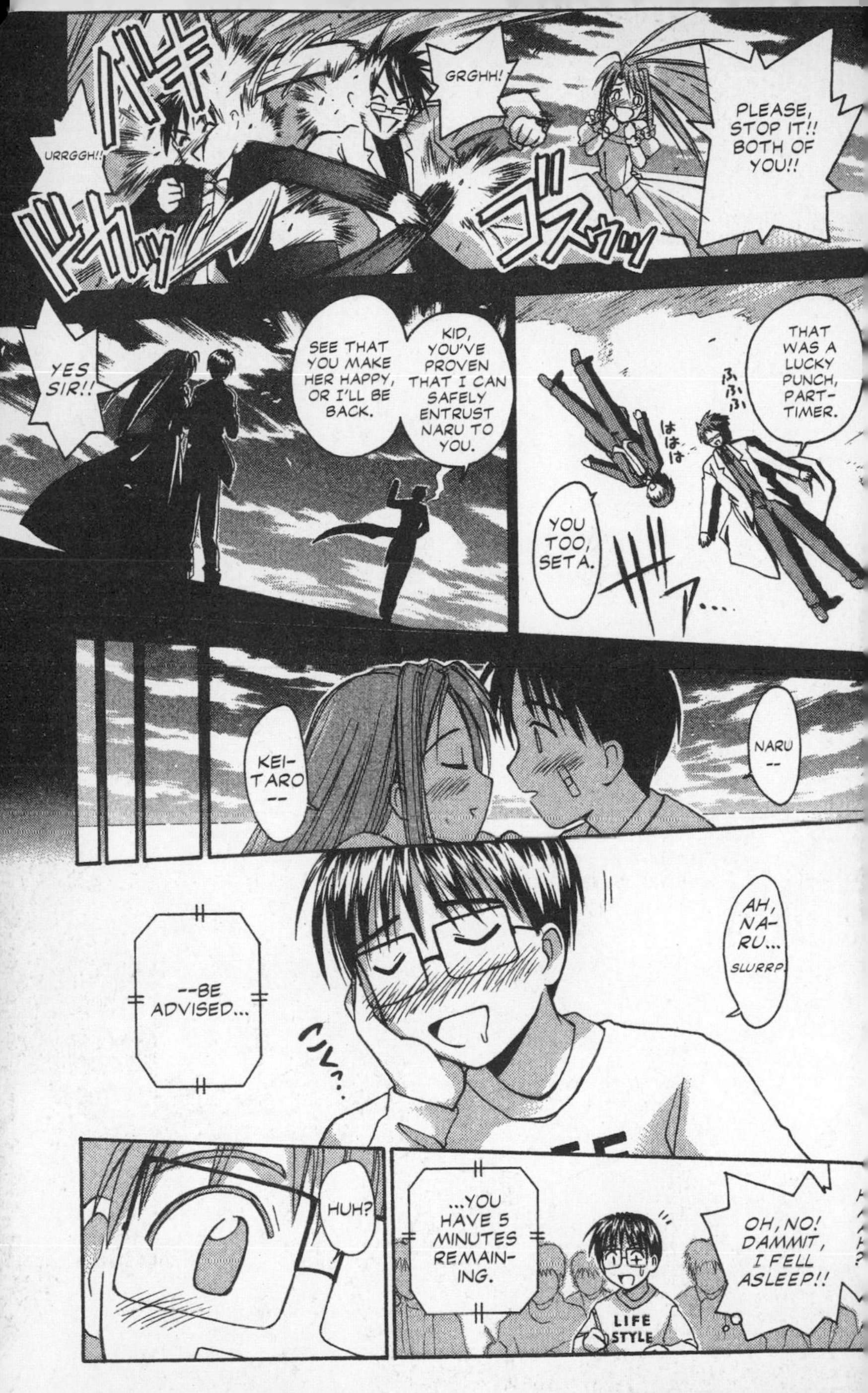
PLEASE, STOP IT!! BOTH OF YOU!!
GRGHH!
URRGGH!!
THAT WAS A LUCKY PUNCH, PART-TIMER.
ふふふ
ははは
YOU TOO, SETA.
KID, YOU'VE PROVEN THAT I CAN SAFELY ENTRUST NARU TO YOU.
SEE THAT YOU MAKE HER HAPPY, OR I'LL BE BACK.
YES SIR!!
NARU --
KEI-TARO --
AH, NA-RU...
SLURRP
--BE ADVISED...
OH, NO! DAMMIT, I FELL ASLEEP!!
...YOU HAVE 5 MINUTES REMAINING.
LIFE STYLE
HUH?

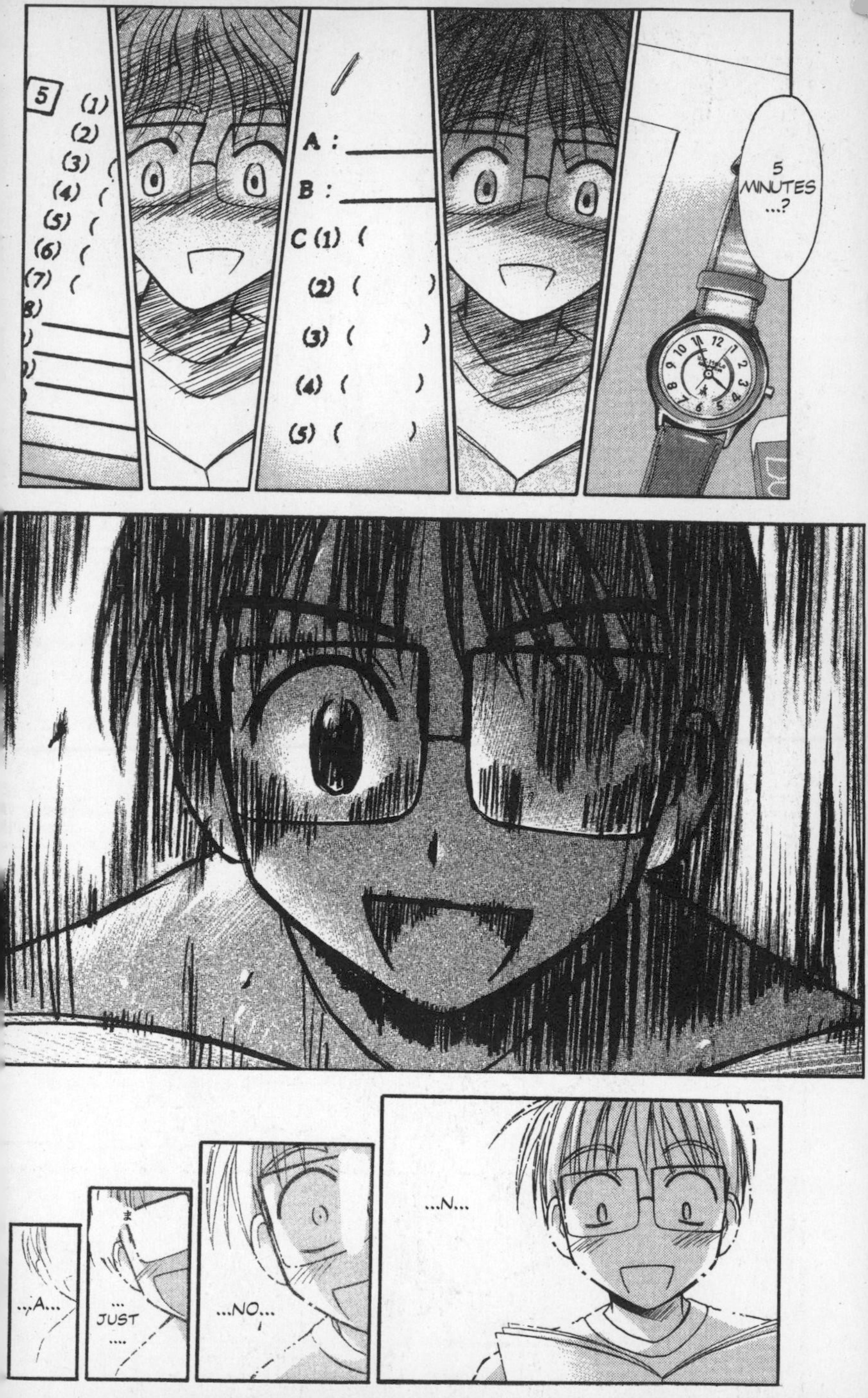

5 MINUTES ...?
...N...
...NO...
... JUST ....
...A...

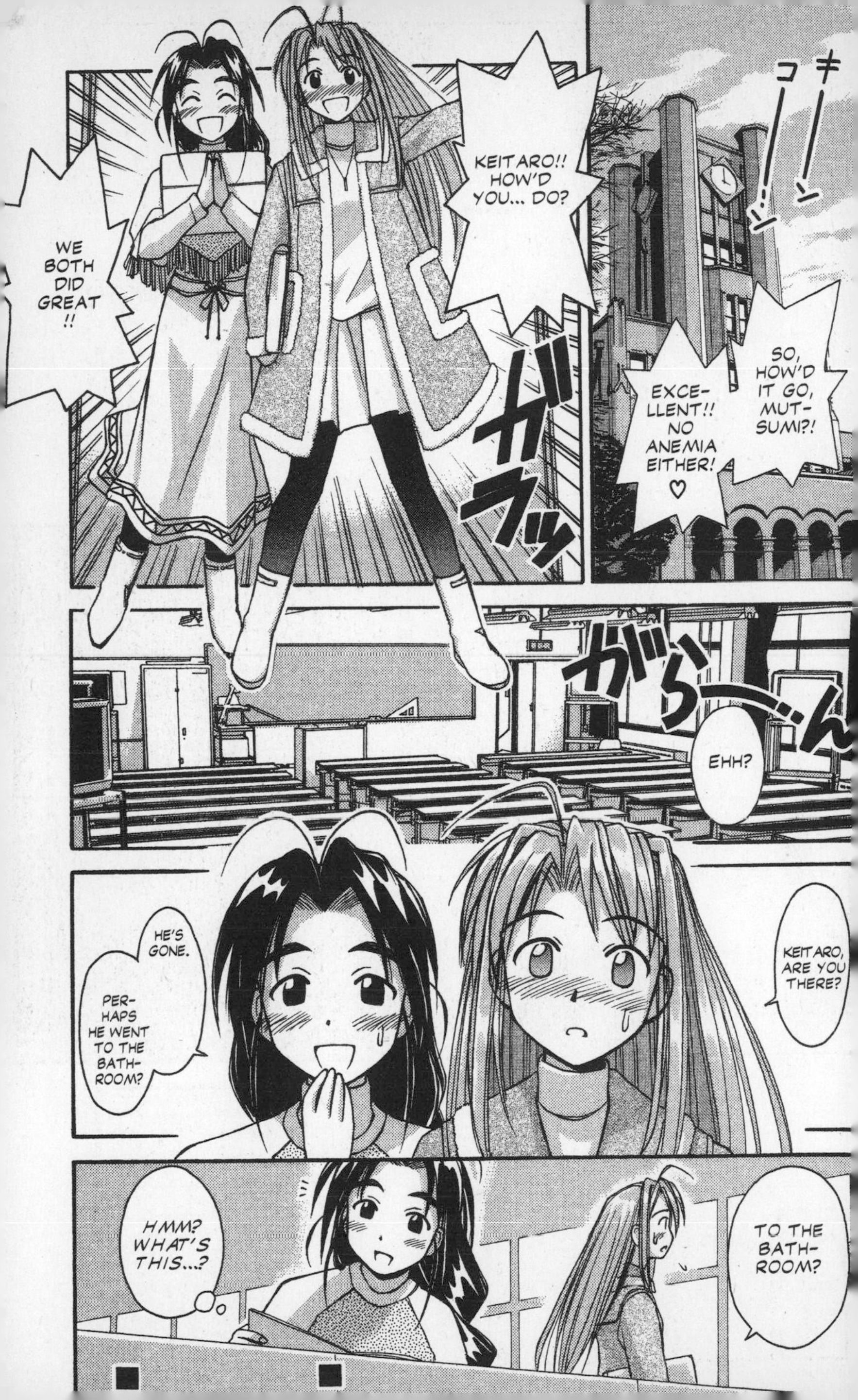
SO, HOW'D IT GO, MUT-SUMI?!
EXCE-LLENT!! NO ANEMIA EITHER! ♡
KEITARO!! HOW'D YOU... DO?
WE BOTH DID GREAT!!
ガラッ
がらーーん
EHH?
KEITARO, ARE YOU THERE?
HE'S GONE.
PER-HAPS HE WENT TO THE BATH-ROOM?
TO THE BATH-ROOM?
HMM? WHAT'S THIS...?

STAFF

Ken Akamatsu
Takashi Takemoto
Kenichi Nakamura
Takaaki Miyahara
Masaki Ohyama
Yumiko Shinohara


EDITOR

Noboru Ohno
Tomoyuki Shiratsuchi
Yasushi Yamanaka


KC Editor

Mitsuei Ishii

# Love Hina

## Preview for Volume Eight

### From Pararakelse With Love

The Tokyo University Entrance Exams have come and gone once again for our trio of intrepid ronins. But as the dust begins to settle, Keitaro goes missing. And before the results are even posted, Naru is off to track down Hinata House's troublemaking landlord.

Keitaro's whimsy leads him to a mysterious island in the South Pacific known as Pararakelse Island, a place rumored to be the home of a legendary civilization of turtles. It is here that a familiar face offers him a new lease on life. Of course, his old life is chasing after him at break neck speed with the exam results.

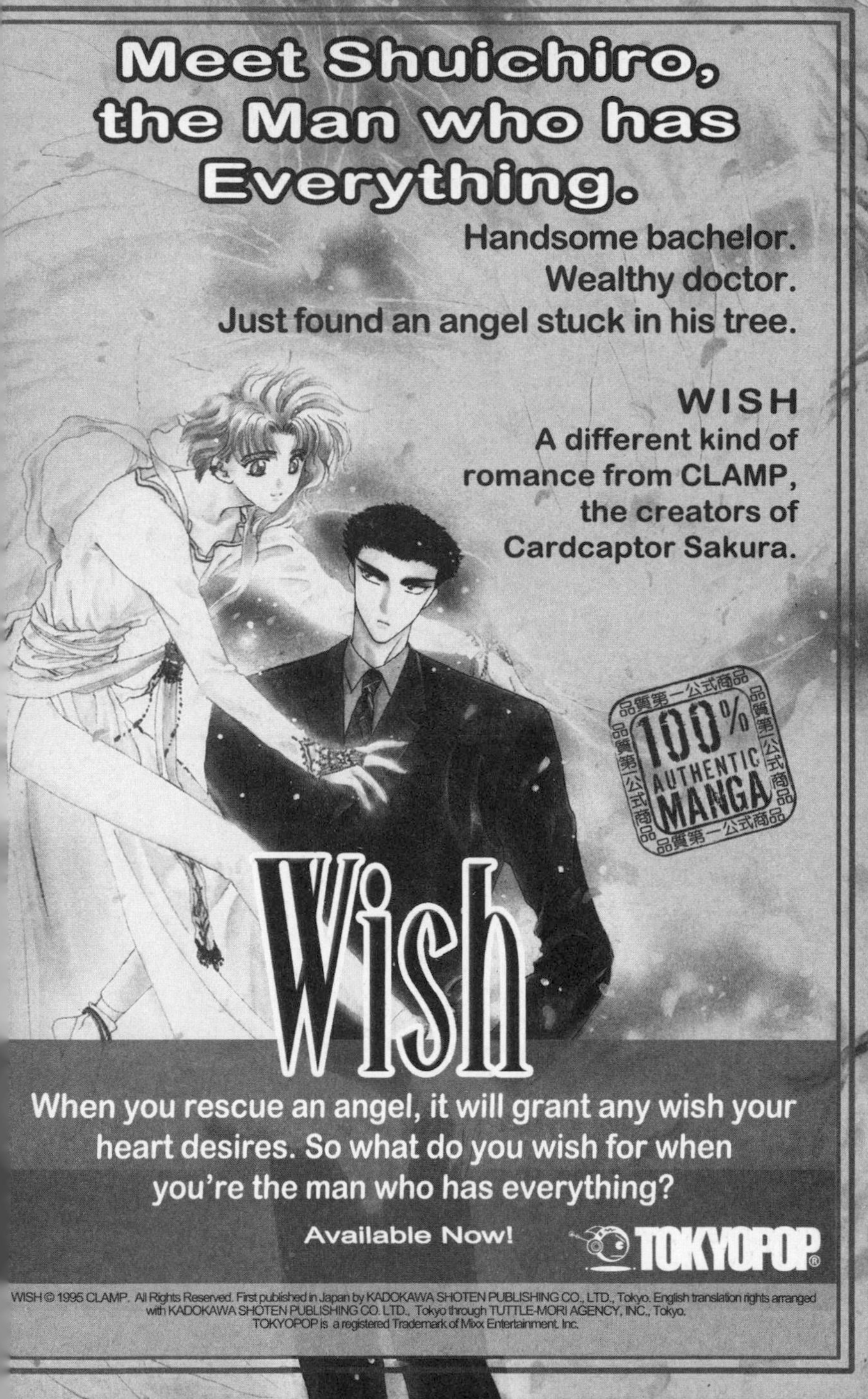

Meet Shuichiro, the Man who has Everything.
Handsome bachelor.
Wealthy doctor.
Just found an angel stuck in his tree.
WISH
A different kind of romance from CLAMP, the creators of Cardcaptor Sakura.
100% AUTHENTIC MANGA
Wish
When you rescue an angel, it will grant any wish your heart desires. So what do you wish for when you're the man who has everything?
Available Now!
TOKYOPOP®
WISH © 1995 CLAMP. All Rights Reserved. First published in Japan by KADOKAWA SHOTEN PUBLISHING CO., LTD., Tokyo. English translation rights arranged with KADOKAWA SHOTEN PUBLISHING CO. LTD., Tokyo through TUTTLE-MORI AGENCY, INC., Tokyo.
TOKYOPOP is a registered Trademark of Mixx Entertainment. Inc.

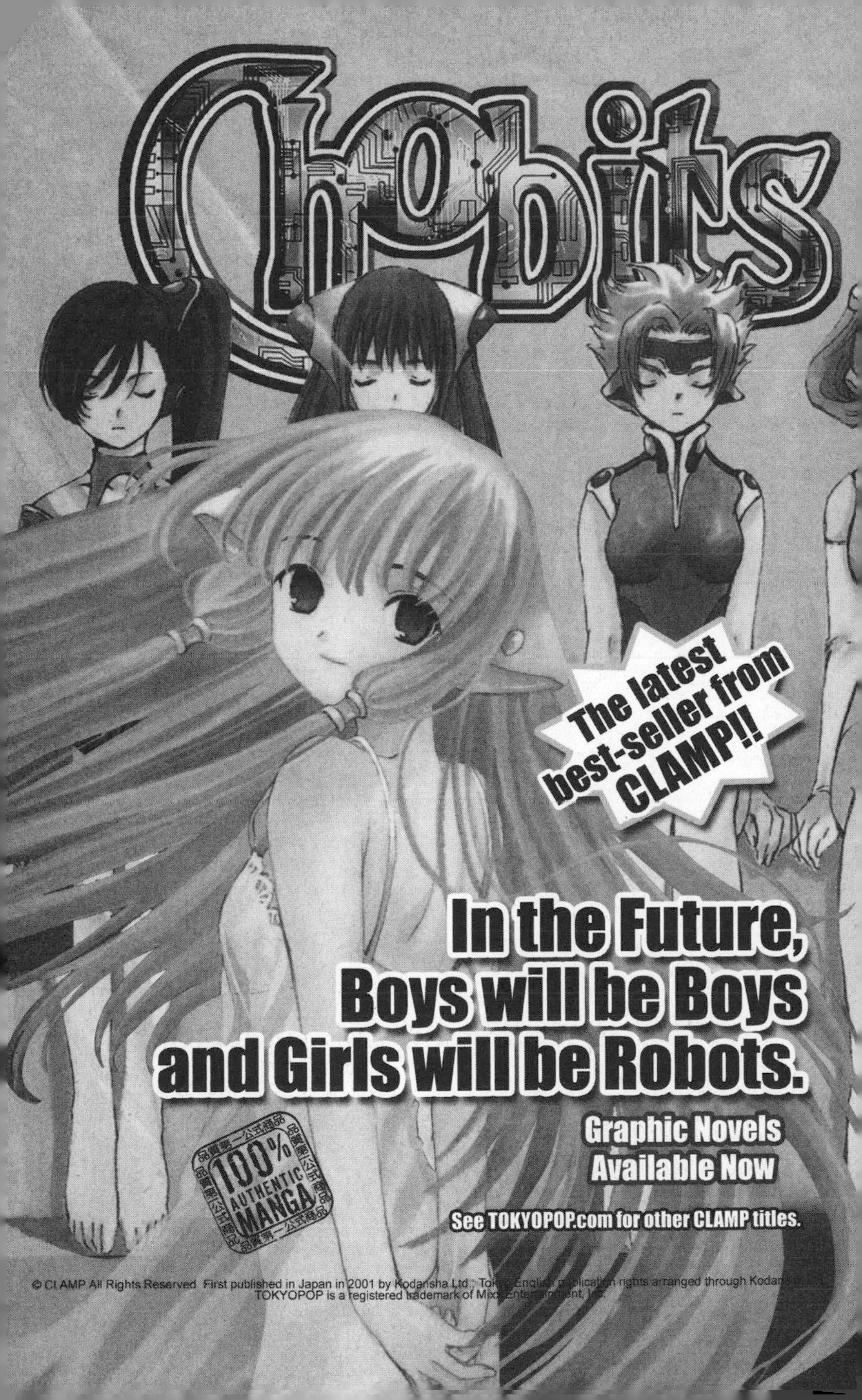
Chobits
The latest best-seller from CLAMP!!
In the Future, Boys will be Boys and Girls will be Robots.
Graphic Novels Available Now
100% AUTHENTIC MANGA
品質第一公式商品
See TOKYOPOP.com for other CLAMP titles.
© CLAMP All Rights Reserved. First published in Japan in 2001 by Kodansha Ltd.,
TOKYOPOP is a registered trademark of

# STOP!

## This is the back of the book.
## ou wouldn't want to spoil a great ending!

This book is printed "manga-style," in the authentic Japanese right-to-left format. Since none of the artwork has been flipped or altered, readers get to experience the story just as the creator intended. You've been asking for it, so TOKYOPOP® delivered: authentic, hot-off-the-press, and far more fun!

# DIRECTIONS

If this is your first time reading manga-style, here's a quick guide to help you understand how it works.

It's easy... just start in the top right panel and follow the numbers. Have fun, and look for more 100% authentic manga from TOKYOPOP®!